My iPhone® for Seniors

SECOND EDITION

Brad Miser

800 East 96th Street,
Indianapolis, Indiana 46240 USA

My iPhone® for Seniors, Second Edition

Copyright © 2016 by Pearson Education, Inc.

ISBN-13: 978-0-7897-5548-3

ISBN-10: 0-7897-5548-3

Library of Congress Control Number: 2015954876

Printed in the United States of America

First Printing: November 2015

Trademarks

Warning and Disclaimer

Special Sales

For information about buying this title in bulk quantities, or for special sales opportunities (which may include electronic versions; custom cover designs; and content particular to your business, training goals, marketing focus, or branding interests), please contact our corporate sales department at corpsales@pearsoned.com or (800) 382-3419.

For government sales inquiries, please contact governmentsales@pearsoned.com.

For questions about sales outside the U.S., please contact international@pearsoned.com.

Editor-in-Chief
Greg Wiegand

Senior Acquisitions Editor
Laura Norman

Senior Development Editor
Laura Norman

Marketing
Dan Powell

Director AARP Books
Jodi Lipson

Managing Editor
Sandra Schroeder

Project Editor
Mandie Frank

Senior Indexer
Cheryl Lenser

Proofreader
Debbie Williams

Content Editor
Bill Baker

Editorial Assistant
Cindy Teeters

Designer
Mark Shirar

Compositor
Mary Sudul

Contents at a Glance

Chapter 1   Getting Started with Your iPhone 3

Chapter 2   Connecting Your iPhone to the Internet, Bluetooth Devices, and iPhones/iPods/iPads 57

Chapter 3   Setting Up and Using iCloud and Other Online Accounts 89

Chapter 4   Configuring an iPhone to Suit Your Preferences 123

Chapter 5   Customizing How Your iPhone Looks and Sounds 163

Chapter 6   Downloading Apps, Music, Movies, TV Shows, and More onto Your iPhone 201

Chapter 7   Managing Contacts 243

Chapter 8   Communicating with the Phone and FaceTime Apps 267

Chapter 9   Sending, Receiving, and Managing Email 317

Chapter 10   Sending, Receiving, and Managing Texts and iMessages 367

Chapter 11   Managing Calendars and Reminders 419

Chapter 12   Working with Siri 479

Chapter 13   Surfing the Web 513

Chapter 14   Working with Photos and Video You Take with Your iPhone 561

Chapter 15   Using Other Cool iPhone Apps and Features 643

             Index 700

Chapter 16   Maintaining and Protecting Your iPhone and Solving Problems .... **ONLINE ONLY**

             Bonus Content: Finding and Listening to Music .... **ONLINE ONLY**

Find the online chapters and other helpful information on this book's website at quepublishing.com/title/9780789755483.

Table of Contents

Using This Book xvi
Getting Started xviii

1 Getting Started with Your iPhone **3**
Getting to Know Your iPhone's External Features 3
Getting to Know Your iPhone's Software 6
    Using Your Fingers to Control Your iPhone 6
    Going Home 7
    Touching the iPhone's Screen 8
    Working with iPhone Apps 13
    Using the Home Screens 18
    Using the iPhone 6 Plus/6s Plus' Split-Screen 19
    Searching on Your iPhone 21
    Working with Siri Suggestions 23
    Working with the Control Center 24
    Working with Notifications and the Notification Center 26
    Using the Do Not Disturb Mode 29
    Working with Text 30
    Dictating Text 39
    Meeting Siri 41
    Understanding iPhone Status Icons 44
    Turning Your iPhone On or Off 45
    Sleeping/Locking and Waking/Unlocking Your iPhone 46
    Signing Into Your Apple ID 48
    Setting the Volume 49
    Using Airplane Mode 50
    Using the Settings App 51
    Printing from Your iPhone 52

2 Connecting Your iPhone to the Internet, Bluetooth Devices, and iPhones/iPods/iPads **57**
Getting Started 58
Securing Your iPhone 59
Using Wi-Fi Networks to Connect to the Internet 63
    Connecting to Open Wi-Fi Networks 64

Connecting to Public Wi-Fi Networks 68
Using Cellular Data Networks to Connect to the Internet 71
Using Bluetooth to Connect to Other Devices 77
Connecting to Bluetooth Devices 78
Connecting Your iPhone to Other iPhones, iPod touches, or iPads 80
Using AirDrop to Share Content with Other iPhones, iPod touches,
iPads, or a Mac 81
Enabling AirDrop 82
Using AirDrop to Share Your Content 84
Using AirDrop to Work with Content Shared with You 87

3   Setting Up and Using iCloud and Other Online Accounts   89

Getting Started 90
Configuring and Using iCloud 91
Obtaining an iCloud Account 92
Signing Into Your iCloud Account 95
Enabling iCloud to Store Your Information on the Cloud 97
Configuring iCloud Drive 99
Configuring iCloud to Store Photos 101
Configuring Your iCloud Backup 104
Configuring Your iCloud Keychain 105
Setting Up Other Types of Built-In Online Accounts on Your iPhone ... 108
Configuring a Google Account 109
Configuring Other Types of Online Accounts 111
Setting Up an Online Account Manually 112
Configuring a Facebook Account 114
Setting How and When Your Accounts Are Updated 116
Configuring How New Data is Retrieved for Your Accounts 117

4   Configuring an iPhone to Suit Your Preferences   123

Getting Started 123
Using the Settings App on Any iPhone 124
Searching for Settings 125
Using the Settings App on an iPhone 6 Plus or 6s Plus 126
Setting Passcode, Touch ID, and Auto-Lock Preferences 128
Securing Your iPhone with Auto-Lock 129
Configuring Your Passcode and Fingerprints (iPhone 5s and later) 130

Setting Keyboard, Language, and Format Options 136
    Setting Keyboard Preferences 137
    Creating and Working with Text Replacements 142
    Setting Language and Region Preferences 143
Setting Do Not Disturb Preferences 147
Setting Accessibility Options 150
Setting Restrictions for Content and Apps 155

5 Customizing How Your iPhone Looks and Sounds   **163**
Getting Started 163
Customizing Your Home Screens 165
    Moving Icons Around Your Home Screens 165
    Creating Folders to Organize Apps on Your Home Screens 168
    Placing Icons in Existing Folders 170
    Configuring the Home Screen Dock 172
    Deleting Icons 174
Setting the Screen's Brightness, View, Text Size, and Wallpaper 175
    Setting the Screen Brightness, View, and Text Size 176
    Setting the Wallpaper on the Home and Lock Screens 180
Choosing the Sounds Your iPhone Makes 186
Setting Up Notifications and the Notification Center 190
    Understanding Notifications and the Notification Center 190
    Setting Global Notification Preferences 194
    Configuring Notifications for Specific Apps 196

6 Downloading Apps, Music, Movies, TV Shows, and More onto Your iPhone   **201**
Getting Started 201
Configuring Store Settings 202
    Configuring Automatic Store Downloads 202
Using the App Store App to Find and Install iPhone Apps 205
    Searching for Apps 206
    Downloading Apps 210
Using the iTunes Store App to Download Music, Ringtones, Movies, and TV Shows 212
    Searching for iTunes Store Content 213
    Browsing for iTunes Store Content 216

Previewing iTunes Store Content 219
Downloading iTunes Store Content 221
Using Your iTunes Store History List 224
Downloading Apps or iTunes Store Content You've Purchased Previously 226
Downloading Previously Purchased App Store Apps 226
Downloading Previously Purchased iTunes Content 228
Using Family Sharing to Share Your Store Downloads with Others 232
Setting Up Family Sharing 232
Adding People to Family Sharing 234
Managing Family Sharing 237
Accessing Shared Content 240

7 Managing Contacts   243

Getting Started 243
Setting Your Contacts Preferences 244
Creating Contacts on Your iPhone 247
Creating New Contacts from Email 247
Creating Contacts Manually 249
Working with Contacts on Your iPhone 257
Using the Contacts App 257
Accessing Contacts from Other Apps 261
Managing Your Contacts on Your iPhone 263
Updating Contact Information 263
Deleting Contacts 265

8 Communicating with the Phone and FaceTime Apps   267

Getting Started 268
Configuring Phone Settings 268
Making Voice Calls 273
Dialing with the Keypad 275
Dialing with Contacts 276
Dialing with Favorites 277
Dialing with Recents 278
Dialing from the SIRI SUGGESTIONS Screen 280
Managing In-Process Voice Calls 281
Entering Numbers During a Call 283

Making Conference Calls 284
Using Another App During a Voice Call 288
Receiving Voice Calls 289
Answering Calls 289
Answering Calls During a Call 292
Managing Voice Calls 292
Clearing Recent Calls 293
Adding Calling Information to Favorites 294
Using the iPhone's EarPods for Calls 296
Using Visual Voicemail 296
Recording a New Greeting 297
Listening to and Managing Voicemails 299
Finding and Listening to Voicemails 300
Listening to and Managing Deleted Voicemails 302
Communicating with FaceTime 304
Configuring FaceTime Settings 305
Making FaceTime Calls 307
Receiving FaceTime Calls 310
Managing FaceTime Calls 312

9 Sending, Receiving, and Managing Email   317
Getting Started 317
Setting Mail App Preferences 318
Working with Email 324
Receiving and Reading Email 326
Receiving and Reading Email on an iPhone 6 Plus or 6s Plus ... 331
Using 3D Touch for Email (iPhone 6s and 6s Plus) 334
Sending Email 337
Using Mail's Suggested Recipients 341
Replying to Email 342
Forwarding Email 344
Managing Email 346
Checking for New Email 347
Understanding the Status of Email 347
Managing Email from the Message Screen 348
Managing Email from an Inbox 349

Managing Multiple Emails at the Same Time 352
Organizing Email from the Message Screen 354
Organizing Email from the Inbox 356
Viewing Messages in a Mailbox 358
Saving Images Attached to Email 359
Searching Your Email 360
Working with VIPs 362
Designating VIPs 363
Accessing VIP Email 363
Managing Junk Email 365

10 Sending, Receiving, and Managing Texts and iMessages   367

Getting Started 367
Preparing Messages for Messaging 368
    Setting Your Text and iMessage Preferences 369
    Blocking People from Messaging or Texting You 377
Sending Messages 378
    Creating and Sending Messages 379
Receiving, Reading, and Replying to Messages 384
    Receiving Messages 384
    Reading Messages 386
    Viewing Images or Video You Receive in Messages 388
    Listening to Audio in Messages You Receive in Messages 390
    Watching Video in Messages You Receive in Messages 392
    Replying to Messages from the Messages App 394
    Replying to Messages from a Banner Alert 395
    Using Quick Actions to Send Messages (iPhone 6s and 6s Plus) ... 396
Working with Messages 397
    Receiving and Reading Messages on an iPhone 6 Plus or 6s Plus ... 398
    Using 3D Touch for Messages (iPhone 6s and 6s Plus) 400
    Adding Images and Video to Conversations 401
    Adding Audio Recordings to Conversations 407
    Adding Video and Photos to Conversations 409
    Adding Locations to Conversations 410
    Browsing Attachments to Conversations 412
    Deleting Messages and Conversations 414
    Deleting Conversations 416

11 Managing Calendars, Reminders, and Clocks   **419**

Getting Started 419

Setting Calendar, Reminder, Date, and Time Preferences 420

Working with Calendars 424

Viewing Calendars and Events 424

Configuring Calendars 425

Navigating Calendars 430

Viewing Calendars 430

Using 3D Touch for Events (iPhone 6s and 6s Plus Only) 434

Adding Events to a Calendar 436

Using Quick Actions with the Calendar App (iPhone 6s and 6s Plus Only) .. 449

Searching Calendars 449

Managing Calendars and Events 451

Working with Reminders 453

Creating Reminders 456

Organizing Reminders with Lists 461

Managing Reminders 463

Working with the Clock 465

Setting and Using Alarms 466

Managing Alarms 470

Using the Stopwatch 472

Using the Timer 474

12 Working with Siri   **479**

Getting Started 479

Setting Up Siri 481

Understanding Siri's Personality 484

Learning How to Use Siri by Example 490

Using Siri to Make Voice Calls 490

Composing New Email with Siri 491

Replying to Emails with Siri 492

Having Messages Read to You 494

Replying to Messages with Siri 495

Sending New Messages with Siri 496

Using Siri to Create Events 497

Using Siri to Create Reminders 499

Using Siri to Get Information 501
Using Siri to Play Music 502
Using Siri to Get Directions 503
Using Dictation to Speak Text Instead of Typing 505
Using Siri to Open Apps 507
Getting Suggestions from Siri 507

13 Surfing the Web   513

Getting Started 513
Setting Safari Preferences 515
Visiting Websites 520
Using Bookmarks to Move to Websites 521
Using Your Favorites to Move to Websites 524
Typing URLs to Move to Websites 526
Using Your Browsing History to Move to Websites 528
Viewing Websites 530
Working with Multiple Websites at the Same Time 534
Opening New Pages in the Background 534
Opening New Pages in a New Tab 535
Using Tab View to Manage Open Web Pages 536
Searching the Web 539
Saving and Organizing Bookmarks 541
Creating Bookmarks 541
Organizing Bookmarks 544
Deleting Bookmarks or Folders of Bookmarks 549
Creating Bookmarks on the Home Screen 550
Using 3D Touch with Safari (iPhone 6s and iPhone 6s Plus Only) 552
Completing Forms on the Web 554
Manually Completing Forms 555
Using AutoFill to Complete Forms 557
Signing In to Websites Automatically 558

14 Working with Photos and Video You Take with Your iPhone   561

Getting Started 561
Setting Your Photos & Camera Preferences 562

Taking Photos and Video with Your iPhone 567
   Taking Photos 573
   Taking Panoramic Photos 577
   Taking Video 579
   Taking Photos and Video from the Lock Screen 581
   Taking Photos and Video from the Control Center 582
   Taking Photos with Quick Actions (iPhone 6s, 6s Plus Only) 583
Viewing, Editing, and Working with Photos on Your iPhone 585
   Finding Photos to Work With by Browsing 585
   Finding Photos to Work With by Searching 593
   Using 3D Touch with Photos (iPhone 6s, 6s Plus Only) 594
   Viewing Photos in Slideshows 595
   Working with Burst Mode Photos 601
   Editing Photos 603
   Enhancing Photos 604
   Straightening, Rotating, and Cropping Photos 606
   Applying Filters to Photos 609
   Removing Red-Eye from Photos 611
   Making Smart Adjustments to Photos 613
   Working with Photos 616
   Sharing Photos via Email 617
   Organizing Photos in a New Album 620
   Adding Photos to an Existing Album 622
   Deleting Photos 624
Viewing, Editing, and Working with Video on Your iPhone 625
   Finding and Watching Videos 625
   Editing Video 627
Using AirPlay to View Photos and Videos on a TV 629
Using iCloud with Your Photos 633
   Sharing Your Photos 633
   Adding Photos to a Shared Album 635
   Working with Photo Albums Shared with You 638

15 **Using Other Cool iPhone Apps and Features**   **643**

Getting Started 643

Touring Other Cool iPhone Apps 644

    Touring Other Cool iPhone Apps Already Installed on Your iPhone 644

    Touring Other Cool iPhone Apps You Can Download onto Your iPhone 647

Listening to Podcasts with the Podcasts App 649

    Setting Your Podcast Preferences 649

    Using the Podcasts App to Subscribe to Podcasts 652

    Choosing a Podcast to Listen To 655

    Listening to Podcasts 658

    Managing Podcasts and Episodes of Podcasts 662

Finding Your Way with Maps 665

Working with the Wallet App and Apple Pay 672

    Working with the Wallet App 672

    Adding Passes or Cards to Your Wallet Using an App 677

    Adding Passes or Cards to Your Wallet by Scanning Their Codes ... 678

    Working with Apple Pay 680

    Adding Credit or Debit Cards to Apple Pay 682

    Managing Apple Pay 684

Managing Your Health with the Health App 686

    Using the Health App to Create a Medical ID 686

    Accessing Your Medical ID 688

    Using the Health App for Health and Fitness Information 689

    Configuring Apps to Report to the Health App 690

    Using the Health App to View Health Information 692

    Managing Sources in the Health App 695

Working Seamlessly Across Your Devices 696

    Working with Handoff 696

    Using Handoff on iOS Devices 697

    Taking Phone Calls on Macs or iPads 699

Index   **700**

16 **Maintaining and Protecting Your iPhone and Solving Problems**   **ONLINE**

Bonus Content: Finding and Listening to Music   **ONLINE**

About the Author

Brad Miser has written extensively about technology, with his favorite topics being the amazing "i" devices, especially the iPhone, that make it possible to take our lives with us while we are on the move. In addition to *My iPhone for Seniors*, Second Edition, Brad has written many other books, including *My iPhone,* 9th Edition and *My Pages, Keynote, and Numbers*. He has also been an author, development editor, or technical editor for more than 50 other titles.

Brad is or has been a sales support specialist, the director of product and customer services, and the manager of education and support services for several software development companies. Previously, he was the lead proposal specialist for an aircraft engine manufacturer, a development editor for a computer book publisher, and a civilian aviation test officer/engineer for the United States Army. Brad holds a bachelor of science degree in mechanical engineering from California Polytechnic State University at San Luis Obispo and has received advanced education in maintainability engineering, business, and other topics.

Brad would love to hear about your experiences with this book (the good, the bad, and the ugly). You can write to him at bradmiser@icloud.com.

About AARP and AARP TEK

AARP is a nonprofit, nonpartisan organization, with a membership of nearly 38 million, that helps people turn their goals and dreams into real possibilities™, strengthens communities, and fights for the issues that matter most to families such as healthcare, employment and income security, retirement planning, affordable utilities, and protection from financial abuse. Learn more at aarp.org.

The AARP TEK (Technology Education & Knowledge) program aims to accelerate AARP's mission of turning dreams into real possibilities™ by providing step-by-step lessons in a variety of formats to accommodate different learning styles, levels of experience, and interests. Expertly guided hands-on workshops delivered in communities nationwide help instill confidence and enrich lives of people 50+ by equipping them with skills for staying connected to the people and passions in their lives. Lessons are taught on touchscreen tablets and smartphones—common tools for connection, education, entertainment, and productivity. For self-paced lessons, videos, articles, and other resources, visit aarptek.org.

Dedication

To those who have given the last full measure of devotion so that the rest of us can be free.

Acknowledgments

To the following people on the *My iPhone for Seniors* project team, my sincere appreciation for your hard work on this book:

Laura Norman, my acquisitions and development editor, who envisioned the original concept for *My iPhone* and works very difficult and long hours to ensure the success of each edition. Laura and I have worked on many books together, and I appreciate her professional and effective approach to these projects. Thanks for putting up with me yet one more time! Frankly, I have no idea how she does all the things she does and manages to be so great to work with, given the incredible work and pressure books like this one involve!

Mandie Frank, my project editor, who skillfully managed the hundreds of files and production process that it took to make this book. Imagine keeping dozens of plates spinning on top of poles and you get a glimpse into Mandie's daily life! (And no plates have been broken in the production of this book!)

Mark Shirar, for the interior design and cover of the book.

Que's production and sales team for printing the book and getting it into your hands.

We Want to Hear from You!

As the reader of this book, *you* are our most important critic and commentator. We value your opinion and want to know what we're doing right, what we could do better, what areas you'd like to see us publish in, and any other words of wisdom you're willing to pass our way.

We welcome your comments. You can email or write to let us know what you did or didn't like about this book—as well as what we can do to make our books better.

Please note that we cannot help you with technical problems related to the topic of this book.

When you write, please be sure to include this book's title and author as well as your name and email address. We will carefully review your comments and share them with the author and editors who worked on the book.

Email: feedback@quepublishing.com

Mail: Que Publishing, ATTN: Reader Feedback
           800 East 96th Street, Indianapolis, IN 46240 USA

Reader Services

Visit our website and register this book at quepublishing.com/register for convenient access to any updates, downloads, or errata that might be available for this book.

Using This Book

This book has been designed to help you transform an iPhone into *your* iPhone by helping you learn to use it easily and quickly. As you can tell, the book relies heavily on pictures to show you how an iPhone works. It is also task-focused so that you can quickly learn the specific steps to follow to do lots of cool things with your iPhone.

Using an iPhone involves lots of touching its screen with your fingers. When you need to tap part of the screen, such as a button or keyboard, you see a callout with the step number pointing to where you need to tap. When you need to swipe your finger along the screen, such as to browse lists, you see the following icons:

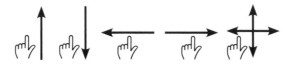

The directions in which you should slide your finger on the screen are indicated with arrows. When the arrow points both ways, you can move your finger in either direction. When the arrows point in all four directions, you can move your finger in any direction on the screen.

To zoom in on the screen, unpinch your figures by placing them together on the center of the screen and then sliding them apart while still touching the screen. To zoom out on screens, place your fingers a little apart on the screen, and then pinch them together. These motions are indicated by the following icons:

When you need to tap once or twice, such as to zoom out or in, you see the following icons matching the number of times you need to tap:

If you use an iPhone 6s or iPhone 6s Plus, you can use pressure on the screen to activate certain functions. The following icons indicate when you should apply some pressure or slightly more pressure:

When you can rotate your iPhone, you see this icon:

Occasionally, you shake the iPhone to activate a control. When you do, you see this icon:

As you can see on its cover, this book provides information about a number of iPhone models, which are the iPhone 4s, iPhone 5, iPhone 5c and 5s, iPhone 6/6s, and iPhone 6/6s Plus. Each of these models has specific features and capabilities that vary slightly from the others. Additionally, they have different screen sizes with the 4s being the smallest and the iPhone 6/6s Plus being the largest.

Because of the variations between the models, the figures you see in this book may be slightly different than the screens you see on your iPhone. For example, the iPhone 6/6s has settings that aren't on the iPhone 5s while the 5s and later models support Touch ID (fingerprint recognition) while the 4s and 5/5c don't. In most cases, you can follow the steps as they are written with any of these models even if there are minor differences between the figures and your screens.

When the model you are using doesn't support a feature being described, such as the Display Zoom that is on the iPhone 6/6s and 6/6s Plus but not on previous models, you can skip the information or read it to help you decide if you want to upgrade to a newer model.

If you have used an iPhone before running an earlier version of its software, you will notice that there are many changes in iOS 9, some are significant and still others are entirely new. In the case of those features that have changed significantly, or are completely new, we have added an indicator to the text and table of contents to help you easily locate them. When you see **New!** be sure to check out those tasks to quickly get up to speed on what's new in iOS 9.

Getting Started

Learning to use new technology can be intimidating. Don't worry, with this book as your guide, you'll be working your iPhone like you've been using it all your life in no time at all.

There are several ways you can purchase an iPhone, such as from an Apple Store, from a provider's store (such as AT&T or Verizon), or from a website. And, you may be upgrading from a previous iPhone or other type of cell phone, in which case, you are using the same phone number, or you might be starting with a completely new phone and phone number. However you received your new phone, you need to turn it on, perform the basic setup (the iPhone leads you through this step-by-step), and activate the phone.

If you purchased your phone in a store, you probably received help with these tasks and you are ready to start learning how to use your iPhone. If you purchased your iPhone from an online store, it came with basic instructions that explain how you need to activate your phone; follow those instructions to get your iPhone ready for action.

For this book, I've assumed you have an iPhone in your hands, you have turned it on, followed the initial setup process it led you through, and activated it.

With your iPhone activated and initial setup complete, you are ready to learn how to use it. This book is designed for you to read and do at the same time. The tasks explained in this book contain step-by-step instructions that guide you; to get the most benefit from the information, perform the steps as you read them. This book helps you learn by doing!

As you can see, this book has quite a few chapters. However, there are only a few that you definitely should read as a group as you get started. You can read the rest of them as the topics are of interest to you. Most of the chapters are designed so that they can be read individually as you move into new areas of your iPhone. For example, when you want to learn how to send messages, read Chapter 10, "Sending, Receiving, and Managing Texts and iMessages."

After you've finished reading this front matter, I recommend you read and work through Chapter 1, "Getting Started with Your iPhone;" Chapter 2, "Connecting Your iPhone to the Internet, Bluetooth Devices, and iPhones/iPods/iPads;" and Chapter 3, "Setting Up and Using iCloud and Other Online Accounts" in their entirety. These chapters give you a good overview of your iPhone and help you set up the basics you use throughout the rest of the book.

From there, read the parts of Chapter 4, "Configuring an iPhone to Suit Your Preferences," and Chapter 5, "Customizing How Your iPhone Looks and Sounds," that are of interest to you (for example, in Chapter 5, you how to change the wallpaper image that you see in the background of the Home and Lock screens). Tasks covering how to protect your iPhone with a passcode and how to have your iPhone recognize your fingerprints to unlock it and to make purchases from the iTunes Store should be high on your priority list (this is covered in Chapter 4). Chapters 4 and 5 are good references whenever you need to make changes to how your iPhone is configured.

After you've finished these core chapters, you're ready to explore the rest of the book in any order you'd like. For example, when you want to learn how to use your iPhone's camera and work with the photos you take, see Chapter 14, "Working with Photos and Video You Take with Your iPhone."

You'll soon wonder how you ever got along without one!

In this chapter, you get introduced to the amazing iPhone! Topics include the following:

→ Getting to know your iPhone's external features
→ Getting to know your iPhone's software

1

Getting Started with Your iPhone

Your iPhone is one of the most amazing handheld devices ever because of how well it is designed. It has only a few external features you need to understand. For most of the things you do, you just use your fingers on your iPhone's screen (which just seems natural), and the iPhone's consistent interface enables you to accomplish most tasks with similar steps.

Getting to Know Your iPhone's External Features

Take a quick look at the iPhone's physical attributes. It doesn't have many physical buttons or controls because you mostly use software to control it.

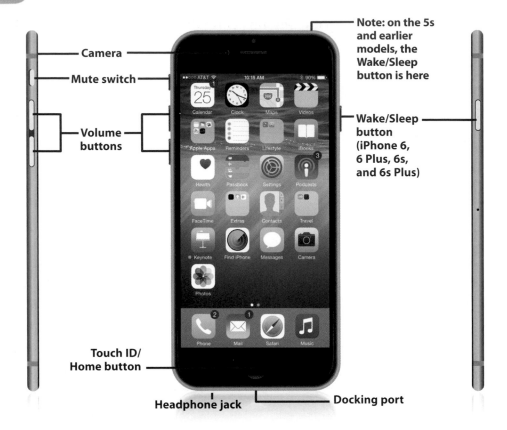

Camera

Mute switch

Volume buttons

Touch ID/
Home button

Headphone jack

Note: on the 5s and earlier models, the Wake/Sleep button is here

Wake/Sleep button (iPhone 6, 6 Plus, 6s, and 6s Plus)

Docking port

- **Cameras**—One of the iPhone's camera lenses is located on its backside near the top-left corner; the other is on the front at the top at the center of the phone. When you take photos or video, you can choose either camera to use. All iPhone models have a flash located near the camera on the backside. The iPhone 6s and 6s Plus also have a flash on the front; for all other models, there is no flash when you use the camera on the front.

- **Wake/Sleep button**—Press this to lock the iPhone's screen and put it to sleep. Press it again to wake the iPhone from Sleep mode. You also use this button to shut down the iPhone and to power it up.

- **Mute switch**—This switch determines whether the iPhone makes sounds, such as ringing when a call comes in or making the alert noise for notifications, such as an event on a calendar. Slide it toward the front of the iPhone to hear sounds. Slide it toward the back of the iPhone to mute all sound. When muted, you see orange in the switch.

- **Headphone jack**—Plug the iPhone's EarPods or self-powered, external speakers into this jack.

- **Volume**—Press the upper button to increase volume; press the lower button to decrease volume. This is contextual; for example, when you are listening to music, it controls the music's volume, but when you aren't, it controls the ringer volume. When you are using the Camera app, pressing either button takes a photo.

- **Docking port**—Use this port, located on the bottom side of the iPhone, to connect it to a computer or power adapter using the included USB cable. There are also accessories that connect to this port. The iPhone 5s, 5c, 6/6s, and 6/6s Plus have the Lightning port, which uses a flat, thin plug. It doesn't matter which side is up when you plug something into this port. The iPhone 4s uses the 30-pin port, which is much larger and has to be inserted "top side up."

- **Touch ID/Home button (iPhone 5s, 6, 6s, 6 Plus, and 6s Plus)**—This serves two functions. The Touch ID sensor recognizes your fingerprint, so you can simply touch it to unlock your iPhone, sign into the iTunes Store, and use Apple Pay to confirm your information to complete a transaction. It also functions just like the Home button described in the following bullet.

- **Home button (iPhone 5c, 5, and 4s)**—When the iPhone is asleep, press it to wake up the iPhone. When the iPhone is awake and unlocked, press this button to move to the all-important Home screens; press it twice quickly to open the App Switcher. Press and hold the Home button to activate Siri to speak to your iPhone.

>>>*Go Further*
SO MANY iPHONES, SO FEW PAGES

The iPhone is now in its ninth generation of software that runs on multiple generations of hardware. Each successive generation has added features and capabilities to the previous version. All iPhone hardware runs the iOS operating system. However, this book is based on the current version of this operating system, iOS 9. Only the iPhone 4s and newer can run this version of the software. If you have an older version of the iPhone, this book helps you see why it is time to upgrade, but most of the information contained herein won't apply to your iPhone until you do.

There are also differences even among the models of iPhones that can run iOS 9. For example, the iPhone 5s, 6, 6 Plus, 6s, and 6s Plus models have Touch ID that uses your fingerprint to unlock your iPhone, to sign into your Apple ID, and for other purposes (such as Apple Pay). The iPhone 4s, 5, and 5c do not have this capability.

This book is primarily based on the latest generation of iPhones, the iPhone 6s and 6s Plus. If you use one of the other models that can run iOS 9, there might be some differences between the details you read in this book and your phone. Those differences aren't significant and shouldn't stop you from accomplishing the tasks as described in this book.

Getting to Know Your iPhone's Software

You might not suspect it based on the iPhone's simple and elegant exterior, but this powerhouse runs very sophisticated software that enables you to do all sorts of great things. The beauty of the iPhone's software is that it is both very powerful and also easy to use—once you get used to its User Interface (UI for the more technical among you). The iPhone's UI is so well designed that after a few minutes, you may wish everything worked so well and was so easy to use.

Using Your Fingers to Control Your iPhone

Apple designed the iPhone to be touched. Most of the time, you control your iPhone by using your fingers on its screen to tap buttons, select items, swipe on the screen, zoom, type text, and so on. If you want to get technical, this method of interacting with software is called the multi-touch interface.

Going Home

Almost all iPhone activities start at the Home screen, or Home screens, to be more accurate, because the Home screen consists of multiple pages. You get to the Home screen by pressing the Touch ID/Home button once. Along the bottom of the Home screen (or along the side on an iPhone 6 Plus or 6s Plus held horizontally) is the Dock, which is always visible on the Home screen. This gives you easy access to the icons it contains (more on the Home screens shortly); up to four icons can be placed on this Dock. Above the Dock are apps that do all sorts of cool things. As you install apps, the number of icons increases. You can also create bookmarks for websites and store them on the Home screens. You can organize the pages of the Home screens in any way you like, and you can place icons into folders to keep your Home screens tidy. At the top of the screen are status icons that provide you with important information, such as whether you are connected to a Wi-Fi network and the current charge of your iPhone's battery.

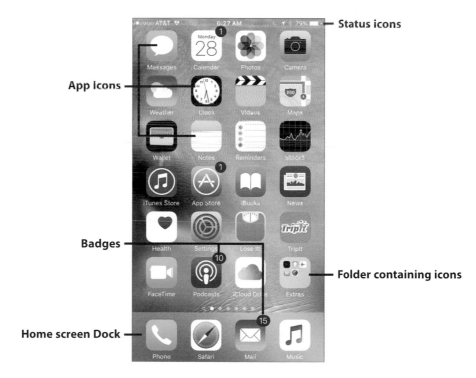

Status icons

App Icons

Badges

Folder containing icons

Home screen Dock

Touching the iPhone's Screen

The following figures highlight the major ways you control an iPhone:

- **Tap:** briefly touch a finger to the iPhone's screen and then lift your finger again. For example, to open an app, you tap its icon.

Tap an app's icon to launch it

- **Double-tap:** tap twice.
- **Swipe:** touch the screen at any location and slide your finger in one direction.

Swipe your finger up and down to browse lists

Tap a letter in the index to jump to it

Tap an item to work with it

- **Drag:** tap and hold an object and move your finger across the screen without lifting it up; the faster you move your finger, the faster the resulting action happens. (You don't need to apply pressure, just make contact.)
- **Pinch or unpinch:** place two fingers on the screen and drag them together or move them apart; the faster and more you pinch or unpinch, the "more" the action happens (such as a zoom in).

Swipe your finger up, down, left, and right to scroll

Unpinch your fingers or tap twice to zoom in

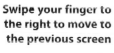

Pinch your fingers or tap twice to zoom out

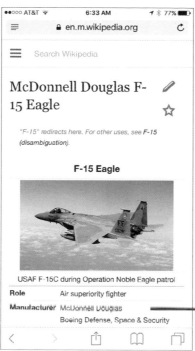

Tap a link to move to it

Swipe your finger to the right to move to the previous screen

Swipe your finger to the left to move to the next screen

Tap the screen to show/hide toolbars

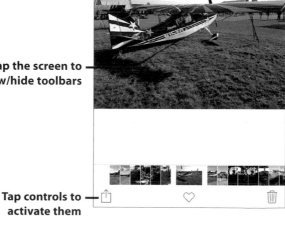

Tap controls to activate them

- Rotate: rotate the iPhone to change the screen's orientation.

Rotate the iPhone to change the screen's orientation

On an iPhone 6s or iPhone 6s Plus, you can take advantage of 3D Touch that enables you to perform tasks by applying pressure on the screen in addition to just touching it.

When you are looking at a preview of something, such as an email, tap and put a small amount of pressure on the screen to perform a Peek. A Peek causes a window to open that shows a preview of the object. You can preview the object in the Peek window; in most cases, when you swipe up on a Peek, you get a menu of commands related to the object. For example, when you perform a Peek on an email and then swipe up on the Peek, you can tap Reply to reply to the email.

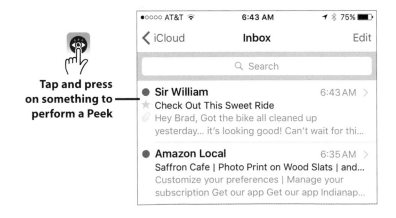

Tap and press on something to perform a Peek

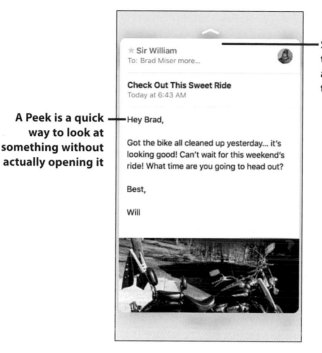

Swipe up on a Peek to reveal menus with actions you can select to perform them

A Peek is a quick way to look at something without actually opening it

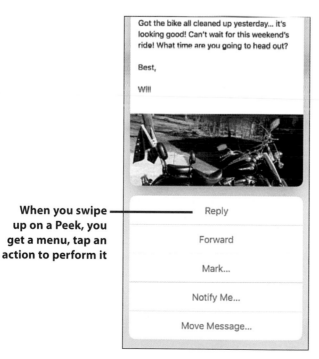

When you swipe up on a Peek, you get a menu, tap an action to perform it

When you are looking at a Peek, apply slightly more pressure on the screen to perform a Pop, which opens the object in its app. For example, you can perform a Peek on a photo's thumbnail to preview it. Apply a bit more pressure (a Pop) on the preview to "pop" it open in the Photos app.

Tap and press on something to perform a Peek

Press slightly harder on a Peek to perform a Pop

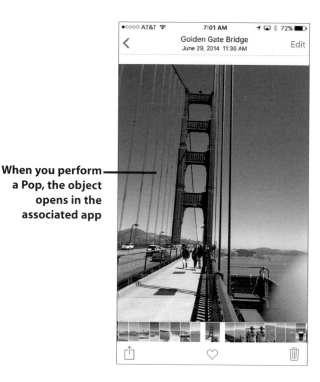

When you perform a Pop, the object opens in the associated app

Peeks and Pops can take a little bit of experimentation to get the amount of pressure you need just right, but after a few tries, you'll find these to be handy techniques to quickly access content.

Working with iPhone Apps

One of the best things about an iPhone is that it can run all sorts of applications, or in iPhone lingo, *apps*. It includes a number of preinstalled apps, such as Mail, Safari, and so on, but you can download and use thousands of other apps through the App Store. You learn about many of the iPhone's preinstalled apps as you read through this book. And as you learned earlier, to launch an app, you simply tap its icon. The app launches and fills the iPhone's screen.

When you tap an app's icon, it opens and fills the iPhone's screen (this is the Podcasts app) —

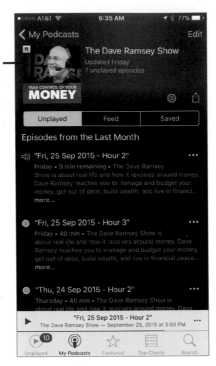

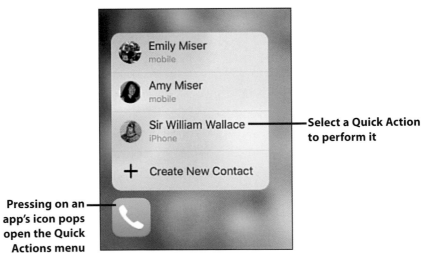

— Select a Quick Action to perform it

Pressing on an app's icon pops open the Quick Actions menu —

On an iPhone 6s or iPhone 6s Plus, 3D Touch enables you to perform tasks by applying pressure on the screen in addition to just touching it. When you press on an app's icon, the Quick Actions menu appears; slide your finger on the menu to highlight an action to take it. For example, when you open the Quick Actions menu for the Phone app, you can place calls to people you have recently communicated with or create a new contact.

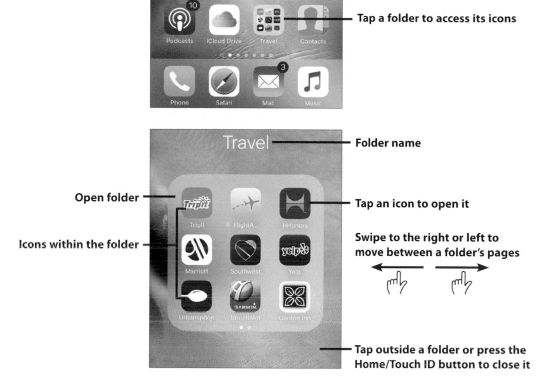

Tap a folder to access its icons

Folder name

Open folder

Tap an icon to open it

Swipe to the right or left to move between a folder's pages

Icons within the folder

Tap outside a folder or press the Home/Touch ID button to close it

In Chapter 5, "Customizing How Your iPhone Looks and Sounds," you learn how you can organize icons in folders to keep your Home screens tidy and make getting to icons faster and easier. To access an icon that is in a folder, tap the folder. It opens and takes over the screen. Under its name is a box showing the apps or website bookmarks it contains. Like the Home screens, folders can have multiple pages. To move between a folder's pages, swipe to the left to move to the next screen or to the right to move to the previous one. Each time you "flip" a page, you see another set of icons. You can close a folder without opening an app by tapping outside its borders or press the Home/Touch ID button.

To launch an app or open a website bookmark within a folder, tap its icon.

When you are done using an app, press the Home button. You return to the Home screen you were most recently using.

When you move out of an app by pressing the Home button, the app moves into the background but doesn't stop running (you can control whether or not apps are allowed to work in the background, as you learn in a later section). So, if the app has a task to complete, such as uploading photos or playing audio, it continues to work behind the scenes. In some cases, most notably games, the app becomes suspended at the point you move it into the background by switching to a different app or moving to a Home screen. In addition to the benefit of completing tasks when you move into another app, the iPhone's capability to multitask means that you can run multiple apps at the same time. For example, you can run an Internet radio app to listen to music while you switch over to the Mail app to work on your email.

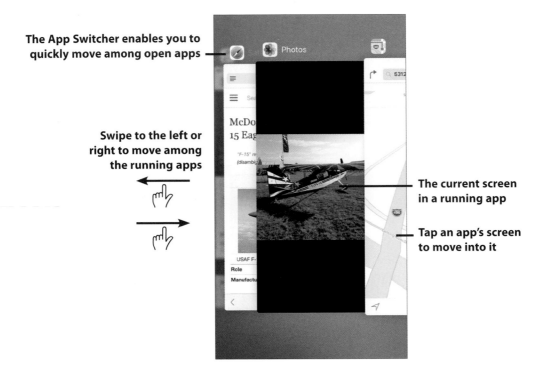

The App Switcher enables you to quickly move among open apps

Swipe to the left or right to move among the running apps

The current screen in a running app

Tap an app's screen to move into it

You can control apps by using the App Switcher. To see this, quickly press the Touch ID/Home button twice. The App Switcher appears.

At the top of the App Switcher, you see icons for apps you have used recently. Under each app's icon, you see a thumbnail of that app's screen. You can swipe to the left or right to move among the apps you see. You can tap an app's screen to move into it. That app takes over the screen, and you can work with it, picking up right where you left off the last time you used it.

When you open the App Switcher, the app you were using most recently comes to the center to make it easy to return to. This enables you to toggle between two apps easily. For example, suppose you need to enter a confirmation number from one app into another app. Open the app into which you want to enter the number. Then open the app containing the number you need to enter. Open the App Switcher and tap the pervious app to return to it quickly so that you can enter the number.

To close the App Switcher without moving into a different app, press the Home/Touch ID button once. You move back into the app or Home screen you were most recently using.

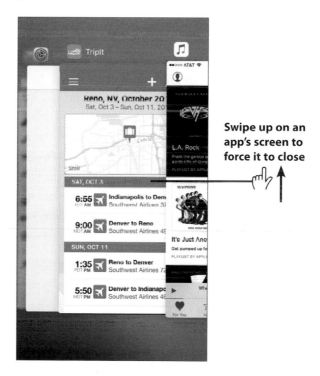

Swipe up on an app's screen to force it to close

In some cases (such as when it's using up your battery too quickly or it has stopped responding to you), you might want to force an app to quit. To do this, open the App Switcher by quickly pressing the Touch ID/Home button twice. Swipe up on the app you want to stop. The app is forced to quit, its icon and screen disappear, and you remain in the App Switcher. You should be careful about this, though, because if the app has unsaved data, that data is lost when you force the app to quit. The app is not deleted from the iPhone—it is just shut down until you open it again (which you can do by returning to the Home screen and tapping the app's icon).

Tap to return to the app you were previously using ⟶

Sometimes, a link in one app takes you into a different app. When this happens, you see the Back to *App* button, where *App* is the name of the app in which you tapped the link, in the upper-left corner of the screen. You can tap this button to return to the app you came from. For example, you can tap a link in a Mail email message to open the associated web page in Safari. To return to the email you were reading in the Mail app, tap the Back to Mail button in the upper-left corner of the screen.

Using the Home Screens

Previously in this chapter, you read that the Home screen is the jumping-off point for many of the things you do with your iPhone because that is where you access the icons you tap to launch things such as apps or website bookmarks you've saved there.

The Home screen has multiple pages. To change the page you are viewing, swipe to the left to move to later pages or to the right to move to earlier pages. The dots above the toolbar represent the pages of the Home screen. The white dot represents the page being displayed. You can also change the page by tapping to the left of the white dot to move to the previous page or to the right of it to move to the next page.

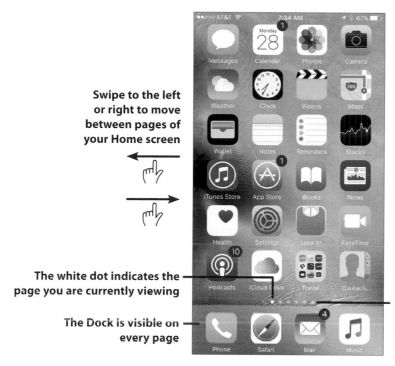

Swipe to the left or right to move between pages of your Home screen

The white dot indicates the page you are currently viewing

The Dock is visible on every page

Tap to the left or right of the current page (white dot) to move to the previous or the next page

When you move to a different page, you see a different set of icons and folders

Using the iPhone 6 Plus/6s Plus' Split-Screen

When you hold an iPhone 6 Plus/6s Plus in the horizontal orientation, you can take advantage of the iPhone 6 Plus/6s Plus' Split-screen feature in many apps (not all apps support this). In Split-screen mode, the screen has two panes. The left pane is for navigation, while the right pane shows the content selected in the left pane. The two panes are independent, so you can swipe up and down on one side without affecting the other. In most apps that support this functionality, there is a button you can use to open or close the split screen. This button changes depending on the app you are using. For example, when you are using Safari to browse the Web, tap the Bookmark button (this looks like an open book) to open the left pane and tap it again to close the left pane (while the left pane is open, you can select bookmarks in the left pane and see the associated web pages in the right pane). As another example, in the Mail app, you tap the Full Screen button (two arrows pointing diagonally away from each other) to open or close the left pane.

Apps that support this functionality include Settings, Mail, Safari, and Messages; you see examples showing how Split-screen works in those apps later in this book. You should hold the iPhone 6 Plus/6s Plus horizontally when using your favorite apps to see if they support this feature.

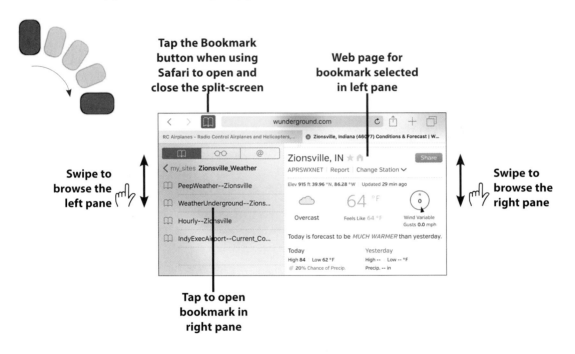

Tap the Bookmark button when using Safari to open and close the split-screen

Web page for bookmark selected in left pane

Swipe to browse the left pane

Swipe to browse the right pane

Tap to open bookmark in right pane

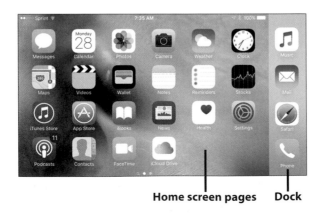

Home screen pages   **Dock**

When you hold the iPhone 6 Plus/6s Plus horizontally and move to the Home screen, the Dock moves to the right side of the screen and you see the Home screen's pages in the left part of the window. Although this looks a bit different, it works the same as when you hold an iPhone vertically.

Searching on Your iPhone

Swipe down from the center part of the screen to open the Spotlight Search tool

You can use the Spotlight Search tool to search your iPhone. To open this tool, move to a Home screen and swipe down from the center part of the screen. (Be careful not to swipe down from the very top of the screen because that opens the Notification Center instead.) The Search bar appears at the top of the screen and the keyboard opens.

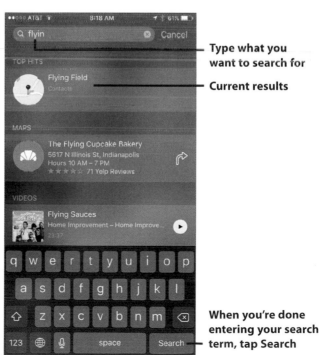

Type what you want to search for

Current results

When you're done entering your search term, tap Search

To perform a search, tap in the Search bar and type the search term using the onscreen keyboard. As you type, items that meet your search are shown on the list below the Search bar. When you finish typing the search term, tap Search.

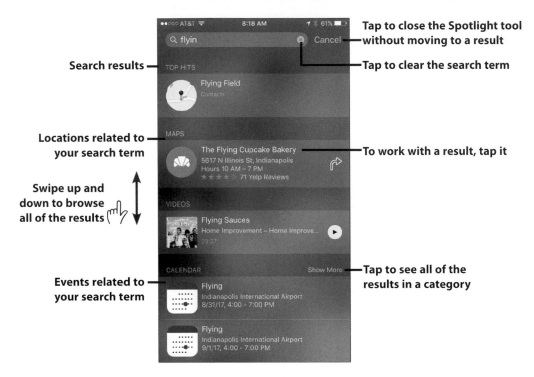

Tap to close the Spotlight tool without moving to a result

Tap to clear the search term

Search results

Locations related to your search term

To work with a result, tap it

Swipe up and down to browse all of the results

Tap to see all of the results in a category

Events related to your search term

The results are organized into sections, such as TOP HITS, CONTACTS, MAIL, MUSIC, and so on. Swipe up and down the screen to browse all of the results. To work with an item you find, such as to view an event you found, tap it; you move into the associated app and see the search result that you tapped. The results remain in the Spotlight Search tool. Move back to the Home screen and open the Spotlight tool again. The results of the most recent search are still listed. To clear the search term, tap the Clear button (x). To close the Spotlight tool without going to one of the results, tap Cancel.

Working with Siri Suggestions

When you move to a Home page and swipe all the way to the right, you see the SIRI SUGGESTIONS page. This page shows you people you communicate with, apps you use, items that might be of interest that are near you, and news you might be interested in. You can also search from this screen just like from other Home screens.

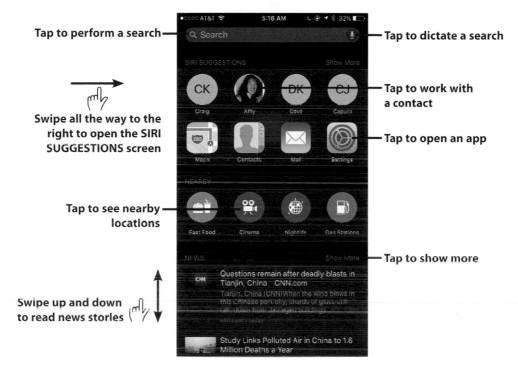

On the SIRI SUGGESTIONS screen, you can do the following tasks:

- Tap in the Search bar to type a search or tap the Microphone to dictate a search. This works just like the searching you learned about in the previous section.

- Tap a contact to reveal options you can use to communicate with her.

- Tap an app you've used recently to return to it.

- Tap a category of location shown in the NEARBY section to move to the Maps app and see a list of places of that type.

- Swipe up and down in the NEWS section to browse news stories. Tap a story to read its detail in the News app.

Working with the Control Center

On the Home screen or when you are using apps, swipe up from the bottom of the screen to open the Control Center

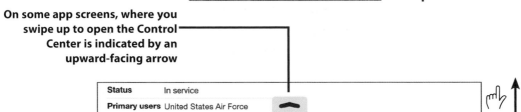

On the Lock screen, the place you swipe up on to open the Control Center is marked with a line

On some app screens, where you swipe up to open the Control Center is indicated by an upward-facing arrow

Status	In service
Primary users	United States Air Force

The Control Center provides quick access to a number of very useful controls. To access it, swipe up from the bottom of the screen. If your iPhone is asleep/locked, press the Sleep/Wake or Touch ID/Home button to wake up the phone and then swipe up from the bottom of the screen from the area of the horizontal line. Sometimes when you are using an app, the place you swipe up on is marked with an upward-facing arrow. Regardless of the screen you are on, when you swipe up, the Control Center opens and gives you quick access to a number of controls.

Control Center Tip

Some apps have a Dock at the bottom of the screen. When you are using such an app, make sure you don't touch a button on the Dock when you are trying to open the Control Center because you'll do whatever the button is for instead. Just swipe up on an empty area of the toolbar and the Control Center opens.

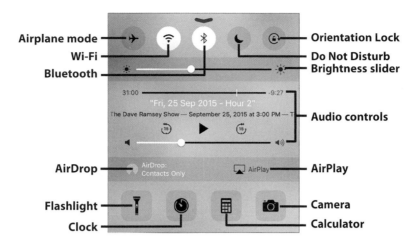

At the top of the Control Center are buttons you can use to turn on or turn off important functions. To activate a function, tap the button, which becomes white to show the function is active. To disable a function, tap the button so that it becomes dark to show you it is inactive. For example, to lock the orientation of the iPhone's screen in its current position, tap the Orientation Lock button so it becomes white. Your iPhone screen's orientation no longer changes when you rotate the phone. To make the orientation change when you rotate the phone again, turn off the Orientation Lock button. You learn about Airplane mode and Do No Disturb later in this chapter. Wi-Fi and Bluetooth are explained in Chapter 2, "Connecting Your iPhone to the Internet, Bluetooth Devices, and iPhones/iPods/iPads."

Below the top function buttons is the Brightness slider. Drag the slider to the right to make the screen brighter or to the left to make it dimmer.

In the center of the Control Center are the audio controls you can use with whatever audio is playing, such as podcasts from the Podcasts app.

The AirDrop button enables you to share content with other iOS device and Mac users in the same vicinity; this is covered in Chapter 2. The AirPlay button enables you to stream your iPhone's music, podcasts, photos, and video onto other devices, such as a TV to which an Apple TV is connected.

At the bottom of the Control Center are four app icons; tap an icon to open the app, just as you do on the Home screens. The Flashlight app uses your iPhone's flash as a flashlight. The Clock app provides you with a number of time-related functions, which are world clocks, alarms, timer, and stopwatch; when you open this app from the Control Center, it opens in the timer, but you can use its other functions by tapping the function you want to use. The Calculator does just what it sounds like it does; when you hold the iPhone vertically, you see a simple calculator, while if you rotate the iPhone to horizontal, the calculator becomes more powerful. The Camera app enables you to capture photos and video (this is covered in Chapter 14 , "Working with Photos and Video You Take with Your iPhone").

Working with Notifications and the Notification Center

Your iPhone has a lot of activity going on, from new emails to reminders to calendar events. The iOS notification system keeps you informed of these happenings through a number of means. Visual notifications include alerts, banners, and badges. Alert sounds can also let you know something has happened, and vibrations make you feel the new activity. There are a variety of notification options for each app. You learn how to customize the notifications your iPhone uses in Chapter 5.

Working with visual notifications is pretty straightforward.

When a banner appears, you can do one of several things. You can view and then ignore it (it rotates off the screen after displaying for a few seconds). You can tap it to move into the app to take some action, such as to read an email. You can swipe up from the bottom of the banner to close it. For some apps, such as Messages, you can swipe down on the banner to respond directly in the notification.

When an alert appears, you must either take action, such as marking a reminder as completed or listening to a voice message, tap the Options button to take one of a number of actions, or tap the Later, Dismiss, Close, or Ignore button (the button you see depends on the app the alert comes from) to close the alert and keep doing what you were doing.

Badges appear on an app's or a folder's icon to let you know something has changed, such as when you have received new email.

Badges are purely informational as are sounds and vibrations; you can't take any action on these directly. They inform you about an event so that you can take action, such as to download and install an update to your iPhone's iOS software.

Notifications on the Lock Screen

Notifications can appear on the Lock screen. This is useful because you can see them when your iPhone is locked. If your phone is asleep, the notifications appear briefly on the screen and then it goes dark again; you can press the Wake/Sleep button or the Touch/ID Home button to see your notifications without unlocking the iPhone. You can swipe up or down the screen to browse the notifications on the Lock screen or swipe to the right on them to move to the related app, too (you need to enter your passcode or touch the Touch ID button to move into the associated app).

The Notification Center organizes and displays a variety of information for you. To open the Notification Center, swipe down from the top of the iPhone's screen; if your iPhone is currently asleep/locked, press the Home/Touch ID or Sleep/Wake button and then swipe down from the top of the screen to open the Notification Center.

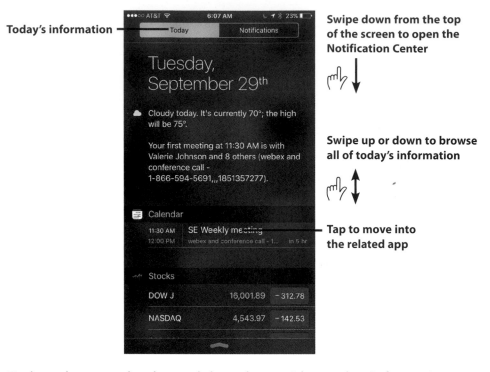

Today's information —— **Swipe down from the top of the screen to open the Notification Center**

Swipe up or down to browse all of today's information

—— **Tap to move into the related app**

Tap the Today tab to see the day and date along with weather information. Under that, you see any information that impacts your day; this information is organized in sections based on its type, such as Reminders, Calendar events, and so on. If you swipe up far enough, you see the Tomorrow section that presents information about tomorrow's activities, too.

Tap the Notifications tab to see all your current notifications, such as for new email or text messages. These are organized by the app from which they come. Like the Today tab, you can swipe up and down to browse all the notifications, tap a notification to move to the related app, and so on. To remove all the notifications for an app, tap its Clear button (x) and then tap Clear.

Active Notifications

Some of the notifications can show more information than can fit on the screen (examples include the Weather and Stocks apps). Swipe to the left or right on these notifications to see more information. Some notifications have links that take you to the Web to get more detailed information.

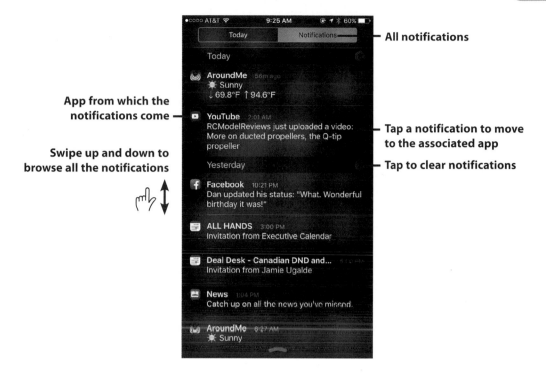

App from which the notifications come —

Swipe up and down to browse all the notifications

All notifications

Tap a notification to move to the associated app

Tap to clear notifications

Using the Do Not Disturb Mode

All the notifications you read about in the previous section are useful, but at times, they can be annoying or distracting. When you put your iPhone in Do Not Disturb mode, its visual, audible, and vibration notifications are disabled so that they won't bother you. It won't ring if someone calls you, unless you specify certain contacts to override the Do Not Disturb.

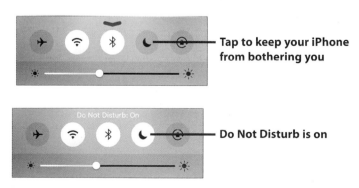

Tap to keep your iPhone from bothering you

Do Not Disturb is on

To put your iPhone in Do Not Disturb mode, open the Control Center and tap the Do Not Disturb button. It becomes white and the Do Not Disturb: On status appears at the top of the Control Center. Your iPhone stops its notifications and does not ring if someone calls. To make your notifications active again, tap the Do Not Disturb button so it is black; your iPhone resumes trying to get your attention when it is needed.

In Chapter 4, "Configuring an iPhone to Suit Your Preferences," you learn how to set a schedule for Do Not Disturb so that your iPhone goes into this mode automatically at certain times, such as from 10 p.m. to 6 a.m. You can also configure certain exceptions, including whose calls come in even when your iPhone is in Do Not Disturb mode.

Working with Text

You can do lots of things with an iPhone that require you to provide text input. There are a couple of ways you can do this, the most obvious of which is by typing. The iPhone's keyboard is quite amazing. Whenever you need it, whether it's for emailing, entering a website URL, performing a search, or any other typing function, it pops up automatically.

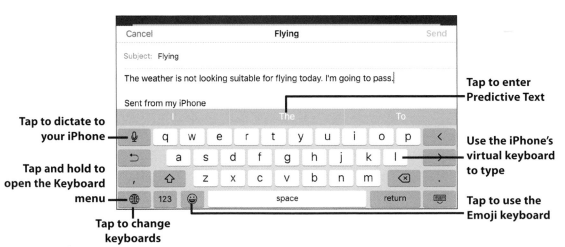

To type, just tap the keys. As you tap each key, you hear audio feedback (you can disable this sound if you want to) and the key you tapped pops up in a magnified view on the screen. The keyboard includes all the standard keys, plus a few for special uses. To change from letters to numbers and special characters, just tap the 123 key. Tap the #+= key to see more special characters. Tap the 123 key to move back to the numbers and special characters or the ABC key to return to letters. The keyboard also has contextual keys that appear when you need them. For example, when you enter a website address, the .com key appears so you can enter these four characters with a single tap.

You can also use Predictive Text, which is the feature that tries to predict text you want to enter based on the context of what you are currently typing and what you have typed before. Predictive Text appears in the bar between the text and the keyboard and presents you with three options. If one of those is what you want to enter, tap it and it is added to the text at the current location of the cursor. If you don't see an option you want to enter, keep typing and the options change as the text changes. You can tap an option at any time to enter it. The nice thing about Predictive Text is that it gets better at predicting your text needs over time. In other words, the more you use it, the better it gets at predicting what you want to type. You can also enable or disable Predictive Text as you see shortly.

Predictive Text Need Not Apply

When you are entering text where Predictive Text doesn't apply, such as when you are typing email addresses, the Predictive Text bar is hidden and can't be enabled. This makes sense because there's no way text in things such as email addresses can be predicted. When you move back into an area where it does apply, Predictive Text becomes active again.

The great thing about a virtual keyboard like the iPhone has is that it can change to reflect the language or symbols you want to type. As you learn in Chapter 4, you can install multiple keyboards, such as one for your primary language and more for your secondary languages. You can also install third-party keyboards to take advantage of their features (this is also covered in Chapter 4).

By default, two keyboards are available for you to use. One is for the primary language configured for your iPhone (for example, mine is U.S. English). The other is the Emoji keyboard (more on this shortly). How you change the keyboard you are using depends on if you have installed additional keyboards and the orientation of the iPhone.

If you haven't installed additional keyboards, you can change keyboards by tapping the Emoji key, which has a smiley face on it.

If you have installed other keyboards, you change keyboards by tapping the Globe key.

Each time you tap this key (Globe if available, Emoji if there isn't a Globe), the keyboard changes to be the next keyboard installed; along with the available keys changing, you briefly see the name of the current keyboard in the Space bar. When you have cycled through all the keyboards, you return to the one where you started.

The Keys, They Are A-Changin'

The keys on the keyboard can change depending on the orientation of the iPhone. For example, when you have more than one keyboard installed and hold the iPhone vertically, the Emoji key disappears and you see only the Globe key. Not to worry though, you can still get to the Emoji keyboard by tapping the Globe key until the Emoji keyboard appears, or by opening the Keyboard menu and tapping Emoji. When you have installed additional keyboards and hold the iPhone horizontally, you see both the Globe and Emoji keys. Tap the Emoji key to switch to that keyboard or the Globe key to cycle through all the keyboards.

You can also select the specific keyboard you want to use and enable/disable Predictive Text by tapping and holding on the Globe key (or the Emoji key, if you don't see the Globe key). The Keyboard menu appears. Tap a keyboard to switch to it. Tap the Predictive Text switch to enable or disable it; when the switch is green, Predictive Text is enabled, when the switch is white, it is disabled.

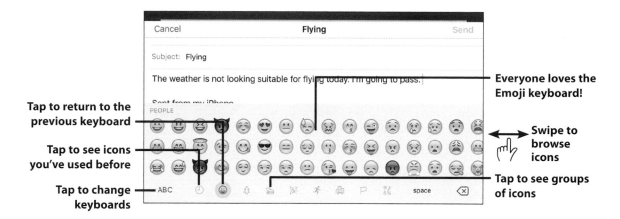

The Emoji keyboard allows you to insert a variety of icons into your text to liven things up, communicate your feelings, or just to have some fun (if you don't have this keyboard installed, see Chapter 4). You can open this keyboard by tapping its key (the smiley face) or by tapping it on the Keyboard menu. You see a palette containing many icons, organized into groups. You can change the groups of icons you are browsing by tapping the buttons at the bottom of the screen. Swipe to the left or right on the icons to browse the icons in the current group. Tap an icon to enter it at the cursor's location in your message, email, or other type of document. To use an icon you've used before, tap the Clock button; you'll probably find that you use this recent set of icons regularly so this can save a lot of time. To return to the mundane world of letters and symbols, tap the Emoji or Globe key again.

Another Reason It's Called a Plus

When you rotate an iPhone 6 Plus or 6s Plus to the horizontal position, the keyboard gains some extra keys. These include Cut (scissors), Copy (two squares), Paste (paper and clipboard), Format (**B**/U), and Undo (curved arrow).

What's Your Typing Orientation?

Like many other tasks, you can rotate the iPhone to change the screen's orientation while you type. When the iPhone is in the horizontal orientation, the keyboard is wider, making it easier to tap individual keys. When the iPhone is in vertical orientation, the keyboard is narrower, but you can see more of the typing area. So, try both to see which mode is most effective for you.

If you type a word that the iPhone doesn't recognize, that word is flagged as a possible mistake and suggestions are made to help you correct it. How this happens depends on whether or not Predictive Text is enabled.

Suspicious word

Tap to change the suspicious word to be the suggested word

If Predictive Text is enabled, potential replacements for suspicious words appear in the Predictive Text bar. Tap a word to replace what you've typed with the suggested word.

Suspicious word

Tap x to reject the suggestion

If Predictive Text isn't enabled, a suspicious word is highlighted and a suggestion about what it thinks is the correct word appears in a pop-up box. To accept the suggestion, tap the Space key. To reject the suggestion, tap the pop-up box to close it and keep what you typed. You can also use this feature for shorthand typing. For example, to type "I've" you can simply type "Ive" and iPhone suggests "I've," which you can accept by tapping the Space key.

Typing Tricks

Many keys, especially symbols and punctuation, have additional characters. To see a character's options, tap it and hold down. If it has options, a menu pops up after a second or so. To enter one of the optional characters, drag over the menu until the one you want to enter is highlighted, and then lift your finger off the screen. The optional character you selected is entered. For example, if you tap and hold on the period, you can select .com, .edu, and so on, which is very helpful when you are typing a website or email addresses.

By default, the iPhone attempts to correct the capitalization of what you type. It also automatically selects the Shift key when you start a new sentence, start a new paragraph, or in other places where its best guess is that you need a capital letter. If you don't want to enter a capital character, simply tap the Shift key before you type. You can enable the Caps Lock key by tapping the Shift key twice. When the key is highlighted, everything you type is in uppercase letters.

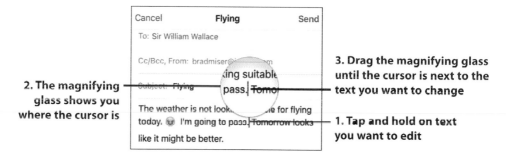

2. The magnifying glass shows you where the cursor is

3. Drag the magnifying glass until the cursor is next to the text you want to change

1. Tap and hold on text you want to edit

To edit text you've typed, tap and hold on the text you want to edit. A magnifying glass icon appears on the screen, and within it you see a magnified view of the location of the cursor. Drag the magnifying glass to where you want to make changes (to position the cursor where you want to start making changes), and then lift your finger from the screen. The cursor remains in that location, and you can use the keyboard to make changes to the text or to add text at that location.

Using 3D Touch with Text

When you are using an iPhone 6s or 6s Plus, you can apply slight pressure when you touch the screen to have the closest word selected automatically; it is highlighted in blue to show you that it is selected. To place the cursor without selecting words that are near your finger, just touch the screen without applying any pressure.

Your Own Text Replacements

You can create your own text shortcuts so you can type something like "eadd" and it is automatically replaced with your email address. See Chapter 4 for the details.

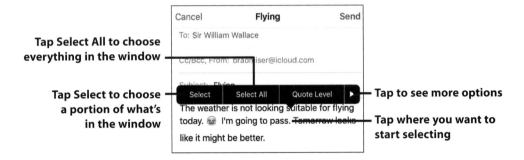

Tap Select All to choose everything in the window

Tap Select to choose a portion of what's in the window

Tap to see more options

Tap where you want to start selecting

You can also select text or images to copy and paste the selected content into a new location or to replace that content. Tap and hold down briefly where you want to start the selection until the magnifying glass icon appears; then lift your finger off the screen. The Select menu appears. Tap Select to select part of the content on the screen, or tap Select All to select everything in the current window.

More Commands

Some menus that appear when you are making selections and performing actions have a right-facing arrow at the right end. Tap this to see a new menu that contains additional commands. These commands are contextual, meaning that you see different commands depending on what you are doing at that specific time. You can tap the left-facing arrow to move back to a previous menu.

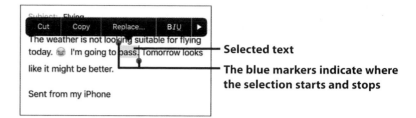

Selected text

The blue markers indicate where the selection starts and stops

You see markers indicating where the selection starts and stops. (The iPhone attempts to select something logical, such as the word or sentence.) New commands appear on the menu; these provide actions for the text currently selected.

Magnified view of what you are selecting

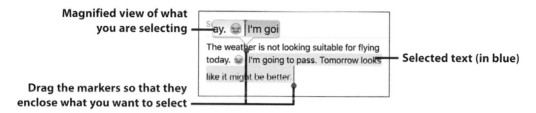

Selected text (in blue)

Drag the markers so that they enclose what you want to select

Drag the two markers so that the content you want to select is between them; the selected portion is highlighted in blue. As you drag, you see a magnified view of where the selection marker is, which helps you place it more accurately. When the selection markers are located correctly, lift your finger from the screen. (If you tapped the Select All command, you don't need to do this because the content you want is already selected.)

Have I Got a Suggestion for You!

Tap the Suggestion option to see items that might be useful to you. These are also contextual. For example, when you have a word selected, one of the suggestions might be Define, which looks up the selected word in the Dictionary (tap Done to return to where you came from). As you use your iPhone, check out the Suggestions because you'll find some very useful options tucked away there.

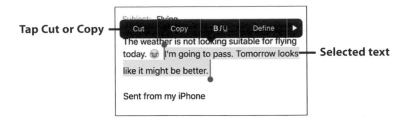

Tap Cut or Copy — Cut | Copy | B*I*U | Define ▶

Selected text — (points to highlighted text "I'm going to pass. Tomorrow looks")

Tap Cut to remove the content from the current window, or tap Copy to just copy it.

Format It!

If you tap the **B/U** button, you can tap Bold, Italics, or Underline to apply those formatting options to the selected text. You also can tap multiple format options to apply them at the same time. You might need to tap the right-facing arrow at the end of the menu to see this command, depending on how many commands are on the menu.

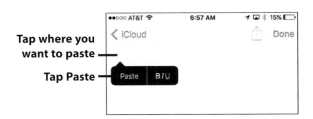

Tap where you want to paste

Tap Paste — Paste | B*I*U

Move to where you want to paste the content you selected; for example, use the App Switcher to change to a different app. Tap where you want the content to be pasted. For a more precise location, tap and hold and then use the magnifying glass icon to move to a specific location. Lift your finger off the screen and the menu appears. Then tap Paste.

Pasted content — I'm going to pass. Tomorrow looks like it might be better.

The content you copied or cut appears where you placed the cursor.

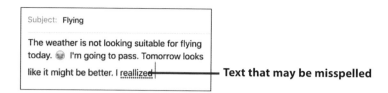

Text that may be misspelled

The iPhone also has a spell-checking feature that comes into play after you have entered text (as opposed to the Predictive Text and autocorrect/suggests feature that change text as you type it). When you've entered text the iPhone doesn't recognize, it is underlined in red.

Tap the correct word

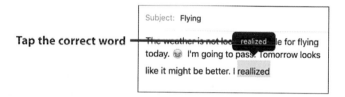

Tap the underlined word. It is shaded in red to show you what is being checked, and a menu appears with one or more replacements that might be the correct spelling. If one of the options is the one you want, tap it. The incorrect word is replaced with the one you tapped.

Contextual Menus and You

In some apps, tapping a word causes a menu with other kinds of actions to appear; you can tap an action to make it happen. For example, in the iBooks app, when you tap a word, the resulting menu enables you to look up the word in a dictionary. Other apps support different kinds of actions, so it's a good idea to try tapping words in apps that involve text to see which commands are available.

Dictating Text

You can also enter text by dictating it. This is a fast and easy way to type and you'll be amazed at how accurate the iPhone is at translating your speech into typed words. Dictation is available almost anywhere you need to enter text. (Exceptions are passcodes and passwords, such as for your Apple ID.)

Tap to put the cursor where you want dictated text to start

Tap the Microphone key to start dictation

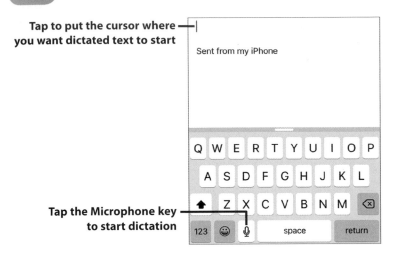

To start dictating, tap the Microphone key. The iPhone goes into Dictation mode. A gray bar appears at the bottom of the window. As the iPhone "hears" you, the line oscillates.

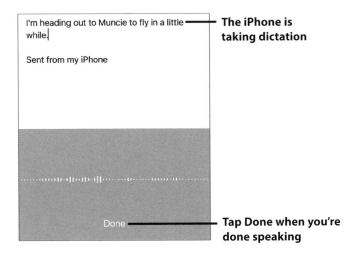

The iPhone is taking dictation

Tap Done when you're done speaking

Start speaking the text you want the iPhone to type. As you speak, the text is entered starting from the location of the cursor.

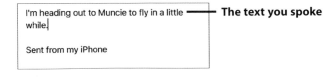

The text you spoke

When you've finished dictating, tap Done. The keyboard reappears and you see the text you spoke. This feature is amazingly accurate and can be a much faster and more convenient way to enter text than typing it.

You can edit the text you dictated just like text you entered using the keyboard.

Meeting Siri

Siri is the iPhone's voice-recognition and control software. This feature enables you to accomplish many tasks by speaking. For example, you can create and send text messages, reply to emails, make phone calls, and much more. (Using Siri is explained in detail in Chapter 12, "Working with Siri.")

When you perform actions, Siri uses the related apps to accomplish what you've asked it to do. For example, when you create a meeting, Siri uses the Calendar app.

Siri is a great way to control your iPhone, especially when you are working in handsfree mode.

Your iPhone has to be connected to the Internet for Siri (and dictation for that matter) to work. That's because the words you speak are sent over the Internet, transcribed into text, and then sent back to your iPhone. If your iPhone isn't connected to the Internet, this can't happen and Siri reports that it can't connect to the network or simply that it can't do what you ask right now.

Using Siri is pretty simple because it follows a consistent pattern and prompts you for input and direction.

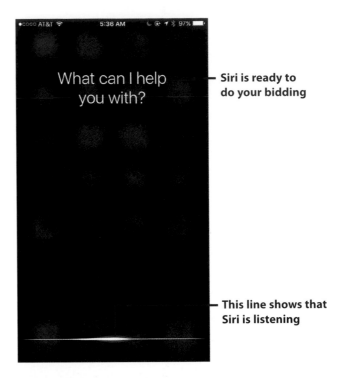

What can I help you with? — Siri is ready to do your bidding

This line shows that Siri is listening

Activate Siri by pressing and holding down the Touch ID/Home button or pressing and holding down the center part of the buttons on the right EarPod wire until you hear the Siri chime. If so configured (see Chapter 12), you can say "Hey Siri" to activate it, too. This puts Siri in "listening" mode and the "What can I help you with?" text appears on the screen. This indicates Siri is ready for your command.

Hey Siri set up a meeting with William Wallace at the park at 11 o'clock on December 15 — What Siri heard you say

Speak your command or ask a question. When you stop speaking, Siri goes into processing mode. After Siri interprets what you've said, it provides two kinds of feedback to confirm what it heard: it displays what it heard on the screen and provides audible feedback to you. Siri then tries to do what it thinks you've asked and shows you what it is doing. If it needs more input from you, you're prompted to provide it and Siri moves into "listening" mode automatically.

Siri is going to invite Sir William to a meeting and needs to know which email address to use

Tell Siri which email to use by saying "work"

If Siri requests that you confirm what it is doing or to make a selection, do so. Siri completes the action and displays what it has done; it also audibly confirms the result.

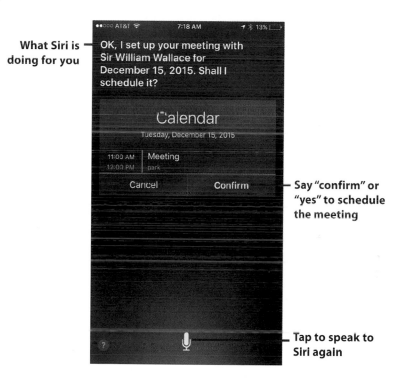

What Siri is doing for you

Say "confirm" or "yes" to schedule the meeting

Tap to speak to Siri again

Siri isn't quite like using the computer on the Starship Enterprise on *Star Trek*, but it's pretty darn close. Mostly, you can just speak to Siri as you would talk to someone else, and it is able to do what you want or asks you the information it needs to do what you want.

Understanding iPhone Status Icons

At the top of the screen is the Status bar with various icons that provide you with information, such as whether you are connected to a Wi-Fi or cellular data network, the time, sync in process, whether the iPhone's orientation is locked, the state of the iPhone's battery, and so on. Keep an eye on this area as you use your iPhone. The following table provides a guide to the most common of these icons.

iPhone Status Icons

Icon	Description	Where to Learn More
	Signal strength—Indicates how strong the cellular signal is.	Chapter 2
AT&T	**Provider name**—The provider of the current cellular network.	Chapter 2
LTE	**Cellular data network**—Indicates which cellular network your iPhone is using to connect to the Internet.	Chapter 2
	Wi-Fi—Indicates your phone is connected to a Wi-Fi network.	Chapter 2
Wi-Fi	**Wi-Fi calling**—Indicates your phone can make voice calls over a Wi-Fi network.	Chapter 2
	Do Not Disturb—Your iPhone's notifications and ringer are silenced.	Chapters 1, 4
	Bluetooth—Indicates if Bluetooth is turned on or off and if your phone is connected to a device.	Chapter 2
97%	**Battery percentage**—Percentage of charge remaining in the battery.	Chapter 16 (online)
	Battery status—Relative level of charge of the battery.	Chapter 16 (online)
	Low Battery status—The battery has less than 20% power remaining.	Chapter 16 (online)

Icon	Description	Where to Learn More
🔋	**Low Power mode**—The iPhone is operating in Low Power mode.	Chapter 16 (online)
🔒	**Orientation Lock**—Your iPhone's screen won't change when you rotate your iPhone.	Chapter 1
🔋⚡	**Charging**—The battery in the iPhone is being charged.	Chapter 16 (online)
➤	**Location Services**—An app is using the Location Services feature to track your iPhone's location.	Chapter 4
✈	**Airplane mode**—The transmit and receive functions are disabled.	Chapter 1

Turning Your iPhone On or Off

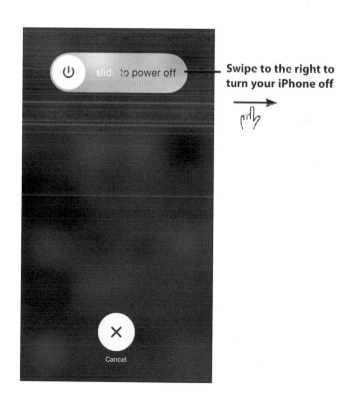

Swipe to the right to turn your iPhone off

If you want to turn off your iPhone, press and hold the Wake/Sleep button until the slider appears at the top of the screen. Swipe the slider to the right to shut down the iPhone. The iPhone shuts down.

To restart your iPhone, press and hold the Wake/Sleep button until the Apple logo appears on the screen, and then let go of the button.

After it starts up, and you have a passcode, you see the Lock screen. Swipe to the right and enter your passcode to start using your phone. (Even if you have Touch ID enabled to unlock your phone, you must enter your passcode the first time you unlock it after a restart.)

If you don't have a passcode configured, you move directly to the Home screen when the phone starts and it's ready for you to use. Keep in mind, if you do not have a passcode configured, your phone is vulnerable to anyone who gets a hold of it.

Sleeping/Locking and Waking/Unlocking Your iPhone

When an iPhone is asleep/locked, you need to wake it up and then unlock it to use it. How you do this depends on the type of iPhone you have.

If you have an iPhone 5s or later, and have configured it to recognize your fingerprint to unlock it, press the Touch ID/Home button once, and then touch the Touch ID button with your finger. When your fingerprint is recognized, your iPhone unlocks and you can start using it.

Be Recognized

To use the Touch ID, you need to train your iPhone to recognize the fingerprints you want to use. You were prompted to configure one fingerprint when you started your iPhone for the first time. You can change or add fingerprints for Touch ID at any time; see Chapter 4 for the details of configuring Touch ID.

Swipe to the right to unlock your iPhone

If you have an iPhone 5c or older, or you don't have any Touch ID configured to unlock your phone, you first press the Wake/Sleep button or the Home button. The iPhone wakes up, the Lock screen appears, and at the bottom of the screen, the Unlock slider appears. Swipe on the slider to the right to unlock the iPhone so you can work with it.

If you require a passcode to unlock your iPhone—which you should for security—type your passcode at the prompt.

When you unlock the phone, or swipe to open it if no passcode is configured, you move to the last screen you were using before it was locked.

The Time Is Always Handy

If you use your iPhone as a watch the way I do, just press the Wake/Sleep button. The current time and date appear; if you don't unlock it, the iPhone goes back to sleep after a few seconds.

Enter your passcode to
start using your iPhone

In most cases, you should just put the iPhone to sleep when you aren't using it
instead of turning it off. It doesn't use much power when it sleeps, and it wakes
up immediately when you want to start using it again. Also, when you put your
iPhone to sleep, it can't be used until it is unlocked. If you set it to require a
passcode to unlock, this also protects your information. (You seldom need to
turn off an iPhone.) Even when the iPhone is asleep, you can receive notifications,
such as when you receive emails or text messages. (See Chapter 4 to configure
which notifications you see on the Lock screen.)

To put your iPhone to sleep and lock it, press the Wake/Sleep button.

Signing Into Your Apple ID

As you learn throughout this book, an Apple ID is useful in many situations, such
as to access iCloud services; purchase music, movies, and other content from the
iTunes Store; download apps from the App Store; and so on. If you have an iPhone
5s or later, you can quickly sign into your Apple ID by using the iPhone's Touch ID/
Home button. (As referenced in the prior note, you need to configure your iPhone
to recognize your fingerprint to use Touch ID; see Chapter 4 for details.)

You need to sign into your Apple ID to complete an action

Touch the Touch ID button to sign in

When you need to sign into your Apple ID, you see a prompt. Simply touch your finger to the Touch ID/Home button. When your fingerprint is recognized, you sign into your Apple ID and can complete whatever your were doing, such as downloading music from the iTunes Store.

You need to sign into your Apple ID to complete an action

Enter your Apple ID password and tap OK

If you have an older model or you don't have the settings configured to enable you to use Touch ID with your Apple ID, you need to provide your Apple ID password to sign in by typing it and tapping OK. Whatever action you were performing is completed.

Setting the Volume

Setting the ringer volume

To change the iPhone's volume, press the up or down Volume button on the side of the iPhone. When you change the volume, your change affects the current activity. For example, if you are on a phone call, the call volume changes or if you are listening to music, the music's volume changes. If you aren't on a screen that shows the Volume slider, an icon pops up to show you the relative volume you are setting and the type, such as setting the ringer's volume. When the volume is right, release the Volume button.

Drag to the left or right to change the volume level

When you are using an audio app, such as the Music app, you can also drag the volume slider in that app or on the Control Center to increase or decrease the volume.

When you use the iPhone's EarPods, you can change the volume by pressing the upper part of the switch on the right EarPod's wire to increase volume or the lower part to decrease it.

Using Airplane Mode

Although there's a debate about whether devices such as iPhones pose any real danger to the operation of aircraft, there's no reason to run any risk by using your iPhone while you are on an airplane. (Besides, not following crew instructions on airplanes can lead you to less-than-desirable interactions with the flight crew.) When you place your iPhone in Airplane mode, its transmitting and receiving functions are disabled, so it poses no threat to the operation of the aircraft. While it is in Airplane mode, you can't use the phone, the Web, Siri, or any other functions that require communication between your iPhone and other devices or networks.

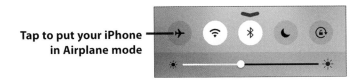

Tap to put your iPhone in Airplane mode

To put your iPhone in Airplane mode, swipe up from the bottom of the screen to open the Control Center and tap the Airplane mode button. All connections to the Internet and the cell network stop, and your iPhone goes into quiet mode in which it doesn't broadcast or receive any signals. The Airplane mode button becomes white and you see the Airplane mode icon at the top of the screen.

In Airplane mode, you can use your iPhone for all your apps that don't require an Internet connection, such as iBooks, Music, Videos, Photos, and so on.

To turn off Airplane mode, open the Control Center and tap the Airplane mode button; it becomes black again and the Airplane mode icon disappears. The iPhone resumes transmitting and receiving signals, and all the functions that require a connection start working again.

Wi-Fi in Airplane Mode

Many airplanes support Wi-Fi on board. To access a Wi-Fi network without violating the requirement not to use a cell network, put the iPhone in Airplane mode, which turns off Wi-Fi. On the Control Center, tap the Wi-Fi button to turn Wi-Fi back on. Wi-Fi starts up and you can select the network you want to join (see Chapter 2). You can use this configuration at other times, too, such as when you want to access the Internet but don't want to be bothered with phone calls. When your iPhone is in Airplane mode and Wi-Fi is on, all your calls (including Wi-Fi calls) go straight to voicemail but you can use your Internet-related apps. (I would never do this, you understand.)

Using the Settings App

The Settings app is where you do almost all of your iPhone's configuration, and you use it frequently throughout this book. To use the Settings app, tap Settings on the Home screen. The app opens. Swipe up and down the screen to browse the various settings tools. Tap an item to configure its settings. For example, to configure your notifications, tap Notifications. (You use the Settings app in a number of chapters in this book, especially in Chapter 4.)

Tap to open the Settings app

Swipe up or down to browse all the settings options

Tap a setting to configure it

Printing from Your iPhone

You can also print from your iPhone to AirPrint-compatible printers.

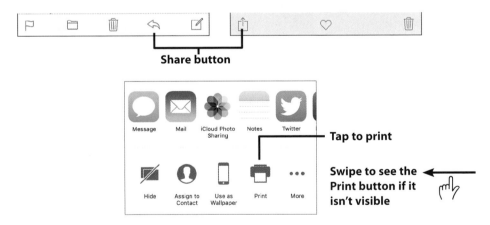

Share button

Tap to print

Swipe to see the Print button if it isn't visible

First, set up and configure your AirPrint printer (see the instructions that came with the printer you use).

It Depends

When you tap the Share button, you might see a menu containing commands instead of the grid of icons shown in the figure. The way it appears is dependent upon the app you are using. Either way, tap Print to move to the Printer Options screen.

When you are in the app from which you want to print, tap the Share button. Tap Print on the resulting menu. You might need to swipe to the right to expose the Print command. (If you don't see the Share button or the Print command, the app you are using doesn't support printing.) The Share button looks a bit different in some apps, but it works similarly.

Tap to select
a printer

Tap the
printer you
want to use

The first time you print, you need to select the printer you want to use. On the Printer Options screen, tap Select Printer. Then tap the printer you want to use. You move back to the Printer Options screen and see the printer you selected.

Don't Have an AirPrint Printer?

If you don't have an AirPrint printer, do a web search for a tool called "AirPrint for Windows" if you have a Windows PC or "handyPrint for Mac" if you have a Mac. Download and install the software on a computer that is capable of sharing its printers. Configure your computer to share the printer you want to use with your iPhone. Then launch the software on your computer and start it. The printers you configure in the AirPrint software are available for printing from your iPhone.

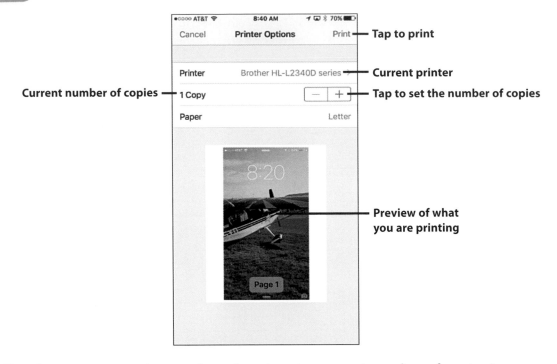

Tap the − or + to set the number of copies; the current number of copies is shown to the left of the buttons. Tap Print to print the document.

The next time you print, if you want to use the same printer, you can skip the printer selection process because the iPhone remembers the last printer you used. To change the printer, tap Printer and tap the printer you want to use.

Connect to the Internet via Wi-Fi or a cellular network

Use AirDrop to share content with other iOS devices

Tap here to join Wi-Fi networks to connect to the Internet and configure Bluetooth to connect to other devices

Take advantage of an Internet connection in many different apps

In this chapter, you explore how to connect your iPhone to the Internet; Bluetooth devices; and other iPhones, iPod touches, and iPads. Topics include the following:

→ Getting started
→ Securing your iPhone
→ Using Wi-Fi networks to connect to the Internet
→ Using cellular data networks to connect to the Internet
→ Using Bluetooth to connect to other devices
→ Connecting your iPhone to other iPhones, iPod touches, or iPads
→ Using AirDrop to share content with Macs, other iPhones, iPod touches, or iPads

2

Connecting Your iPhone to the Internet, Bluetooth Devices, and iPhones/iPods/iPads

Your iPhone has many functions that rely on an Internet connection. Fortunately, you can easily connect your iPhone to the Internet by connecting it to a Wi-Fi network that provides Internet access. You can connect your phone to the Internet even more easily through a cellular data network operated by your cell phone provider because that happens automatically.

Using Bluetooth, you can wirelessly connect your iPhone to other devices, including keyboards, headsets, headphones, and so on.

There are a number of ways to connect your iPhone to other iPhones, iPod touches, iPads, and Macintosh computers. This is useful to use collaborative apps, play games, and share information. For example, using AirDrop, you can quickly and easily share photos and other content with other people using iOS devices or a Mac computer.

Getting Started

The bad news is that there are lots of complex-sounding terms that you hear and see when you are connecting your iPhone to the Internet and other devices. The good news is that you don't need to understand these terms in-depth to be able to connect your iPhone to the Internet and other devices because the iPhone manages the complexity for you. You just need to make a few simple settings, and you'll be connected in no time. Here's a quick guide to the most important concepts you encounter in this chapter:

- **Wi-Fi**—This acronym stands for Wireless Fidelity and encompasses a whole slew of technical specifications around connecting devices together without using cables or wires. Wi-Fi networks have a relatively short range and are used to create a Local Area Network (LAN). The most important thing to know is that you can use Wi-Fi networks to connect your iPhone to the Internet. This is great because Wi-Fi networks are available in many places you go. You probably have a Wi-Fi network available in your home, too. (If you connect your computers to the Internet without a cable from your computer to a modem or network hub, you are using a Wi-Fi network.) You can connect your iPhone to your home's Wi-Fi network, too.

- **Cellular data network**—In addition to your voice, your iPhone can transmit and receive data over the cellular network to which it is connected. This enables you to connect your iPhone to the Internet just about anywhere you are. You use the cellular network provided by your cell phone company. There are many different cell phone providers that support iPhones. In the United States, these include AT&T, Sprint, T-Mobile, and Verizon. You don't need to configure your iPhone to use the cellular data network, as it is set up from the start to do so.

- **3G/4G/LTE**—The speed of the connection you have when using a cellular data network varies, which means the things you do on the Internet (such as browsing a web page) will be faster or slower depending on the current connection speed. These terms (this is not an exhaustive list; you may see these networks called by other names) refer to various types of cellular data networks you can use with your iPhone. Each type has a different speed. LTE networks are currently the fastest type. You usually don't choose which type of network you use because the iPhone connects to the fastest one available automatically.

- **Data Plan**—When you use your iPhone on the Internet (for web browsing, email, and apps), data is transmitted to your iPhone and the iPhone transmits data back to the Internet. Your cellular account includes a data plan that defines how much data you can send/receive during a specific time period (usually per month) based on how much you pay per month. It's important to know the size of your data plan so that you can be aware of how much of it you are using per month.

- **Overage charge**—If you use more data than is allowed under your data plan, you can be charged a fee. These fees can be quite expensive so you need to be aware of how much data you are using so that you can avoid overage charges.

- **Roaming charge**—Your cellular provider's network covers a defined geographic area. When you leave your provider's network coverage area, your iPhone automatically connects to another provider's network when one is available. When your iPhone is connected to a different provider's network, this is called roaming. You need to be aware when you are roaming because you can incur additional fees while using the roaming network.

- **Bluetooth**—This is the name of a technology that is used to wirelessly connect devices together. It is widely used for many different kinds of devices. Your iPhone can use Bluetooth to connect to speakers, the audio system in your car, keyboards, and headphones.

- **AirDrop**—This is Apple's technology for connecting iPhones, iPads, iPod touches, and Macintosh computers together to share information. AirDrop is a short-range technology—typically, the devices need to be in the same room or area for it to work. For example, you can use AirDrop to send photos from your iPhone to someone's iPad. The nice thing about AirDrop is that it requires very little setup and is quite easy to use, as you will see in this chapter.

Securing Your iPhone

Even though you won't often be connecting a cable to it, an iPhone is a connected device, meaning that it sends information to and receives information from other devices, either directly or via the Internet, during many different activities. Some are obvious, such as sending text messages or browsing the Web, while others might not be so easy to spot, such as when an app is determining your iPhone's location. Whenever data is exchanged between your iPhone and other devices, there is always a chance your information will get intercepted by someone you didn't intend or that someone will access your iPhone without you knowing about it.

The good news is that with some simple precautions, the chances of someone obtaining your information or infiltrating your iPhone are quite small (much less than the chance of someone obtaining your credit card number when you use it in public places, for example). Following are some good ways to protect the information you are using on your iPhone:

- Configure a passcode and fingerprint (if your iPhone supports Touch ID, which is Apple's fingerprint recognition technology) on your iPhone so that the passcode must be entered, or your fingerprint scanned, to be able to use it. Configuring a passcode is explained in Chapter 4, "Configuring an iPhone to Suit Your Preferences."

- Never let someone you don't know or trust use your iPhone, even if he needs it "just for a second to look something up." If you get a request like that, look up the information for the person and show him rather than letting him touch your iPhone.

- Learn how to use the Find My iPhone feature in case you lose or someone steals your iPhone. This is explained in Chapter 16, "Maintaining and Protecting Your iPhone and Solving Problems," which you'll find on this book's website (see the back cover for the information you need to access it).

- Never respond to an email that you aren't expecting requesting that you click a link to verify your account. If you haven't requested some kind of change, such as signing up for a new service, virtually all such requests are scams, seeking to get your account information, such as username and password, or your identification, such as full name and Social Security number. And many of these scam attempts look like email from actual organizations; for example, I receive many of these emails that claim, and sometimes even look like, they are from Apple, but Apple doesn't request updates to account information using a link in an email unless you have made some kind of change, such as registering a new email address for iMessages. Legitimate organizations never include links in an email to update account information when you haven't requested or made any changes. Requests from legitimate organizations will provide instructions for you to visit a website to provide needed information.

- To reinforce this concept, there are two types of requests for verification you might receive via email. The legitimate type is sent to you after you sign up for a new service, such as creating a new account on a website, to confirm that the email address you provided is correct and that you are really you. If you make changes to an existing account, you might also receive confirmation request emails. You should respond to these requests to finish the configuration of your account.

    If you receive a request for account verification, but you haven't done anything with the organization from which you received the request, don't respond to it. For example, if you receive a request that appears to be from Apple, PayPal, or other organizations, but you haven't made any changes to your account, the email request is bogus and is an attempt to scam you. Likewise, if you have never done anything with the organization apparently sending the email, it is also definitely an attempt to scam you.

    If you have any doubt, contact the organization sending the request before responding to the email.

- If you need to change or update account information, always go directly to the related website using an address that you type in or have saved as a bookmark.

- Be aware that when you use a Wi-Fi network in a public place, such as a coffee shop, hotel, or airport, there is a chance that the information you send over that network might be intercepted by others. The risk of this is usually quite small, but you need to be aware that there is always some level of risk. To have the lowest risk, don't use apps that involve sensitive information, such as an online banking app, when you are using a Wi-Fi network in a public place.

- If you don't know how to do it, have someone who really knows what they are doing set up a wireless network in your home. Wireless networks need to be configured properly, so they are secure. Your home's Wi-Fi network should require a password to join. (Fortunately, as you learn shortly, your iPhone remembers your password, so you only have to enter it once.)

- For the least risk, only use your home's Wi-Fi network (that has been configured properly) or your cellular data connection (you can turn Wi-Fi off when you aren't home) for sensitive transactions, such as accessing bank accounts or other financial information.

- Never accept a request to share information from someone you don't know. Later in this chapter, you learn about AirDrop, which enables you to easily share photos and lots of other things with other people using iOS devices. If you receive an AirDrop request from someone you don't recognize, always decline it. In fact, if you have any doubt, decline such requests. It's much easier for someone legitimate to confirm with you and resend a request than it is for you to recover from damage that can be done if you inadvertently accept a request from someone you don't know.

- Only download apps through Apple's App Store through the App Store app on your iPhone. Fortunately, the way the iPhone is set up, you have to do something very unusual to install apps outside of the App Store. As long as you download apps only as described in this book, you are free of apps that can harm your information because Apple has strict controls over the apps that make it into the App Store. (Downloading apps is explained in Chapter 6, "Downloading Apps, Music, Movies, TV Shows, and More onto Your iPhone.")

Reality Check

Internet security is a complex topic, and it can be troublesome to think about. It's best to keep in mind the relative level of risk when you use your iPhone compared to other risks in the physical world that most of us don't think twice about. For example, every time you hand your credit card to someone, there is a chance that that person will record the number and use it without your knowledge or permission. Even when you swipe a credit card in a reader, such as at a gas station, that information is communicated across multiple networks and can be intercepted. (For example, there have been numerous compromises of credit card information at a number of well-known retailers.) If you take basic precautions like those described here, the risks to you when you are using your iPhone are similar to the other risks we all face in everyday life. My recommendation is to take the basic precautions, and then don't worry about it overly much. It might be a good idea to have identity theft insurance (try to find a company that assigns someone to do the work of recovering for you should your identity be stolen).

Using Wi-Fi Networks to Connect to the Internet

Much of the iPhone's amazing functionality relies on an Internet connection. Fortunately, you can easily connect your iPhone to Wi-Fi networks to get to the Internet, and Wi-Fi networks are available just about everywhere these days.

Almost all Wi-Fi networks broadcast their information so that you can easily see them with your iPhone; these are called *open networks* because anyone who is in range can attempt to join one since they appear on Wi-Fi devices automatically. The Wi-Fi networks you can access in public places (such as airports and hotels) are all open, and you can see them on your iPhone. Likewise, any Wi-Fi networks in your home or office are very likely to be open as well. Connecting to an open network typically requires selecting the network you want to join, based on its name, and then entering its password (if required).

By default, when you access one of your iPhone's Internet functions, such as Safari, your iPhone automatically searches for Wi-Fi networks to join, if you aren't already connected to one. A box appears showing all the networks available. You can select and join one of these networks. You learn how to do this in the following steps.

Connecting to Open Wi-Fi Networks

To connect to a Wi-Fi network, perform the following steps:

(1) On the Home screen, tap Settings. Next to Wi-Fi, you see the status of your Wi-Fi connection. It is Off if Wi-Fi is turned off, Not Connected if Wi-Fi is turned on and your phone isn't currently connected to Wi-Fi, or the name of the Wi-Fi network to which your iPhone is connected.

(2) Tap Wi-Fi.

(3) If Wi-Fi isn't enabled already, slide the Wi-Fi switch to on (green) to allow your iPhone to start searching for available networks. When Wi-Fi is turned on, a list of available networks is displayed in the CHOOSE A NETWORK section (it can take a moment or two for your iPhone to list all the networks in the area). Along with each network's name, icons indicating whether it requires a password (the padlock icon) to join and the current signal strength (the radio signal icon) are displayed.

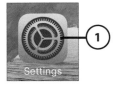

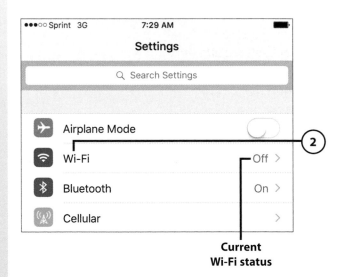

Current Wi-Fi status

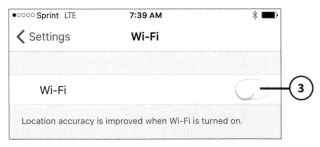

4 Tap the network you want to join. If a network requires a password, you must know what that password is to be able to join it. Another consideration should be signal strength; the more waves in the network's signal strength icon, the stronger the connection will be.

5 At the prompt, enter the password for the network. If you aren't prompted for a password, you selected a network that doesn't require one and you can skip to step 7. You're likely to find networks that don't require a password in public places (hotels, airports, and so on); see the next section for information on using these types of networks.

6 Tap Join. If you provided the correct password, your iPhone connects to the network and gets the information it needs to connect to the Internet. If not, you're prompted to enter the password again. After you successfully connect to the network, you return to the Wi-Fi screen.

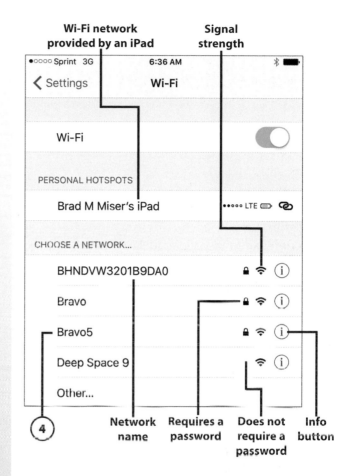

Wi-Fi network provided by an iPad   Signal strength

Network name   Requires a password   Does not require a password   Info button

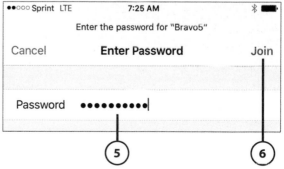

Typing Passwords

As you type a password, each character is hidden by dots in the Password field except for the last character you entered, which is displayed on the screen for a few moments. This is helpful because you see each character as you type it, so you always see the most recent character you entered, which can prevent you from getting all the way to the end of a long password only to discover you've made a mistake along the way and have to start all over again.

(7) Review the network information. The network to which you are connected appears just below the Wi-Fi switch and is marked with a check mark. You also see the signal strength for that network. (This indication is typically more accurate than the one you see before you are connected.) Assuming the Wi-Fi network is providing Internet access, you're able to use apps that require the Internet to work.

The network your
iPhone is using

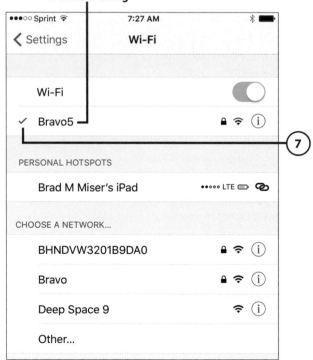

Changing Networks

You can use these same steps to change the Wi-Fi network you are using at any time. For example, if you have to pay to use one network while a different one is free, simply choose the free network in step 4.

8 Try to move to a web page, such as www.weather.com, to test your Wi-Fi connection. (See Chapter 13, "Surfing the Web," for details on using the web browser.) If the web page opens, you are ready to use the Internet on your phone. If you are taken to a login web page for a Wi-Fi provider, rather than the page you were trying to access, see the next task. If you see a message saying the Internet is not available, there is a problem with the network you joined. Go back to step 4 to select a different network.

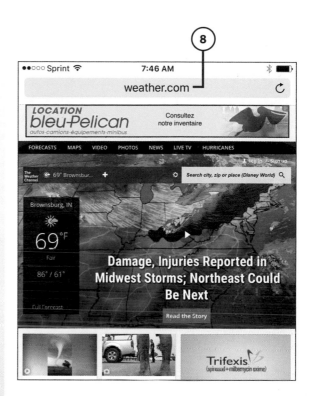

Be Known

After your iPhone connects to a Wi-Fi network successfully, it becomes a known network. This means that your iPhone remembers its information so you don't have to enter it again. Your iPhone automatically connects to known networks when it needs to access the Internet.

>>>Go Further

PERSONAL HOTSPOTS

In the PERSONAL HOTSPOTS section, you might see networks being provided by individual devices such as iPhones and iPads. These devices can share their cellular Internet connection with other devices. The icons for these networks are a bit different; along with the name of the network, you see its type of connection (such as LTE), the charge state of the device providing the network, and two connected loops that indicate the network is from a hotspot. You can select and use these networks just like the other types of networks being described in this chapter. Select the hotspot you want to use, and enter the correct password to join it. Once you've joined a hotspot's network, you can access the Internet. The speed of your access is determined mostly by the speed of the device's cellular data connection.

Connecting to Public Wi-Fi Networks

Many Wi-Fi networks in public places, such as hotels or airports, require that you pay a fee or provide other information to access the Internet through that network; even if access is free, you usually have to accept the terms and conditions for the network to be able to use it.

When you connect to one of these public networks, you're prompted to provide whatever information is required. This can involve different details for different networks, but the general steps are the same. You're prompted to provide whatever information is required. Then, follow the instructions that appear.

Following are the general steps to connect to many types of public Wi-Fi networks:

1. Use the steps in the previous task to move to and tap the public network you want to join. The iPhone connects to the network, and you see the Log In screen for that network.

2. If prompted to do so, provide the information required to join the network, such as a name and room number. If a fee is required, you'll have to provide payment information. In almost all cases, you at least have to indicate that you accept the terms and conditions for using the network, which you typically do by checking a check box.

3. Tap the button to join the network. This button can have different labels depending on the type of access, such as Authenticate, Done, Free Access, Login, and so on.

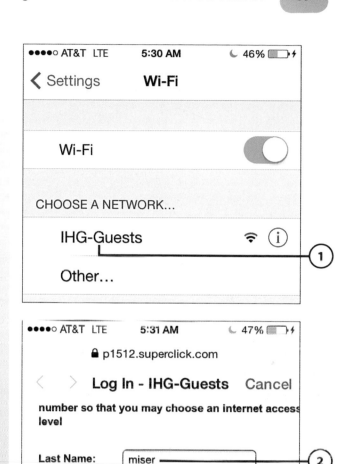

No Prompt?

Not all public networks prompt you to log in as these steps explain. Sometimes, you use the network's website to log in instead. After you join the network (step 1), your iPhone is connected to the network without any prompts. When you try to move to a web page as explained in step 4, you're prompted to log in to or create an account with the network's provider on the web page that appears.

(4) Try to move to a web page, such as www.wikipedia.org, to test your Wi-Fi connection. (See Chapter 13 for details.) If the web page opens, you are ready to use the Internet on your phone. If you are taken to a login web page for the Wi-Fi network's provider, you need to provide the required information to be able to use the Internet.

A Closed Network

Some Wi-Fi networks are closed, which means they don't broadcast their names. This means that you don't see closed networks listed in the CHOOSE A NETWORK on the Wi-Fi screen. To be able to access a closed network, you need to know its name, its password, and the type of security it uses. With this information in hand, tap Other in the CHOOSE A NETWORK section. Type the network's name. Tap Security, choose the appropriate type, and tap Back. Enter the required password and tap Join.

Cell Phone Provider Wi-Fi Networks

Many cell phone providers also provide other services, particularly public Wi-Fi networks. In some cases, you can access that provider's Internet service through a Wi-Fi network that it provides; often, you can do this at no additional charge. So, you can take advantage of the speed a Wi-Fi connection provides without paying more for it. Check your provider's website to find out whether it offers this service and where you can access it.

Using Cellular Data Networks to Connect to the Internet

The provider for your iPhone also provides a cellular data connection your iPhone uses to connect to the Internet automatically when a Wi-Fi connection isn't available. (Your iPhone tries to connect to an available Wi-Fi network before connecting to a cellular data connection because Wi-Fi is typically less expensive and faster to use.) These networks cover large geographic areas and the connection to them is automatic. Access to these networks is part of your monthly account fee; you choose from among various amounts of data per month at different monthly charges.

Most providers have multiple cellular data networks, such as a low-speed network that is available widely and one or more higher-speed networks that have a more limited coverage area.

The speed and name of the cellular data networks you can use are determined based on your provider, your data plan, the model of iPhone you are using, and your location within your provider's networks or the roaming networks available when you are outside of your provider's coverage area. The iPhone automatically uses the fastest connection available to it at any given time (assuming you haven't disabled that option, as explained later).

This iPhone is connected to a
high-speed LTE cellular network

Whenever you are connected to a cellular data network, you can access the Internet for web browsing, email, etc.

One thing you do need to keep in mind when using a cellular network is that your account might include a limited amount of data per month. When your data use exceeds this limit, you might be charged overage fees, which can be very expensive. Most providers send you warning texts or emails as your data use approaches your plan's limit, at which point you need to be careful about what you do while using the cellular data network to avoid an overage fee. Some tasks, such as watching YouTube videos or downloading large movie files, can chew up a lot of data and should be saved for when you are on a Wi-Fi network to avoid running out of data. Others, such as using email, typically don't use very much data.

An App for That

Various apps are available in the App Store that you can install on your iPhone that monitor how much data you are using. These apps are a good way to know where your data use is relative to your plan's monthly allowance so that you can avoid an overage situation. To get information on finding, downloading, and installing apps, see Chapter 6. (To find an app for this purpose, search for "data monitoring app.")

When you are outside of your primary provider's coverage area, a different provider might provide cellular phone or data access, or both. The iPhone automatically selects a roaming provider. Roaming charges can be associated with calls or data use. These charges are often very expensive. The roaming charges associated with phone calls are easier to manage, since it's more obvious when you make or receive a phone call in a roaming area. However, data roaming charges are much more insidious, especially if Push functionality (where emails are pushed to your iPhone from the server automatically) is active. And when you use some applications, such as Maps to navigate, you don't really know how much data is involved. Because data roaming charges are harder to notice, the iPhone is configured by default to prevent data roaming. When data roaming is disabled, the iPhone is unable to access the Internet when you are outside of your cellular network, unless you connect to a Wi-Fi network. (You can still use the cellular roaming network for telephone calls.)

You can configure some aspects of how your cellular network is used, as this task demonstrates. You can also allow individual apps to use, or prevent them from using, your cellular data network. This is important when your data plan has a monthly limit. In most cases, the first time you launch an app, you're prompted to allow or prevent it from using cellular data. At any time, you can use the Cellular Data options in the Settings app to enable or disable an app's access to your cellular data network.

To configure how your iPhone uses its cellular network for data, perform the following steps:

(1) Open the Settings app.

(2) Tap Cellular.

(3) To disable all cellular data connections, set the Cellular Data switch to off (white) and skip the rest of these steps. The iPhone is no longer able to connect to any cellular data networks. To use the Internet when the Cellular Data switch is off, you have to connect to a WI-FI network that provides Internet access.

(4) To disable the high-speed network, set the Enable *high-speed network*, where *high-speed* network is the network name (such as LTE) switch to off (white). The iPhone is no longer able to use the higher-speed network, but can access other, slower cellular data networks.

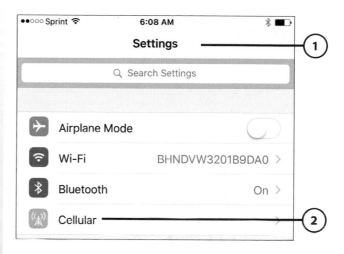

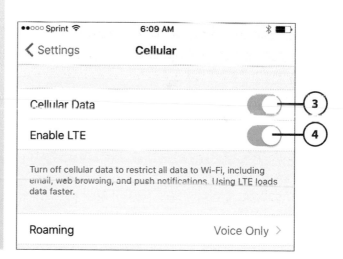

Monitoring Data Use

In the CELLULAR DATA USAGE section toward the bottom of the Cellular screen, you see how much data you've used for the current period and how much you've used while roaming. This can help you see where your use is compared to your monthly plan allowance, so you know whether you are getting close to exceeding that allowance (thus incurring overage charges).

Provider Differences

The configuration of roaming depends on the provider your iPhone is connected to. Steps 4 through 9 show the details for Sprint in the United States. Other providers have different options. You can configure cellular data use by apps for all providers as shown, starting with step 10.

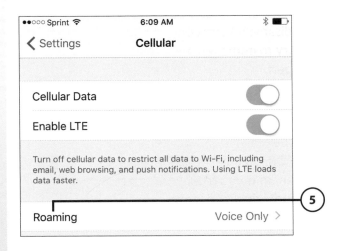

(5) To configure roaming, tap Roaming.

(6) To prevent voice calls when you are roaming, set the Voice Roaming switch to off (white). (Not all providers allow for preventing voice roaming, so you might not see this option.) When you are outside of your provider's network, you won't be able to make or receive voice calls. When you disable Voice Roaming, Data Roaming is disabled automatically so you can skip to step 9.

(7) If you want to allow data roaming, slide the Data Roaming switch to the on (green) position. When you move outside your primary network, data comes to your iPhone via an available roaming cellular data network. You should disable it again by sliding the Data Roaming switch to off (white) as soon as you're done with a specific task to limit roaming charges.

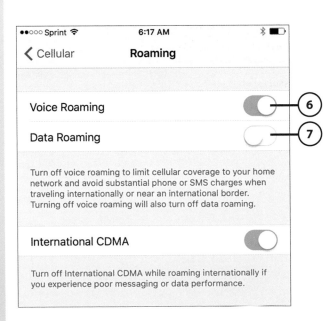

8 Use the other options you see to complete the Roaming configuration. For example, if your phone uses a CDMA (Code Division Multiple Access) network, you can disable International CDMA to try to improve your phone's performance.

9 Tap Cellular.

10 Swipe up the screen until you see the USE CELLULAR DATA FOR: section. This section enables you to allow or prevent individual apps from accessing a cellular data network. To limit the amount of data you use, it's a good idea to review this list and allow only those apps that you rely on to use the cellular data network. (Of course, if you are fortunate enough to have an unlimited data plan, you can leave all the apps enabled.)

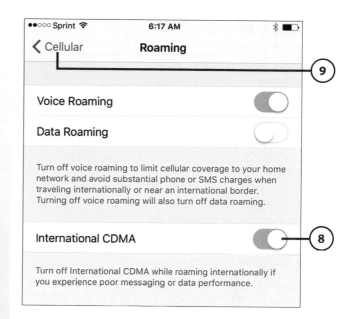

Monitoring an App's Data Use

Just under each app's name, you see a number that shows you how much data the app has used since the counter was last reset. The magnitude of this number can help you determine how much data a particular app is using. For example, if an app's use is shown in Mega Bytes (MB), it's used a lot more data than an app whose use is shown in Kilo Bytes (KB). This information can help you identify apps that might be causing you to exceed your data plan's monthly limit.

(11) Set an app's switch to on (green) if you want it to be able to use a cellular data network.

(12) Set an app's switch to off (white) if you want it to be able to access the Internet only when you are connected to a Wi-Fi network.

(13) Tap Settings when you're done configuring your cellular network use.

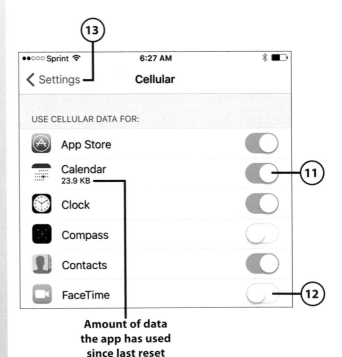

Amount of data the app has used since last reset

Using Bluetooth to Connect to Other Devices

Bluetooth is a short-range wireless communication technology that enables mobile and other devices to communicate with each other. Bluetooth is widely used on computers, mobile phones, tablets, and even home electronics, such as televisions. The iPhone includes built-in Bluetooth support so you can use this wireless technology to connect to other Bluetooth-capable devices. The most likely devices to connect to an iPhone in this way are Bluetooth headphones or headsets or car audio/entertainment/information systems, but you can also use Bluetooth to connect to other kinds of devices, most notably keyboards, computers, iPod touches, iPads, and other iPhones.

To connect Bluetooth devices together, you *pair* them. In Bluetooth, pairing enables two Bluetooth devices to communicate with each other. For devices to find and identify each other so they can communicate, one or both must be *discoverable*, which means they broadcast a Bluetooth signal other devices can detect and connect to.

There is also a "sometimes" requirement, which is a pairing code, passkey, or PIN. All those terms refer to the same thing, which is a series of numbers, letters, or both, entered on one or both devices being paired. Sometimes you enter this code on both devices, whereas for other devices you enter the first device's code on the second device. Some devices don't require a pairing code at all.

When you have to pair devices, you're prompted to do so, and you have to complete the actions required by the prompts to communicate via Bluetooth. This might be just tapping Connect, or you might have to enter a passcode on one or both devices.

Also, because Bluetooth works over a relatively short range, the devices have to be in the same proximity, such as in the same room.

Connecting to Bluetooth Devices

This task demonstrates pairing an iPhone with a Bluetooth keyboard; you can pair it with other devices similarly.

1. Move to the Settings screen. The current status of Bluetooth on your iPhone is shown.

2. Tap Bluetooth.

3. If Bluetooth isn't on (green), tap the Bluetooth switch to turn it on. If it isn't running already, Bluetooth starts up. The iPhone immediately begins searching for Bluetooth devices. You also see the status Now Discoverable, which means other Bluetooth devices can discover the iPhone. In the OTHER DEVICES section, you see the devices that are discoverable to your iPhone but that are not paired with it.

4. If the device you want to use isn't shown in the OTHER DEVICES section, put it into Discoverable mode. (Not shown, see the instructions provided with the device.) When it is discoverable, it appears in the OTHER DEVICES section.

5. Tap the device to which you want to connect. If a passkey is required, you see a prompt to enter it on the device with which you are pairing.

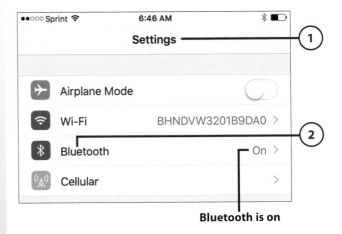

Bluetooth is on

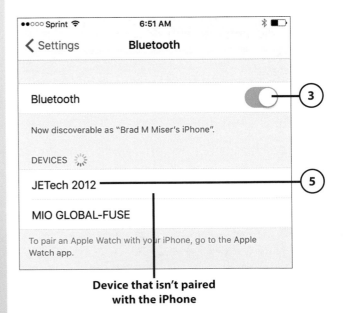

Device that isn't paired with the iPhone

6 If it is required, the code is displayed on your iPhone. You input the pairing code, passkey, or PIN on the device, such as typing the passkey on a keyboard if you are pairing your iPhone with a Bluetooth keyboard.

7 If required, tap Connect (not shown in the figures)—some devices connect as soon as you enter the passkey and you won't need to do this. If a passkey isn't required, such as with a Bluetooth speaker, you tap Connect without entering a passkey. You see the device to which the iPhone is connected in the MY DEVICES section of the Bluetooth screen, and its status is Connected, indicating that your iPhone can communicate with and use the device.

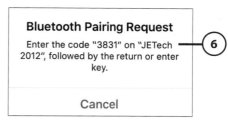

Bluetooth Pairing Request

Enter the code "3831" on "JETech 2012", followed by the return or enter key.

Cancel

6

This keyboard is now connected and can be used

●●○○○ Sprint 🔶   6:51 AM   ✳ ■⬤

‹ Settings   **Bluetooth**

Bluetooth   ⬤

Now discoverable as "Brad M Miser's iPhone".

MY DEVICES

JETech 2012   Connected ⓘ

OTHER DEVICES

MIO GLOBAL-FUSE

To pair an Apple Watch with your iPhone, go to the Apple Watch app.

>>>Go Further

MANAGING BLUETOOTH

Following are a few pointers for using Bluetooth with other devices:

- Like other connections you make, the iPhone remembers Bluetooth devices to which you've connected before and reconnects to them automatically, which is convenient—most of the time anyway. If you don't want your iPhone to keep connecting to a device, move to the Bluetooth screen and tap the device's Info (i) button. If you just want to stop using the device, but keep the pairing in place, tap Disconnect. Tap the Forget this Device button, and then tap Forget Device to completely remove the pairing. Of course, you can always pair the devices again at any time.

- A device that is already paired can still have the Not Connected status. You need to connect it to use it. Move to the Bluetooth screen and tap the device to connect it to your iPhone. Once its status becomes Connected, your iPhone can communicate with the device again.

- You can use multiple Bluetooth devices with your iPhone at the same time. For example, you might want to be connected to a Bluetooth speaker and a keyboard at the same time.

Connecting Your iPhone to Other iPhones, iPod touches, or iPads

The iPhone (and other devices that run the iOS software, including Apple Watch, iPod touch, and iPad) supports peer-to-peer connectivity, which is the technical way of saying that these devices can communicate with one another directly via a Wi-Fi network or Bluetooth. This capability is used in a number of apps, especially multiplayer gaming, for information sharing, and for other collaborative purposes.

If the app you want to use communicates over a Wi-Fi network, all the devices with which you want to communicate must be on that same network. If the application uses Bluetooth, you must enable Bluetooth on each device and pair them (as described in the previous task) so they can communicate with one another.

The specific steps you use to connect to other iOS devices using a collaborative app depend on the specific app you are using. The general steps are typically as follows:

1. Ensure the devices can communicate with each other. If the app uses Wi-Fi, each device must be connected to the same Wi-Fi network (see "Using Wi-Fi Networks to Connect to the Internet" earlier in this chapter). If the app uses Bluetooth, the devices must be paired.

2. Each person opens the app on his device.

3. Use the app's controls to select the devices with which you'll be collaborating. Usually, this involves a confirmation process in which one person selects another person's device and that person confirms that the connection should be allowed.

4. Use the app's features to collaborate. For example, if the app is a game, each person can interact with the group members. Or, you can directly collaborate on a document with all parties providing input into the document.

---

iPhone and Apple Watch

The Apple Watch is designed to be a perfect partner device for your iPhone and can work with it in many ways. For detailed information about the Apple Watch, see the book *My Apple Watch, 2nd edition* (Que Publishing, ISBN: 9780789756626).

Using AirDrop to Share Content with Other iPhones, iPod touches, iPads, or a Mac

You can use the iOS AirDrop feature to share content directly with people using a Mac running OS X Yosemite or later, or using a device running iOS 7 or later. For example, if you capture a great photo on your iPhone, you can use AirDrop to instantly share that photo with iOS devices and Mac users near you.

AirDrop can use Wi-Fi or Bluetooth to share, but the nice thing about AirDrop is that it manages the details for you. You simply open the Share menu—which is available in most apps—and in the AirDrop section of the menu tap the people with whom you want to share.

When you activate AirDrop, you can select Everyone, which means you will see anyone who has AirDrop enabled on a Mac running OS X Yosemite or later, or an iOS device running version iOS 7 or later. They also need to be on the same Wi-Fi network with you (or have a paired Bluetooth device). Or, you can select Contacts Only, which means only people who are in your Contacts app are able to use AirDrop to communicate with you. In most cases, you should choose the Contacts Only option so you have more control over who uses AirDrop with you.

When enabled, you can use AirDrop by opening the Share menu while using an app. Then, tap the people with whom you want to share content.

Is AirDrop Safe?

Anything you share with AirDrop is encrypted, so the chances of someone else being able to intercept and use what you share are quite low. Likewise, you don't have to worry about someone using AirDrop to access your information or to add information to your device without your permission. However, like any networking technology, there's always some chance—quite small in this case—that someone will figure out how to use this technology for nefarious purposes. The best thing you can do is ensure that any requests you receive to share information are from people you know and trust before you accept them.

Enabling AirDrop

To use AirDrop, you must enable it on your iPhone.

1. Swipe up from the bottom of the screen to open the Control Center.

(2) If AirDrop is not active—
indicated by the text "AirDrop"
being in black—tap AirDrop. If
it is active, the "AirDrop" text is
in white and you see its status
(Everyone or Contacts Only); if
it is already active, skip the next
two steps.

(3) Tap Contacts Only to allow
only people in your Contacts
app to communicate with you
via AirDrop, or tap Everyone to
allow anyone using a device
running iOS 7 or later or a Mac
running OS X Yosemite or later
in your area to do so.

(4) Swipe down from the top of the
Control Center to close it. You're
ready to use AirDrop to share
content such as photos and
documents.

Share and Share Alike?

You should disable AirDrop when
you aren't using it, especially if
you use the Everyone option.
By disabling it, you avoid having people in your area be able
to try to communicate with you
without you wanting them to do
so. Generally, you should enable
AirDrop only when you are actively using it and disable it when you
aren't. To disable AirDrop, open
the Control Center, tap AirDrop,
and then tap Off.

**Current AirDrop
status (disabled)**

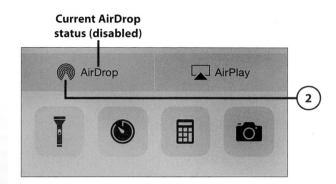

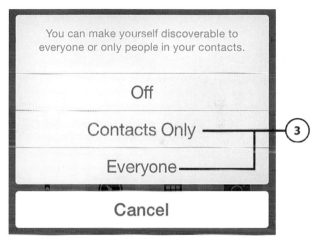

**People in your Contacts app can use
AirDrop to communicate with you**

Using AirDrop to Share Your Content

To use AirDrop to share your content, do the following:

(1) Open the content you want to share. This example shows sharing a photo using the Photos app. The steps to share content from any other app are quite similar.

(2) Tap the Share button.

(3) You see icons for each person in your area who has AirDrop enabled that you have permission to access (such as being in her Contacts app if she is using the Contacts Only option).

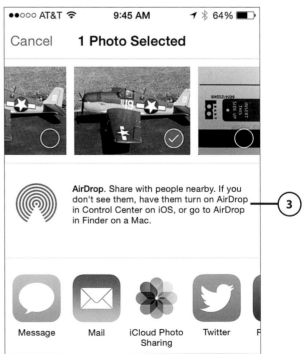

4 Swipe to the left or right to browse all the people with whom you can share.

5 Tap the people with whom you want to share the content. A sharing request is sent to those peoples' devices. Under their icons, the Waiting status is displayed. When a recipient accepts your content, the status changes to Sent. If a recipient rejects your content, the status changes to Declined.

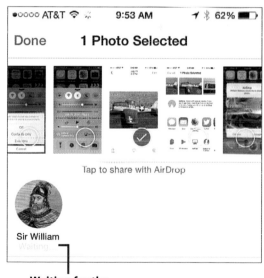

Waiting for the recipient to accept or decline your sharing

(6) If the app supports it, browse and select more content to share.

(7) Tap the people with whom you want to share the content.

(8) When you're done sharing, tap Done.

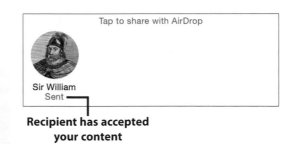

Tap to share with AirDrop

Sir William
Sent

**Recipient has accepted
your content**

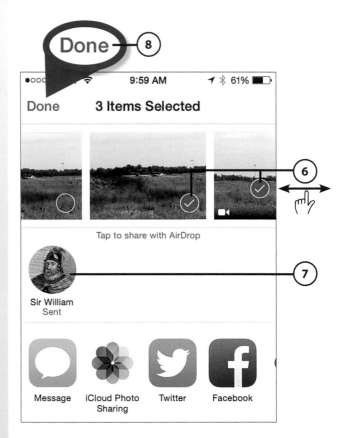

Done (8)

Done   3 Items Selected   9:59 AM   61%

(6)

Tap to share with AirDrop

Sir William
Sent

(7)

Message   iCloud Photo   Twitter   Facebook
            Sharing

Using AirDrop to Work with Content Shared with You

When someone wants to share content with you, you receive an AirDrop sharing request; if you have previously accepted content from that person, you might not receive a sharing request because it is accepted by default. Respond to sharing requests by doing the following:

(1) Make sure you know the person attempting to share with you.

(2) Make sure the content being shared with you is something you want. In this case, a photo is being shared.

(3) To accept the content on your iPhone, tap Accept. To reject it, tap Decline.

(4) After you accept content, swipe up and down the screen to see the detail of what you are accepting, or use the app's controls to edit it.

(5) Use the app's controls to work with the shared content. For example, the Photos app provides tools to edit and share photos that are shared with you. In some cases, such as saving a contact shared with you, you need to tap Save to save the content on your iPhone or Cancel to not save it. (Other apps provide different controls depending on the type of content and the app it opens in.)

Go here to configure and manage iCloud and your other online accounts

Store files on the cloud

Use iCloud and other accounts to store the data your apps use on the cloud

In this chapter, you learn how to connect your iPhone to various types of accounts, such as iCloud and Google, so that apps on your iPhone can access your data stored on the Internet cloud. Topics include the following:

→ Getting started
→ Configuring and using iCloud
→ Setting up other types of built-in online accounts on your iPhone
→ Configuring other types of online accounts
→ Setting how and when your accounts are updated

Setting Up and Using iCloud and Other Online Accounts

No iPhone is an island. Connecting your iPhone to the Internet enables you to share and sync a wide variety of content using popular online accounts such as iCloud and Google. Using iCloud, you can put your email, contacts, calendars, photos, and more on the Internet so that multiple devices—most importantly your iPhone—can connect to and use that information. (There's a lot more you can do with iCloud, too, as you learn throughout this book.) There are lots of other accounts you might also want to use, such as Google for email, calendars, and contacts as well as Facebook for accessing social networks.

You need to configure these accounts on your iPhone to be able to use them; in this chapter, you'll see sections for several different accounts you might want to use. Of course, you only need to refer to the sections related to the accounts you want to use. You should also understand how you can determine how and when your information is updated along with tasks you might find valuable as you manage the various accounts on your iPhone.

Getting Started

One of the best things about using an iPhone is that you can configure it to use various types of online accounts that offer different types of services and information to you. Here are some of the key getting started terms for this chapter:

- **iCloud**—This is Apple's online service that offers lots of great features that you can use for free. It includes email, online photo storage and sharing, backup, calendars, Find My iPhone, and much more. You'll learn how to set up iCloud on your iPhone in this chapter and will see examples of how you can use it in many others.

- **Family Sharing**—This Apple service allows you to share content with a group of people. (They don't actually have to be related to you.) For example, you can share music you download from the iTunes Store with others automatically—when you set them up in your "family" group. It is also free.

- **Google account**—A Google account is similar to an iCloud account except it is provided by Google instead of Apple. It also offers lots of features, such as email, calendars, and contacts. You can use iCloud and a Google account on your iPhone at the same time.

- **Facebook**—Facebook is one of the largest social media sites that people and organizations use to share information, events, photos, and more. You can log into your Facebook account on your iPhone and use the Facebook app along with sharing information via that account in a number of apps (such as Photos).

- **Push, Fetch, or Manual**—Information has to get from your online account onto your iPhone. For example, when someone sends you an email, it actually goes to an email server, which then sends the message to devices that are configured with your email account. You can choose how and when new data is provided to your phone. Push means updates happen in real time; for example, as soon as a new email reaches the server, it is sent directly to your iPhone. Fetch means your phone connects to the servers periodically to retrieve new information. Manual means that new information is only retrieved when you cause it to be, such as by opening the Mail app.

Configuring and Using iCloud

iCloud is a service provided by Apple that provides you with your own storage space on the Internet. You can store content from your computer or devices in your storage space on the cloud, and because it is on the Internet, all your devices are able to access that information at the same time. This means you can easily share your information between your iPhone, a computer, an iPad, and so on, so that the same information and content is available to you no matter which device you are using at any one time.

Although your iPhone can work with many types of online/Internet accounts, iCloud is integrated into the iPhone like no other type of account (not surprising because the iPhone and iCloud are both Apple technology). An iCloud account is really useful in a number of ways. For example, iCloud can be used for the following:

- **Family Sharing**—With Family Sharing, you can designate up to six people with whom you want to automatically share your iTunes and apps downloads, calendars, reminders, and more.

- **Files**—iCloud Drive enables you to store your documents and other files on the cloud so that you can seamlessly work with them using different devices.

- **Photos**—You can store your photos in iCloud to back them up and to make them easy to share.

- **Email**—An iCloud account includes an @icloud.com email address. You can configure any device to use your iCloud email account, including an iPhone, an iPad, an iPod touch, and a computer.

- **Contacts**—You can store your contact information in iCloud.

- **Calendars**—Putting your calendars in iCloud makes it much easier to manage your time.

- **Reminders**—Through iCloud, you can be reminded of things you need to do or anything else you want to make sure you don't forget.

- **Safari**—iCloud can store your bookmarks, letting you easily access the same websites from all your devices. And you can easily access websites currently open on other devices, such as a Mac, on your iPhone.

- **Notes**—With the Notes app, you can create text notes for many purposes; iCloud enables you to use these notes on any iCloud-enabled device.

- **News**—iCloud can store information from the News app online, making reading news on multiple devices easier.

- **Wallet**—The Wallet app stores coupons, tickets, boarding passes, and other documents so you can access them quickly and easily. With iCloud, you can ensure that these documents are available on any iCloud-enabled device.

- **Backup**—You can back up your iPhone to the cloud so that you can recover your data and your phone's configuration should something ever happen to it.

- **Keychain**—The Keychain securely stores sensitive data, such as passwords, so that you can easily use that data without having to remember it.

- **Find My iPhone**—This service enables you to locate and secure your iPhone and other devices.

You'll learn about iCloud's many useful features throughout this book (such as using iCloud with your photos, which is covered in Chapter 14, "Working with Photos and Video You Take with Your iPhone"). The tasks in this chapter show you how to set up and configure the iCloud features you want to use.

Obtaining an iCloud Account

Of course, to use iCloud on your iPhone, you need to have an iCloud account. The good news is that you probably already have one. The other good news is that even if you don't, obtaining one is simple and free.

If you have any of the following accounts, you already have an iCloud account and are ready to start using iCloud and can skip ahead to the next section:

- **iTunes Store**—If you've ever shopped at the iTunes Store, you created an account with an Apple ID and password. You can use that Apple ID and password to access iCloud.

- **Apple Online Store**—As with the iTunes Store, if you made purchases from Apple's online store, you created an account with an Apple ID and password that also enables you to use iCloud.

- **Find My iPhone**—If you obtained a free Find My iPhone account, you can log in to iCloud using that Apple ID.

During the initial iPhone startup process, you were prompted to sign into or create an iCloud account. If you created one at that time, you are also good to go and can move to the next task.

If you don't have an iCloud account, you can use your iPhone to create one by performing the following steps:

1. On the Home screen, tap Settings.
2. Swipe up the screen and tap iCloud.
3. Tap Create a new Apple ID.

4 Provide the information required on the following screens; tap Next to move to the next screen after you've entered the required information. You start by entering your birthday.

During the process, you'll be prompted to use an existing email address or to create a free iCloud email account. You can choose either option. The email address you use becomes your Apple ID that you use to sign into iCloud. If you create a new iCloud email account, you can use that account from any email app on any device, just like other email accounts you have.

You'll also create a password, set up security questions, enter a rescue email address (optional), choose email updates you want to receive, and agree to license terms. When your account has been created, you're prompted to enter your password.

After you successfully create your password, you are logged into your iCloud account and might be prompted to merge information already stored on your iPhone, such as Safari bookmarks, onto iCloud. Tap Merge to copy your existing information onto the cloud or Don't Merge to keep it out of the cloud.

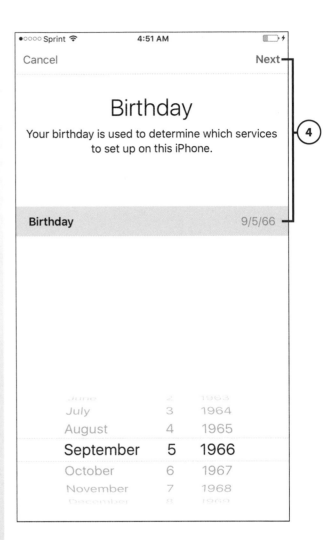

When you've worked through merging your information, you see that iCloud tracks the location of your iPhone through the Find My iPhone feature.

(5) Tap OK. You are ready to complete the configuration of your iCloud account, which is covered in the next section.

Find My iPhone Enabled

This allows you to locate, lock, or erase your iPhone. Your Apple ID and password will be required to reactivate your iPhone.

OK ————————— (5)

Multiple iCloud Accounts

You can have more than one iCloud account. However, you can have only one iCloud account active on your iPhone at a time.

Signing Into Your iCloud Account

To be able to use an iCloud account on your iPhone, you need to first sign into your account, and then enable the services you want to use and disable those that you don't want to use. After iCloud is set up on your iPhone, you rarely need to change your account settings. If you restore your iPhone at some point, you might need to revisit these steps to ensure iCloud remains set up as you want it.

To get started, sign into your iCloud account—if you created your iCloud account on your iPhone, you don't need to perform these steps because you signed in when you created the account; in that case, skip to the next task.

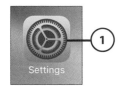

1. On the Home screen, tap Settings.

2. Swipe up the screen and tap iCloud.

3. Enter your Apple ID. If you see account information instead of the Apple ID field, an iCloud account is already signed into on the iPhone. If it is your account, skip to the next task. If it isn't your account, swipe up the screen and tap Sign Out; tap Delete to delete various data from your iPhone at the prompts and continue with these steps.

4. Enter your Apple ID password.

5. Tap Sign In. You are logged in to your iCloud account.

6. If prompted to do so, tap Merge to merge existing data, such as Safari bookmarks, already stored on the iPhone onto the cloud.

7. At the prompt, tap OK indicating that you realize Find My iPhone is enabled. You're ready to configure the rest of iCloud's services.

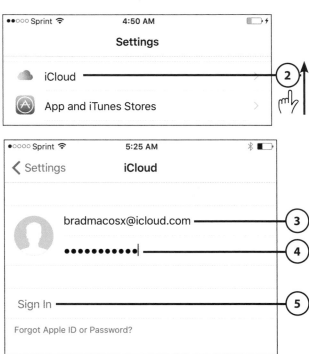

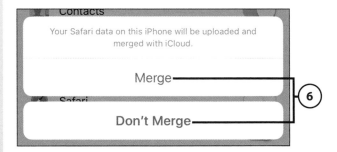

Enabling iCloud to Store Your Information on the Cloud

One of the best things about iCloud is that it stores email, contacts, calendars, reminders, bookmarks, notes, photos, and other data on the cloud so that all your iCloud-enabled devices can access the same information. You can choose the types of data stored on the cloud by performing the following steps:

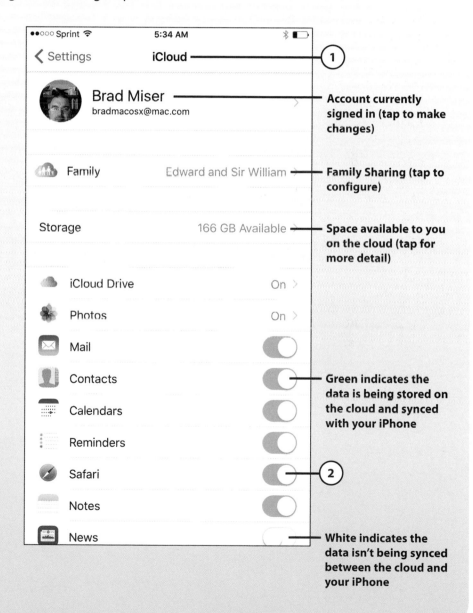

(1) Move to the iCloud screen by tapping Settings, iCloud. Just below the Storage information are the iCloud data options. Some of these have a right-facing arrow that you tap to configure options, while others have a two-position switch. When a switch is green, it means that switch is turned on and the related data is stored to your iCloud account and kept in sync with the information on the iPhone.

Share and Share Alike

Family Sharing enables you to share iTunes and App Store downloads, reminders, photos, and other information with a group of people. Configuring Family Sharing is explained in "Using Family Share to Share your iTunes Store Content" in Chapter 6, "Downloading Apps, Music, Movies, TV Shows, and More onto Your iPhone."

(2) If you don't want a specific type of data to be stored on the cloud and synced to your iPhone, tap its switch to turn that data off (the switch becomes white instead of green). The types of data that have switches are: Mail, Contacts, Calendars, Reminders, Safari, Notes, News, and Wallet.

When you turn a switch off because you don't want that information stored on the cloud any more, you might be prompted to keep the associated information on your iPhone or delete it.

If you choose Keep on My iPhone, the information remains on your iPhone but is no longer connected to the cloud; this means any changes you make exist only on the iPhone. If you choose Delete from My iPhone, the information is erased from your iPhone. Whether you choose to keep or delete the information, any information of that type that was previously stored on the cloud remains available there; the delete action only impacts the information stored on the iPhone.

After you've configured each data switch on the iCloud screen, you're ready to configure the rest of the data options, which are explained in the following tasks.

Configuring iCloud Drive

iCloud Drive, which is enabled by default, stores files (such as Pages documents) on the cloud so that you can work with those documents on any device. For example, you can create a letter in Pages on a Mac and then access it on your iPhone to edit it. To configure your iCloud Drive, perform the following steps:

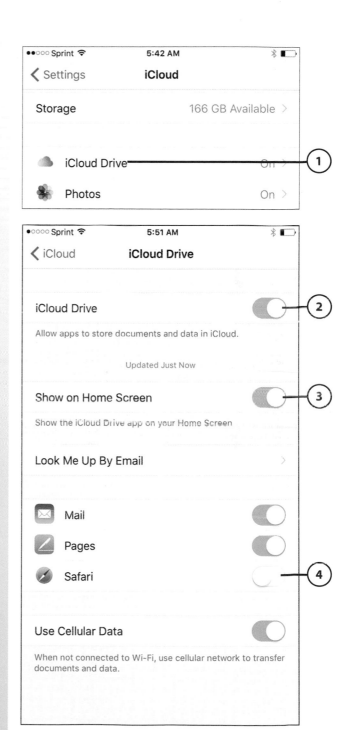

1. On the iCloud screen in the Settings app, tap iCloud Drive.

2. To enable your files to be stored in iCloud, set the iCloud Drive switch to on (green).

3. To show the iCloud Drive icon on the Home screens, set the Show on Home Screen switch to on (green). Using this icon, you can open and view files in folders just like on a computer. If you prefer not to display the icon, your apps can still use the iCloud Drive, you just can't get to the files stored there without using an app.

4. Set the switch to off (white) for any apps currently saving data to your iCloud Drive that you don't want to use your iCloud Drive; set the switch to on (green) for those apps that you do want to use the iCloud Drive to store data.

5 To prevent file data from being copied to and from the cloud while your iPhone is using a cellular data network, set the Use Cellular Data switch to off (white). If you do turn this off, when your iPhone connects to a Wi-Fi network, your documents are synced with the cloud.

6 Tap iCloud.

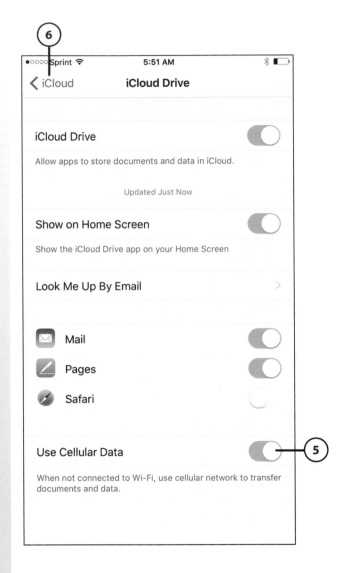

Configuring iCloud to Store Photos

Storing your photos on the cloud provides many benefits, not the least of which is that the photos you take with your iPhone are automatically saved on the cloud. You can access photos in iCloud from computers and other iOS devices (such as iPads) and your photos remain available even if something happens to your iPhone, such as you lose it. Using iCloud also makes it easy for you to share your photos with others. To configure your photos to be stored in iCloud, do the following:

(1) On the iCloud screen, tap Photos.

(2) To store your entire photo library on the cloud, set the iCloud Photo Library switch to on (green). This stores all of your photos and video in iCloud, which both protects them by backing them up and makes them accessible on other iOS devices (iPads, iPod touches, and iPhones) and computers, either through an app, such as Apple's Photos, or via the Web. If you set this switch to off (white), skip to step 4.

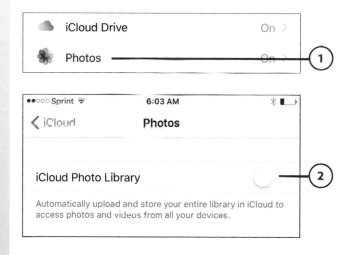

Photos Revealed
Using the iCloud-enabled photo features is explained in detail in Chapter 14.

3 If you enable the iCloud Photo Library feature, tap Optimize iPhone Storage to keep lower resolution versions of photos and videos on your iPhone (this means the file sizes are smaller so that you can store more of them on your phone) or Download and Keep Originals if you want to keep the full-resolution photos on your iPhone. In most cases, you should choose the Optimize option so that you don't use as much of your iPhone's storage space for photos.

4 Ensure the Upload to My Photo Stream switch is on (green) (if you aren't using the iCloud Photo Library, this switch is called My Photo Stream); if you disabled this, skip to step 6. Any photos you take with the iPhone's camera are copied onto iCloud, and from there they are copied to your other devices on which the Photo Stream is enabled. Note that Photo Stream only affects photos that you take with the iPhone from the time you enable it, while the iCloud Photo Library feature uploads all of your photos, those you took in the past and will take in the future.

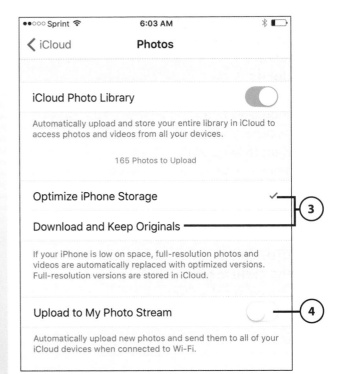

5 If you want all of your burst photos (see Chapter 14) to be uploaded to iCloud, set the Upload Burst Photos switch to on (green). In most cases, you should leave this off (white) because you typically don't want to keep all the photos in a burst. When you review and select photos to keep, the ones you keep are uploaded through Photo Stream.

6 To be able to share your photos and to share other people's photos, set the iCloud Photo Sharing switch to on (green).

7 Tap iCloud.

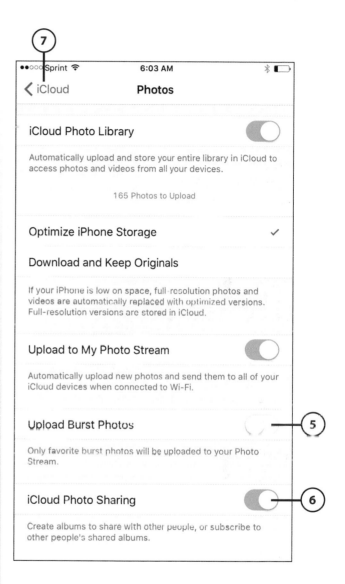

7

•• ○○○ Sprint 🔋   6:03 AM   ✳ ▬

❮ iCloud   **Photos**

iCloud Photo Library

Automatically upload and store your entire library in iCloud to access photos and videos from all your devices.

165 Photos to Upload

Optimize iPhone Storage   ✓

Download and Keep Originals

If your iPhone is low on space, full-resolution photos and videos are automatically replaced with optimized versions. Full-resolution versions are stored in iCloud.

Upload to My Photo Stream

Automatically upload new photos and send them to all of your iCloud devices when connected to Wi-Fi.

Upload Burst Photos   **5**

Only favorite burst photos will be uploaded to your Photo Stream.

iCloud Photo Sharing   **6**

Create albums to share with other people, or subscribe to other people's shared albums.

Configuring Your iCloud Backup

Like other digital devices, it is important to back up your iPhone's data so that you can recover should something bad happen to your iPhone. You can back up your iPhone's data and settings to iCloud, which is really useful because that means you can recover the backed-up data using a different device, such as a replacement iPhone. Configure your iCloud backup with the following steps:

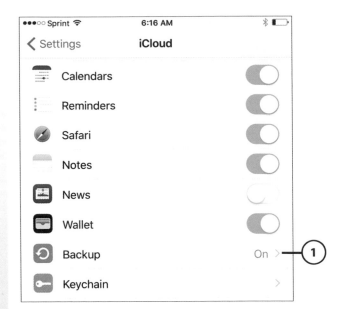

(1) On the iCloud screen, tap Backup.

(2) Set the iCloud Backup switch to on (green). Your iPhone's data and settings are backed up to the cloud automatically.

(3) Tap iCloud.

Back Me Up on This

You can manually back up your iPhone's data and settings at any time by tapping Back Up Now on the Backup screen. This can be useful to ensure recent data or settings changes are captured in your backup. For example, if you know you are going to be without a Wi-Fi connection to the Internet for a while, back up your phone to ensure that your current data is saved in the backup.

Configuring Your iCloud Keychain

A keychain can be used to store user-names, passwords, and credit cards so you can access this information without retyping it every time you need it. Enabling keychain syncing through iCloud makes this informa-tion available on multiple devices. For example, if you've configured a credit card on your keychain on a Mac, that credit card is available though the keychain being synced via iCloud. Follow these steps to enable keychain syncing through iCloud:

Assumptions

These steps assume you have a keychain already configured for iCloud syncing on another device, such as a Mac or iPad, and that you know your security code. If not, your steps may be slightly different than those shown here. For example, you create a security code if this is the first time you set up keychain syncing.

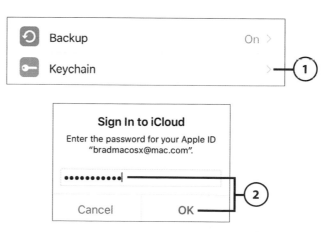

1. On the iCloud screen, tap Keychain.

2. Enter your Apple ID password and tap OK. Next, you need to approve with your security code or via another device that uses your keychain.

3 Set the iCloud Keychain switch to on (green). You need to verify you want the keychain to be enabled on the device. You can do this by entering your security code or approving on another device that has access to your keychain. When you enable the keychain, approval requests are sent to the other devices that have access to your keychain. You can enter your Apple ID password at the prompt on those devices to approve the keychain on your iPhone or continue with these steps to use your security code to do so.

4 Tap Approve with Security Code.

5 Enter your security code. You're prompted to enter a verification code, which is texted to your phone.

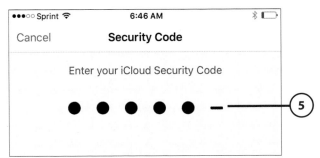

6 Enter the verification code you receive via text. Your keychain syncing starts and your keychain information is stored on the cloud and synced onto your iPhone.

Advanced Keychain Syncing

When keychain syncing has been enabled, Advanced appears on the Keychain screen. Tap this to access additional Keychain commands. Use the Approve with Security Code switch to determine if your code can be used to set up keychain syncing on other devices. Tap Change Security Code to change your security code. Use the controls in the VERIFICATION NUMBER section to see or change the phone number to which the verification code is texted.

It's Not All Good

If you store a lot of sensitive information in your keychain on a Mac, such as usernames and passwords to websites, credit cards, and such, be careful about enabling keychain syncing. When you enable that, all this data becomes available on your iPhone and can be used by anyone who can use your phone. Assuming you have a passcode to the phone, you are protected from someone using your phone without you knowing it, but if you let someone use your phone, they can also use your sensitive information. You may choose to leave keychain syncing off and just keep a minimum amount of sensitive information on your phone.

>>>*Go Further*

CONFIGURING FIND MY iPHONE

Find My iPhone enables you to locate and secure your iPhone if you lose it. This feature is enabled by default when you sign into your iCloud account (you can find a detailed explanation of how to use Find My iPhone in Chapter 16, "Maintaining and Protecting Your iPhone and Solving Problems," which is available on this book's website). You should usually leave it enabled so that you have a better chance of locating your iPhone should you lose it or to be able to delete its data should you decide you won't be getting it back. There are a couple of configuration tasks you can do for Find My iPhone:

- To disable Find My iPhone, open Settings and tap the iCloud option, and then tap Find My iPhone. Set the Find My iPhone switch to off (white) and enter your Apple ID password at the prompt. You can longer access your iPhone via the Find My iPhone feature.

- To send the last known location of the iPhone to Apple when power is critically low, open the Find My iPhone screen and set the Send Last Location switch to on (green). When your iPhone is nearly out of power, its location is sent to Apple. You can contact Apple to try to locate your iPhone should it run out of power while it isn't in your possession.

Setting Up Other Types of Built-In Online Accounts on Your iPhone

Many types of online accounts provide different services, including email, calendars, contacts, social networking, and so on. To use these accounts, you need to configure them on your iPhone. The process you use for most types of accounts is similar to the steps you used to set up your iCloud account. In this section, you'll learn how to configure a Google account.

Configuring a Google Account

A Google account provides email, contacts, calendar, and note syncing that is similar to iCloud. To set up a Google account on your iPhone, do the following:

(1) On the Home screen, tap Settings.

(2) Tap Mail, Contacts, Calendars.

(3) Tap Add Account.

(4) Tap Google.

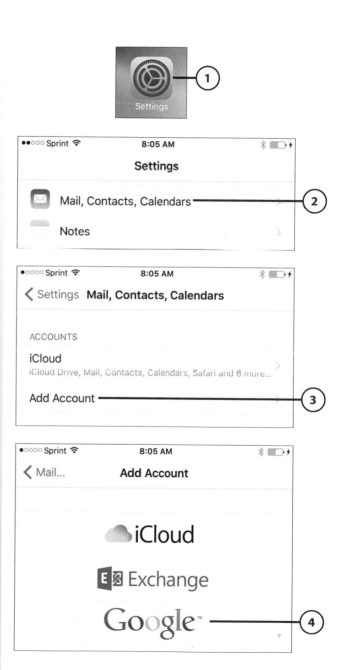

(5) Enter your Google email address.

(6) Enter your Google account password.

(7) Tap Sign In.

(8) Tap Allow to allow Google to use your information or Deny to prevent it.

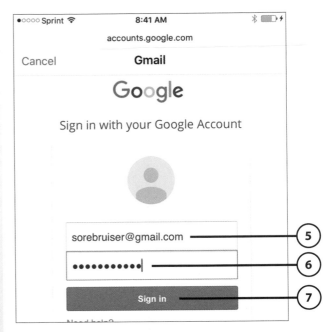

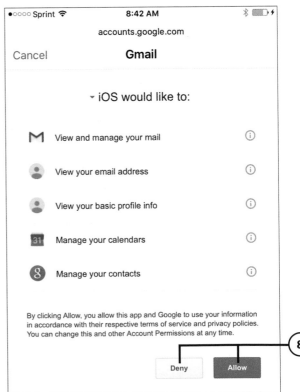

9. Enable the features of the account you want to access on the iPhone, which are Mail, Contacts, Calendars, and Notes.

10. Tap Save. The account is saved, and the data you enabled becomes available on your iPhone.

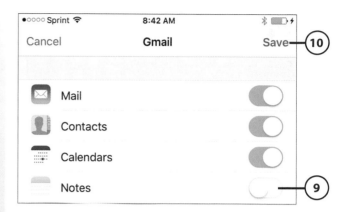

Configuring Other Types of Online Accounts

You can access many types of online accounts on your iPhone. These include accounts that are "built in," which include iCloud, Exchange, Google, Yahoo!, AOL, and Outlook.com. Setting up an Exchange, Yahoo!, AOL, or Outlook.com account is similar to the built-in accounts you learned to configure earlier in this chapter (iCloud and Google). Just select the account type you want to use and provide the information for which you are prompted.

There are lots of other accounts you might want to use. An email account included with an Internet access account, such as one from a cable Internet provider, is one example. Support for these accounts isn't built in to the iOS; however, you can usually set up such accounts on your iPhone fairly easily.

When you obtain an account, such as email accounts that are part of your Internet service, you should receive all the information you need to configure those accounts on your iPhone. If you don't have this information, visit the provider's website and look for information on configuring the account in an email application. You need to have this information to configure the account on the iPhone.

Setting Up an Online Account Manually

With the configuration information for the account in hand, you're ready to set it up:

(1) In the Settings app, move to the Mail, Contacts, Calendars screen and tap Add Account.

(2) Tap Other.

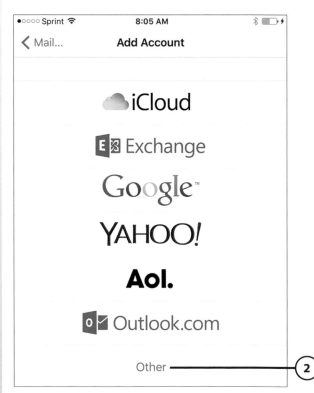

3 Tap the type of account you want to add. For example, to set up an email account, tap Add Mail Account.

4 Enter the information by filling in the fields you see; various types of information are required for different kinds of accounts. You just need to enter the information you received from the account's provider.

5 Tap Next. If the iPhone can set up the account automatically, its information is verified and it is ready for you to use (if the account supports multiple types of information, you can enable or disable the types with which you want to work on your iPhone). If the iPhone can't set up the account automatically, you're prompted to enter additional information to complete the account configuration. When you're done, the account appears on the list of accounts and is ready for you to use.

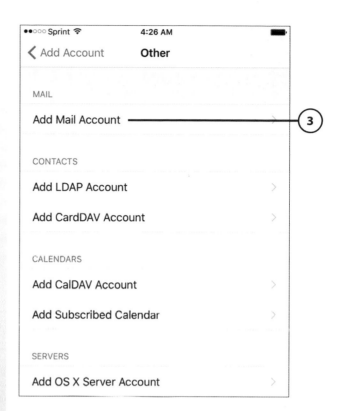

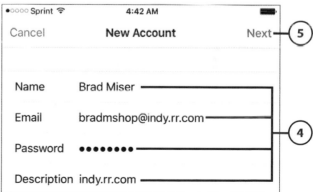

⑥ Configure the switches for the data sync options you see.

⑦ Tap Save. The account you configured is available in the related app, such as Mail if you set up an email account.

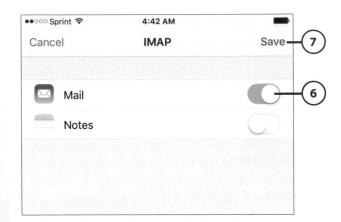

Multiple Accounts

There is no limit (that I have found so far) on the number of online accounts (even of the same type, such as Gmail) that you can access on your iPhone.

Configuring a Facebook Account

Facebook is one of the most popular social media channels you can use to keep informed about other people and inform them about you. Facebook is integrated into the iOS so you can share photos, messages, and such via your Facebook page, along with using the Facebook app.

To configure Facebook, perform the following steps:

① Move to the Home screen and tap Settings.

② Swipe up the screen and tap Facebook. If you see INSTALLED at the top of the screen, the Facebook app is installed on your iPhone and you can get

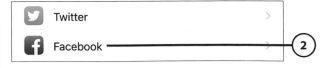

right into your account. If not, tap INSTALL to install the app (download and installing apps is covered in Chapter 6); when the app is done installing, continue with these steps.

No Facebook Account?

If don't have a Facebook account, tap Create New Account and follow the onscreen instructions to create one. When you are done creating the new account, you're signed into it automatically.

(3) Type your Facebook username.

(4) Type your Facebook password.

(5) Tap Sign In. Your account information is verified and you are signed into your account.

(6) Tap Sign In.

(7) To prevent apps from accessing your Facebook information, slide their switches to the off position (white).

(8) Tap Update All Contacts. Facebook attempts to match as much of your contact information with your friends as it can. When the process is complete, you are ready to access your Facebook account within the Facebook app or in any number of other apps.

More Facebook Settings

If you tap Settings on the Facebook Settings screen, you can do some additional configuration such as enabling or disabling sound and vibration for Facebook notifications. If you tap your name on that screen, you can change your password (which you might need to do from time to time).

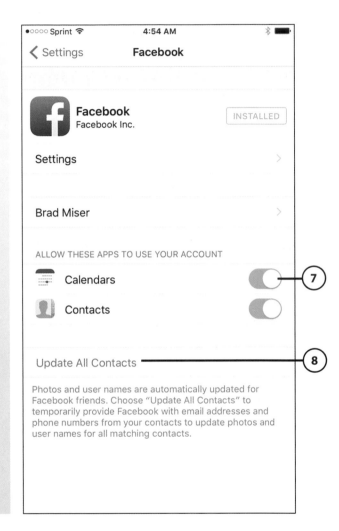

Setting How and When Your Accounts Are Updated

The great thing about online accounts is that their information can be updated any time your iPhone can connect to the Internet. This means you have access to the latest information, such as new emails and changes to your calendars.

As you learned in the "Getting Started" section, there are three ways that information on your iPhone is updated: Push, Fetch, and Manual. You can choose the methods that are used to update the information on your iPhone.

Push automatically provides the most current information, but also uses the most power, which shortens how long you can use your iPhone between charges. Fetch updates information automatically though less frequently, but uses less power than Push, so your battery lasts longer. Manual requires that you take action to update information.

You can configure the update method that is used globally, and you can set the method for specific accounts. Some account types, such as iCloud, support all three options while others might support only Fetch and Manual. The global option for updating is used unless you override it for individual accounts. For example, you might want your personal account to be updated via Push so your information there is always current, while configuring Fetch on a club email account may be frequently enough.

Configuring How New Data is Retrieved for Your Accounts

To configure how your information is updated, perform the following steps:

1. Move to the Mail, Contacts, Calendars screen of the Settings app.

2. Tap Fetch New Data.

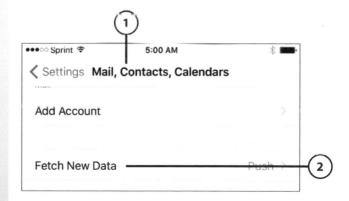

3 To enable data to be pushed to your iPhone, slide the Push switch to on (green). To disable push to extend battery life, set it to off (white). This setting is global, meaning that if you disable Push here, it is disabled for all accounts even though you can still configure Push to be used for individual accounts. For example, if your iCloud account is set to use Push but Push is globally disabled, the iCloud account's setting is ignored and data is fetched instead.

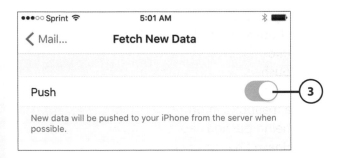

4 To change how an account's information is updated, tap it. The account's screen displays. The options on this screen depend on the kind of account it is. You always have Fetch and Manual; Push is displayed only for accounts that support it.

5 Tap the option you want to use for the account: Push, Fetch, or Manual.

If you choose Manual, information is retrieved only when you manually start the process by opening the related app (such as Mail to fetch your email) or by using the refresh gesture (swiping down from the top of the screen), regardless of the global setting.

If you choose Fetch, information is updated according to the schedule you set in step 9.

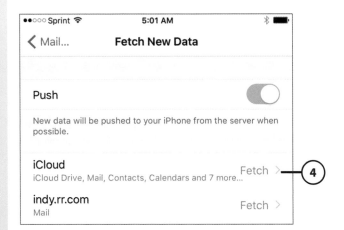

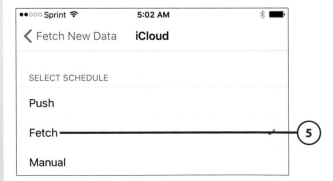

6 If you choose the Push option, choose the mailboxes whose information you want to be pushed by tapping them so they have a check mark; to prevent a mailbox's information from being pushed, tap it so that it doesn't have a check mark. (The Inbox is selected by default and can't be unselected.)

7 Tap Fetch New Data.

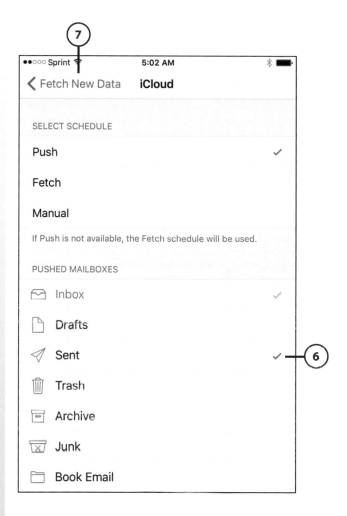

7

●●○○○ Sprint 🔋   5:02 AM   ❊ ▬▬

❮ Fetch New Data   iCloud

SELECT SCHEDULE

Push   ✓

Fetch

Manual

If Push is not available, the Fetch schedule will be used.

PUSHED MAILBOXES

✉ Inbox   ✓

🗋 Drafts

✒ Sent   ✓ — **6**

🗑 Trash

🗃 Archive

🗑 Junk

🗀 Book Email

8 Repeat steps 5-7 until you have set the update option for each account. (The current option is shown to the right of the account's name.)

9 Tap the amount of time when you want the iPhone to fetch data when Push is turned off globally or for those accounts for which you have selected Fetch or that don't support Push; tap Manually if you want to manually check for information for Fetch accounts or when Push is off. Information for your accounts is updated according to your settings.

How information is being updated for the account

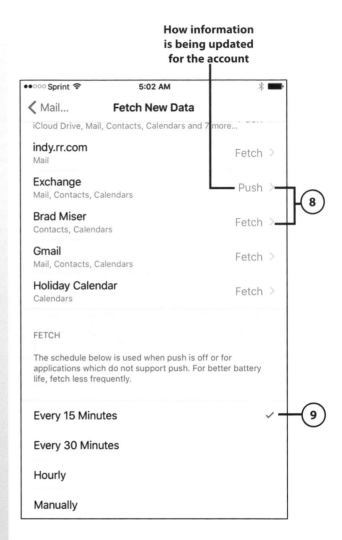

>>>Go Further

TIPS FOR MANAGING YOUR ACCOUNTS

As you add and use accounts on your iPhone, keep the following points in mind:

- You can temporarily disable any data for any account by moving to the Mail, Contacts, Calendars screen and tapping that account. Set the switch for the data you don't want to use to off (white). You might be prompted to keep or delete that information; if you choose to keep it, the data remains on your iPhone but is disconnected from the account and is no longer updated. If you delete it, you can always recover it again by simply turning that data back on. For example, suppose you are going on vacation and don't want to deal with club email. Move to your club account and disable all its data. That data disappears from the related apps; for example, the account's mailboxes no longer appear in the Mail app. When you want to start using the account again, simply re-enable its data.

- If you want to completely remove an account from your iPhone, move to its configuration screen, swipe up the screen, and tap Delete Account. Tap Delete in the confirmation dialog box and the account is removed from your iPhone. (You can always re-create the account to start using it again.)

- You can have different notifications for certain aspects of an account, such as email. See Chapter 5, "Customizing How Your iPhone Looks and Sounds," for the details of configuring and using notifications.

- You can change how information is updated at any time, too. If your iPhone is running low on battery, disable Push and set Fetch to Manually so you can control when the updates happen. When your battery is charged again, you can re-enable Push or set a Fetch schedule.

Tap to personalize
your iPhone to
make it your own

In this chapter, you learn how to make an iPhone into your iPhone. Topics include the following:

→ Getting started
→ Setting Passcode, Touch ID, and Auto-Lock preferences
→ Setting keyboard, language, and format options
→ Configuring the Control Center
→ Setting Do Not Disturb preferences
→ Setting accessibility options
→ Setting Restrictions for Content and Apps

Configuring an iPhone to Suit Your Preferences

The iPhone can be configured to make it look and work how you want it to. Taking the time to tailor your iPhone to your personal preferences and how you want to use it makes the iPhone easier, better, and more fun to use.

Getting Started

As you've seen in previous chapters, the Settings app enables you to configure various aspects of your iPhone, such as connecting your iPhone to a Wi-Fi network and configuring iCloud. The Settings app provides many other configuration tools that you can use to tailor how your iPhone works to suit your preferences. Perhaps the most important of these is the security of your iPhone that you can configure by setting a passcode and fingerprint recognition using Touch ID. You can also configure the keyboards available, language and region format options, the Control Center, Do Not Disturb hours, accessibility options, and how content on your phone can be accessed. You use the Settings app to customize the iPhone in all of these areas as you see throughout this chapter.

Using the Settings App on Any iPhone

You can work with the Settings app on any iPhone as follows:

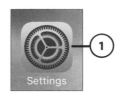

(1) On the Home screen, tap Settings. The Settings app opens. The app is organized in sections starting at the top with Airplane Mode, Wi-Fi, Bluetooth, and Cellular.

(2) Swipe up or down the screen to get to the settings area you want to use.

(3) Tap the area you want to configure, such as Sounds.

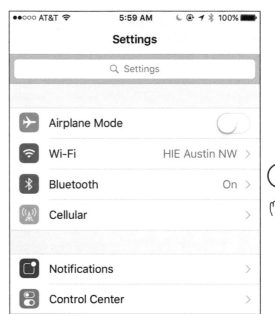

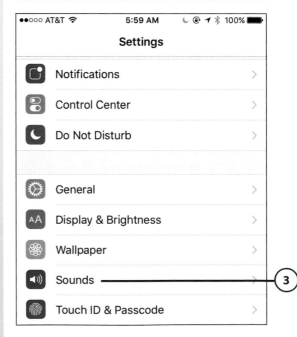

(4) Use the resulting controls to configure that area. The changes you make take effect immediately.

(5) When you're done, you can leave the Settings app where it is or tap the back button, which is always located in the upper-left corner of the screen, until you get back to the main Settings screen to go into other Settings areas.

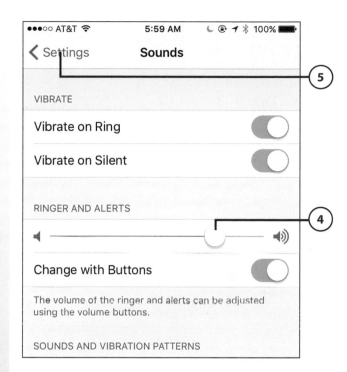

Searching for Settings

New! You can quickly find settings you need by searching for them:

(1) Move into the Settings app.

(2) Tap in the Search bar; if you don't see the Search bar, swipe down from the top of the Settings screen until it appears.

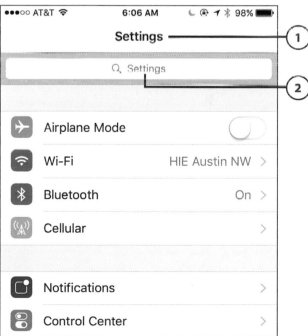

3 Type the setting for which you want to search. As you type, potential matches are shown on the list of results. Matches can include a settings area, such as Sounds, and specific settings, such as the ringtone and vibrations used when you receive a call.

4 Tap the setting you want to use.

5 Configure the setting you selected in the previous step.

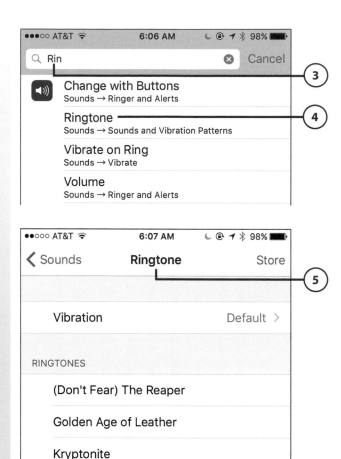

Using the Settings App on an iPhone 6 Plus or 6s Plus

When you hold an iPhone 6 Plus or 6s Plus in the horizontal orientation and use the Settings app, you can take advantage of the iPhone 6 Plus' or 6s Plus' split-screen feature as follows:

1. Hold the iPhone 6 Plus or 6s Plus so it is horizontal.

2. Tap the Settings app to open it. In the left pane, you see the areas of the Settings app that you can configure. In the right pane, you see tools you can use to configure the selected function. The two panes are independent, making navigation easier than with other iPhones.

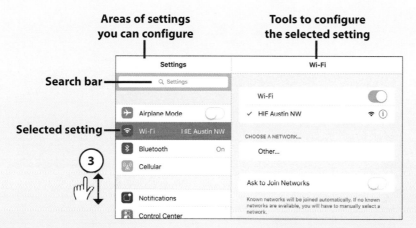

3. Swipe up or down on the left pane until you see the function, feature, or app you want to configure.

4. Tap the function, feature, or app you want to configure, such as Sounds. Its controls appear in the right pane.

5. Swipe up or down on the right pane until you see the specific setting you want to change.

6. Tap the setting you want to configure, such as Ringtone. Its controls appear in the right pane.

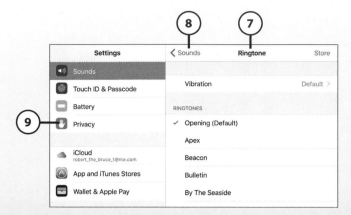

7. Use the tools in the right pane to configure the setting you selected in step 6. These work just as described in the previous task and throughout this chapter except that you move within the right pane instead of changing the entire screen.

8. To move back through the screens in the right pane, use the back button, which is labeled with the name of the screen you came from.

9. Tap another area in the left pane to configure it. As you can see, the split screen makes it very easy to quickly switch between areas in the Settings app.

Setting Passcode, Touch ID, and Auto-Lock Preferences

Your iPhone contains data you probably don't want others to access. You can (and should) require a passcode so your iPhone can't be unlocked without the proper passcode being entered. This gives you a measure of protection should you lose control of your phone. If you have an iPhone 5s or later, you can record your fingerprints so that you can unlock your phone (by automatically entering the passcode for you) and enter your Apple ID password by touching the Touch ID/Home button. The capability can also be used in other apps and services that require confirmation, such as Apple Pay.

The Auto-Lock feature automatically locks your phone after a specific period of time. This is useful because your iPhone automatically locks and, assuming you require a passcode, the passcode or fingerprint must be provided to be able to unlock your phone.

Securing Your iPhone with Auto-Lock

To configure your phone so it locks automatically, perform the following steps:

① On the Settings screen, tap General.

② Swipe up the screen until you see Auto-Lock.

③ Tap Auto-Lock.

④ Tap the amount of idle time you want to pass before the iPhone automatically locks and goes to sleep. You can choose from 1 to 5 minutes; choose Never if you only want to manually lock your iPhone. I recommend that you keep Auto-Lock set to a relatively small value to conserve your iPhone's battery and to make it more secure. Of course, the shorter you set this time to be, the more frequently you have to unlock your iPhone.

⑤ Tap General. You're ready to configure your passcode and fingerprints (iPhone 5s and later).

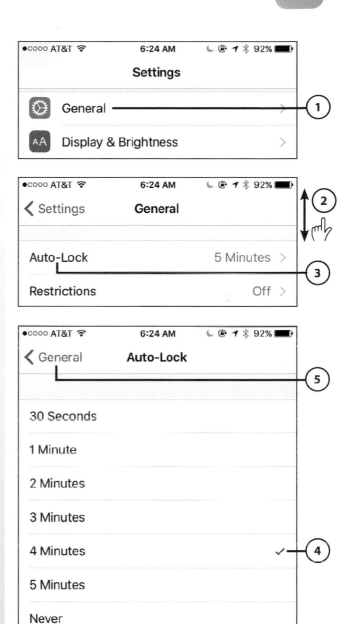

Configuring Your Passcode and Fingerprints (iPhone 5s and later)

To configure the passcode you have to enter to unlock your iPhone, perform the following steps (note these steps show an iPhone that has Touch ID; if your model doesn't have this, the steps will be slightly different as you will only be configuring a passcode):

① On the Settings screen, tap Touch ID & Passcode.

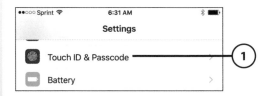

Already Have a Passcode?

When you first turned your iPhone on, you were prompted to enter a passcode and to record a finger-print for Touch ID. If your iPhone already has a passcode set, when you perform step 1, you're prompt-ed to enter your current passcode. When you enter it correctly, you move to the Touch ID & Passcode (iPhone 5s and later) or Passcode (other models) screen and you can make changes to the current pass-code, add new fingerprints, and so on. In this case, you can skip direct-ly to step 5. If you want to change your current passcode, tap Change Passcode and follow steps 3 and 4 to change it. Then continue with step 5.

(2) Tap Turn Passcode On.

(3) Enter a six-digit passcode.

(4) Reenter the passcode. If the two passcodes match, the passcode is set.

(5) Tap Require Passcode; when you use Touch ID to unlock your iPhone, you don't have an option for when the passcode is required and can skip to step 8.

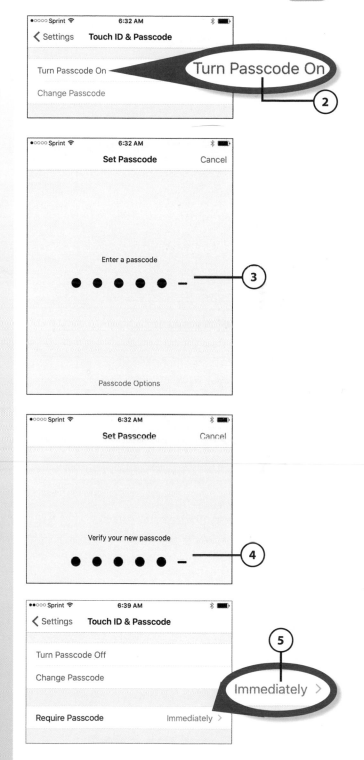

6 Tap the amount of time the iPhone is locked before the passcode takes effect. The shorter this time is, the more secure your iPhone is, but also the more times you'll have to enter the passcode if your iPhone locks frequently.

7 Tap Touch ID & Passcode.

8 If you have an iPhone 5s or later, tap Add a Fingerprint and continue to step 9; if you have a model that doesn't support Touch ID, skip to step 17.

9 Touch the finger you want to be able to use to unlock your phone and enter your Apple ID password to the Touch ID/Home button, but don't press it. An image of a fingerprint appears.

10 Leave your finger on the Touch ID/Home button until you feel the phone vibrate, which indicates part of your fingerprint has been recorded and you see some segments turn red. The parts of your fingerprint that are recorded are indicated by the red segments, gray segments are not recorded yet.

11 Take your finger off the Touch ID/Home button and touch the button again, adjusting your finger on the button to record other parts that currently show gray lines instead of red

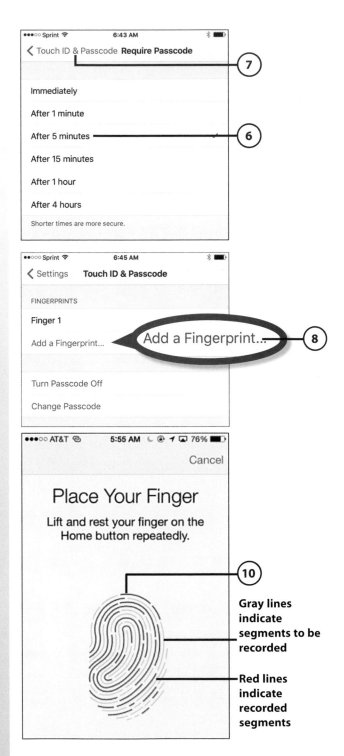

Gray lines indicate segments to be recorded

Red lines indicate recorded segments

ones. Other segments of your fingerprint are recorded.

(12) Repeat step 11 until all the segments are red. You are prompted to change your grip so you can record more of your fingerprint.

(13) Tap Continue.

(14) Repeat step 11, again placing other areas of your finger to fill in more gray lines with red ones. When the entire fingerprint is covered in red lines, you see the Complete screen.

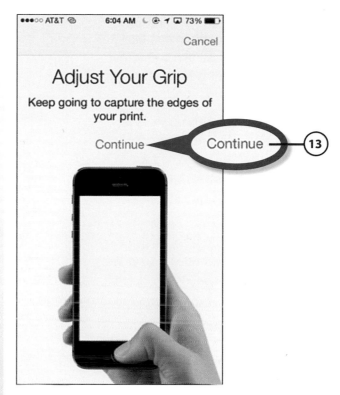

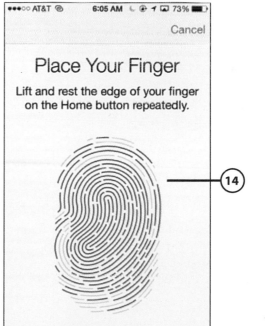

(15) Tap Continue. The fingerprint is recorded and you move back to the Touch ID & Passcode screen. You see the fingerprint that has been recorded.

(16) Repeat steps 8 through 15 to record up to five fingerprints. These can be yours or someone else's if you want to allow another person to access your iPhone.

(17) To be able to use Touch ID to unlock your iPhone, ensure the iPhone Unlock switch is set to on (green).

(18) To use your fingerprint to make Apple Pay payments, set the Apple Pay switch to on (green).

(19) If you want to also be able to enter your Apple ID password by touching your finger to the Touch ID/Home button, set the App and iTunes Stores switch to on (green).

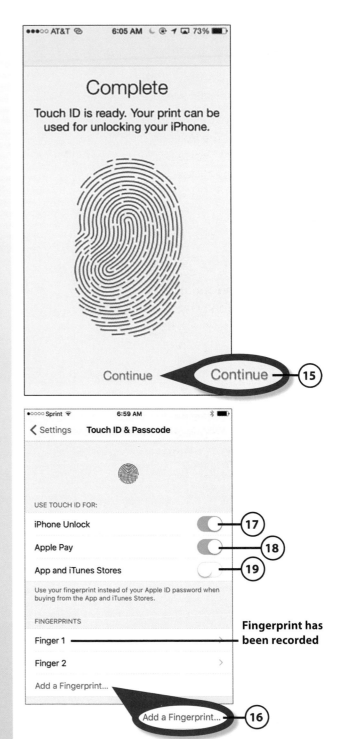

Fingerprint has been recorded

20 Enter your Apple ID password and tap OK.

21 Swipe up the screen until you see the Voice Dial switch.

22 To prevent Voice Dial from working, set the Voice Dial switch to off (white). (Voice Dial enables you to make calls by speaking even if you don't use Siri.)

23 Use the switches in the ALLOW ACCESS WHEN LOCKED: section to enable or disable the related functions when your iPhone is locked. The options are Today (the Today tab on the Notification Center), Notifications View (the Notifications tab of the Notification Center), Siri, Reply with Message, and Wallet. If you set a switch to off (white), you won't be able to access the corresponding function when your iPhone is locked.

24 If you don't want the iPhone to automatically erase all your data after an incorrect passcode has been entered 10 times, set the Erase Data switch to off (white).

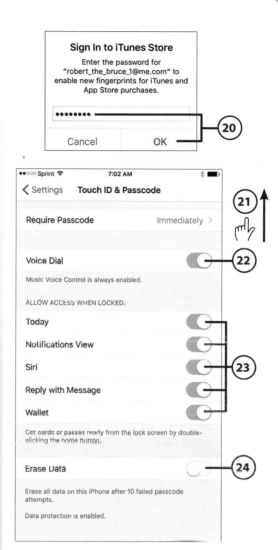

Automatic Erase

When you have enabled the Erase Data function and you enter an incorrect passcode when unlocking your iPhone, you see a counter showing the number of unsuccessful attempts. When this reaches 10, all the data on your iPhone will be erased on the next unsuccessful attempt.

Making Changes

Any time you want to make changes to your passcode and/or fingerprint settings, go to the Touch ID & Passcode (iPhone 5s or later) or Passcode (other models) Settings screen. Before you can move to this screen, you must enter your current passcode at the prompt. After you enter your current passcode, you move to the Touch ID & Passcode or Passcode screen. To disable the passcode, tap Turn Passcode Off, tap Turn Off, and enter the passcode. To change your passcode, tap Change Passcode. Enter your current passcode, and then enter your new passcode twice. You return to the Passcode Lock screen, and the new passcode takes effect. You can change the other settings similar to how you set them initially as described in the "Setting Passcode, Touch ID, and Auto-Lock Preferences" task. For example, you can add or remove fingerprints. To remove a fingerprint, move to the Fingerprints screen, swipe to the left on the fingerprint you want to remove, and tap Delete. You can rename a fingerprint by tapping it, editing its name on the resulting screen, and tapping Done (for example, you might want to name the fingerprints so you recognize them, such as My Right Thumb or Jim's Left Thumb).

Setting Keyboard, Language, and Format Options

You'll be working with text in many apps on your iPhone. You can customize a number of keyboard- and format-related options so text appears and behaves the way you want it to.

Setting Keyboard Preferences

You use the iPhone's keyboard to input text in many apps, including Mail, Messages, and so on. A number of settings determine how the keyboard works.

(1) On the Settings screen, tap General.

(2) Swipe up the screen.

(3) Tap Keyboard.

(4) Tap Keyboards. This enables you to activate more keyboards so that you can choose a specific language's keyboard when you are entering text. At the top of the screen, you see the keyboards that are available to you.

(5) Tap Add New Keyboard.

Fun in Text

The Emoji keyboard allows you to include a huge variety of smiley faces, symbols, and other icons whenever you type. The Emoji keyboard is active by default; however, if you don't see it on the list of active keyboards, you can use these steps to activate it.

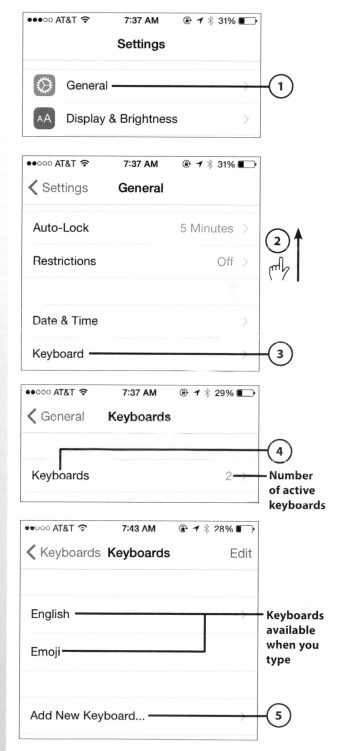

Number of active keyboards

Keyboards available when you type

(6) Swipe up and down the screen to browse the available keyboards.

(7) Tap the keyboard you want to add.

(8) Tap the keyboard you added in step 7.

(9) Tap the keyboard layout you want to use.

(10) Tap Keyboards.

Third-party keyboards available

THIRD-PARTY KEYBOARDS
When using one of these keyboards, the keyboard can access all the data you type. About Third-Party Keyboards & Privacy...

SwiftKey

OTHER IPHONE KEYBOARDS

English (Australia)

English (Canada)

English (India)

English (Singapore)

English (UK)

11 Repeat steps 5–10 to add and configure additional keyboards.

12 Tap Keyboards. (Note that the Text Replacement option is explained in the next task.)

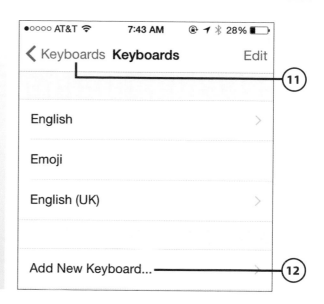

>>>Go Further

THIRD-PARTY KEYBOARDS

You can install and use keyboards that third parties provide (meaning not Apple) on your iPhone. To do this, open the App Store app and search for "keyboards for iPhone" or you can search for a specific keyboard by name if you know of one you want to try. (See Chapter 6, "Downloading Apps, Music, Movies, TV Shows, and More onto Your iPhone," for help using the App Store app.) After you have downloaded the keyboard you want to use, use steps 1 through 5 to move back to the Keyboards Settings screen. When you open the Add New Keyboard screen, you see a section called THIRD-PARTY KEYBOARDS in which you see the additional keyboards you have installed. Tap a keyboard in this section to activate it as you do with the default keyboards. When you move back to the Keyboards screen, you see the keyboard you just activated. Tap it to configure its additional options. Then you can use the new keyboard just like the others you have activated. Make sure you check out the documentation for any keyboards you download so you take advantage of all of their features.

(13) To prevent your iPhone from automatically capitalizing as you type, set Auto-Capitalization to off (white). The iPhone no longer changes the case of letters as you type them.

(14) To disable the automatic spell checking/correction, set Auto-Correction to off (white). Your iPhone no longer automatically suggests corrections to what you type.

(15) To disable the Caps Lock function, set the Enable Caps Lock to off (white). The Caps Lock function won't be available to you when you tap the Shift key twice.

(16) To prevent the character you type from being shown in a magnified pop-up as you type it, set the Character Preview switch to off (white). You won't see a bubble quote with the character you type as you type it.

(17) To disable the shortcut that types a period followed by a space when you tap the spacebar twice, set the "." Shortcut switch to off (white). You must tap a period and the spacebar to type these characters when you end a sentence.

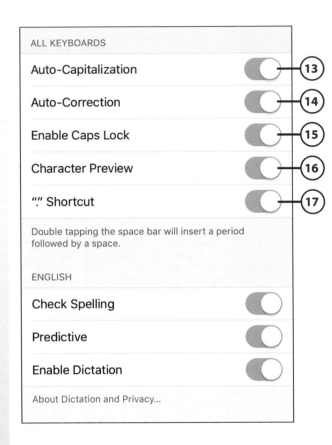

18 To disable the iPhone's Spell Checker, set the Check Spelling switch to off (white). You'll be on your own spelling-wise.

19 To disable the iPhone's Predictive Text feature (see Chapter 1, "Getting Started with Your iPhone"), set the Predictive switch to off (white). You won't be able to use the predictive text bar to enter text.

20 To disable the iPhone's dictation feature, set the Enable Dictation switch to off (white). The microphone key won't appear on the keyboard and you won't be able to dictate text.

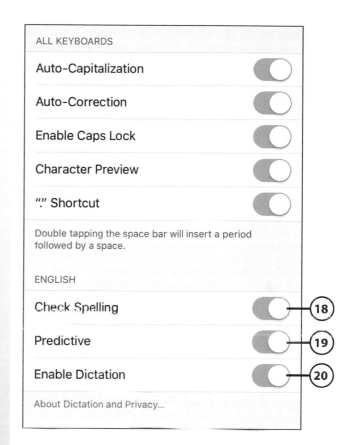

Changing Keyboards

To delete a keyboard, move to the Keyboards Settings screen and swipe to the left on the keyboard you want to remove. Tap Delete. The keyboard is removed from the list of activated keyboards and is no longer available to you when you type. (You can always activate it again later.) To change the order in which keyboards appear, move to the Keyboards screen, tap Edit, and drag the keyboards up and down the screen. When you've finished, tap Done.

Creating and Working with Text Replacements

Text replacements are useful because you can use just a few letters to type a series of words. You type the replacement, and it is replaced by the phrase with which it is associated. To configure your text replacements, do the following:

1. Move to the Keyboards screen as described in steps 1–3 in the previous task.

2. Tap Text Replacement.

3. Swipe up and down to review the current replacements.

4. To add a replacement, tap Add (+).

5. Type the phrase for which you want to create a replacement.

6. Type the shortcut you want to be replaced by the phrase you created in step 5.

7. Tap Save. If the replacement doesn't contain any disallowed characters, it is created and you move back to the Text Replacement screen where you see your new text replacement. If there is an error, you see an explanation of the error; you must correct it before you can create the replacement.

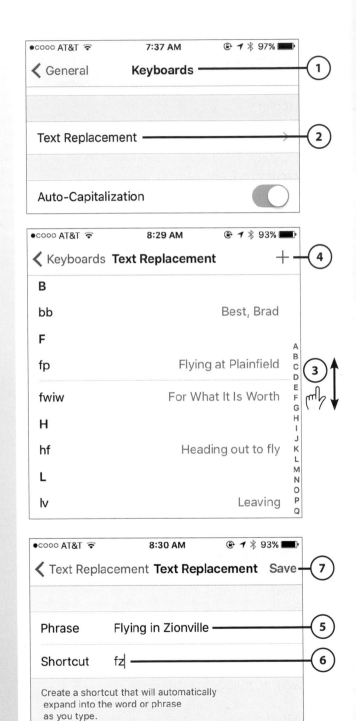

8 Repeat steps 4–7 to create other text replacements.

9 When you've created all the replacements you want, tap Keyboards.

Shortcuts to Replacements

To change a replacement, tap it. Use the resulting screen to change the phrase or shortcut, and tap Save to update the replacement. To remove a replacement, swipe to the left on it and tap Delete. To search for a replacement, tap in the Search bar at the top of the screen and type the replacements you want to see; you can also use the index along the right side of the screen to find replacements. You can also tap Edit on the Shortcuts screen to change your replacements.

Setting Language and Region Preferences

There are a number of formatting preferences you can set that determine how information is formatted in various apps. For example, you can choose how addresses are formatted by default by choosing the region whose format you want to follow.

1 On the Settings screen, tap General.

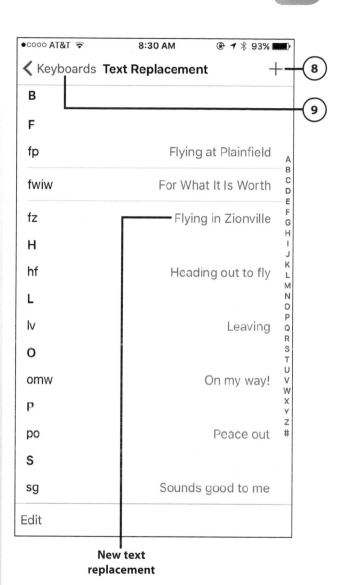

New text replacement

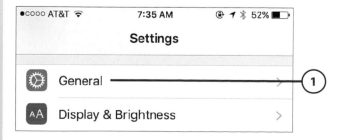

(2) Swipe up the screen.

(3) Tap Language & Region.

(4) Tap iPhone Language.

(5) Swipe up and down the screen to view the languages with which your iPhone can work or tap in the Search bar and type a language you want to use to find it. The current language is marked with a check mark.

(6) Tap the language you want to use.

(7) Tap Done.

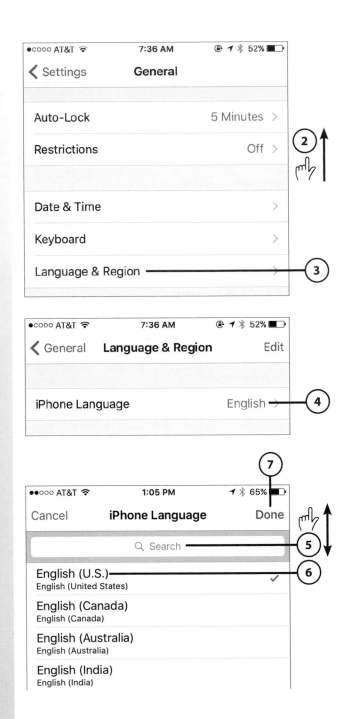

8 Tap to confirm the change in language you indicated. Your iPhone screen goes dark while the iPhone switches to the new language. When it comes back, you return to the Language & Region screen, and the language you selected starts being used.

9 Tap Add Language.

10 Using steps 5 through 7, find and tap a secondary language. This language is used when your primary language can't be, such as on websites that don't support your primary language

11 Tap Done.

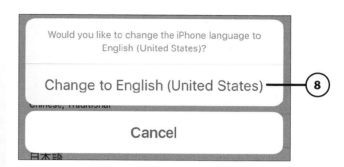

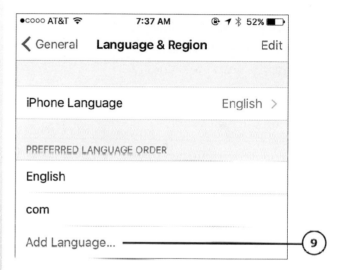

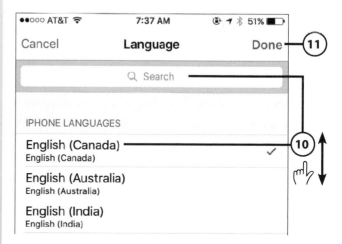

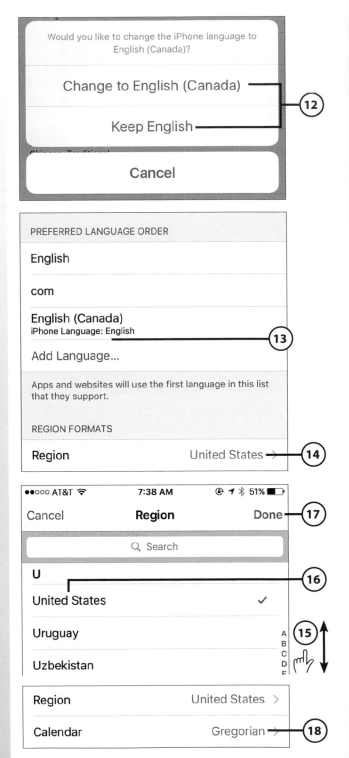

(12) Tap the language you want to be primary to confirm it. The language you selected is configured and you move back to the Language & Region screen. The new language is shown on the list in the center of the screen.

(13) To add more languages, tap Add Language and follow steps 10 through 12 to add more languages.

Order, Order!

To change the order of preference for the languages you have configured, tap Edit, drag the languages up or down the screen to set their order, and tap Done to save your changes.

(14) Tap Region.

(15) Swipe up and down the regions available to you. The current region is marked with a check mark.

(16) Tap the region whose formatting you want to use; if there are options within a region, you move to an additional screen and can tap the specific option you want to use.

(17) Tap Done. Your iPhone starts using the formatting associated with the region you selected.

(18) Tap Calendar.

(19) Tap the calendar you want your iPhone to use.

(20) Tap Language & Region. You move back to the Language & Region screen. Swipe up until you see the bottom of the screen where there are examples of the format options you have selected, such as the time and date format.

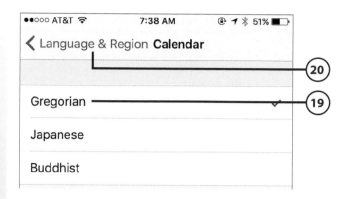

Setting Do Not Disturb Preferences

The Do Not Disturb feature enables you to temporarily silence notifications; you can also configure quiet times during which notifications are automatically silenced.

You can set an automatic Do Not Disturb schedule by performing the following steps:

(1) On the Settings screen, tap Do Not Disturb.

(2) To activate Do Not Disturb manually, set the Manual switch to on (green). (This does the same thing as activating it from the Control Center.)

(3) To configure Do Not Disturb to activate automatically on a schedule, slide the Scheduled switch to on (green).

(4) Tap the From and To box.

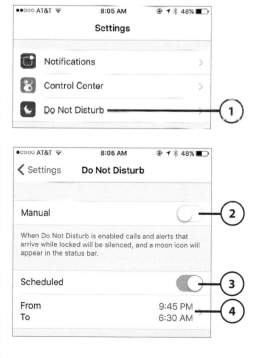

5 Tap From.

6 Swipe on the time selection wheels to select the hour and minute (AM or PM) when you want the Do Not Disturb period to start.

7 Tap To.

8 Swipe on the time selection wheels to set the hour and minute (AM or PM) when you want the Do Not Disturb period to end.

9 Tap Do Not Disturb.

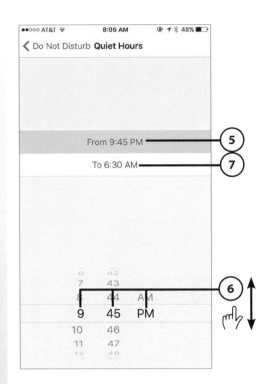

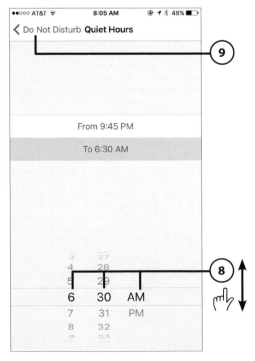

10 Tap Allow Calls From.

11 Tap the option for whose calls should be allowed during the Do Not Disturb period. The options are Everyone, which doesn't prevent any calls; No One, which sends all calls to voicemail; Favorites, which allows calls from people on your Favorites lists to come through but all others go to voicemail; or one of your contact groups, which allows calls from anyone in the selected group to come through while all others go to voicemail.

12 Tap Do Not Disturb.

13 Set the Repeated Calls switch to on (green) if you want a second call from the same person within three minutes to be allowed through. This feature is based on the assumption that if a call is really important, someone will try again immediately.

14 If you want notifications to be silenced only when your phone is locked, tap Only while iPhone is locked during the Do Not Disturb period. Tap Always if you want notifications to be silenced regardless of the Lock status.

15 Tap Settings. During the Do Not Disturb period, your iPhone is silent, except for any exceptions you configured. When the scheduled Do Not Disturb period ends, your iPhone resumes its normal notification activity.

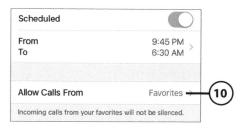

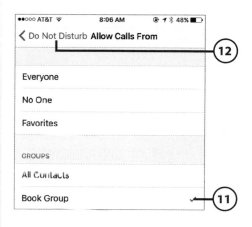

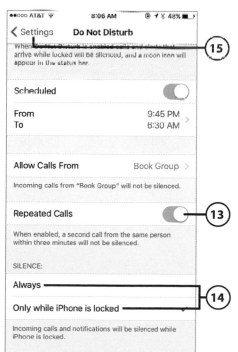

Setting Accessibility Options

The iPhone has many features designed to help people who are hearing-impaired, visually-impaired, or who have other physical challenges, to be able to use it effectively.

The Accessibility features can be enabled and configured on the Accessibility Settings screen.

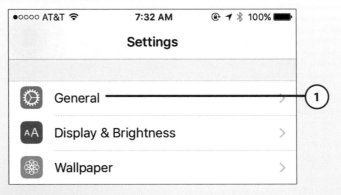

1 On the Settings screen, tap General.

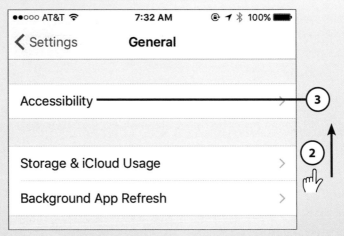

2 Swipe up the screen until you see Accessibility.

3 Tap Accessibility. The Accessibility screen is organized into different sections for different kinds of limitations. The first section is VISION, which includes options to assist people who are visually impaired.

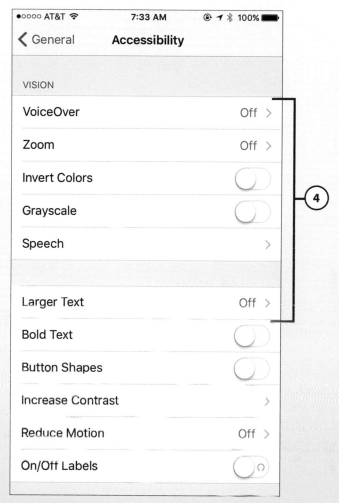

4. Use the controls in the VISION section to change how the iPhone's screens appear. Some of the options include:

- **VoiceOver**—The iPhone guides you through screens by speaking their contents. To set this, tap VoiceOver and set the VoiceOver switch to on (green) to turn it on. The rest of the settings configure how VoiceOver works. For example, you can set the rate at which the voice speaks, what kind of feedback you get, and many more options.

- **Zoom**—This magnifies the entire screen. Tap Zoom and then turn Zoom on. Use the other settings to change how the zoom works, such as whether it follows where you are focused on the screen or remains fixed.

- **Invert Colors**—This switch changes the screen from dark characters on a light background to light characters on a dark background.

- **Grayscale**—This option causes the screen to use grayscale instead of color.
- **Speech**—Under the Speech option, Speak Selection causes a Speak button to appear when you select text, Speak Screen provides the option to have the screen's content spoken, and Speak Auto-text has the iPhone speak corrections it suggests to you, such as auto-capitalizations.
- **Larger and Bold Text**—These increase the text size and add bold; these are in addition to the Text Size and Bold settings that you learn about in Chapter 5, "Customizing How Your iPhone Looks and Sounds." You can make the text even larger than with those settings.
- **Other options**—You can also change button shapes, change contrast, reduce motion, and turn labels on or off.

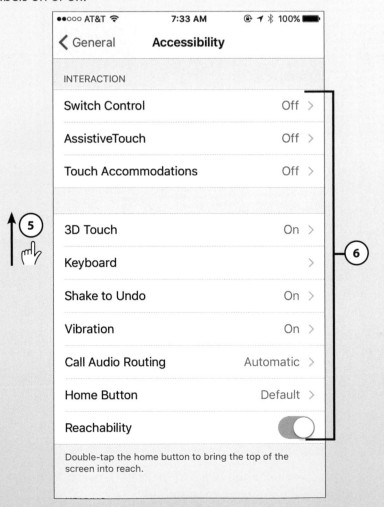

(5) Swipe up to see the INTERACTION section.

(6) Use the controls in this section to adjust how you can interact with the iPhone. The controls here include:

- **Switch Control**—The controls on this screen enable you to configure an iPhone to work with an adaptive device so that you can control the iPhone with that device.

- **Assistive Touch**—These controls make an iPhone easier to manipulate; if you enable this, a white button appears on the screen at all times. You can tap this to access the Home screen, Notification Center, and other areas. You can also create new gestures to control other functions on the iPhone.

- **Touch Accommodations**—You can use the Touch Accommodation options to make it easier for you to use the touch screen. For example, you can change the amount of time you must touch the screen before it is recognized as a touch.

- **3D Touch**—This setting, which is only available on an iPhone 6s or 6s Plus, enables you to turn the Touch 3D feature off or on. If 3D Touch is on, you can determine how much pressure you need to apply to the screen to activate it.

- **Keyboard**—Using these options, you can show or hide lowercase letters and change how the keys react to your touches.

- **Shake to Undo**—This setting enables you to turn off the shake motion to undo your most recent action.

- **Vibration**—This setting enables you to enable or disable vibrations.

- **Call Audio Routing**—Use this to configure where audio is heard during a phone call or FaceTime session, such as headset or speaker.

- **Home Button**—Use this switch to set the rate at which you press the Home/Touch ID button to register as a double- or triple-press.

- **Reachability**—When this switch is on, you can press the Home/Touch ID button twice to bring the top of the screen into view.

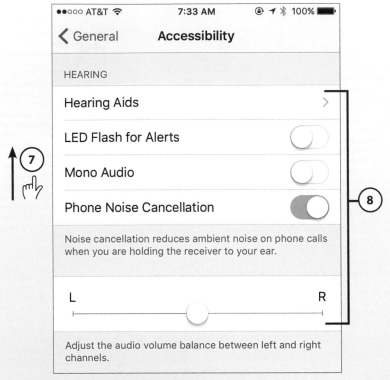

7) Swipe up to see the HEARING section.

8) Use the controls in this section to configure sounds and to configure the iPhone to work with hearing-impaired people. The controls in this section include:

- **Hearing Aids**—You can pair an iPhone to work with a Bluetooth-capable hearing aid and put it in hearing aid mode.

- **LED Flash for Alerts**—When you set this switch to on (green), the flash flashes whenever an alert plays on the phone.

- **Mono Audio**—This causes the sound output to be in mono instead of stereo.

- **Phone Noise Cancellation**—This switch turns noise cancellation on and off. Noise cancellation reduces ambient noise when you are using the Phone app.

- **Balance**—Use this slider to change the balance of stereo sound between left and right.

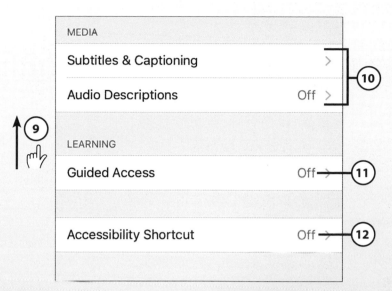

(9) Swipe up to see the MEDIA section.

(10) Use the controls in this section to add features to video playback, including:

- **Subtitles & Captioning**—Use these controls to enable subtitles and captions for video and choose the style of those elements on the screen.

- **Audio Descriptions**—This causes an audio description of media to be played when available.

(11) Use the Guided Access setting if you want to limit the iPhone to using a single app and to further configure the features, such as Passcode Settings and Time Limits.

(12) Use the Accessibility Shortcut control to determine what happens when you press the Touch ID/Home button three times.

Setting Restrictions for Content and Apps

You can restrict the access to specific content and apps on your phone. Suppose you let other people borrow your iPhone but don't want them to use certain apps or to see data you'd rather keep to yourself. You can enable a restriction to prevent someone from accessing these areas without entering the restriction code. You can also restrict the use of apps, movies, music, and other content based on the age rating that the app or other content has.

To restrict access to content or apps, perform the following steps:

1. On the Settings screen, tap General.

2. Swipe up the screen until you see Restrictions.

3. Tap Restrictions.

4. Tap Enable Restrictions.

5. Create a Restrictions Passcode. You have to enter this passcode to change the content restrictions or to be able to access restricted content.

6. Reenter your Restrictions Passcode. You return to the Restrictions screen, and the ALLOW switches are enabled.

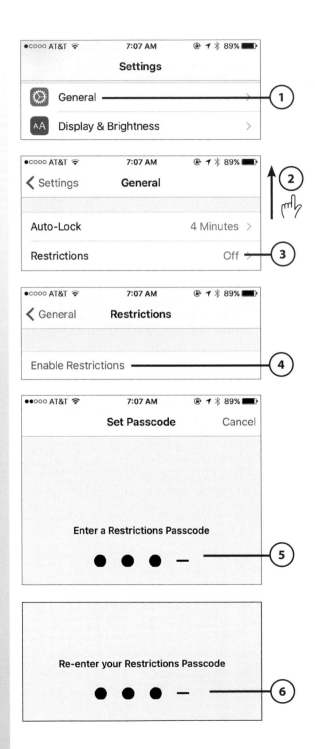

Dueling Passcodes

There are two passcodes: the Lock passcode and the Restrictions passcode. Each controls access to its respective functions. Limiting access to content and apps likely means you will be letting someone else use your phone, so the person who will be using your iPhone might need to be able to unlock it unless you want to have to unlock it for them. If you want to allow them to unlock the phone, but want to restrict access to your Apple Pay information or Apple ID, create a fingerprint for that person, but disable Touch ID for Apple Pay and App and iTunes Stores (see the task, "Configuring Your Passcode and Fingerprints (iPhone 5s and later)" earlier in this chapter for details). This enables the person to unlock and use your iPhone, but you can control what they can do by setting a Restrictions passcode and configuring permissions as described in these steps. (You don't want to give the person the passcode to the phone as that defeats the purpose of configuring restrictions.)

(7) In the ALLOW section, set the switch next to each function you want to disable to off (white). For example, to prevent web browsing, set the Safari switch to off (white); the Safari icon is removed from the Home screen and can't be used. With the other controls, you can prevent access to the Camera, FaceTime, iTunes Store, and so on.

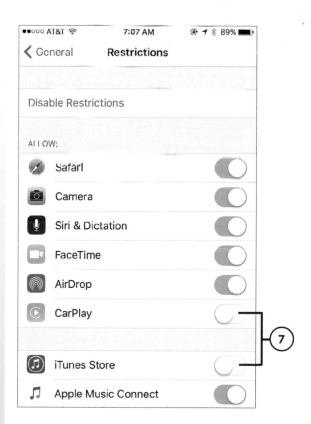

In-app Purchases

Some apps, especially games, allow you to make purchases while you are using the app. For example, you can buy additional levels for a game. To prevent in-app purchases, set the In-App Purchases switch to off (white). This is especially important if you let your phone be used by children or others who might inadvertently make purchases you don't want made.

8 Swipe up to see the ALLOWED CONTENT section.

9 Tap Ratings For.

10 Tap the country whose rating system you want to use for content on your iPhone.

Whose Ratings?

The country you select in step 10 determines the options you see in the remaining steps because the restrictions available depend on the location you select. These steps show the United States rating systems; if you select a different country, you see rating options for that country instead.

11 Tap Restrictions.

12 Tap Music, Podcasts, News & iTunes U.

13 To prevent content tagged as explicit from being played, set the EXPLICIT switch to off (white). Explicit content will not be available in the associated apps, such as Music or News.

14 Tap Back.

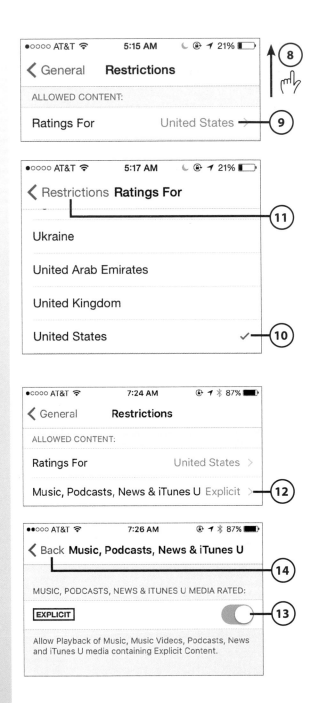

15 Tap Movies.

16 Tap the highest rating of movies that you want to be playable (for example, tap PG-13 to prevent R and NC-17 movies from playing); tap Allow All Movies to allow any movie to be played; or tap Don't Allow Movies to prevent any movie content from playing. Prevented movie ratings are highlighted in red.

17 Tap Restrictions.

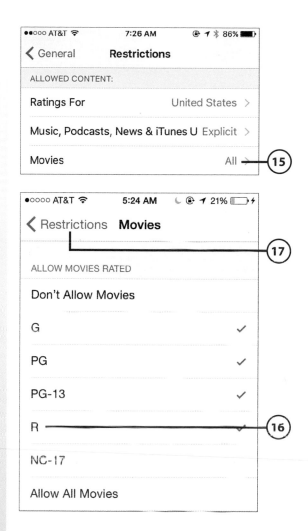

(18) Tap TV Shows and use the
resulting screen to set the
highest rating of TV shows that
you want to be playable (for
example, tap TV-14 to prevent
TV-MA shows from playing);
tap Allow All TV Shows to allow
any show to be played; or tap
Don't Allow TV Shows to prevent
any TV content from playing.
Prevented ratings are highlighted
in red. Tap Restrictions to return
to the Restrictions screen.

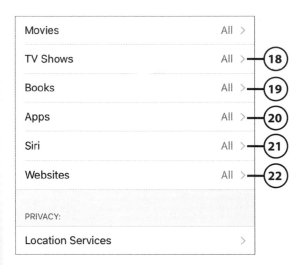

(19) Use the Books option to enable
or disable access to sexually
explicit books.

(20) Tap Apps and set the highest
rating of app that you want to
be available (for example, tap
12+ to prevent 17+ applications
from working); tap Allow All
Apps to allow any application
to be used; or tap Don't Allow
Apps to prevent all applications.
Tap Restrictions to return to the
Restrictions screen.

(21) Use the Siri option to restrict
explicit language for searching
the Web.

(22) Use the Websites option to
control the websites that can
be accessed. The options are to
limit sites with adult content or
to allow only specific websites
to be visited. When you select
this option, you can create a list
of sites and only those sites can
be visited.

23 Swipe up the screen until you see the PRIVACY section.

24 Use the settings in the PRIVACY section to determine whether apps can access information stored in each area and whether they should be locked in their current states. For example, you can prevent apps from accessing your calendars or photos.

25 Swipe up the screen until you see the ALLOW CHANGES section.

26 Tap areas that you want to restrict, such as Cellular Data Use and then tap Don't Allow Changes to prevent changes to that area.

27 To prevent multiplayer games in the Game Center, set the Multiplayer Games switch to off (white). Users will no longer be able to play games against other people.

28 To prevent new friends from being added in the Game Center, set the Adding Friends switch to off (white). Players will be restricted to the friends already allowed.

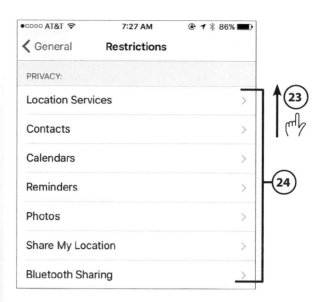

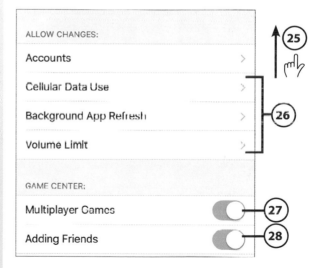

Removing Restrictions

To remove all restrictions, move to the Restrictions screen (your Restrictions passcode is required) and tap Disable Restrictions. Enter your Restrictions passcode, and the restrictions are removed.

Choose the image you want as wallpaper

Customize the layout of the icons on your Home screens by placing icons where you want them

Tap to configure notifications and sounds

Place icons in folders to keep your Home screens organized

In this chapter, you learn how to make an iPhone look and sound the way you want it to. Topics include the following:

→ Getting started
→ Customizing your Home screens
→ Setting the screen's brightness, view, text size, and wallpaper
→ Choosing the sounds your iPhone makes
→ Setting up notifications and the Notification Center

5

Customizing How Your iPhone Looks and Sounds

There are lots of ways that you can customize an iPhone to make it *your* iPhone so that it looks and sounds the way you want it to.

Getting Started

In Chapter 4, "Configuring an iPhone to Suit Your Preferences," you learned how to change many aspects of how your iPhone works. This chapter focuses on how you can change the way you interact with your iPhone and how it interacts with you. Following are key areas you can configure to personalize your iPhone's personality:

- **Home screens.** The iPhone's Home screens are the starting point for most everything you do because these screens contain the icons that you tap to access the apps and web page icons that you want to use. You see and use the Home screens constantly, so it's a good idea to customize them to your preferences. You can place icons on specific screens, and you can use folders to make your Home screens work better for you.

- **Screen brightness, view, text size, and wallpaper.** Because you continually look at your iPhone's screen, it should be the right brightness level for your eyes. However, the screen is also a large user of battery power, so the dimmer an iPhone's screen is, the longer its battery lasts. You should find a good balance between viewing comfort and battery life. Fortunately, your iPhone has an Auto-Brightness feature that automatically adjusts for current lighting conditions.

  The iPhone 6/6 Plus and 6s/6s Plus offer two views. The Standard view maximizes screen space and the Zoomed view makes things on the screen larger, making them easier to see but less content fits on the screen. You can choose the view that works best for you.

  As you use your iPhone, you'll be constantly working with text so it's also important to configure the text size so that it is easy to read. Making text larger improves its readability, but also means that less text fits on the screen so you have to move on the screen more to read all of it.

  Although it doesn't affect productivity or usability of the iPhone, choosing the images you see in the background of the Home and Lock screens makes your iPhone more personal to you and is just plain fun.

- **Sounds.** Sound is one important way your iPhone uses to communicate with you. The most obvious of these sounds is the ringtone that plays when you receive a call. However, there are many other sounds you can choose to help you know when something is happening. You can also choose to disable sounds so that your iPhone isn't so noisy.

- **Notifications.** Many apps use notifications to communicate information to you, such as to inform you about status updates, email messages, text messages, and other events. You can use the Notifications settings to enable or disable notifications and to configure them for specific apps. Configuring notifications is one of the most important ways to customize your iPhone so that it keeps you informed as much as you want it to without overwhelming you.

Customizing Your Home Screens

The Home screens come configured with icons in default locations. You can change the location of these icons to be more convenient for you. As you install more apps and create your own web page icons, it's a good idea to organize your Home screens so that you can quickly get to the items you use most frequently. You can move icons around the same screen, move icons between the pages of the Home screen, and organize icons within folders. You can even change the icons that appear on the Home screens' Dock. You can also delete icons you no longer need.

Moving Icons Around Your Home Screens

You can move icons around on a Home screen, and you can move icons among screens to change the screen on which they are located.

1. Press the Touch ID/Home button to move to a Home screen if you aren't there already.

2. Swipe to the left or right across the Home screen until the page containing an icon you want to move appears.

3. Tap and hold any icon. After a moment, the icons begin jiggling and you can then move icons on the Home screens. You also see Delete buttons (an x) in the upper-left corner of some icons, which indicate that you can delete both the icon and app or the web page link (more on this later in this section).

4 Tap and hold an icon you want to move; it becomes larger to show that you have selected it.

5 Drag the icon to a new location on the current screen; as you move the icon around the page, other icons separate and are reorganized to enable you to place the icon in its new location.

Touch But Don't Press (6s or 6s Plus)

If you are working with an iPhone 6s or 6s Plus, don't press on icons when you want to move them, just touch your finger to the screen. If you apply pressure, you may open the Quick Action menu instead. When you just touch an icon and leave your finger on the screen, the icons will become fuzzy briefly and then start jiggling indicating you can move them.

6 When the icon is in the location you want, lift your finger up. The icon is set in that place.

7 Tap and hold on an icon you want to move to a different page.

8 Drag the icon to the left edge of the screen to move it to a previous page or to the right edge of the screen to move it to a later page. As you reach the edge of the screen, you move to the previous or next page.

9 Drag the icon around on the new screen until it is in the location where you want to place it.

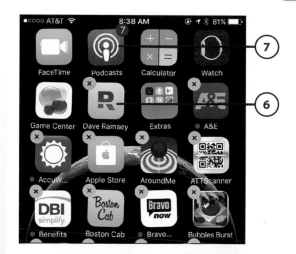

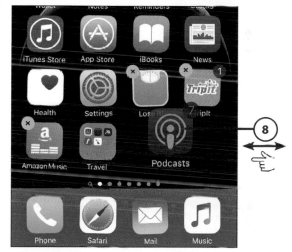

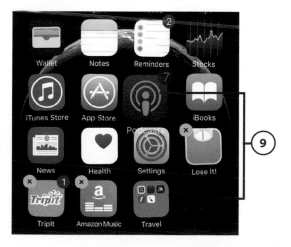

(10) Lift your finger up. The icon is set in its new place.

(11) Continue moving icons until you've placed them in the locations you want; then press the Touch ID/Home button. The icons are locked in their current positions, they stop jiggling, and the Delete buttons disappear.

Creating Folders to Organize Apps on Your Home Screens

You can place icons into folders to keep them organized and to make more icons available on the same page. To create a folder, do the following:

(1) Move to the Home screen containing two icons you want to place in a folder.

(2) Tap and hold an icon until the icons start jiggling; the Delete buttons appear.

(3) Drag one icon on top of another one that you want to be in the new folder together.

(4) When the first icon is on top of the second and a border appears around the second icon, lift your finger. The two icons are placed into a new folder, which is named based on the type of icons you place within it. The folder opens and you see its default name.

(5) To edit the name, tap in the name field.

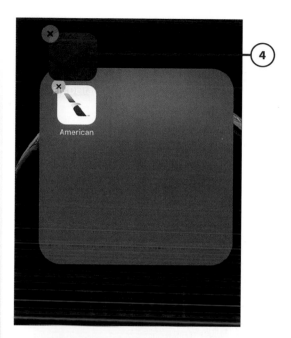

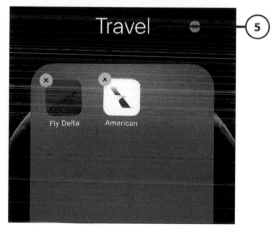

(6) Edit the folder's name.

(7) Tap Done.

(8) Tap outside the folder to close it.

(9) If you're done organizing the Home screen, press the Touch ID/Home button. The icons stop jiggling.

Locating Folders

You can move a folder to a new location in the same way you can move any icon. Tap and hold an icon until the icons start jiggling. Drag the folder icon to where you want it to be.

Placing Icons in Existing Folders

You can add icons to an existing folder like so:

(1) Move to the Home screen containing an icon you want to place in a folder.

(2) Tap and hold an icon until the icons start jiggling and the Delete buttons appear.

New folder containing two icons

3 Drag the icon you want to place into a folder on top of the folder's icon so that the folder's icon enlarges. (The icon doesn't have to be on the same Home screen page; you can drag an icon from one page and drop it on a folder on a different page.)

4 When the folder opens, lift up your finger. The icon is placed within the folder and you see its current location within the folder. (If you don't want to change the icon's location when you place it in the folder, lift up your finger as soon as the folder's icon enlarges; this places the icon in the folder but doesn't cause the folder to open. This is more efficient when you want to place multiple icons within a folder during the same time period.)

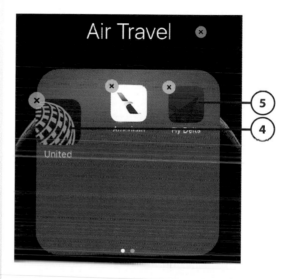

5 Drag the new icon to its location within the folder.

6 Tap outside the folder. The folder closes.

7 When you're done adding icons to folders, press the Touch ID/Home button.

Removing Icons from Folders

To remove an icon from a folder, tap the folder from which you want to remove the icon to open it. Tap and hold the icon you want to remove until it starts jiggling. Drag the icon you want to remove from inside the folder to outside the folder. When you cross the border of the folder, the folder closes and you can place the icon on a Home screen.

Folders and Badges

When you place an icon that has a badge (the red circle with a number in it that indicates the number of new items in an app) in a folder, the badge transfers to the folder so that you see it on the folder's icon. When you place more than one app with a badge in the same folder, the badge on the folder becomes the total number of new items for all the apps in the folder. You need to open a folder to see the badges for individual apps it contains.

Configuring the Home Screen Dock

The Dock on the bottom of the Home screen appears on every page. You can place any icons on the Dock that you want, including folder icons.

① Move to the Home screen containing an icon you want to place on the Dock.

② Tap and hold an icon until the icons start jiggling and the Delete buttons appear.

3 Drag an icon that is currently on the Dock from the Dock onto the Home screen to create an empty space on the Dock.

4 Drag an icon or folder containing icons from the Home screen onto the Dock.

5 Drag the icons on the Dock around so they are in the order you want them to be.

6 Press the Touch ID/ Home button to set the icons in their current places.

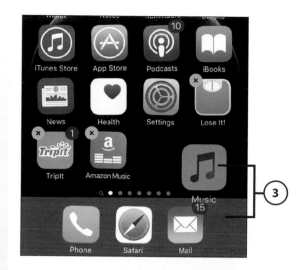

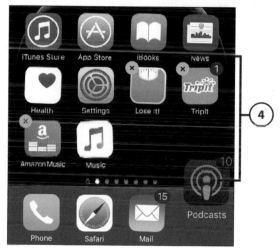

Deleting Icons

You can delete icons from a Home screen to remove them from your iPhone. When you delete an app's icon, its data is also deleted and you won't be able to use the app anymore (of course, you can download it again if you change your mind). When you delete a web page's icon (see Chapter 13, "Surfing the Web," for information on creating web page icons), the bookmark to that web page is deleted.

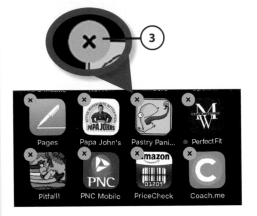

1. Move to the Home screen containing an icon you want to delete.

2. Tap and hold an icon until the icons start jiggling and the Delete buttons appear (you can delete icons that are inside folders, too).

3. Tap the icon's Delete button.

4. Tap Delete. If the icon was for an app, it and any associated data on your iPhone are deleted. If the icon was for a bookmark, the bookmark is deleted.

>>>Go Further
MORE ON ORGANIZING HOME SCREENS

Organizing your Home screens can make the use of your iPhone more efficient. Here are a few more things to keep in mind:

- You can place many icons in the same folder whose name you want to change. When you add more than nine, any additional icons are placed on new pages within the folder. As you keep adding icons, pages keep being added to the folder so that it opens. You can swipe to the left or right within a folder to move among its pages, just as you can to move among your Home screens.

- To change a folder's name, move to a screen showing the folder. Tap and hold an icon until the icons jiggle. Tap the folder so that it opens, and then tap the current name. Edit the name, tap Done, and tap outside the folder to close it. Press the Touch ID/Home button to complete the process.

- To delete a folder, remove all the icons from it. The folder is deleted as soon as you remove the last icon from within it.

- You can only delete icons for things you've added to your iPhone, which are either apps you've installed or bookmarks to web pages you've added. You can't delete any of the default apps, which is why their icons don't have Delete buttons like apps that you install do. If you don't use some of these default apps, move them to pages of your Home screen that you don't use very often so they don't get in your way, or create a folder for unused icons and store them there, out of your way.

- To return your Home screens to how they were when you first started using your iPhone, open the Settings app, tap General, Reset, Reset Home Screen Layout, and Reset Home Screen. The Home screens return to their default configurations. Icons you've added are moved onto the later pages.

Setting the Screen's Brightness, View, Text Size, and Wallpaper

In this section, you learn how to configure three functional aspects of your iPhone's screen, which are its brightness, view, and text size, along with one that is just for fun, which is the image you see in the background of the Home screens and on the Lock screen (this is called wallpaper).

Setting the Screen Brightness, View, and Text Size

To set the screen brightness, perform the following steps:

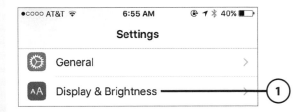

① In the Settings app, tap Display & Brightness.

② Drag the slider to the right to raise the base brightness or to the left to lower it. A brighter screen uses more power but is easier to see.

③ If you don't want to use the Auto-Brightness feature, slide the switch to off (white) to disable this feature. The Auto-Brightness feature adjusts the screen brightness based on the lighting conditions in which you are using the iPhone. You'll get more battery life with Auto-Brightness on, but you might not be comfortable with the brightness of the screen when you use the iPhone where there isn't a lot of ambient light.

④ Tap View; if you don't see this option, your iPhone doesn't support it and you can skip to step 17. The View settings screen enables you to set the zoom level you want to use.

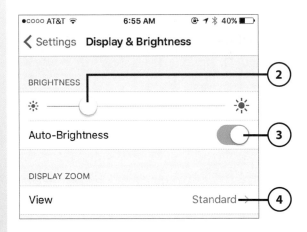

(5) Tap Standard.

(6) Look at the sample screen.

(7) Swipe to the left or right to see examples of what other screens look like in the Standard view.

(8) Look at the next sample screen.

(9) Swipe to the left or right to see examples of what other screens look like in the Standard view.

(10) Tap Zoomed. The sample screens change to reflect the Zoomed view.

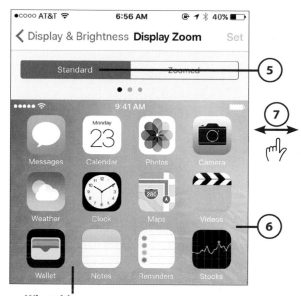

What this screen looks like in Standard view

(11) Swipe to the left and right to preview the other sample screens in the Zoomed view.

(12) If you want to keep the current view, tap Cancel and skip to step 16.

(13) To change the view, tap the view you want.

(14) Tap Set (if Set is grayed out, the view you selected is already set and you can skip to step 17).

(15) Tap Use Zoomed (this is Use Standard if you are switching to the Standard view). Your iPhone restarts and uses the new view.

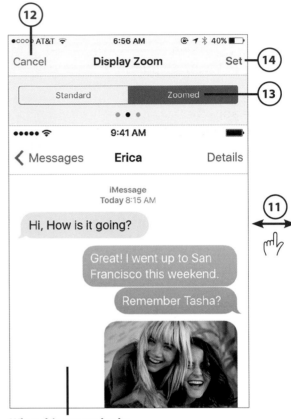

What this screen looks like in Zoomed view

16 Move back into the Settings app and then to the Display & Brightness screen.

17 Tap Text Size. This control changes the size of text in all the apps that support the iPhone's Dynamic Type feature.

18 Drag the slider to the right to increase the size of text or to the left to decrease it. As you move the slider, the text at the top of the screen resizes so you can see the impact of the change you are making.

19 When you are happy with the size of the text, tap Display & Brightness.

20 If you want to make all of the text on your iPhone bold, set the Bold Text switch to on (green) and move to step 21. If you don't want to bold the text, skip the next step.

21 Tap Continue. Your iPhone restarts. All the text is in bold, making it easier to read.

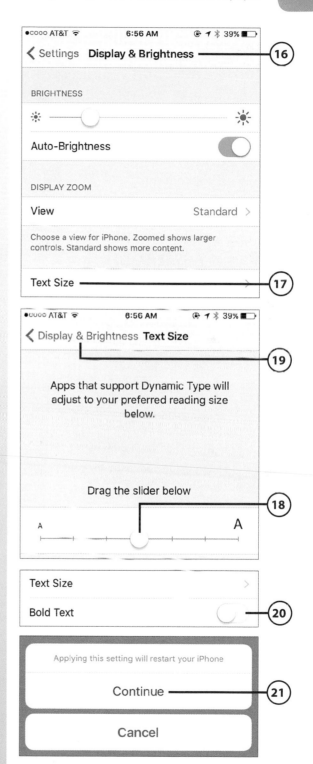

Setting the Wallpaper on the Home and Lock Screens

When you choose your wallpaper, you can use the iPhone's default images, or you can use any photo you have taken on your iPhone. You can set the wallpaper on Home screens and on the Lock screen (you can use the same image in both places or use a different one for each). To configure your wallpaper, perform the following steps:

1. In the Settings app, tap Wallpaper. You see the current wallpaper set for the Lock and Home screens.

2. Tap Choose a New Wallpaper. The Choose screen has two sections. The APPLE WALLPAPER section enables you to choose one of the default wallpaper images while the PHOTOS section shows you the photos available on your iPhone. If you don't have any photos stored on your iPhone, you can only choose from the default images. To choose a default image, continue with step 3; to use one of your photos as wallpaper, skip to step 8.

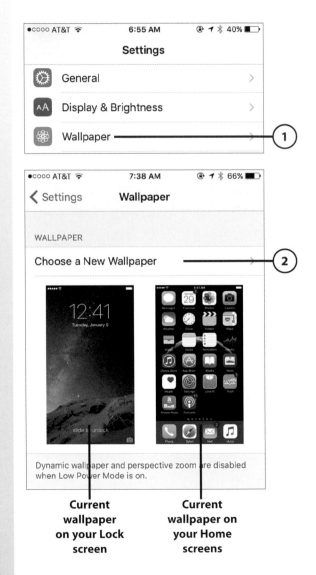

Current wallpaper on your Lock screen

Current wallpaper on your Home screens

3 Tap Dynamic if you want to use dynamic wallpaper, Stills if you want to use a static image, or Live if you want to use a Live Photo. These steps show selecting a Live Photo, but using a dynamic or still image is similar.

Wallpaper Options Explained

Dynamic wallpaper has motion (kind of like a screen saver on a computer). Stills are static images. Live Photos show motion when you tap and hold on them. Live Photos are available only on iPhone 6s or iPhone 6s Plus. On other models, you only see the Dynamic and Stills options.

4 Swipe up and down the screen to browse the images available to you.

5 Tap the image you want to use as wallpaper.

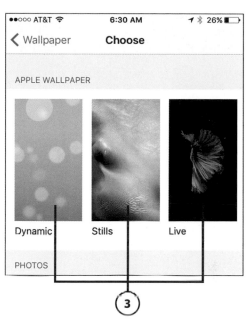

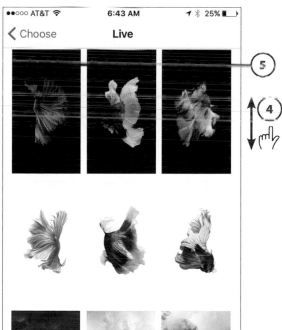

6 Tap Perspective to use the Perspective view of the wallpaper (see the sidebar "More on View Options"), tap Still to use a static version of the image, or tap Live Photo to use a Live Photo.

7 Tap Set and move to step 15.

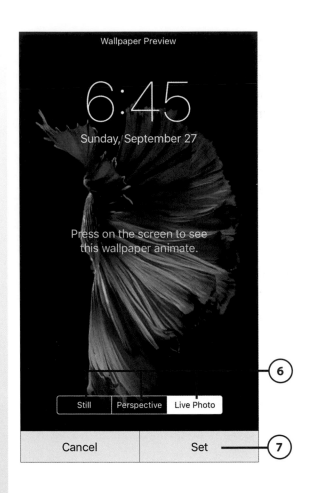

Wallpaper Preview

6:45

Sunday, September 27

Press on the screen to see this wallpaper animate.

Still   Perspective   Live Photo

Cancel   Set

More on View Options

The Perspective view can be a bit difficult to describe because it is subtle. This view magnifies the wallpaper image when you tilt your iPhone. It is sometimes noticeable and sometimes not, depending on the image you are using for wallpaper. The best thing to do is to enable it to see if you notice any difference or disable it if you prefer not to use it for the specific images you use as wallpaper. You can enable or disable it anytime for your wallpaper on the Lock and Home screens. To change the view without changing the wallpaper, move to the Wallpaper screen and tap the wallpaper (tap the Lock or Home screen) you want to change. Tap Perspective to use the Perspective view or Set if you don't want to use it. To save the view, tap Set or to leave it as it is, tap Cancel.

When you choose a Live Photo as wallpaper, you can touch and hold on the screen to see the image's motion. Note that when you apply a Live Photo to the Home screen wallpaper, it becomes a static image for which you can choose the Still or Perspective view.

8. To use a photo as wallpaper, swipe up the screen to browse the sources of photos available to you; these include All Photos, Favorites, albums, and so on.

Working with Photos

To learn how to work with the photos on your iPhone, see Chapter 14, "Working with Photos and Video You Take with Your iPhone."

9. Tap the source containing the photo you want to use.

10. Swipe up and down the selected source to browse its photos.

11. Tap the photo you want to use. The photo appears on the Move and Scale screen, which you can use to resize and move the image around.

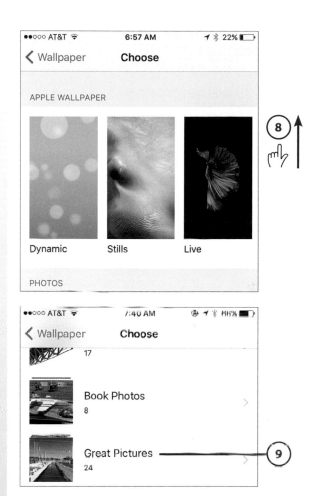

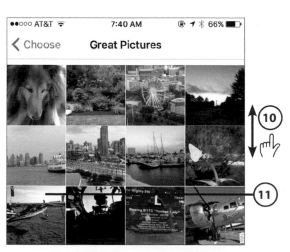

(12) Use your fingers to unpinch to zoom in or pinch to zoom out, and hold down and drag the photo around the screen until it appears how you want the wallpaper to look.

(13) Tap Perspective to use the Perspective view of the wallpaper (see the sidebar "More on View Options"), tap Still to use a static version of the image, or tap Live Photo to use a Live Photo (only available on iPhone 6s or iPhone 6s Plus).

(14) Tap Set.

(15) Tap Set Lock Screen or Set Home Screen to apply the wallpaper to only one of those screens; tap Set Both to apply the same wallpaper in both locations. The next time you move to the screen you selected, you see the wallpaper you chose.

16 If you set the wallpaper in only one location, tap Choose to move back to the Choose screen and repeat steps 3–15 to set the wallpaper for the other location.

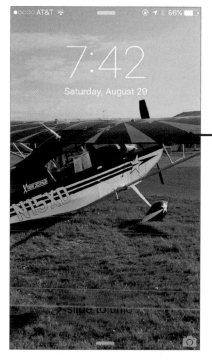

New wallpaper on the Lock screen

New wallpaper on the Home screen

Choosing the Sounds Your iPhone Makes

You can configure the sounds the phone uses in two ways. One is by choosing the general sounds your iPhone makes, which is covered in this section. You can also configure sounds specific apps use to notify you about certain events; this is covered in the next section.

To configure your iPhone's general sounds, do the following:

1. On the Settings screen, tap Sounds.

2. If you want your iPhone to also vibrate when it rings, set the Vibrate on Ring switch to on (green).

3. If you want your iPhone to vibrate when you have it muted, set the Vibrate on Silent switch to on (green).

4. Set the volume of the ringer and alert tones by dragging the slider to the left or right.

5. If you want to also be able to change this volume using the volume buttons on the side of the phone, set the Change with Buttons switch to on (green).

6. Tap Ringtone. On the resulting screen, you can set the sound and vibration your iPhone uses when a call comes in.

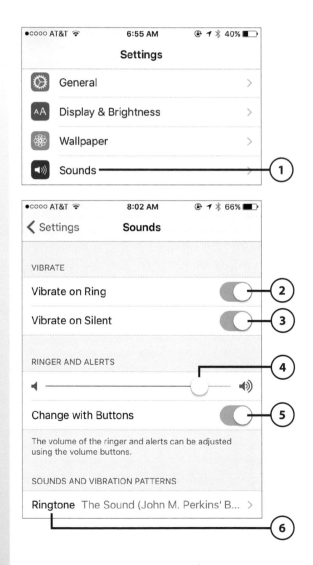

(7) Swipe up and down the screen to see all the ringtones available to you. There are two sections of sounds on this screen: RINGTONES and ALERT TONES. These work in the same way; alert tones tend to be shorter sounds. At the top of the RINGTONES section, you see any custom ringtones you have configured on your phone; a dark line separates those from the default ringtones that are below the custom ones.

(8) Tap a sound, and it plays.

(9) Repeat steps 7 and 8 until you have selected the sound you want to have as your general ringtone.

(10) If necessary, swipe down the screen so you see the Vibration section at the top.

(11) Tap Vibration. A list of Standard and Custom vibrations is displayed.

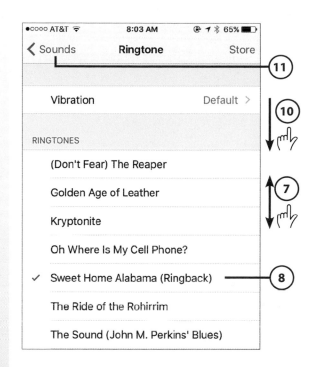

Individual Ringtones and Vibrations

The ringtone and vibration you set in steps 6–14 are the default or general settings. These are used for all callers except for people in your Contacts app for whom you've set specific ringtones or vibrations. In that case, the contact's specific ringtone and vibration are used instead of the defaults. See Chapter 7, "Managing Contacts," to learn how to configure specific ringtones and vibrations for contacts.

12 Swipe up and down the screen to see all the vibrations available. The STANDARD section contains the default vibrations while the CUSTOM section shows vibrations you have created.

13 Tap a vibration. It "plays" so you can feel it.

14 Repeat steps 12 and 13 until you've selected the general vibration you want to use; you can tap None at the bottom of the Vibration screen below the CUSTOM section if you don't want to have a general vibration.

15 Tap Ringtone.

16 Tap Sounds. The ringtone you selected is shown on the Sounds screen next to the Ringtone label.

17 Tap Text Tone.

18 Use steps 7–14 and tap Text Tone to set the sound and vibration used when you receive a new text. The process works the same as for ringtones, though the screens look a bit different. For example, the ALERT TONES section is at the top of the screen because you are more likely to want a short sound for new texts.

19 When you're done setting the text tone, tap Sounds.

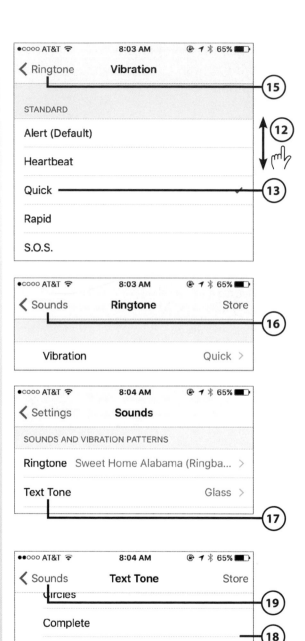

(20) Using the same pattern as you did for ringtones and text tones, set the sound and vibrations for the rest of the events in the list.

(21) If you don't want your iPhone to make a sound when you lock it, slide the Lock Sounds switch to off (white). Your iPhone no longer makes this sound when you press the Sleep/Wake button to put it to sleep and lock it.

(22) If you don't like the audible feedback when you tap keys on the iPhone's virtual keyboard, slide the Keyboard Clicks switch to off (white) to disable that sound. The keyboard is silent as you type on it.

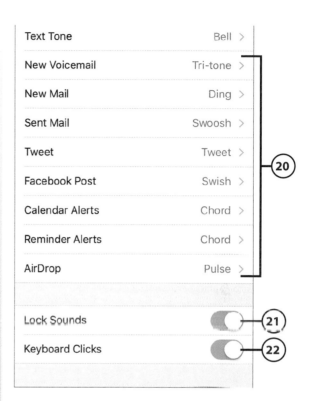

Text Tone	Bell >
New Voicemail	Tri-tone >
New Mail	Ding >
Sent Mail	Swoosh >
Tweet	Tweet >
Facebook Post	Swish >
Calendar Alerts	Chord >
Reminder Alerts	Chord >
AirDrop	Pulse >
Lock Sounds	
Keyboard Clicks	

>>>Go Further

SOUNDING OFF

Following are some other sound- and vibration-related pointers:

- You can tap the Store button on the Ringtone, Text Tone, and other screens to move to the iTunes Store, where you can download ringtones and other sounds to your iPhone. See Chapter 6, "Downloading Apps, Music, Movies, TV Shows, and More onto Your iPhone," for more information about downloading content from the iTunes Store.

- You can create custom vibration patterns, too. On the Vibration screen, tap Create New Vibration. Tap the vibration pattern you want to create; when you're done tapping, tap Stop. Tap Record to start over if you don't like the one you created. When you're done, tap Save. Name the pattern and tap Save. The patterns you create are available in the CUSTOM section on the Vibration screen, so you can use them just like the iPhone's default vibration patterns. To remove a custom pattern, swipe to the left on it and tap Delete.

Setting Up Notifications and the Notification Center

Your iPhone uses notifications, which can be messages on the screen, sounds, or vibrations, to let you know when something has happened that you might want to know about. Since there is a lot of activity on your phone, it's important that you choose which events you want to be notified about. You want to strike a balance so that you are informed about what is important to you while not receiving so many notifications that they are annoying or disruptive.

Understanding Notifications and the Notification Center

There are several types of notifications, which include badges, banners, alerts, vibrations, and sounds.

Number of new items in the app

Badges are the counters that appear on an app's or folder's icon to let you know how many new of something you have, such as email messages, texts, event invitations, and so on. You can enable or disable the badge for an app's icon. (Remember that when a badge appears on a folder's icon, it counts all the events for all the apps it contains.)

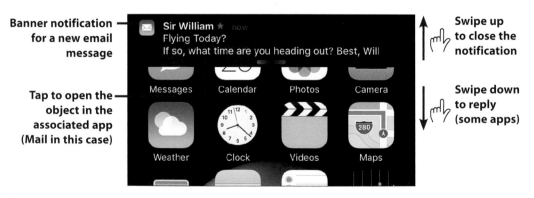

Banner notification for a new email message

Tap to open the object in the associated app (Mail in this case)

Swipe up to close the notification

Swipe down to reply (some apps)

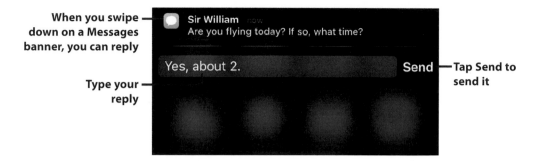

When you swipe down on a Messages banner, you can reply

Type your reply

Tap Send to send it

Banners are small messages that appear at the top of the screen when something happens, such as when you receive an email message. Banners contain the icon of the app from which they come, and they can show a preview (if you enable the preview setting). Banners are nice because they don't interfere with what you are doing. If you ignore a banner, after a few seconds, it disappears. If you tap a banner, you move into the app producing the banner and can work with whatever the banner is for, such as a new email message. You can swipe up on a banner to close it. You can swipe down on a banner to reply (for some apps, such as Messages). When you receive a new banner when one is visible on the screen, the first one rotates out of the way so the newest one is displayed. If you receive a lot of notifications at the same time, you see a summary of how many you have received.

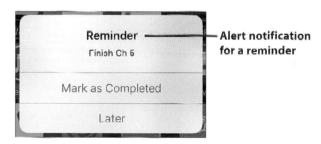

Alert notification for a reminder

Alerts are another means that apps can use to communicate with you. There are alerts for many types of objects, such as texts, emails, reminders, missed call notifications, and so on. The differences between a banner and an alert are that alerts appear in the center of the screen and you must do something to make the alert go away, such as listen to or ignore a voice message. Some alerts have an Options button; tap this button to see and do actions related to the notification. Alerts can contain a variety of other options depending on the app that sent the alert; for example, you can mark a reminder as complete or tap Later to reset the reminder's alert.

Cellular Emergency Notifications

Depending on where you live and which provider you use, you might receive emergency notifications from government agencies for such things as weather emergencies, Amber Alerts (in the United States, these are issued when a child is abducted), and so on. These alerts appear on your iPhone when they are issued to keep you informed of such events. You can enable or disable certain of these notifications.

You should use alerts when you want to be sure to take action on the occurrence about which an alert is sent. For example, you might want to use alerts for calendar events so you have to respond to the notice that the event is coming up, such as the start of a meeting. Banners are better for those notifications that you want to be aware of but that you don't want to interrupt what you are doing, such as email messages. (If an alert appears each time you receive an email message, they can be very disruptive.)

Sounds are audible indicators that something has happened. For example, when something happens in the Game Center, you can be notified via a sound. Earlier in this chapter, you learned how to configure your iPhone's general sounds. You also can configure the sounds used for a specific app's notifications.

Vibrations are a physical indicator that something has happened. Like sounds, you can configure general vibrations, and you can also configure an app's vibration pattern for its notifications.

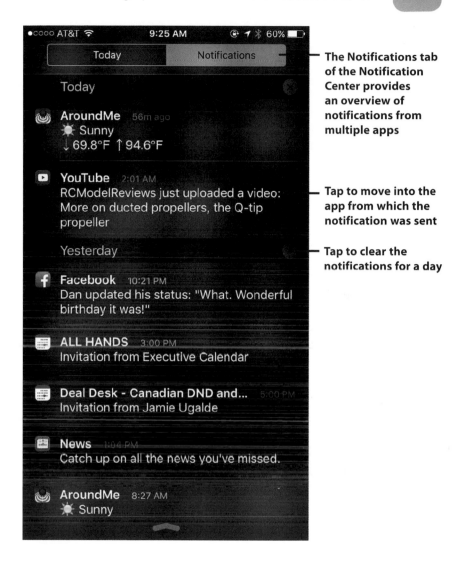

The Notifications tab of the Notification Center provides an overview of notifications from multiple apps

Tap to move into the app from which the notification was sent

Tap to clear the notifications for a day

The Notification Center enables you to access all your notifications on one screen. As you learned in Chapter 1, "Getting Started with Your iPhone," swipe down from the top of the screen to reveal the Notification Center. Tap the Notifications tab, and you see your current notifications grouped by the day on which those notifications occurred. Swipe up and down the screen to review them. Tap the delete (x) button and tap Clear to clear all of the notifications for a day. Tap a notification to move into the app from which the notification was sent. You can configure which apps provide notifications on the Notification Center and how many are allowed.

Setting Global Notification Preferences

Use the following steps to configure general notification settings:

1. On the Settings screen, tap Notifications.

2. In the NOTIFICATIONS VIEW section, tap Sort Order.

3. Tap Recent if you want the notifications shown in the Notification Center to be organized based on the most recent information being toward the top of the screen, and then skip to step 6.

4. Tap Manual if you want to set the order (from top to bottom) of notifications in the Notification Center.

5. Drag apps by their order button up and down to change the order in which their notifications appear in the Notification Center.

6. Tap Notifications.

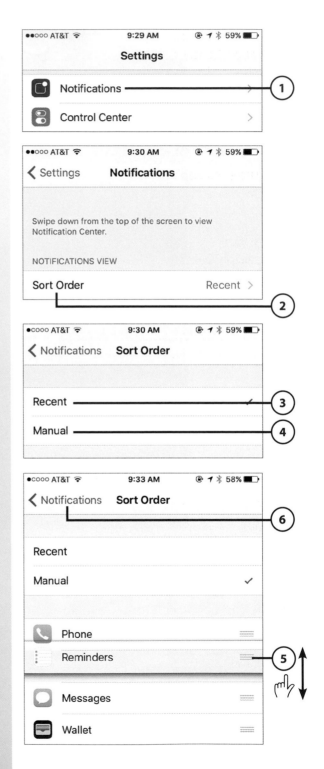

7 To have notifications on the Notification Center grouped by app instead of by time, set the Group By App switch to on (green); this option is only available if the Sort Order is set to Recent as explained in step 3.

8 Configure each app's notification settings; the details of this are explained in the next task.

9 Swipe up the screen until you see the GOVERNMENT ALERTS section.

More Alerts

Depending on where you live, you might see a different set of alert options in the GOVERNMENT ALERTS section. You can enable or disable any of the alerts you see in this section as explained in steps 8 and 9.

10 If you don't want to receive AMBER alert notifications, set the AMBER Alerts switch to off (white).

11 If you don't want to receive other types of emergency alerts, set the Emergency Alerts switch to off (white).

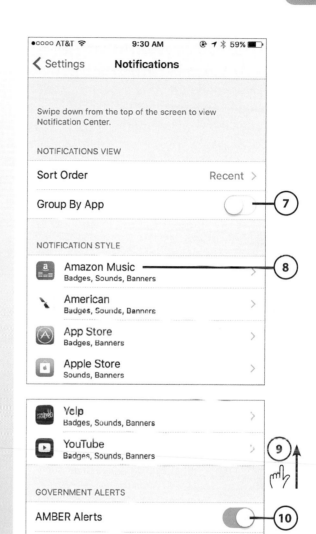

Configuring Notifications for Specific Apps

You can configure how apps can provide notifications and, if you allow notifications, which type. You can also configure other aspects of notifications, such as whether an app displays in the Notification Center or whether its notifications appear on the Lock screen. Not all apps support all notification options. Some apps, such as Mail, support notification configuration by account (for example, you can set a different alert sound for new mail in each account). You can follow the same general steps to configure notifications for each app; you should explore the options for the apps you use most often to ensure they work the best for you.

The following steps show how to configure Mail's notifications, which is a good example because it supports a lot of notification features; other apps might have fewer features or might be organized slightly differently. But, configuring the notifications for any app follows a similar pattern.

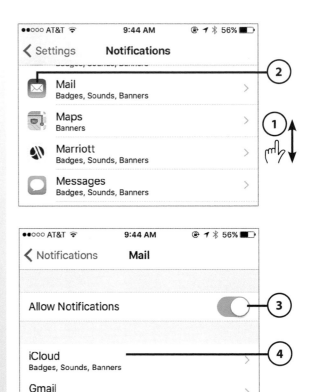

1. Continuing in the Notification Center screen from the previous task, swipe up and down to browse all of the apps installed on your iPhone that support notifications.

2. Tap the app whose notifications you want to configure.

3. If you want the app to provide notifications, set the Allow Notifications switch to on (green) and move to step 4. If you don't want notifications from the app, set the Allow Notifications switch to off (white) and skip the rest of these steps.

4. Tap the account for which you want to configure notifications.

5 To show notifications from the app/account in the Notification Center, set the Show in Notification Center switch to on (green); if you set this to off (white), notifications from the app/account are not shown in the Notification Center.

6 Tap Sounds.

7 Use the resulting Sounds screen to choose the alert sound and vibration for new email messages to the account (refer to the section on setting general sound preferences earlier in this chapter for details on choosing sounds and vibrations).

8 Tap the back button located in the upper-left corner of the screen (it is labeled with the account's name).

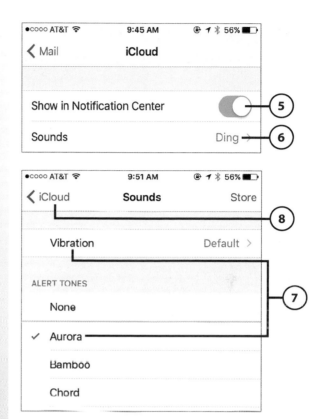

9 To display the app's badge, set the Badge App Icon switch to on (green).

10 If you want the app's notifications for the account to appear on the Lock screen, slide the Show on Lock Screen switch to on (green).

11 Choose the type of notification you want by tapping None, Banners, or Alerts. You know which alert type is currently selected because its name appears in an oblong button.

12 If you don't want a preview to appear in the app's notifications, slide the Show Previews switch to off (white). For example, you might want to keep some types of messages private when you receive a notification; to do so, disable the Show Previews option for that account.

13 Tap the back button, which is located in the upper-left corner of the window and is labeled with the app you are configuring (Mail, in this example).

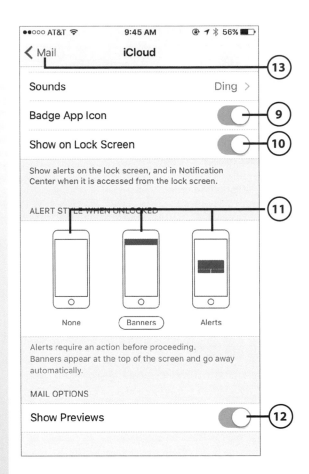

Installed App Not Shown?

You must have opened an app at least once for it to appear on the Notifications screen.

(14) Configure notifications for the other accounts used in the app.

(15) Configure notifications for VIP email and threads.

(16) Tap Notifications.

(17) Repeat these steps for each app shown on the Notification Center screen. Certain apps might not have all the options shown in these steps, but the process to configure their notifications is similar.

VIPs Are Special

Mail supports VIPs, which are people from whom email messages are treated specially, such as having a dedicated mailbox in the Mail app. You can apply specific notification settings to VIP messages using the VIP option. These override the notification settings for the email account to which messages from VIPs are sent.

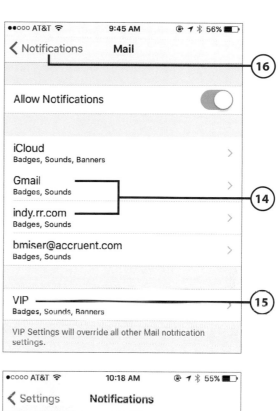

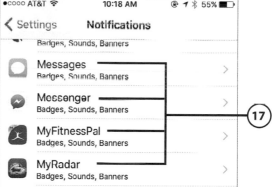

Use the App Store app to download and install cool and useful apps on your iPhone

Use the iTunes Store app to load up your phone with great music, movies, TV shows, and more

Use the Settings app to configure your store preferences

In this chapter, you learn how to add apps, music, TV shows, and other content onto your iPhone, and how to share your goodies with others. Topics include the following:

→ Getting started
→ Configuring store settings
→ Using the App Store app to find and install iPhone apps
→ Using the iTunes Store app to download music, ringtones, movies, and TV shows
→ Downloading apps or iTunes Store content you've purchased previously
→ Using Family Sharing to share your store downloads with others

Downloading Apps, Music, Movies, TV Shows, and More onto Your iPhone

Developers around the world have created many thousands of apps available in the App Store app to download and install on your iPhone. Along with all these great apps, there are also lots of music, movies, TV shows, ebooks, audiobooks, and much more content available to enjoy on your iPhone; using the iTunes Store app, you can easily find content and download it to your iPhone.

Getting Started

Because adding the apps you want to use along with the music and other content you want to enjoy is part of making *an* iPhone into *your* iPhone, you'll need to know how to download items to your iPhone. Here are the major concepts related to this topic:

- **App Store**—This is both a location where all the apps are available for your iPhone and an app on your iPhone that you use to download apps.

- **iTunes Store**—Like the App Store, this is both a store and an app on your iPhone. You use the iTunes Store app to download content, such as music, ringtones, and books, onto your iPhone.

- **Family Sharing**—You can define a group of up to six people (they don't have to be actual family members) with whom you want to share content you download. The people in your Family Sharing group can download and use your content without having to pay for it again. When people put you in their Family Sharing group, you can use the content they purchase.

Configuring Store Settings

You can configure your iPhone so that music, apps, and books that you download from any of your devices are automatically downloaded to your phone as well. For example, if you purchase an album on your iPad, that same album is immediately downloaded to your iPhone, too. You can also have any updates to apps installed on your iPhone downloaded and installed automatically so you don't have to wonder if you are using the current versions.

Configuring Automatic Store Downloads

To have content you purchase from the iTunes Store be automatically downloaded to your iPhone and configure when password entry is required to download content, perform the following steps:

1. Tap Settings.

2. Tap App and iTunes Stores.

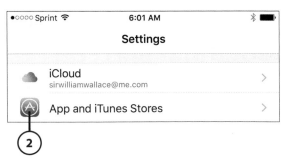
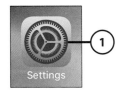

3 Tap Password Settings; if you don't see Password Settings, Touch ID is configured for the App and iTunes Stores and you can skip to step 7. (Touch ID makes it much easier to securely download content from the stores. To learn how to configure Touch ID, see "Setting Passcode, Touch ID, and Auto-Lock Preferences" in Chapter 4, "Configuring an iPhone to Suit Your Preferences.")

4 Tap Always Require if you want your password to be required for every download from either store, or tap Require After 15 Minutes if you want downloads within 15 minutes of the most recent purchase to be allowed without entering your password again.

5 If you want to have to enter your password to download free content, set the Require Password switch to on (green). If other people use your phone, it's a good idea to set this to on so they don't load up your phone with content you don't want.

6 Tap App and iTunes Stores.

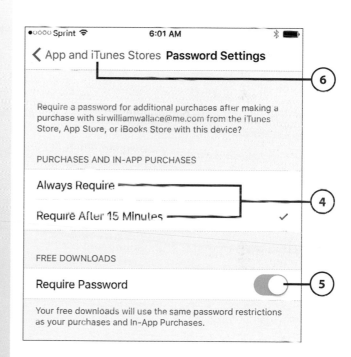

(7) Slide the switches to on (green) for the types of content you want to be downloaded to your iPhone automatically; the options are Music, Apps, Books, and Updates (which causes any updates to the apps installed on your iPhone to be downloaded and installed automatically).

(8) If you don't have an unlimited cellular data plan, you might want to set the Use Cellular Data to off (white) so content is downloaded only when you are on a Wi-Fi network.

(9) If you want apps that are currently installed on your phone to be suggested to you based on your current location and app use, set the Installed Apps switch to on (green). With this enabled, as you change locations, apps that are relevant to that location are suggested on the Lock screen and in the App Switcher. Apps are also suggested in these locations based on the apps that you use.

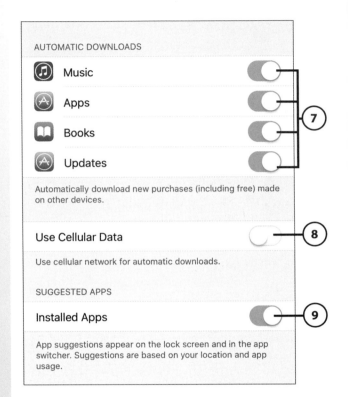

Apple ID

To work with the Apple ID you use in the App and iTunes Stores, tap the account shown at the top of the App and iTunes Store screen. On the resulting prompt, you can view your Apple ID, sign out of your account, or reset your password (the iForgot option). If you sign out of your account, the Store screen only has the Sign In button. Tap this and sign into the Apple ID you want to configure for the stores.

Using the App Store App to Find and Install iPhone Apps

The App Store app enables you to quickly and easily browse and search for apps, view information about them, and then download and install them on your iPhone with just a few taps.

When you use the App Store app, you can find apps to download using any of the following options:

- **Categories**—This link shows you various categories of apps that you can browse.
- **Featured**—This tab takes you to apps featured in the App Store. This screen organizes apps in several categories. These categories change from time to time, but they typically include "best new" types of apps (such as games), apps for specific purposes (for example, travel), and so on. Swipe up and down the screen to see all the categories available.
- **Top Charts**—This takes you to lists of the top iPhone apps. This screen has three tabs at the top of the screen: Paid shows you the top apps for which you have to pay a license fee; Free shows you a similar list containing only free apps; and Top Grossing shows the apps that have been downloaded the most.
- **Explore**—This option shows apps that are popular or relevant based on your current location.
- **Search**—This tool enables you to search for apps. You can search by name, developer, and other keywords.
- **Updates**—Through this option, you can get to the Purchased screen, which enables you to find and download apps you have previously downloaded to

your iPhone or other device, and shows you the update status of your apps on your iPhone (this topic is covered in the last section of this chapter).

Finding and downloading any kind of app follows this same pattern:

1. **Find the app you are interested in.** You can use the options described in the previous list, find apps by browsing for them, or use the search option to find a specific app quickly and easily.

2. **Evaluate the app.** The information screen for apps provides lots of information that you can use to decide whether you want to download an app (or not). The information available includes a text description, screenshots, ratings and reviews of other users, and so on.

3. **Download and install the app.**

The following tasks provide detailed examples for each of these steps.

Searching for Apps

If you know something about an app, such as its name, its developer, or just about anything else, you can quickly search the App Store to find the app. Here's how to search for an app:

1. Move to the Home screen and tap App Store.

2. Tap Search.

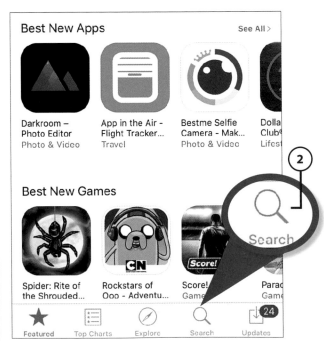

③ Tap in the Search box.

④ Type a search term. This can be the type of app you are looking for based on its purpose (such as travel) or the name of someone associated with the app, its title, its developer, or even a topic. As you type, the app suggests searches that are related to what you are typing.

⑤ Tap the search you want to perform (to see the full list of search results, tap Search). The apps that meet your search term appear.

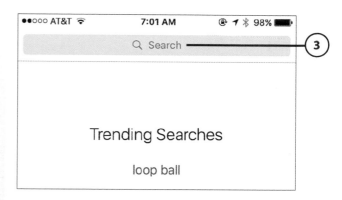

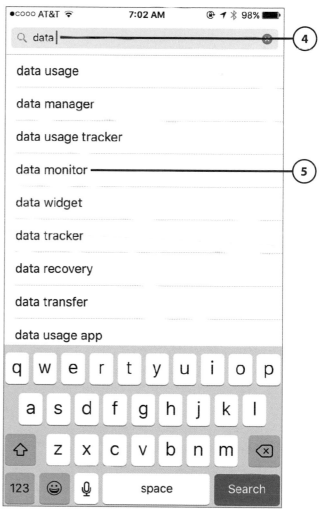

6 Swipe up and down on the screen to review the apps that were found by your search.

Related Apps

When the search results are on the screen, at the top (just under the Search bar), you see app searches that are related to the one you performed in some way in the Related bar. Tap a related search on this bar to use it to find other apps. As you use related searches, back (<) and forward (>) buttons appear in the Related bar so that you can move back and forth among the searches you have done. For example, tap the back button to get back to previous search results.

7 If none of the apps are what you are looking for, tap the x in the Search box and repeat steps 4–6 (or use the Related searches as described in the Related Apps note).

8 When you find an app of interest to you, tap it. You move to the app's information screen.

9 Use the app's information on the information screen to evaluate the app and decide if you want to download it. You can read about the app, see screenshots, and read other peoples' reviews to help you decide. If you want to download the app, see "Downloading Apps" later in this chapter for the details.

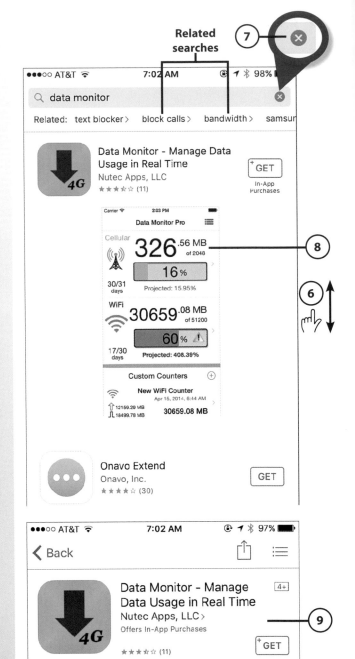

Follow the Trends?

Before you enter a search term on the Search screen, you see the trending searches, which are the searches that are being performed most frequently. You can tap one of these to use it to search for apps.

>>>Go Further

MORE ON FINDING APPS

Following are a few pointers to help you use the App Store:

- You can browse for apps in the App Store by clicking on the text and graphics you see. You can also tap the Categories button in the upper-left corner of the screen and choose a category of apps in which you are interested. Then browse the result list of apps to explore what is available in that category. Browsing for apps is similar to browsing for content in the iTunes Store; see "Browsing for iTunes Store Content" later in this chapter for details.

- When you see a "+" inside an app's price or Get button, that means the app is a universal app, which means it runs equally as well on iPhones, iPads, and iPod touches.

- Some apps include video previews. When you see the Play button on an image, it is a video preview. Tap the Play button to watch it. Tap the Done button in the upper left corner of the screen to move back to the screenshots.

- You can read user reviews of the apps in the App Store. You should take these with a grain of salt. Some people have an issue with the developer, or even the type of app, are viewing an older version of the app, or are commenting on issues unrelated to the app itself, and that causes them to provide low ratings. The most useful individual user reviews are very specific as in "I wanted the app to do x, but it only does y." It can be more helpful to look at the number of reviews and the average user rating than reading the individual reviews.

Downloading Apps

Downloading and installing apps is about as easy as things get, as you can see:

1. In the App Store, view the app you want to download.

2. Tap GET (for free apps) or the price. The button then becomes INSTALL, if it is a free app, or BUY, if it has a license fee.

3. Tap INSTALL or BUY. Depending on your App and iTunes Stores settings, you might be prompted to sign in with your Apple ID and password to start the download. If you aren't prompted to confirm the download, you can skip the next step because the app starts downloading immediately.

4. If you are prompted to confirm the download, and you are using an iPhone 5s or later and have enabled Touch ID for store downloads, touch the Touch ID/Home button at the prompt; if you are using another model, or you don't use Touch ID for store downloads, type your Apple ID password, and then tap OK.

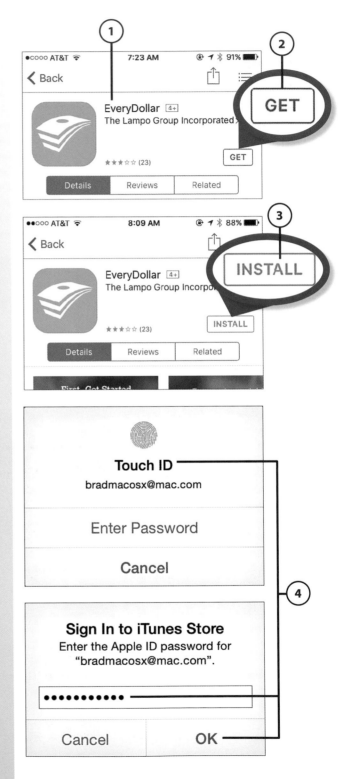

You see the progress of the process.

When the process is complete, the status information is replaced by the OPEN button.

This app is almost fully downloaded

This app is installed and ready to use

>>>Go Further
MORE ON APPS

As you use the App Store app to install apps on your iPhone, keep the following hints handy:

- Like other software, apps are updated regularly to fix problems, add features, or make other changes. If you set the App and iTunes Store AUTOMATIC DOWNLOADS Updates setting to on (green) as described earlier in this chapter, updates to your apps happen automatically in the background. Your apps are always current, so you don't have to update them manually. (More information on updating apps is in the online Chapter 16, "Maintaining and Protecting Your iPhone and Solving Problems.")

- If you see the Download button (a cloud with a downward-pointing arrow) next to an app rather than Get or Buy, that means you have previously downloaded (and paid for if it isn't free) the app but it is not currently installed on your iPhone. Tap the button to download and install it (you only have to pay for an app once).

- To let someone else know about an app, tap the Share button and then tap how you want to let him know; the options are AirDrop, Message, Mail, Twitter, and Facebook. To give the app to someone, tap Gift.

- Using the Family Sharing feature, you can share apps you download with others. You learn about this in "Using Family Sharing to Share Your Store Downloads with Others," at the end of this chapter.

- After you install an app, move to the Settings screen and look for the app's icon. If it is there, the app has additional settings you can use to configure the way it works. Tap the app's icon in the Settings app and use its Settings screen to configure it.

Using the iTunes Store App to Download Music, Ringtones, Movies, and TV Shows

You can use the iPhone's iTunes Store app to download audio and video content from the iTunes Store directly onto your iPhone. You can listen to music you download in the Music app, watch movies and TV shows in the Videos app, and use tones for ringtones and alert tones.

Using the iTunes Store app involves the following general steps:

- **Find the content you are interested in**—Like the App Store app, there are a number of ways to do this. You can search for specific content, or you can browse for content by type, which includes the following (to get to some of these, such as Genius, tap the More button and then tap the item of interest to you):

  - Music enables you to download music.

  - Movies takes you to the movies in the iTunes Store so you can browse, preview, and download them.

  - TV Shows does the same for TV programming.

  - Tones enables you to purchase ringtones and alert tones that you can use as various sounds on your iPhone.

  - Genius shows you recommendations based on content you have previously downloaded that you might also be interested in.

- **Preview the content**—You can sample content before you download it. For example, you can listen to a preview of songs (typically 90 seconds' worth), watch movie trailers, listen to tones, and so on.

- **Download the content**—You can download content with just a couple of taps. After you download content to your iPhone, it immediately becomes available in the related app.

In the following tasks, you see examples of each of these steps.

Searching for iTunes Store Content

When you know something about the content you want, searching is a good way to find it because it is easy and fast. Also, when you search, your results can include multiple types of content. For example, searching on a title can yield an album, a movie, song, or TV show. Here's how to search in the Store:

(1) On the iPhone's Home screen, tap iTunes Store. You move to the iTunes Store app. At the bottom of the screen, you choose how you want to look for content by tapping one of the buttons on the iTunes Store Dock.

(2) Tap Search.

More Trends

Similar to the App Store app, when you haven't entered a search term on the Search screen, you see the searches that are trending. You can tap a trending search to see its results.

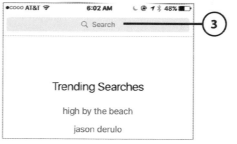

(3) Tap in the Search box.

4 Type a search criterion, such as an artist's name, a movie title, or even a general topic (for example, a franchise, such as *Star Trek*). As you type, content that matches your search appears under the Search bar.

5 When you see something of interest on the results list, tap it, or to see the entire list of search results, tap Search and then tap the result you want to explore.

6 Swipe up, down, right, and left to browse the search results, which are organized into categories, such as Movies, Albums, Songs, Ringtones, Music Videos, and so on.

7 To limit the results to a specific type of content, tap the related tab. For example, to see the movies related to what you searched for, tap Movies.

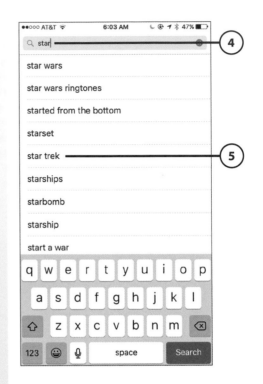

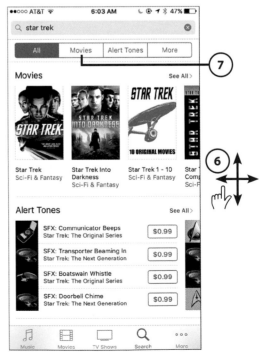

8 Swipe on the screen to browse the list of results for the type of content you selected.

9 When you see something of interest, tap it. You see the Information screen for that content.

10 Use the Information screen to preview and explore the content. Details are provided later in this chapter in the task titled, "Previewing iTunes Store Content."

Stop the Search!

To clear a search, tap the Clear button (x) in the Search bar. Swipe down on the keyboard to close it so that you can see the iTunes Dock at the bottom of the screen again.

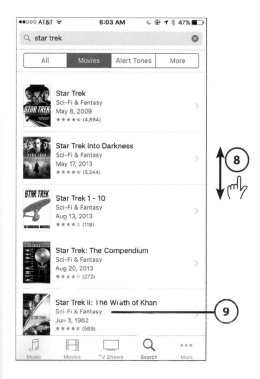

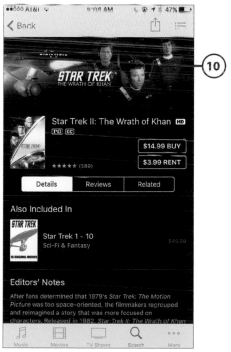

Browsing for iTunes Store Content

Even though browsing isn't as efficient as searching, it is a good way to discover content you might not know about. The details of browsing depend on the type of content for which you are looking. To demonstrate the general process, the task that follows shows browsing music:

1. On the iPhone's Home screen, tap iTunes Store. You move to the iTunes Store app. At the bottom of the screen, you can choose how you want to look for content by tapping one of the buttons on the iTunes Store Dock.

2. Tap Music. You move to the Music Home page. At the top of the screen, you see options you can use to browse: Genres, Featured (the default), and Charts.

3. Swipe the screen to browse the current contents. The rest of these steps show browsing by genre. The steps for using the other browse options are similar.

4. Tap Genres. You see the list of genres.

5 Swipe up and down the screen to browse the list of genres.

6 Tap the genre you want to explore.

7 Swipe the screen to browse the contents being displayed.

8 Tap something of interest to see more detail. For example, tap the See All link for a category to see all the items in that category.

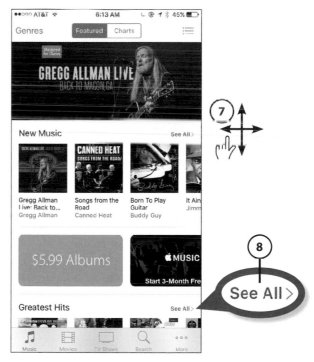

(9) Swipe the results to browse them.

(10) Tap an item for which you'd like to see more detail.

(11) Use the Information screen to preview and explore the content. Details are provided in the task "Previewing iTunes Store Content."

But Wait, There's More

You can access additional categories of content by tapping the More button. On the More screen, you see Tones and Genius. Tap Tones to download sound snippets from songs or special effects to use as ringtones or alert tones. Tap Genius to see recommended content based on content you have downloaded or content related to content you have downloaded.

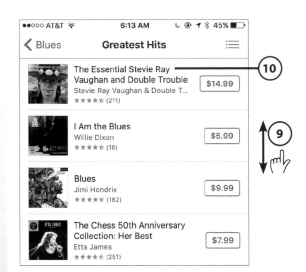

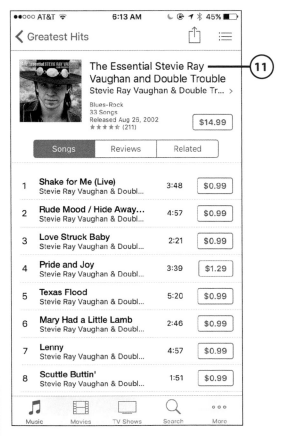

Previewing iTunes Store Content

You can use the Information screen to explore content in which you are interested. This screen looks a bit different for various kinds of content, such as a movie versus an album. However, the general features of this screen are similar, so the following steps showing an album's Information screen will get you started:

1. Move to the Information screen for content you might want to download.

2. Review the summary information at the top of the screen.

3. On the Songs tab (this is called Details for some other types of content), tap More.

4. Read the detailed description/notes. (Be aware that not all content has notes or other information about it.)

5. Tap the Reviews tab.

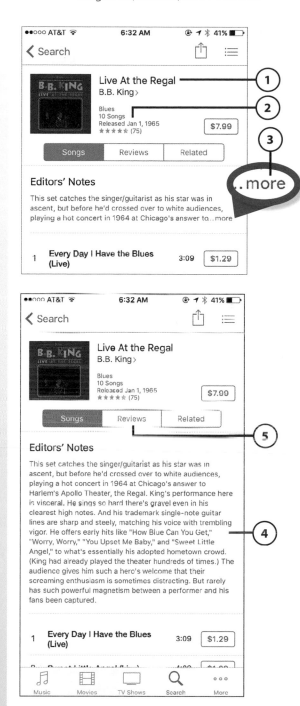

(6) Swipe up and down the screen to read all the review information. At the top, you see an overview of the reviews, indicated by the star ratings. Toward the bottom of the screen, you can read the individual reviews.

(7) Tap Songs.

(8) Swipe up the screen to see the list of songs the album or collection contains.

(9) To preview a track, tap it. A short preview plays. While it's playing, the track's number is replaced by the Stop button, which you can tap to stop the preview.

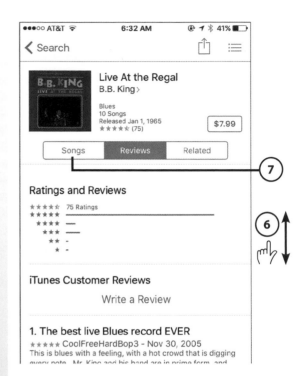

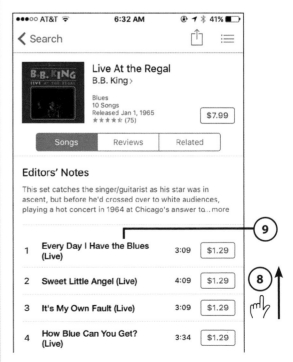

10 Continue previewing the content until you are ready to make a decision to download it—or not.

More on Previewing Content

When you are previewing songs and other audio, you can continue to browse around the store; as you do, a preview bar appears at the top of the screen. This bar shows the content currently playing. You can tap its playback button to stop the preview. When you preview video content, such as watching a trailer for a movie, it plays in a video player. Use the playback controls to watch the video. Tap Done to close the video player.

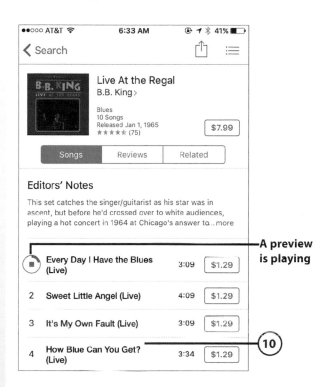

A preview is playing

Downloading iTunes Store Content

Like downloading apps, downloading movies, tones, songs, albums, and so on is just a tap away:

1 Move to the Information screen for content you want to download.

2 Tap the appropriate buy button, which shows the price of the item. For example, to buy an album, tap its price button. To buy a song, tap its price button instead. The button changes to show what you are buying.

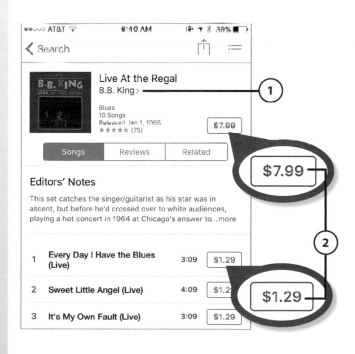

3 Tap the Buy button again, such as BUY ALBUM. If you're prompted to sign into your account, go to step 4. If you recently signed in, the download starts without you signing in and you can skip step 4.

4 If you are using an iPhone 5s or later, at the prompt, touch the Touch ID/Home button. If you are using a different model, enter the password for your Apple ID and tap OK.

The badge on the More button updates to show you how many items are being downloaded to the iPhone. The download process starts and you can continue to shop in the Store or move into a different app; the download process occurs in the background. If you want to, you can monitor the download process by continuing with these steps.

5 Tap More.

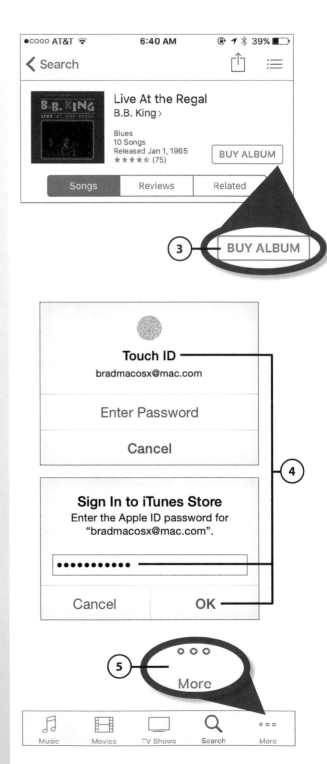

6 Tap Downloads. You move to the Downloads screen, which displays the progress of the tracks you are purchasing.

When the process is complete, the Downloads screen is empty indicating that all the content you purchased has been added to the iPhone.

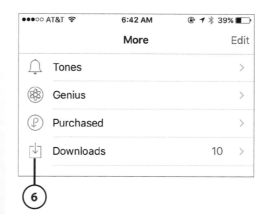

Procrastinate If You Want

When you download some content that is large, such as a movie, you have the option to download it later. For example, you might decide you want a movie while you are using your cellular data network but don't want to use a lot of your data plan's monthly allocation to download it. Tap the Later button to defer the download to a later time. You can do the same thing with the Pause button for any content that is downloaded. Tap the Pause button and the download stops where it is. Tap the Resume button to complete the download (for example, when you return to a Wi-Fi network).

Tap to pause a download

These songs are being downloaded

Using Your iTunes Store History List

As you are looking at content in the iTunes Store, you'll likely encounter music, movies, and so on that you are interested in but are not sure you want to download. It would be a pain to get back to content via searching or browsing. Fortunately, you can use the History List to go back to content you have previewed.

The History List contains content that you've interacted with in the following ways:

- **Wish List**—To add something to your Wish List, open an item's information screen, tap the Share button, and then tap Add to Wish List.

- **Siri** —When music is playing around you, activate Siri and say "What song is this?" Siri identifies the music playing and adds it to your History List. This is a great way to add music that you hear when you are out and about so you can easily find it again later.

- **Radio**—Songs you listen to via iTunes Radio are added to your History List automatically so that you can purchase them easily. So, if you remember that you heard a great song on iTunes Radio, but don't remember who performed it, you can use this option to easily find it.

- **Preview**—Any content you preview is added to your History List automatically.

You can use your History List to find, preview, and download content similarly to how you do these things from other areas. The following example shows content captured by previewing it, but the other options work in the same way.

(1) Tap the History List button.

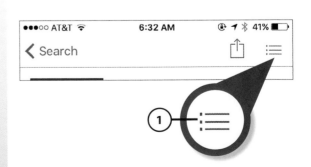

2 Tap the source of content you want to see. For example, tap Previews to see the content you have previewed.

3 Swipe the screen to browse the list of items.

4 To move to an item's Information screen, tap its title.

5 To preview an item, tap its icon.

6 To buy an item, tap its price button and then tap its BUY button.

7 If you've purchased something on this list, tap PLAY to play it.

8 To clear your list, tap Clear and then tap Clear History.

9 To close the list, tap Done.

>>>Go Further

SHOPPING LIKE A PRO

Here are a few more pointers to make your iTunes Store experience even better:

- **Preorder**—You can order content that isn't released yet, such as movies, or a full season of a TV show that is in a current season. When the content you have preordered becomes available, it is downloaded to your iPhone automatically.

- **Renting**—You can rent movies, too. This is less expensive than buying them, but it comes with limitations. You can keep a rented movie for only 30 days. And, after you start watching it, it will play for a 24-hour period (48 hours in some locations). When either of these time periods is up, the rented movie is deleted from your iPhone automatically.

- **Share and Share Alike**—Tap the Share button at the top of iTunes screens to share the content you are exploring. You can share by email, message, Twitter, and Facebook. The messages you send contain a link to the item. Tap Gift to give the content to someone else.

- **Clear History**—The Clear button on the History List deletes only the items from the tab you are currently viewing. For example, if you use it on the Previews tab, all the items you have previewed are erased. To clear the other lists, tap the tab for the content you want to clear, tap Clear, and then tap Clear History at the prompt.

- **Automatic Downloads**—If you have other iOS devices or iTunes on your computers configured to automatically download iTunes Store purchases, the content is downloaded to those locations, too.

Downloading Apps or iTunes Store Content You've Purchased Previously

You can download any content you've purchased from the App or iTunes Stores again without paying a fee (rented movies are an exception because you can download those only once). For example, you might delete music from your iPhone to free up some memory, and then download it again later when you want to listen to it.

Downloading Previously Purchased App Store Apps

To download apps you previously purchased, perform the following steps:

1. Tap the App Store icon to open the app.

2 Tap Updates.

3 Tap Purchased.

4 If you've configured Family Sharing (see "Using Family Sharing to Share Your Store Downloads with Others" later in this chapter), tap My Purchases to download content you've purchased or tap a person whose content is being shared with you to download content that person has purchased. (The rest of these steps show the My Purchases option.)

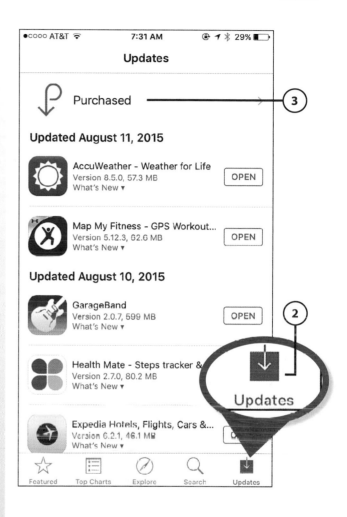

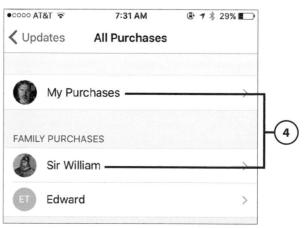

5 Tap Not on This Phone.

6 Swipe up and down the list to browse the apps you've downloaded, but that are not currently installed on your iPhone.

7 Tap the Download button for the app that you want to re-install; if prompted to do so, confirm your Apple ID by tapping the Touch ID button or entering your Apple ID and tapping OK. The app is downloaded and installed on your iPhone. When the process is complete, the OPEN button appears. This indicates that the app has been re-installed on your iPhone and is ready for you to use.

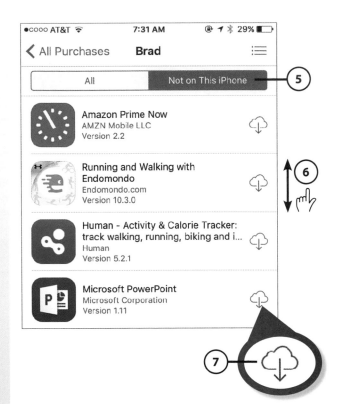

Downloading Previously Purchased iTunes Content

To download music, movies, or other content you previously downloaded, perform the following steps:

1 Open the iTunes Store app.

2 Tap More.

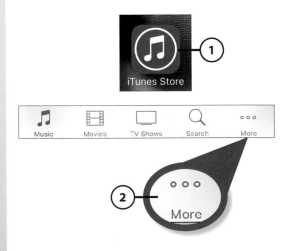

3 Tap Purchased.

4 If you've configured Family Sharing (see "Using Family Sharing to Share Your Store Downloads with Others" later in this chapter), tap Music, Movies, or TV Shows in the MY PURCHASES section to download content you've purchased or tap a person whose content is being shared with you to download content that person has purchased. The rest of these steps show the Music category in the MY PURCHASES section; the other options work similarly.

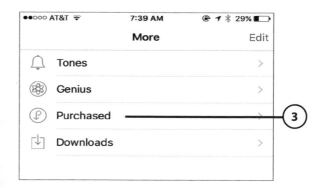

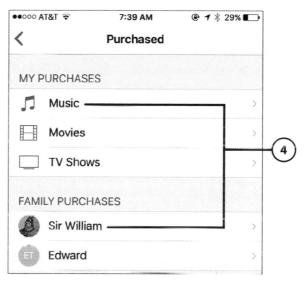

(5) Tap Not on This iPhone. The list shows all the music you've purchased from the iTunes Store but that is not currently stored on your iPhone.

(6) Swipe up and down to browse the list.

(7) Tap the artist whose music you want to download. A list of content for that artist, organized into categories such as albums or songs, is displayed.

(8) Swipe up and down the screen to browse the content you have from the artist (if you have content from only one album, skip to step 12).

(9) To download an entire album, tap its Download button and skip to step 15.

(10) To download all of the content from that artist, tap Download All and skip to step 15.

(11) To download individual songs, tap the album containing the songs you want to download.

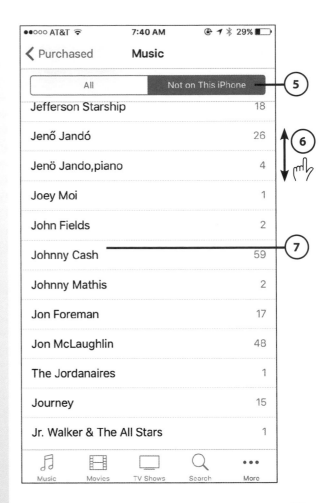

12 Browse the contents of the album.

13 Tap a song's Download button to download it and skip to step 15.

14 To download all of the album's songs, tap its Download button.

15 If prompted and you are using an iPhone 5s or later, touch the Touch ID/Home button; if you are using a different model, enter your Apple ID password and tap OK. The content is downloaded to your iPhone. When that process is complete, you can watch or listen to it in the related app, such as the Music app for songs you download.

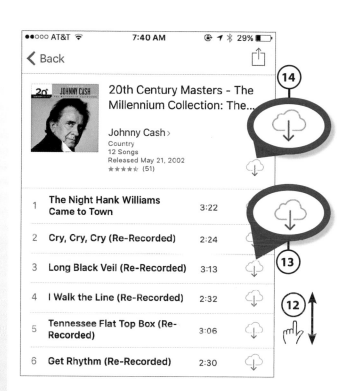

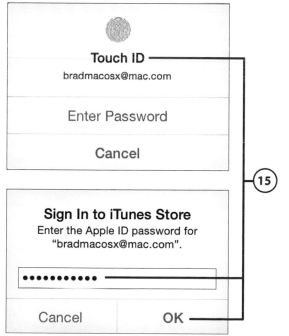

Using Family Sharing to Share Your Store Downloads with Others

With Family Sharing, you can share your apps and content with up to six other people. The people with whom you share content don't have to be related to you in any way despite the name of this feature. People with whom you share content can then download content you have purchased to their devices without needing to use your Apple ID or password.

To start using Family Sharing, you need to set it up and then designate the people with whom you will share content.

Setting Up Family Sharing

To set up Family Sharing on your iPhone, do the following:

1. Open the Settings app.
2. Tap iCloud.
3. Tap Set Up Family Sharing.

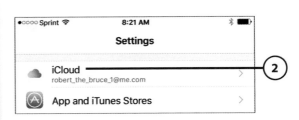

4 Tap Get Started.

5 If you want to share content under your current iCloud account, tap Continue; if you want to change accounts, tap the link at the bottom of the screen and follow the onscreen instructions to change the account you are configuring.

6 Click Agree to accept the terms and conditions (if you don't accept them, you can't use Family Sharing).

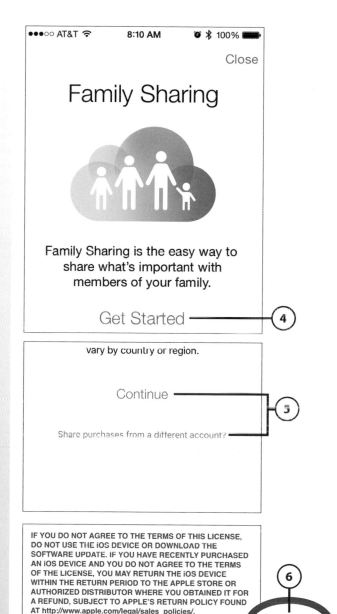

7. Tap Agree to confirm you accept the terms and conditions.

8. To accept changes on the credit card currently associated with your Apple ID, tap Continue; to change the payment method, tap Managing Family Purchases and follow the prompts to make changes.

9. To share your location with the people in your Family Sharing group, tap Share Your Location; if you prefer to not share your location, tap Not Now. You move to the Family screen and are ready to share content with others as described in the next task.

Adding People to Family Sharing

To be able to share content with someone, she must be using a device running iOS 8 or later or a Mac running OS X Yosemite or later. To share your content with someone else, add them to your Family Sharing as follows:

1. If you just completed the previous task and are still on the Family screen, skip to step 4; if this isn't the case, open the Settings app.

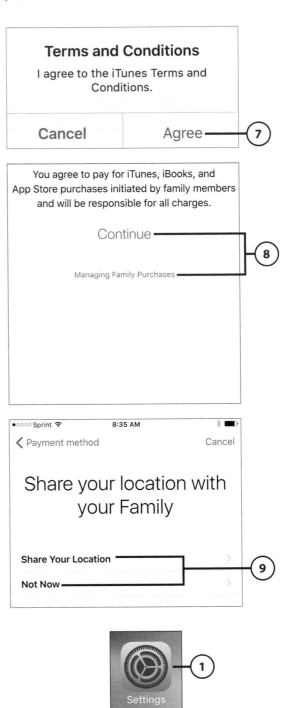

(**2**) Tap iCloud.

(**3**) Tap Family.

(**4**) Tap Add Family Member.

(**5**) Enter the email address of the person with whom you are sharing content and then select the person when he appears on the list. An invitation is sent to the person with whom you are sharing content.

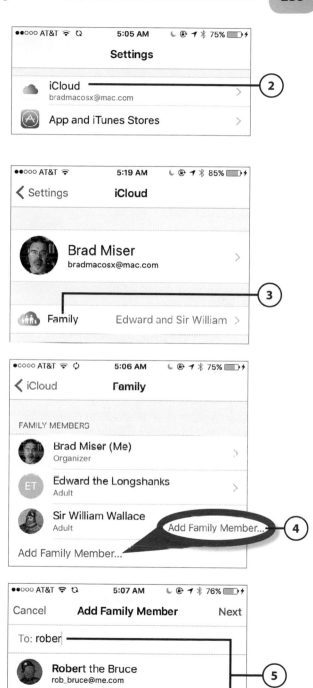

6 Enter your Apple ID password and tap OK.

7 Enter the three-digit security code located on the back of the credit card associated with your account.

8 Tap Next. An invitation is sent to the person you are inviting to share your content.

You return to the Family screen where you see the person whom you invited to share content. You see the Invitation sent status under the person's name.

When the person receives your invitation and taps Get Started, he is led through the process of accepting your invitation. Once accepted, the person's status becomes "Adult" or "Child" on your Family screen. This means the person can download content you've purchased from the App or iTunes Stores just like you can download your own content (see "Accessing Shared Content" later in this chapter for details).

Sign In to iCloud

Enter the password for your Apple ID "bradmacosx@mac.com".

Cancel   OK

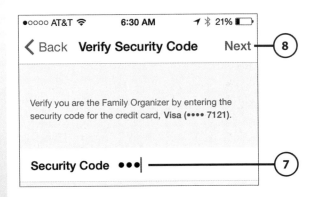

‹ Back   **Verify Security Code**   Next

Verify you are the Family Organizer by entering the security code for the credit card, Visa (•••• 7121).

Security Code •••

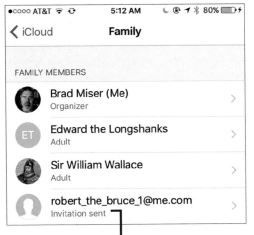

‹ iCloud   **Family**

FAMILY MEMBERS

Brad Miser (Me)
Organizer

Edward the Longshanks
Adult

Sir William Wallace
Adult

robert_the_bruce_1@me.com
Invitation sent

This person will be able to share your content when he accepts your invitation

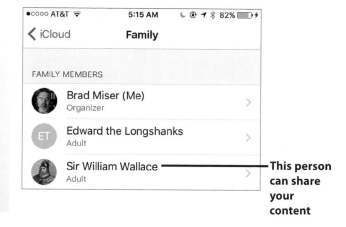

This person can share your content

Create an Apple ID for a Child

If the person with whom you want to share content doesn't have an account, you can create an Apple ID for that person. Tap Create an Apple ID for a child at the bottom of the Family screen. Tap Next. You then have to indicate you had parental consent, confirm your payment information, enter the child's birthday, enter the child's name, create the Apple ID and password, and configure security questions. (A child is considered to be 13 or under.) You then turn Ask to Buy on or off. If you leave it on, you will have to approve a purchase the child tries to make; if you turn it off, you won't have to approve purchases. Note that any purchases the child makes use the payment information associated with your account. Finally, you accept the terms and conditions. Once the account is created, provide the Apple ID and password to the child, and he will be able to purchase apps and iTunes Store content under your account.

Birthdays

If the person whom you are trying to add to Family Sharing doesn't have a birthday configured in her iCloud settings, you might not be able to complete the process. Ask that person to update her birthday in her iCloud settings, either on her iOS device or via the iCloud website.

Managing Family Sharing

You can use the Family screen to manage the people with whom you are sharing content. When you access the Family screen, you see the people with whom you are sharing content and their status.

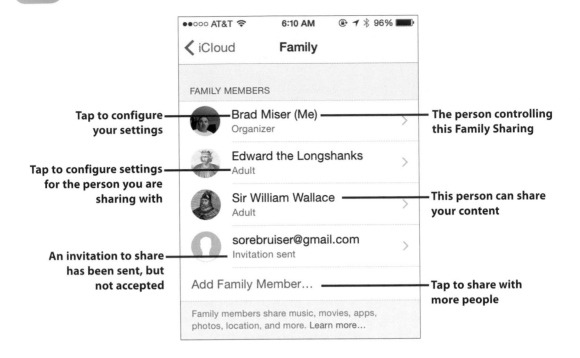

Tap to configure your settings → Brad Miser (Me) Organizer — ← The person controlling this Family Sharing

Tap to configure settings for the person you are sharing with → Edward the Longshanks Adult

Sir William Wallace Adult — ← This person can share your content

An invitation to share has been sent, but not accepted → sorebruiser@gmail.com Invitation sent

Add Family Member... — ← Tap to share with more people

Tap your name (the organizer) to perform the following tasks:

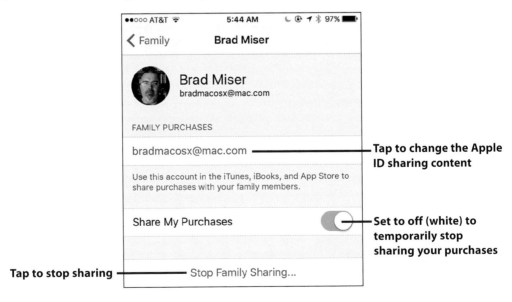

bradmacosx@mac.com — ← Tap to change the Apple ID sharing content

Share My Purchases — ← Set to off (white) to temporarily stop sharing your purchases

Tap to stop sharing — Stop Family Sharing...

- If you tap the email address, you can change the Apple ID being used to share. People who are currently sharing your content will lose access to your content if you change the account being used to share.

- Set the Share My Purchases switch to off (white) if you don't want those with whom you are sharing to be able to share your content. Set the Share My Purchases switch to on (green) to resume sharing your content.

- Tap Stop Family Sharing and then tap Stop Sharing at the prompt to turn Family Sharing off (see the following It's Not All Good before doing this).

It's Not All Good

You can only stop Family Sharing twice during a year. If you stop it twice, you're unable to use it again until a year passes. If you want to prevent others from sharing your content, set the Share My Purchases switch to off (white) because this doesn't limit your ability to access Family Sharing.

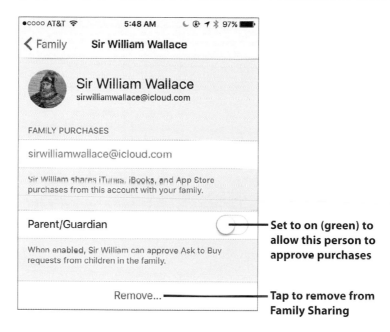

Tap the name of people with whom you are sharing to perform the following tasks:

- Set the Parent/Guardian switch to on (green) to allow the person to approve purchases others make.

- Tap Remove and then tap Remove at the prompt to remove the person from Family Sharing. He is no longer able to access shared content and disappears from the list of people shown on the Family screen.

Accessing Shared Content

Accessing content being shared via Family Sharing is very similar to downloading apps and iTunes Store content previously purchased (see "Downloading Previously Purchased App Store Apps" and "Downloading Previously Purchased iTunes Content"). Following is an example of downloading iTunes content being shared with you (other people can use the same steps to download content you are sharing with them):

1. Using steps 1 through 3 in "Downloading Previously Purchased iTunes Content," move to the Purchased screen of the iTunes app.

2. Tap the person sharing content with you.

3. Tap the type of content you want to download.

4. Tap Not on This iPhone. You see the content being shared with you.

5. Tap the content you want to download.

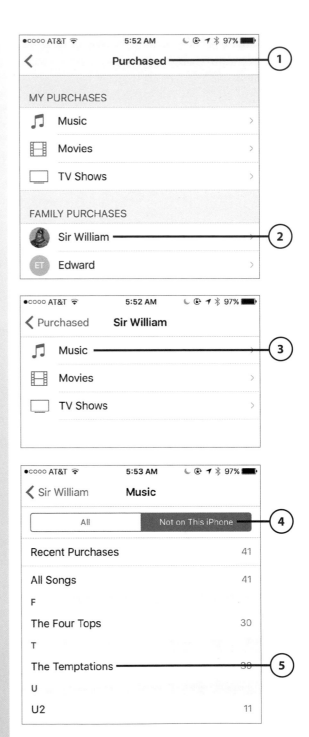

6 Tap Download All to download all the content you see. Tap the download button next to individual items to download specific content, or tap an item (such as album) to explore its content. These options work just like downloading content you purchased from the iTunes Store. When the content is downloaded to your iPhone, you can use the related app to listen to or watch it.

Share and Share Alike

When a person is added to the group shown on the Family tab, any content purchased by any member is immediately available to be shared with all the other members of the group. You should periodically check the Not on This iPhone tab for the people sharing with you to see what new content is available.

Use Settings to configure how contacts are displayed

Tap here to work with your contact information

Use your contact information in many apps

In this chapter, you learn how to ensure that your iPhone has the contact information you need when you need it. Topics include the following:

→ Getting started
→ Setting your Contacts preferences
→ Creating contacts on your iPhone
→ Working with contacts on your iPhone
→ Managing your contacts on your iPhone

Managing Contacts

You'll be using your iPhone to make calls, get directions, send emails, and for many other tasks that require contact information, including names, phone numbers, email addresses, and physical addresses. It would be time consuming and a nuisance to have to remember and re-type this information each time you use it. Fortunately, you don't have to do either because the Contacts app puts all your contact information at your fingertips (literally).

Getting Started

The Contacts app makes using your contact information extremely easy. This information is readily available on your phone in all the apps, such as Mail, Messages, and Phone, in which you need it. And, you don't need to remember or type the information because you can enter it by choosing someone's name, a business' name, or other information that you know about the contact. You can also access your contact information directly in the Contacts app and take action on it (such as placing a call).

To use contact information, it must be in the Contacts app. This can be accomplished in several ways. When you configure an online account on your iPhone, such as iCloud or Google, to include contact information, the contact information stored in that account is immediately available on your phone without you having to do anything else. (See Chapter 3, "Setting Up and Using iCloud and Other Online Accounts" for the steps to enable contact information in online accounts.) You can manually add new contact information to the Contacts app by capturing that information when you perform tasks (such as reading email). You can also enter new contact information directly in the Contacts app.

The Contacts app also makes it easy to keep your contact information current, such as adding more information, updating existing contacts, or removing contacts you no longer need.

Setting Your Contacts Preferences

Using the Settings app, you can determine how contacts are sorted and displayed, if or how names are shortened on various screens, your contact information, and which account should be the default for contact information.

Following is an example showing how to configure your information in the Contacts app. This is an important setting because it is how your phone identifies you, such as when Siri says your name, when you want to get directions home, or when you have Safari automatically fill in forms. You can configure other Contacts settings using similar steps and the descriptions of the settings in the table that follows these steps.

(1) On the Home screen, tap Settings.

(2) Swipe up the screen until you see Mail, Contacts, Calendars.

(3) Tap Mail, Contacts, Calendars.

(4) Swipe up the screen until you see the Contacts section.

(5) Tap My Info.

(6) Browse or search the All Contacts screen (to learn different ways to browse this screen, jump ahead to the section called "Using the Contacts App," and then come back here).

(7) Tap your name. This tells the Contacts app your contact information, which it can insert for you in various places; your contact information is indicated by the label "me" next to the alphabetical index. You return to the Mail, Contacts, Calendars screen where your name appears next to My Info. The following table explains the rest of the Contacts settings options in case you want to make changes to them.

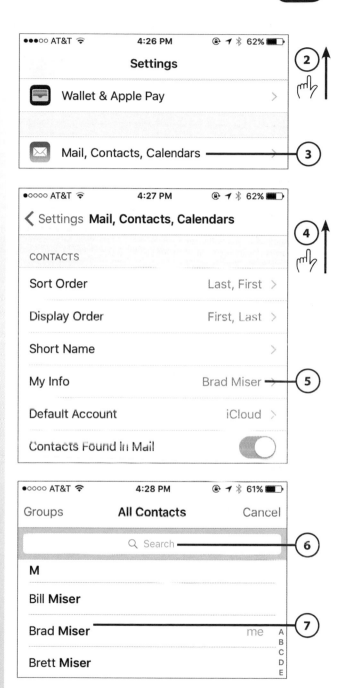

Contacts Settings on the Mail, Contacts, Calendars Screen

Setting	Description
Sort Order	Tap First, Last to have contacts sorted by first name and then last name or tap Last, First to have contacts sorted by last name and then first name.
Display Order	To show contacts in the format *first name, last name,* tap First, Last. To show contacts in the format *last name, first name,* tap Last, First.
Short Name	You can choose whether short names are used and, if they are, what form they take. Short names are useful because more contact information can be displayed in a smaller area, and they look "friendlier." To use short names, move the Short Name switch to the on position (green). Tap the format of short name you want to use. You can choose from a combination of initial and name or just first or last name. If you want nicknames for contacts used for the short name when available, set the Prefer Nicknames switch to on (green).
My Info	Use this setting to find and tap your contact information in the Contacts app, which it can insert for you in various places and which Siri can use to call you by name; your current contact information is indicated by the label "me" next to the alphabetical index.
Default Account	Tap the account in which you want new contacts to be created by default (which is then marked with a check mark); if you want new contacts to be created on your iPhone instead of under an account, tap On My iPhone. If you have only one account configured for contacts, you don't have this option.
Contacts Found in Mail	If you don't want contact information in the Mail app to be used, such as to automatically complete addresses when you create emails, or try to identify callers when a number calling you is unknown, set the Contacts Found in Mail switch to off (white). You typically should leave this on (green) unless you find the automatic contact suggestions annoying or not helpful.

Where Contacts are Stored

You can store your contacts in an online account (for example, iCloud or Google), which is good because it makes the information accessible on many devices and keeps it backed up. If you don't have an online account, contact information is stored on your iPhone. This is not ideal because, if something happens to your phone, you can lose all of your contacts. You should use at least one online account for storing your contacts (see Chapter 3, "Setting Up and Using iCloud and Other Online Accounts," for detailed information about online accounts).

Creating Contacts on Your iPhone

In this section, you learn how to create a new contact starting with information in an email message and how to create a new contact manually.

Creating New Contacts from Email

When you receive an email, you can easily create a contact to capture the email address.

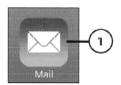

① On the Home screen, tap Mail.

② Use the Mail app to read an email message (see Chapter 9, "Sending, Receiving, and Managing Email," for details).

③ Tap the email address from which you want to create a new contact. You see as much information as could be gleaned from the email address, which is typically the sender's name and email address.

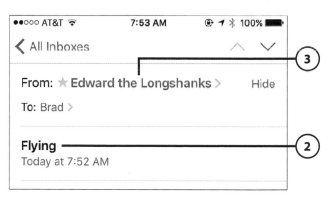

4) Tap Create New Contact. The New Contact screen appears. The name, email address, and any other information that can be identified is added to the new contact.

5) Use the New Contact screen to enter more contact information or update the information that was added. This works just like when you create a new contact manually, except that you already have some information filled in for you—most likely, a name and an email address. For details on adding and changing more information for the contact, see the next task, which is "Creating Contacts Manually."

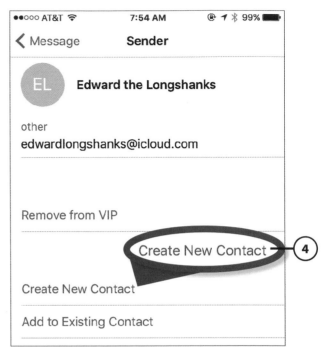

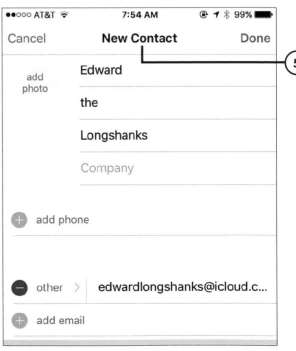

>>>Go Further

MORE ON CREATING CONTACTS FROM APPS

It's useful to be able to create contact information by starting with some information in an app. Keep these points in mind:

- Mail is only one of the apps from which you can create contacts. You can start a contact in just about any app you use to communicate or get information, such as Messages and Maps. The steps to start a contact in these apps are similar to those for Mail. Tap the person or address for which you want to create a contact, and then tap Create New Contact. The Contacts app fills in as much of the information as it can, and you can complete the rest yourself.

- You can also add more contact information to an existing contact from an app you are currently using. You can do this by tapping Add to Existing Contact instead of Create New Contact. You then search for and select the contact to which you want to add the additional information. After it's saved, the additional information is associated with the contact you selected. For example, suppose you have created a contact for a company but all you have is its phone number. You can quickly add the address to the contact by using the Maps app to look it up and then add the address to the company's existing contact information by tapping the location, tapping Add to Existing Contact, and selecting the company in your contacts.

Creating Contacts Manually

Most of the time, you'll want to get the information for a new contact from an app, as the previous task demonstrated, or through an online account, such as contacts stored in your iCloud account. If these aren't available, you can start a contact from scratch and manually add all the information you need to it. Also, you use the same steps to add information to or change information for an existing contact that you do to create a new one, so even if you don't start from scratch often, you do need to know how to add and update contact information.

The Contacts app leads you through creating each type of information you might want to capture. You can choose to enter some or all of the default information on the New Contact screen, or add additional fields as needed. The following steps show creating a new contact containing the most common contact information you are likely to need:

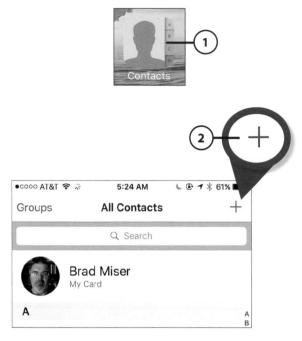

(1) On the Home screen, tap Contacts. (If you don't see the Contacts app on the Home screen, open the Extras folder to see if it is in there.) The All Contacts screen displays.

If you see the Groups screen instead, tap Done to move to the All Contacts screen.

If you have only one account that provides contact information, you see its contact list rather than the All Contacts screen, and you are ready to create a new contact.

(2) Tap the Add button. The New Contact screen appears with the default fields.

(3) To associate a photo with the contact, tap add photo. You can choose a photo already on your phone or take a new photo. These steps show using an existing photo. (See the "Taking Photos" note for the steps to take a new photo.)

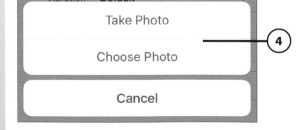

(4) Tap Choose Photo.

(5) Use the Photos app to move to, select, and configure the photo you want to associate with the contact (see Chapter 14, "Working with Photos and Video You Take with Your iPhone," for help with the Photos app).

(6) Tap Choose.

(7) Tap in the First field and enter the contact's first name; if you are creating a contact for an organization only, leave both name fields empty.

(8) Tap in the Last field and enter the contact's last name.

(9) Enter the organization, such as a company, with which you want to associate the contact, if any.

(10) To add a phone number, tap add phone. A new phone field appears along with the numeric keypad.

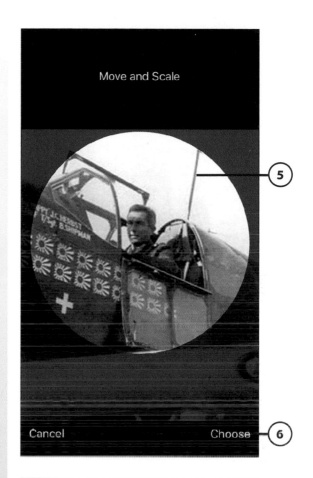

Taking Photos

To take a new photo for a contact, tap Take Photo in step 4 instead of Choose Photo. The Camera app opens. Use that app to take the photo (see Chapter 14). Then use the Move and Scale screen to adjust the photo so it is what you want to use. When it looks right, tap Use Photo.

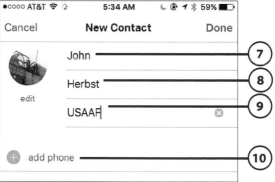

11 Use the numeric keypad to enter the contact's phone number. Include any prefixes you need to dial it, such as area code and country code. The app formats the number for you as you enter it.

12 Tap the label for the phone number, such as home, to change it to another label.

13 Swipe up and down the Label screen to see all the options available.

14 Tap the label you want to apply to the number, such as iPhone.

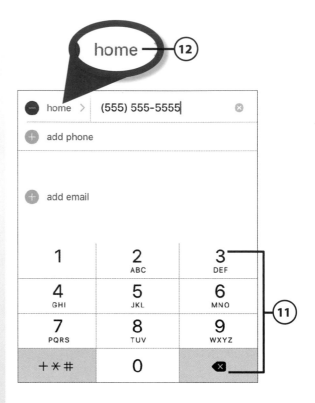

15 Repeat steps 10–14 to add more phone numbers to the contact.

16 Swipe up the screen until you see add email.

17 Tap add email. The keyboard appears.

18 Type the contact's email address.

19 Tap the label for the email address to change it.

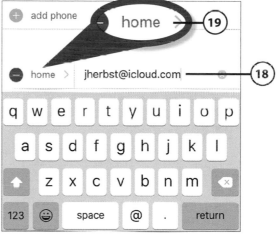

20. Tap the label you want to apply to the email address.

21. Repeat steps 17–20 to add more email addresses.

22. Swipe up the screen until you see Ringtone.

23. Tap Ringtone. The list of ringtones and alert tones available on your iPhone appears.

24. Swipe up and down the list to see all of the tones available.

25. Tap the ringtone you want to play when the contact calls you. When you tap a ringtone, it plays so you can experiment to find the one that best relates to the contact. Setting a specific ringtone helps you identify a caller without looking at the phone.

26. Tap Done. You return to the New Contact screen, where the tone you selected appears.

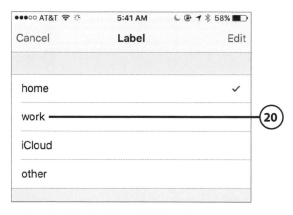

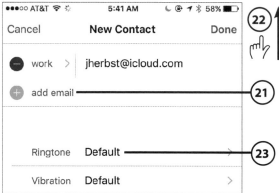

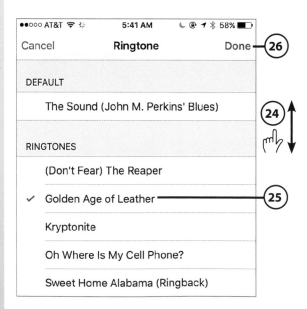

27) Using the pattern you have learned in the previous steps, move to the next item you want to set and tap it.

28) Use the resulting screens to enter the information you want to configure for the contact. After you've done a couple of the fields, it is easy to do the rest because the same pattern is used throughout.

29) When you've added all the information you want to capture, tap Done. The New Contact screen closes and the new contact is created and ready for you to use whenever you need the information it contains. It is also moved onto other devices with which your contact information is synced.

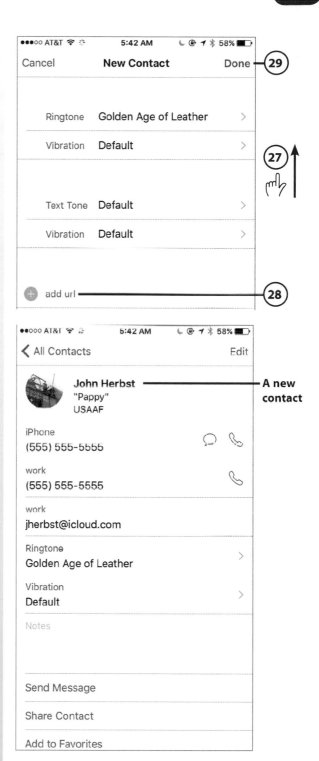

A new contact

>>>Go Further

CREATING CONTACTS EXPANDED

Contacts are useful in many ways so you should make sure you have all the contact information you need. Here are a few points to ponder:

- You can (and should) sync contacts on multiple devices (computers and other iOS devices) by using iCloud, Gmail, or other similar accounts to store your contact information on the cloud from where all your devices can access it. Refer to Chapter 3 for the details of setting up an account through which you can sync your contacts.

- By the way, syncing your contacts works in both directions. Any new contacts you create, or any changes you make to existing contact information on your iPhone, move back to your other devices through the sync process. The bottom line is that you always have the same contact information available no matter which device you are using.

- To remove a field in which you've entered information, tap the red circle with a dash in it next to the field and then tap Delete. If you haven't entered information into a field, just ignore it because empty fields don't appear on a contact's screen.

- The address format on the screens in the Contacts app is determined by the country you associate with the address. If the current country isn't the one you want, tap it and select the country in which the address is located before you enter any information. The fields appropriate for that country's addresses appear on the screen.

- If you want to add a type of information that doesn't appear on the New Contact screen, swipe up the screen and tap add field. A list of additional fields you can add displays. Tap a field to add it; for example, tap Nickname to add a nickname for the contact. Then, enter the information for that new field.

- When you add more fields to contact information, those fields appear in the appropriate context on the Info screen. For example, if you add a nickname, it is placed at the top of the screen with the other "name" information. If you add an address, it appears with the other address information.

Working with Contacts on Your iPhone

There are many ways to use contact information. The first step is always finding the contact information you need, typically by using the Contacts app. Whether you access it directly or through another app (such as Mail), it works the same way. Then, you select the information you want to use or the action you want to perform.

Using the Contacts App

You can access your contact information directly in the Contacts app. For example, you can search or browse for a contact and then view the detailed information for the contact in which you are interested.

(1) On the Home screen, tap Contacts. The Contacts screen displays.

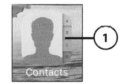

The title of the screen depends on what you have selected to view. The screen is labeled All Contacts or Contacts. If the label is Contacts, you are browsing only some of your contacts based on the contact groups you have elected to view. (If the Groups screen appears, tap Done. You move back to the All Contacts or Contacts screen.)

You can find a contact to view by browsing (step 2), using the index (step 3), or searching (step 4). You can use combinations of these, too, such as first using the index to get to the right area and then browsing to find the contact in which you are interested.

2 Swipe up or down to scroll the screen to browse for contact information; swipe up or down on the alphabetical index to browse rapidly.

3 Tap the index to jump to contact information organized by the first letter of the format selected in the Contact Preferences (last name or first name).

4 Use the Search tool to search for a specific contact; tap in the tool, type the name (you can type last, first, company, or nickname), and then tap the contact you want to view on the results list.

5 To view a contact's information, tap the contact you want to see.

6 Swipe up and down the screen to view all the contact's information.

7 Tap the data or icons on the screen to perform actions, including the following:

- **Phone numbers**—Tap a phone number or the receiver icon to call it.

- **Email addresses**—Tap an email address to create a new message to it.

- **URLs**—Tap a URL to open Safari and move to the associated website.

- **Addresses**—Tap an address to show it in the Maps app.

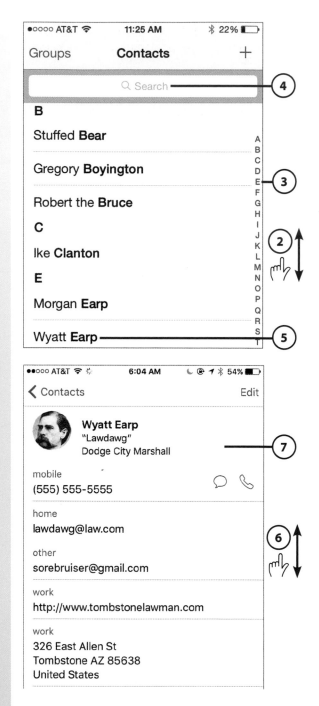

- **FaceTime**—Tap FaceTime to start a FaceTime call with the contact.

- **Text**—Tap Send Message, or the quote bubble icon, and choose the phone number or email address to which you want to send a text message.

- **Share Contact**—Tap Share Contact. The Share menu appears. To share the contact via email, tap Mail; to share it via a text, tap Message; or to share it using AirDrop, tap AirDrop. You can also share via Twitter or Facebook. Then, use the associated app to complete the task.

- **Favorites**— Tap Add to Favorites and choose the phone number or email address you want to designate as a favorite. You can use this in the associated app to do something faster. For example, if it's the Phone app, you can tap the Favorites tab to see your favorite contacts and quickly dial one by tapping it. You can add multiple items (such as cell and work phone numbers) as favorites for one contact.

(**8**) To return to the Contacts list without performing an action, tap Contacts.

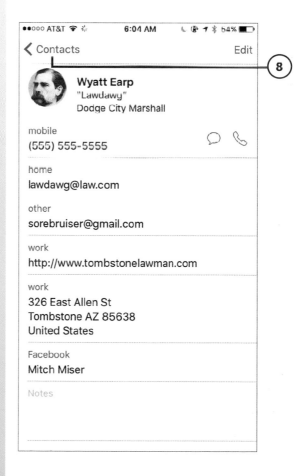

>>>Go Further

MAKE CONTACT

When working with your contacts, keep the following points in mind:

- **Last known contact**—The Contacts app remembers where you last were and takes you back there whenever you move into the Contacts app. For example, if you view a contact's details and then switch to a different app to send a message, and then back to Contacts, you are returned to the screen you were last viewing. To move back to the main Contacts screen, tap Contacts in the upper-left corner of the screen.

- **Groups**—In a contact app on a computer, such as Contacts on a Mac, contacts can be organized into groups, which in turn can be stored in an online account, such as iCloud. When you sync, the groups of contacts move onto the iPhone. You can limit the contacts you browse or search; tap Groups on the Contacts screen.

  The Groups screen displays the accounts (such as iCloud or Google) with which you are syncing contact information; under each account are the groups of contacts stored in that account. If a group has a check mark next to it, its contacts are displayed on the Contacts screen. To hide a group's contacts, tap it so that the check mark disappears. To hide or show all of a group's contacts, tap the All account, where account is the name of the account in which those contacts are stored. To make browsing contacts easier, tap Hide All Contacts to hide all the groups and contacts; then, tap each group whose contacts you want to show on the Contacts screen.

  Tap Done to move back to the Contacts screen.

- **Speaking of contacts**—You can use Siri to speak commands to work with contacts, too. You can get information about contacts by asking for it, such as "What is William Wallace's work phone number?" If you want to see all of a contact's information, you can say "Show me William Wallace." When Siri displays contact information, you can tap it to take action, such as tapping a phone number to call it. (See Chapter 12, "Working with Siri," for more on using Siri.)

Accessing Contacts from Other Apps

You have access to information stored in the Contacts app while you are using a different app. For example, you can use a contact's email address when you create an email message. When you perform such actions, the app you are in uses the information stored in the Contacts app to find and select the contact information you want to use. The following example shows using contact information to send an email message. The steps for accessing your contact information from other apps (such as Phone or Messages) are similar.

1. Open the app from which you want to access contact information (this example uses Mail).

2. Tap the New Message button.

3. In the To: field, tap the Add button.

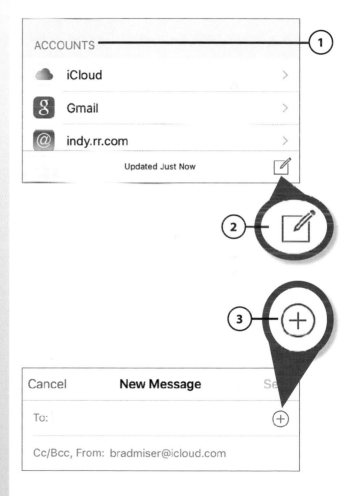

(4) Search, browse, or use the index to find the contact whose information you want to use.

(5) Tap the contact whose information you want to use. (If a contact doesn't have relevant information, for example, if no email address is configured when you are using the Mail app, that contact is grayed out and can't be selected.)

If the contact has only one type of the relevant information (such as a single email address, if you started in the Mail app), you immediately move back to the app. The appropriate information is entered, and you can skip to step 7.

(6) If the contact has multiple entries of the type you are trying to use, tap the information you want to use—in this case, the email address. The information is copied into the app and entered in the appropriate location.

(7) Complete the rest of the task you are doing, such as sending an email message.

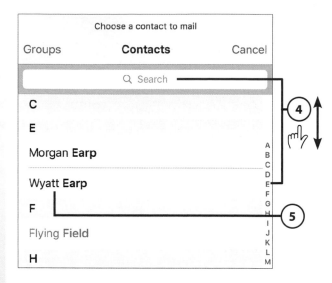

The email address from the Contacts app

Managing Your Contacts on Your iPhone

When you sync contacts with an iCloud, Google, or other account, the changes go both ways. For example, when you change a contact on the iPhone, the synced contact manager application, such as Outlook, makes the changes for those contacts on your computer. Likewise, when you change contact information in a contact manager on your computer, those changes move to the iPhone. If you add a new contact in a contact manager, it moves to the iPhone, and vice versa. You can also change contacts manually in the Contacts app.

Updating Contact Information

You can change any information for an existing contact, such as adding new email addresses, deleting outdated information, and changing existing information.

(**1**) View the contact's Info screen.

(**2**) Tap Edit. The Info screen moves into Edit mode, and you see Unlock buttons.

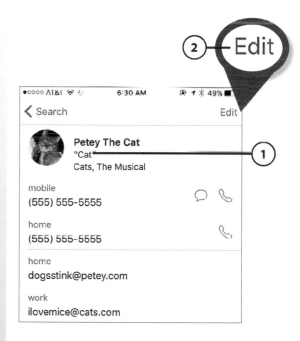

3 Tap current information to change it; you can change a field's label by tapping it, or you can change the data for the field by tapping the information you want to change. Use the resulting tools, such as the phone number entry keypad, to make changes to the information. These tools work just like when you create a new contact (refer to "Creating Contacts Manually," earlier in this chapter).

4 To add more fields, tap add in the related section, such as add phone in the phone number section; then, select a label for the new field and complete its information. This also works just like adding a new field to a contact you created manually.

5 To remove information from the contact, tap its Unlock button.

6 Tap Delete. The information is removed from the contact.

7 To change the contact's photo, tap the current photo, or the word *edit* under the current photo, and use the resulting menu and tools to select a new photo, take a new photo, delete the existing photo, or edit the existing one.

8 When you finish making changes, tap Done. Your changes are saved, and you move out of Edit mode.

No Tones or Vibes?

If you leave the default tones or vibration patterns set for a contact, you won't see those fields when you view the contact. However, when you edit a contact, all the fields you need to add these to a contact become available.

Adding Information to an Existing Contact While Using Your iPhone

As you use your iPhone, you'll encounter information related to a contact that isn't currently part of that contact's information. For example, a contact might send you an email from a different email address than the one you have stored for her. When this happens, you can easily add the new information to the existing contact. Tap the information (such as an email address) to select it, and then tap Add to Existing Contact. Next, select the existing contact to which you want to add the new information. The selected information is added to the contact. Tap Done to save the information and return to the app you were using.

Deleting Contacts

To get rid of contacts, you can delete them from the Contacts app.

1. Find and view the contact you want to delete.

2. Tap Edit.

3. Swipe to the bottom of the Info screen.

4. Tap Delete Contact.

5. Tap Delete Contact again to confirm the deletion. The app deletes the contact, and you return to the Contacts screen.

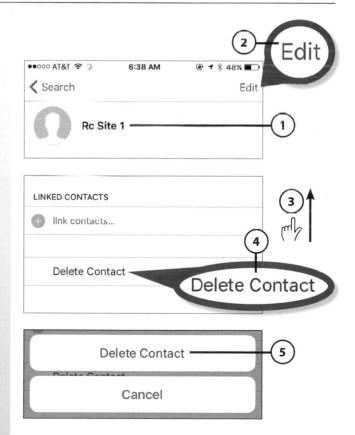

Tap to configure Phone and FaceTime settings

Tap to hear *and see* the person with whom you want to talk

Tap to make calls, listen to voicemail, and more

In this chapter, you explore all the cell phone and FaceTime functionality that your iPhone has to offer. The topics include the following:

→ Getting started
→ Configuring phone settings
→ Making voice calls
→ Managing in-process voice calls
→ Receiving voice calls
→ Managing voice calls
→ Using visual voicemail
→ Communicating with FaceTime

8

Communicating with the Phone and FaceTime Apps

Although it's also a lot of other great things, such as a music player, web browser, email tool, and such, there's a reason the word *phone* is in *iPhone*. It's a feature-rich cell phone that includes some amazing features, two of which are visual voicemail and FaceTime. Other useful features include a speakerphone, conference calling, and easy-to-use onscreen controls. Plus your iPhone's phone functions are integrated with its other features. For example, when using the Maps application, you might find a location, such as a business, that you're interested in contacting. You can call that location just by tapping the number you want to call directly on the Maps screen.

Getting Started

Some of the key concepts you'll learn about in this chapter include:

- **Phone App**—The iPhone can run many different kinds of apps that do all sorts of useful things. The iPhone's cell phone functionality is provided by the Phone app. You use this app whenever you want to make calls, answer calls, or listen to voicemail.

- **Visual Voicemail**—The Phone app shows you information about your voicemails, such as the person who left each message, a time and date stamp, and the length of the message. The Phone app provides a lot more control over your messages, too; for example, you can easily fast forward to specific parts of a message that you want to hear. (This is particularly helpful for capturing information, such as phone numbers.)

- **FaceTime**—This app enables you to have videoconferences with other people so that you can both see and hear them. Using FaceTime is intuitive so you won't find it any more difficult than making a phone call.

- **FaceTime Audio Only**—You can make FaceTime calls using only audio; this is similar to making a phone call. One difference is that when you are using a Wi-Fi network to place a FaceTime audio call, there are no extra costs for the call, no matter if you are calling someone next-door or halfway around the world.

Configuring Phone Settings

Use the iPhone's Sounds settings to configure custom or standard ringtones and other phone-related sounds, including the new voicemail sound. These are explained in Chapter 5, "Customizing How Your iPhone Looks and Sounds."

You can also have different ringtones for specific people so you can know who is calling just by the ringtone (configuring contacts is explained in Chapter 7, "Managing Contacts").

And, you'll want to configure notifications for the Phone app. These include alerts, the app's badge, and notification sounds. Configuring notifications is also explained in Chapter 5.

There are a number of Phone-specific options you can configure using the Settings app. Following is an example showing how to enable other devices you have to be able to answer calls coming to your iPhone and place calls through your phone. For example, if you are using an iPad when a call comes to your iPhone, you can answer the call on the iPad and have the conversation with it, even though the caller called your iPhone. You can configure other Phone app settings using similar steps and the descriptions of the Phone app settings in the table that follows these steps. To enable other devices to take and place calls through your iPhone, perform the following steps:

1. On the Home screen, tap Settings.

2. Swipe up the screen until you see Phone.

3. Tap Phone.

4. Tap Calls on Other Devices.

5. Set the Allow Calls on Other Devices switch to on (green). You see other devices on which you are signed into the same iCloud account and are also using that account for FaceTime (you learn how to configure this later in this chapter).

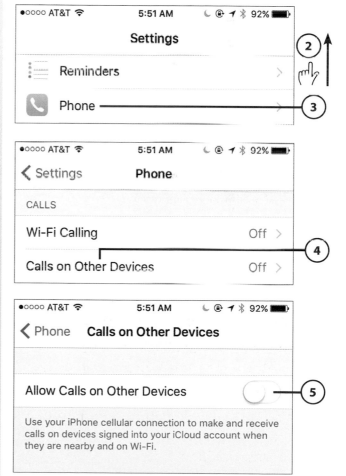

6 To enable a device to receive or place calls, set its switch to on (green). (A device must be on the same Wi-Fi network as your iPhone to be able to receive calls.)

7 To prevent calls from coming to a device, set its switch to off (white).

8 Tap Phone. You can also change the other Phone settings, which are described in the following table.

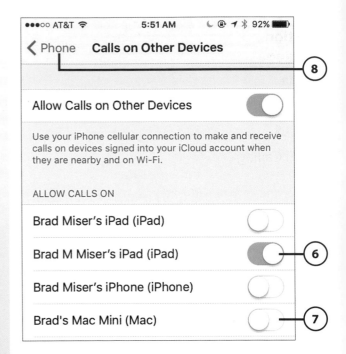

Provider Differences

The settings for the Phone app depend on the cell phone provider you use. The table lists most, but certainly not all, of the options you may have available. Depending on the provider you use, you may see more, fewer, or different settings than shown in the table. It's a good idea to open your Phone settings to see the options available to you.

Phone Settings

Section Setting	Description
None	
My Number	Shows your phone number for reference purposes.
CALLS	
Wi-Fi Calling	When enabled, you can place and receive calls via a Wi-Fi network. This is particularly useful when you are in a location with poor cellular reception, but you have access to a Wi-Fi network. When you set the Wi-Fi Calling on This iPhone switch to on (green), you're prompted to confirm your information. When you do, the service starts and you see the Update Emergency Address option; this is used to record your address so if you can place emergency calls via Wi-Fi, your location can be determined. Note that even when you see this option, it might not be supported in your area yet.
Calls on Other Devices	When enabled, and your iPhone is on the same network as other iOS devices (such as iPads) or Macs, you can take incoming calls and place calls from those devices. This can be useful when you aren't near your phone or simply want to use a different device to have a phone conversation. It can also be annoying because when a call comes in, all the devices using this feature start "ringing." When the Allow Calls on Other Devices switch is on (green), you can choose the specific devices calls are allowed on by setting their switches to on (green).
Respond with Text	When calls come in, you have the option to respond with text. For example, you might want to say "Can't talk now, will call later." There are three default text responses or you can use this setting to create your own custom text responses.

Section Setting	Description
Call Forwarding	Enables you to forward incoming calls to a different phone number.
Call Waiting	Enables or disables the call waiting feature.
Show My Caller ID	Shows or hides your caller id information when you place a call.
Blocked	Enables you to block incoming calls and text messages. Step-by-step instructions to block calls are in the online Chapter 16, "Maintaining and Protecting Your iPhone and Solving Problems."
TTY	TTY devices enable hearing-impaired people to use a telephone. To use TTY with your iPhone, you need an adapter to connect your iPhone to a TTY device. You also need to turn on TTY support by turning the TTY switch to on (green).
None	
Change Voicemail Password	Use this option to change your voicemail password.
Dial Assist	Enable the Dial Assist feature, if you want the correct country code to be added to numbers in your country when dialing those numbers from outside your country or if you want the correct area codes to be added when you dial a local number. For example, if you live in the United States and don't want the correct prefixes added to U.S. phone numbers when you dial them from outside the United States, turn Dial Assist off (white). You then have to add any prefixes manually when dialing a U.S. number from outside the United States.

Section Setting	Description
SIM PIN	Your iPhone uses a Subscriber Identity Module (SIM) card to store certain data about your phone; the SIM PIN setting enables you to associate a personal ID number (PIN) with the SIM card in an iPhone. To use your account with a different phone, you can remove the SIM card from your iPhone and install it in other phones that support these cards. If you set a PIN, that PIN is required to use the card in a different phone.
Provider Services, where *Provider* is the name of your provider	This area provides information about your account such as the numbers you can dial for checking balances, paying bills, and other account management. You can also access your account by tapping the link at the bottom of the screen.

Making Voice Calls

There are a number of ways to make calls with your iPhone; after a call is in progress, you can manage it in the same way no matter how you started it.

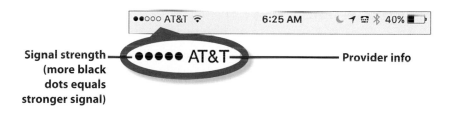

Signal strength (more black dots equals stronger signal)

Provider info

You can tell you are able to make a call or receive calls using your cellular network when you see your provider's information at the top of the screen along with strength of the signal your phone is receiving. As long as you see at least one dark dot, you should be able to place and receive calls via the cellular network. More dots are better because they mean you have a stronger signal, meaning the call quality will be better.

If the Wi-Fi calling feature is enabled and your phone is connected to a Wi-Fi network, you see the Wi-Fi calling icon for your provider at the top of the screen.

With a reasonably strong cellular signal or connection to a Wi-Fi network with Wi-Fi calling enabled, you are ready to make calls.

Which Network?

When you leave the coverage area for your provider and move into an area that is covered by another provider that supports roaming, your iPhone automatically connects to the other provider's network. When you are roaming, you see a different provider near the signal strength indicator at the top of the screen. For example, if AT&T is your provider and you travel to Toronto, Canada, the provider might become Rogers instead of AT&T, which indicates you are roaming. (In some cases, your provider might send you a text message explaining the change in networks, including information about roaming charges.) Although the connection is automatic, you need to be very aware of roaming charges, which can be significant depending on where you use your iPhone and what your default network is. Before you travel outside of your default network's coverage area, check with your provider to determine the roaming rates that apply to where you are going. Also, see if there is a discounted roaming plan for that location. If you don't do this before you leave, you might get a nasty surprise when the bill arrives showing substantial roaming charges.

Dialing with the Keypad

The most obvious way to make a call is to dial the number.

1. On the Home screen, tap Phone. The Phone apps opens.

2. If you don't see the keypad, tap Keypad.

3. Tap numbers on the keypad to dial the number you want to call. If you dial a number associated with one or more contacts, you see the contact's name and the type of number you've dialed just under the number. (If you make a mistake in the number you are dialing, tap the Delete button located to the right of the number you are dialing at the top of the screen to delete the most recent digit you entered.)

4. Tap the receiver button. The app dials the number, and the Call screen appears.

5. Use the Call screen to manage the call; see "Managing In-Process Voice Calls" later in this chapter for the details.

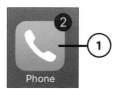

Number you are calling

Delete

Contact whose number it is

Dialing with Contacts

As you saw in Chapter 7, the Contacts app is a complete contact manager so you can store various kinds of phone numbers for people and organizations. To make a call using a contact, follow these steps.

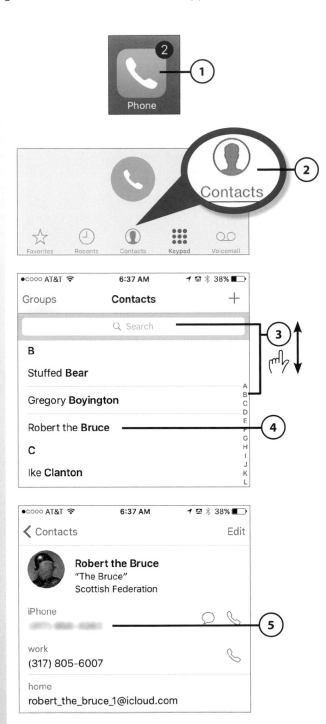

1. On the Home screen, tap Phone.

2. Tap Contacts.

3. Browse the list, search it, or use the index to find the contact you want to call. (Refer to Chapter 7 for information about using the Contacts app.)

4. Tap the contact you want to call.

5. Tap the number you want to dial (if the contact has only one phone number, you skip this step). The app dials the number, and the Call screen appears.

6. Use the Call screen to manage the call; see "Managing In-Process Voice Calls" later in this chapter for the details.

Dialing with Favorites

You can save contacts and phone numbers as favorites to make dialing them even simpler. (You learn how to save favorites in various locations later in this chapter. You learn how to make a contact into a favorite in Chapter 7.)

1. On the Home screen, tap Phone.

2. Tap the Favorites button.

3. Browse the list until you see the favorite you want to call. Along the right side of the screen, you see the type of favorite, such as a phone number (identified by the label in the Contacts app, for example, iPhone or mobile) or FaceTime.

4. Tap the favorite you want to call; to place a voice call, tap a phone number (if you tap a FaceTime contact, a FaceTime call is placed instead). The app dials the number, and the Call screen appears.

5. Use the Call screen to manage the call; see "Managing In-Process Voice Calls" later in this chapter for the details.

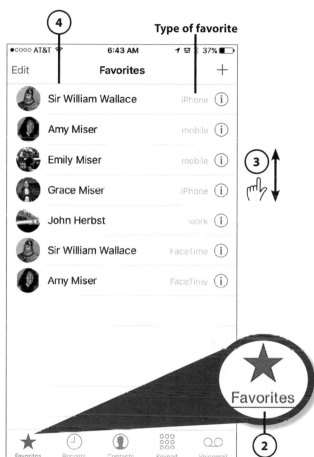

Type of favorite

Nobody's Perfect

If your iPhone can't complete the call for some reason, such as not having a strong enough signal, the Call Failed screen appears. Tap Call Back to try again or tap Done to give up. When you tap Done, you return to the screen from which you came.

Dialing with Recents

As you make, receive, or miss calls, your iPhone keeps tracks of all the numbers for you on the Recents list. You can use the Recents list to make calls.

1. On the Home screen, tap Phone.

2. Tap Recents.

3. Tap All to see all calls.

Info on the Recents Screen

If you have a contact on your iPhone associated with a phone number, you see the person's name and the label for the number (such as mobile). If you don't have a contact for a number, you see the number itself. If a contact or number has more than one call associated with it, you see the number of recent calls in parentheses next to the name or number. If you initiated a call, you see the phone icon next to the contact's name and label.

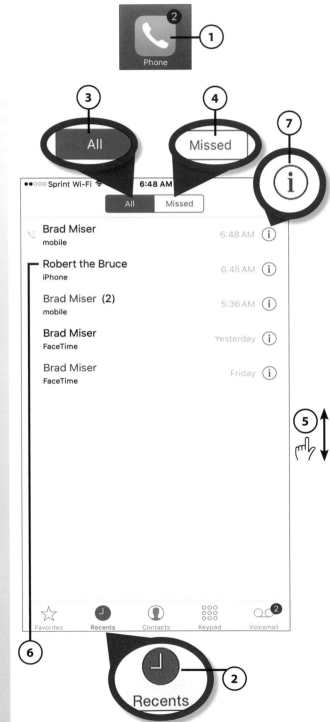

4. Tap Missed to see only calls you missed.

5. If necessary, browse the list of calls.

6. To call the number associated with a recent call, tap the title of the call, such as a person's name, or the number if no contact is associated with it. The app dials the number, and the Call screen appears. Skip to step 10.

7. To get more information about a recent call, tap its Info button. The Info screen appears.

8) Read the information about the call or calls. For example, if the call is related to someone in your Contacts list, you see detailed information for that contact. If there are multiple recent calls, you see information for each call, such as its status (Canceled Call or Outgoing Call, for example) and time.

9) Tap a number on the Info screen. The app dials the number, and the Call screen appears.

Going Back

To return to the Recents screen without making a call, tap Recents.

10) Use the Call screen to manage the call; see "Managing In-Process Voice Calls" later in this chapter for the details.

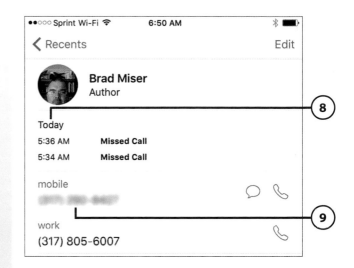

Dialing from the SIRI SUGGESTIONS Screen

New! Using the SIRI SUGGESTIONS screen, you can quickly call someone you have recently communicated with or someone with whom you communicate regularly. The steps are as follows:

1. On the Home screen, swipe to the right until you see the SIRI SUGGESTIONS screen. At the top of the screen, you see the top four people with whom you have recently communicated.

2. To see the full list, tap Show More. The list expands.

3. Tap the person you want to call. The ways you are able to contact the person appear next to the person's icon at the top of the screen; phone numbers are represented by the receiver icon.

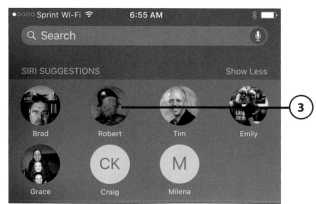

④ Tap the receiver icon.

⑤ Tap the number you want to call. The app dials the number you tapped.

⑥ Use the Call screen to manage the call; see the next section for the details.

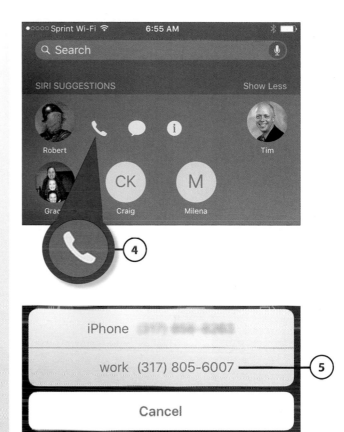

Managing In-Process Voice Calls

When you place a call, there are several ways to manage it. The most obvious is to place your iPhone next to your ear and use your iPhone like any other phone you've ever used. As you place your iPhone next to your ear, the controls on its screen become disabled so you don't accidentally tap onscreen buttons with the side of your face or your ear. When you take your iPhone away from your ear, the Call screen appears again and the Phone app's controls become active again.

When you are on a call, press the Volume buttons on the left side of the iPhone to increase or decrease its volume. Some of the other things you can do while on a call might not be so obvious, as you'll learn in the next few tasks.

Following are some of the buttons on the Call screen that you can use to manage an active call:

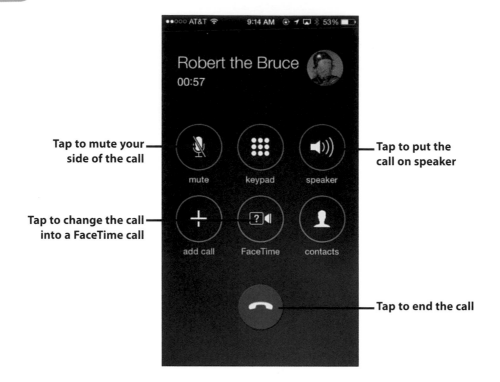

To mute your side of the call, tap mute. You can hear the person on the other side of the call, but he can't hear anything from your side.

Tap speaker to use the iPhone's speakers to hear the call. You can speak with the phone held away from your face, too.

Tap FaceTime to convert the voice call into a FaceTime call (more on FaceTime later in this chapter).

When you're done with the call, tap the receiver button.

Contact Photos on the Call Screen

If someone in your contacts calls you, or you call her, the photo associated with the contact appears on the screen. Depending on how the image was captured, it either appears as a small icon at the top of the screen next to the contact's name or fills the entire screen as the background wallpaper.

Entering Numbers During a Call

You often need to enter numbers during a call, such as to log in to a voicemail system, access an account, or enter a meeting code for an online meeting.

1. Place a call using any of the methods you've learned so far.

2. Tap Keypad.

3. Tap the numbers you want to enter.

4. When you're done, tap Hide. You return to the Call screen.

Making Conference Calls

Your iPhone makes it easy to talk to multiple people at the same time. You can have two separate calls going on at any point in time. You can even create conference calls by merging them together. Not all cell providers support two on-going calls or conference calling, though. If yours doesn't, you won't be able to perform the steps in this section.

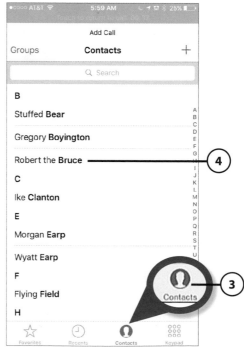

1. Place a call using any of the methods you've learned so far.

2. Tap add call.

3. Tap the button you want to use to place the next call. Tap Favorites to call a favorite, tap Recents to use the Recents list, tap Contacts to place the call via contacts, or tap Keypad to dial the number.

4. Place the call using the option you selected in step 3. Doing so places the first call on hold and moves you back to the Call screen while the Phone app makes the second call. The first call's information appears at the top of the screen, including the word hold so you know the first call is on hold. The app displays the second call just below that, and it is currently the active call.

Similar but Different

If you tap contacts instead of add call, you move directly into the Contacts screen. This might save you one screen tap if the person you want to add to the call is in your Contacts app.

(5) Talk to the second person you called; the first remains on hold.

(6) To switch to the first call, tap it on the list or tap swap. This places the second call on hold and moves it to the top of the call list, while the first call becomes active again.

(7) To join the calls so all parties can hear you and each other, tap merge calls. The iPhone combines the two calls, and you see a single entry at the top of the screen to reflect this.

Merging Calls

As you merge calls, your iPhone attempts to display the names of the callers at the top of the Call screen. As the text increases, your iPhone scrolls it so you can read it. Eventually, the iPhone replaces the names with the word Conference.

Number of Callers

Your provider and the specific technology of the network you use can limit the number of callers you place in a conference call. When you reach the limit, the add call button is disabled.

The first call is placed on hold

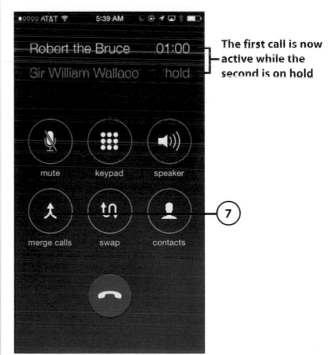

The first call is now active while the second is on hold

8 To add another call, repeat steps 2–7. Each time you merge calls, the second line becomes free so you can add more calls.

9 To manage a conference call, tap the Info button at the top of the screen.

10 To speak with one of the callers privately, tap Private. Doing so places the conference call on hold and returns you to the Call screen showing information about the active call. You can merge the calls again by tapping merge calls.

11 To remove a caller from the call, tap End. The app disconnects that caller from the conference call. You return to the Call screen and see information about the active call.

12 To move back to the Call screen, tap Back. You move to the Call screen and can continue working with the call, such as adding more people to it.

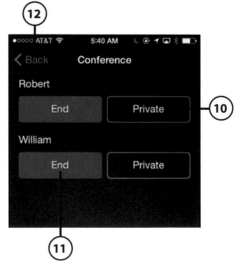

(13) To end the call for all callers, tap the receiver button.

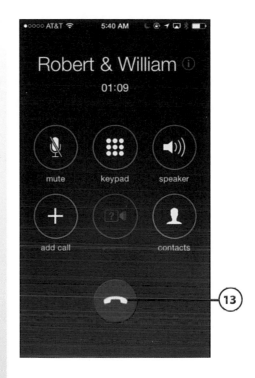

It's Not All Good

When you have multiple calls combined into one, depending on your provider, the minutes for each call can continue to count individually. So if you've joined three people into one call, each minute of the call may count as three minutes against your calling plan. Before you use this feature, check with your provider to determine what policies govern conference calling for your account.

Using Another App During a Voice Call

Tap to return to the call ——————

A call is active, and you can use other apps while still talking

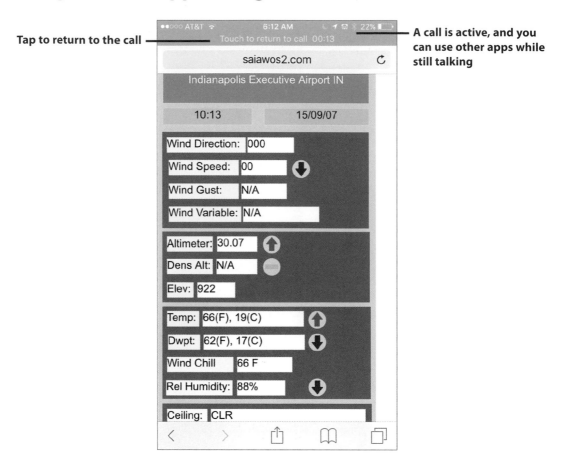

If your provider's technology supports it, you can use your iPhone for other tasks while you are on a call. When you are on a call, press the Touch ID/Home button once to move to the Home screen and then tap a different app (placing the call in speaker mode before you switch to a different app or using the headphones is best for this). Or, you can press the Touch ID/Home button twice and use the App Switcher to move into a different app. The call remains active and you see the active call information in a green bar at the top of the screen. You can perform other tasks, such as looking up information, sending emails, and visiting websites. You can continue to talk to the other person just like when the Call screen is showing. To return to the call, tap the green bar.

Receiving Voice Calls

Receiving calls on your iPhone enables you to access the same great tools you can use when you make calls, plus a few more for good measure.

Answering Calls

Person calling you —

Tap to decline and be reminded of the call later — Remind Me

Tap to decline and respond with a message — Message

Tap to decline and send the call to voicemail — Decline

Tap to answer — Accept

If you configured the ringer to ring, you hear your default ringtone or the one associated with the caller's contact information when a call comes in. If vibrate is turned on, your iPhone vibrates whether the ringer is on or not. And if those two ways aren't enough, a message appears on iPhone's screen to show you information about the incoming call. If the number is in your Contacts app, you see the contact with which the number is associated, the label for the number, and the contact's image if there is one. If the number isn't in your contacts, you see the number only.

Wallpaper

If the photo associated with a contact was taken with your iPhone or came from a high-resolution image, you see the contact's image at full screen when the call comes in, instead of the small icon at the top of the screen.

Calls on Other Devices

By default, when you receive a call on your iPhone, it also comes to any iOS 8 or later devices or Macs running OS X Yosemite or later that are on the same Wi-Fi network, and you can take the call on those devices. To disable this, set the Calls on Other Devices setting to off as described earlier in this chapter.

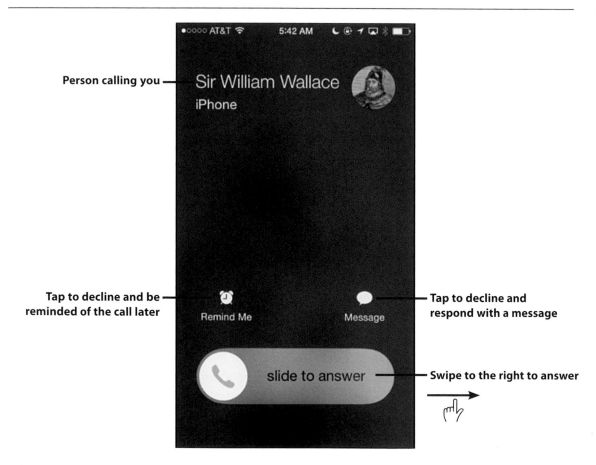

Person calling you — Sir William Wallace / iPhone

Tap to decline and be reminded of the call later — Remind Me

Tap to decline and respond with a message — Message

slide to answer — Swipe to the right to answer

If your iPhone is locked when a call comes in, swipe the slider to the right to answer it or use the Remind Me and Message icons, which work just like they do when a call comes in when the iPhone isn't locked.

When you receive a call, you have the following options:

- **Answer**—Tap Accept (if the iPhone is unlocked) or swipe the slider to the right (if the iPhone is locked) to take the call (you don't have to unlock the phone to answer a call). You move to the Call screen and can work with the call just like calls you place. For example, you can add a call, merge calls, place the call on hold, or end the call.

- **Decline**—If you tap Decline (when the iPhone is unlocked), the Phone app immediately routes the call to voicemail. You can also decline a call by quickly pressing the Sleep/Wake button twice.

- **Silence the ringer**—To silence the ringer without sending the call directly to voicemail, press the Sleep/Wake button once or press either volume button. The call continues to come in, and you can answer it even though you shut off the ringer.

- **Respond with a message**—Tap Message to send the call to voicemail and send a message back in response. You can tap one of the default messages, or you can tap Custom to create a unique message (earlier in the chapter, you learned where you can configure these messages). Of course, the device the caller is using to make the call must be capable of receiving messages for this to be useful.

- **Decline the call but be reminded later**—Tap Remind Me and the call is sent to voicemail. Tap In 1 hour, When I get home, When I get to work, or When I leave to set the timeframe in which you want to be reminded. A reminder is created in the Reminders app to call back the person who called you, and it is set to alert you at the time you select.

Silencio!

To mute your iPhone's ringer, slide the Mute switch located above the Volume switch toward the back so the orange line appears. The Mute icon (a bell with a slash through it) appears on the screen to let you know you turned off the ringer. To turn it back on again, slide the switch forward. The bell icon appears on the screen to show you the ringer is active again. To set the ringer's volume, use the Volume controls (assuming that setting is enabled) when you aren't on a call and aren't listening to an app, such as the Music app.

Answering Calls During a Call

As you saw earlier, your iPhone can manage multiple calls at the same time. If you are on a call and another call comes in, you have a number of ways to respond.

- **Decline incoming call**—Tap Send to Voicemail to send the incoming call directly to voicemail.

- **Place the first call on hold and answer the incoming call**—Tap Hold & Accept to place the current call on hold and answer the incoming one. After you do this, you can manage the two calls just as when you call two numbers from your iPhone. For example, you can place the second call on hold and move back to the first one, merge the calls, and add more calls.

- **End the first call and answer the incoming call**—Tap End & Accept to terminate the active call and answer the incoming call.

- **Respond with message or get reminded later**—These options work just as they do when you are dealing with any incoming phone call.

Auto-Mute

If you are listening to music or video when a call comes in, the app providing the audio, such as the Music app, automatically pauses. When the call ends, that app picks up right where it left off.

Managing Voice Calls

You've already learned most of what you need to know to use your iPhone's cell phone functions. In the following sections, you learn the rest.

Clearing Recent Calls

Previously in this chapter, you learned about the Recents tool that tracks call activity on your iPhone. Over time, you'll build up a large Recents list, which you can easily clear.

(1) Tap Phone.

(2) Tap Recents.

(3) Tap Edit.

(4) To clear the entire list, tap Clear; to delete a specific recent call, skip to step 6.

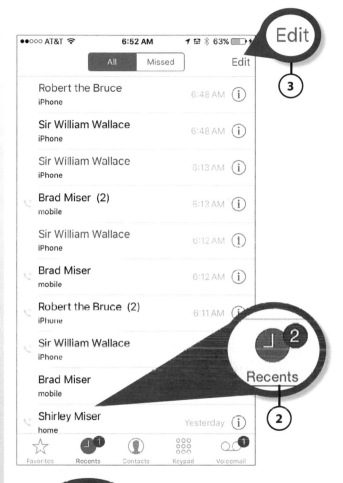

(5) Tap Clear All Recents. The Recents list is reset.

Clear All Recents ─── **(5)**

Cancel

Delete Faster

On the Recents screen, you can delete an individual recent item by swiping to the left on it (starting to the left of the i button) and tapping Delete.

(6) Tap a recent item's unlock button.

(7) Tap Delete. The recent item is deleted.

(8) When you are done managing your recent calls, tap Done.

Adding Calling Information to Favorites

Earlier you learned how simple it is to place calls to someone on your Favorites list. There are a number of ways to add people to this list, including adding someone on your Recents list.

(1) Move to the Recents list.

(2) Tap the Info button for the person you want to add to your favorites list. The Info screen appears. If the number is associated with a contact, you see that contact's information.

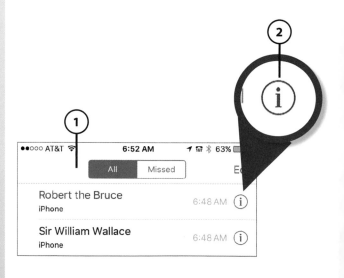

③ Swipe up to move to the bottom of the screen.

Make Contact First

To make someone a favorite, he needs to be a contact in the Contacts app. Refer to Chapter 7 to learn how to make someone who has called you into a contact.

④ Tap Add to Favorites. If the person has multiple numbers associated with his contact information, you see each available number. Numbers that are already set as favorites are marked with a blue star. If the contact has email addresses, you can set them as favorites for FaceTime conversations (video or audio only). In other words, you see all the options you can use to communicate with the contact based on his information.

⑤ Tap the number or email address you want to add as a favorite.

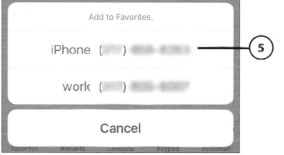

⑥ Repeat steps 4 and 5 if you want to add the contact's other numbers to the favorites list. Any numbers or email addresses that are set as favorites are highlighted in blue and marked with a blue star. If all the numbers and email addresses are assigned as favorites, the Add to Favorites button doesn't appear on the contact's screen.

Using the iPhone's EarPods for Calls

Your iPhone includes an EarPods headset with a microphone on one of its cords. The mic includes a button in the center of the switch on the right side of the EarPod's cable that you can use to do the following:

- **Answer**—Press the mic button once to answer a call.

- **End a call**—Press the mic button while you are on a call to end it.

- **Decline a call**—Press and hold the mic button for about two seconds. Two beeps sound when you release the button to let you know that your iPhone sent the call to voicemail.

- **Put a current call on hold and switch to an incoming call**—Press the mic button once and then press again.

- **End a current call on hold and switch to an incoming call**—Press the mic button once and hold for about two seconds. Release the button and you hear two beeps to let you know you ended the first call. The incoming call is ready for you.

- **Activate Siri**—Press and hold the mic button until you hear the Siri chime. This is useful when you want to make a call to someone without looking at or touching your phone.

Oh, That Ringing in My Ears

When you have EarPods plugged into your iPhone and you receive a call, the ring-tone plays on both the iPhone's speaker (unless the ringer is muted, of course) and through the EarPods.

Using Visual Voicemail

Visual voicemail just might be the best of your iPhone's many great features. No more wading through long, uninteresting voicemails to get to one in which you are interested. You simply jump to the message you want to hear. And because voicemails are stored on your iPhone, you don't need to log in to hear them. If that isn't enough for you, you can also jump to any point within a voicemail to hear just that part, such as to repeat a phone number that you want to write down.

Recording a New Greeting

The first time you access voicemail, you are prompted to record a voicemail greeting. Follow the onscreen instructions to do so.

You can also record a new greeting at any time.

(**1**) Move to the Phone screen and tap Voicemail.

(**2**) Tap Greeting.

(**3**) To use a default greeting that provides only the iPhone's phone number, tap Default and skip to step 10.

(4) To record a custom greeting, tap Custom. If you have previously used a custom greeting, it is loaded into the editor. You can replace it by continuing with these steps.

(5) Tap Record. Recording begins.

(6) Speak your greeting. As you record your message, the red area of the timeline indicates (relatively) how long your message is.

(7) When you're done recording, tap Stop.

For the First Time

Some providers require that you dial into your voicemail number the first time you use it. If you tap Voicemail and the phone starts to dial instead of you seeing Visual Voicemail as shown in these figures, this is your situation. You call the provider's voicemail system, and you're prompted to set up your voicemail. When you've completed that process, you can use these steps to record your greeting.

(8) Tap Play to hear your greeting.

(9) If you aren't satisfied, drag the Playhead to the beginning and repeat steps 5–8 to record a new message.

(10) When you are happy with your greeting, tap Save. The Phone app saves the greeting as the active greeting and returns you to the Voicemail screen.

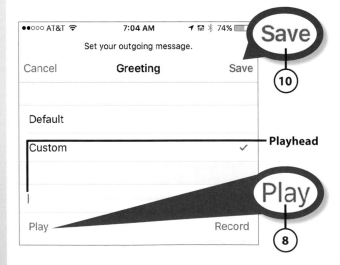

No Visual Voicemail?

If your voicemail password isn't stored on your iPhone when you tap Voicemail, your phone dials into your voicemail instead of moving to the Voicemail screen. If that happens, something has gone wrong with your password and you need to reset it. Follow your provider's instructions to reset the password. When you have the new password, open the Phone Settings screen, tap Change Voicemail Password, enter the reset password, create a new password, and re-enter your new password. (You need to tap Done after each time you enter a password.)

Change Greeting

To switch between the default and the current custom greeting, move to the Greeting screen, tap the greeting you want to use (which is marked with a check mark), and tap Save. When you choose Custom, you use the custom greeting you most recently saved.

Listening to and Managing Voicemails

Unless you turned off the voicemail sound, you hear the sound you selected each time a caller leaves a voicemail for you. The number in the badge on the Phone icon and on the Voicemail button on the Phone screen increases by 1 (unless you've disabled the badge). (Note that the badge number on the Phone icon includes both voicemails left for you and missed calls, while the badge number on the Voicemail button indicates only the number of voicemails left for you.) (A new voicemail is one to which you haven't listened, not anything to do with when it was left for you.)

If you receive a voicemail while your iPhone is locked, you see a message on the screen alerting you that your iPhone received a voicemail (unless you have disabled these notifications from appearing on the Lock screen). (It also indicates a missed call, which is always the case when a call ends up in voicemail.) Swipe to the right on the notification to jump to the Voicemail screen so that you can work with your messages.

And in yet another scenario, if you are using your iPhone when a message is left, you see a notification (either a banner or an alert unless you have turned off notifications for the Phone app) that enables you to ignore the new message or to listen to it.

Missing Password

If something happens to the password stored on your iPhone for your voicemail, such as if you restore the iPhone, you are prompted to enter your password before you can access your voicemail. Do so at the prompt and tap OK. The iPhone signs you in to voicemail, and you won't have to enter your password again (unless something happens to it again of course).

Contacts or Numbers?

Like phone calls, if a contact is associated with a number from which you've received a voicemail, you see the contact's name associated with the voicemail message. If no contact exists for the number, you see the number only.

Finding and Listening to Voicemails

Working with voicemails is simple and quick.

1. Move into the Phone app and tap Voicemail (if you tapped a new voicemail banner or the Listen button on an alert, you jump directly to the Voicemail screen).

2. Swipe up and down the screen to browse the list of voicemails. Voicemails you haven't listened to are marked with a blue circle.

3. To listen to a voicemail, tap it. You see the timeline bar and controls and the message plays.

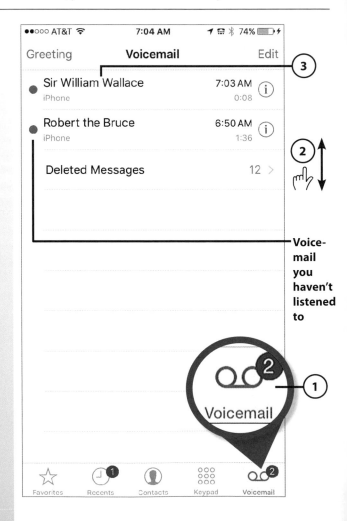

Voicemail you haven't listened to

4 To pause a message, tap its Pause button.

5 To hear the message on your iPhone's speaker, tap Speaker.

6 To move to a specific point in a message, drag the Playhead to the point at which you want to listen.

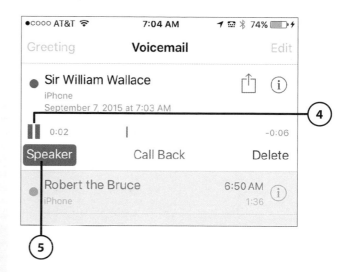

Moving Ahead or Behind

You can also drag the Playhead while a message is playing to rewind or fast-forward it. This is also helpful when you want to listen to specific information without hearing the whole message again.

7 Tap the Play button.

8 To call back the person who left the message, tap Call Back.

9 To delete the message, tap Delete.

10 To share the message, tap the Share button and then tap how you want to share it, such as Message or Mail. For example, when you tap Mail, you send the voicemail to someone else using the Mail app so he can listen to it.

11 To get more information about a message, tap its Info button. The Info screen appears. If the person who left the message is on your contacts list, you see her contact information. The number associated with the message is highlighted in blue.

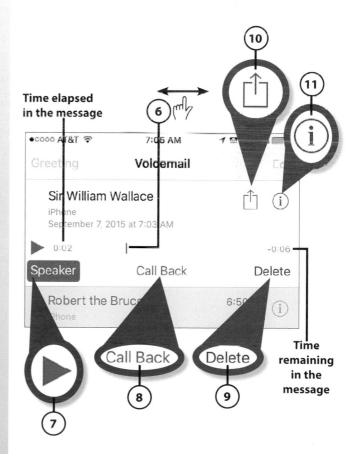

Time elapsed in the message

Time remaining in the message

(12) Swipe up or down the screen to review the caller's information.

(13) Tap Voicemail.

(14) To listen to a message you have listened to before (one that doesn't have a blue dot), tap the message and then tap the Play button. It begins to play.

Deleting Messages

To delete a voicemail message that isn't the active message, tap it so it becomes the active message and then tap Delete. Or swipe to the left on the message you want to delete and tap Delete.

Listening to and Managing Deleted Voicemails

When you delete messages, they are moved to the Deleted Message folder. You can work with deleted messages as follows:

(1) Move to the Voicemail screen.

(2) If necessary, swipe up the screen until you see the Deleted Messages option.

(3) Tap Deleted Messages.

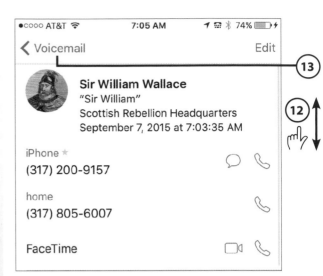

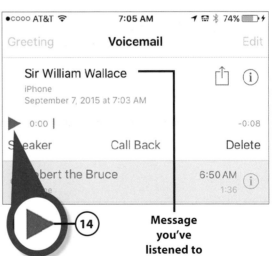

Message you've listened to

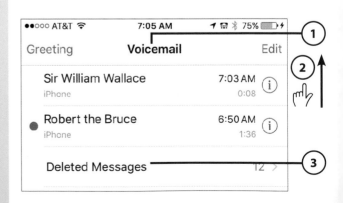

What's Missed?

In case you're wondering, your iPhone considers any call you didn't answer as a missed call. So if someone calls and leaves a message, that call is included in the counts of both missed calls and new voicemails. If the caller leaves a message, you see an alert informing you that you have a new voicemail and showing who it is from (if available). If you don't answer and the caller doesn't leave a message, it's counted only as a missed call and you see an alert showing a missed call along with the caller's identification (if available).

4 Swipe up or down the screen to browse all the deleted messages.

5 Tap a message to listen to it.

6 Tap the Play button. You can use the other playback tools just like you can with undeleted messages.

7 Tap Undelete to restore the deleted message. The iPhone restores the message to the Voicemail screen.

8 To remove all deleted messages permanently, tap Clear All. (If this is disabled, close the open message by tapping it.)

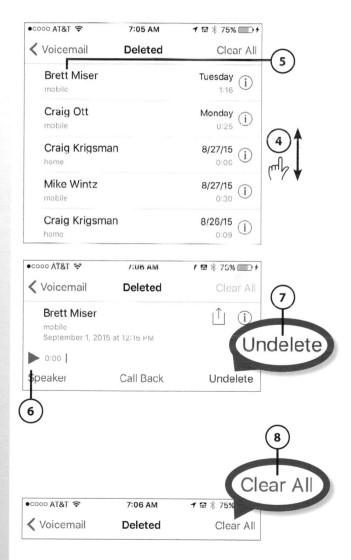

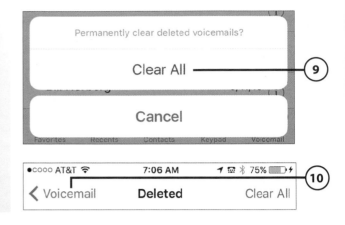

(9) Tap Clear All at the prompt. The deleted messages are erased and you return to the Deleted screen.

(10) To return to the Voicemail screen, tap Voicemail.

Lost/Forgot Your Password?

If you have to restore your iPhone or it loses your voicemail password for some other reason and you can't remember it, you need to have the password reset to access your voicemail on the iPhone. For most cell phone providers, this involves calling the customer support number and accessing an automated system that sends a new password to you via a text message. For AT&T, which is one of the iPhone providers in the United States, call 611 on your iPhone and follow the prompts to reset your password (which you receive via a text). No matter which provider you use, it's a good idea to know how to reset your voicemail password because it is likely you will need to do so at some point.

Communicating with FaceTime

FaceTime enables you to see, as well as hear, people with whom you want to communicate. This feature exemplifies what's great about the iPhone; it takes complex technology and makes it simple. FaceTime works great, but there are two conditions that have to be true for you and the people you want some FaceTime with. To be able to see each other, both sides have to use a device that has the required cameras (this includes iPhone 4s and newer, iPod touches third generation and newer, iPad 2s and newer, and Macs running Snow Leopard and newer), and have FaceTime enabled (via the settings on an iOS device as you see in the next task or via the FaceTime application on a Mac). And, each device has to be able to communicate over a network; an iPhone or cellular iPad can use a cellular data network (if that setting is enabled) or a Wi-Fi network while Macs have to be connected to the Internet through a Wi-Fi or other type of network. When these conditions are true, making and receiving FaceTime calls are simple tasks.

In addition to making video FaceTime calls, you can also make audio-only FaceTime calls. These work similarly to making a voice call except the minutes don't count against your voice plan when you use a Wi-Fi network (if you are making the call over the cellular network, the data does count against your data plan so be careful about this).

Assuming you are in a place where you don't have to pay for the data you use, such as when you use a Wi-Fi network, you don't have to pay for a FaceTime call (video or audio-only) either.

Configuring FaceTime Settings

FaceTime is a great way to use your iPhone to hear and see someone else. There are a few FaceTime settings you need to configure for FaceTime to work. You can connect with other FaceTime users via your phone number, an email address, or your Apple ID.

1. Move to the Settings screen.

2. Tap FaceTime.

3. If the FaceTime switch is off (white), tap the FaceTime switch to turn it on (green). If the FaceTime switch is on and you see an Apple ID, you are already signed into an account; in this case, you see the current FaceTime settings and can follow along starting with step 7 to change these settings. You can sign out of the current account by tapping it, and then tapping Sign Out; proceed to step 4 to sign in with a different account.

4 To use your Apple ID for FaceTime calls, tap Use your Apple ID for FaceTime. If you don't sign in to an Apple ID, you can still use FaceTime but it is always via your cellular connection, which isn't ideal because then FaceTime counts under your voice minutes on your calling plan or as data on your data plan.

5 Enter your Apple ID and password. (An Apple ID might be entered already; if so, you can use it or replace it with a different one.)

6 Tap Sign In.

7 Configure the email addresses you want people to use to contact you for FaceTime sessions by tapping them to enable each address (enabled addresses are marked with a check mark) or to disable addresses (these don't have a check mark). (If you don't have any email addresses configured on your iPhone, you are prompted to enter email addresses.)

8 Tap the phone number or email address by which you will be identified to the other caller during a FaceTime call.

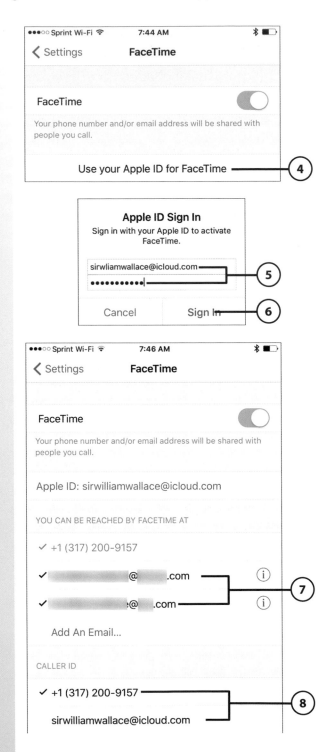

Managing Addresses

You can add more email addresses at any time by tapping Add Another Email and following the onscreen prompts to add and confirm the new addresses. To remove an address from FaceTime, tap its Info button (i) and then tap Remove This Email.

Blocking FaceTime

If you tap Blocked at the bottom of the FaceTime Settings screen, you can block people from making calls, sending messages, or making FaceTime requests to your iPhone. Tap Add New and then tap the contact you want to block.

Making FaceTime Calls

FaceTime is a great way to communicate with someone because you can hear and see him (or just hear him if you choose an audio-only FaceTime call). Because iPhones have cameras facing each way, it's also easy to show something to the person you are talking with. You make FaceTime calls starting from the FaceTime, Contacts, or Phone apps and from the SIRI SUGGESTIONS screen. No matter which way you start a FaceTime session, you manage it in the same way.

Careful

If your iPhone is connected to a Wi-Fi network, you can make all the FaceTime calls you want because you have unlimited data. However, if you are using the cellular data network, be aware that FaceTime calls may use data under your data plan. If you have a limited plan, it's a good idea to use FaceTime primarily when you are connected to a Wi-Fi network. (Refer to Chapter 2, "Connecting Your iPhone to the Internet, Bluetooth Devices, and iPhones/iPods/iPads," for information on connecting to Wi-Fi networks.)

To start a FaceTime call from the Contacts app, do the following:

1 Use the Contacts app to open the contact with whom you want to chat (refer to Chapter 7 for information about using the Contacts app).

2 To place an audio-only FaceTime call, tap the FaceTime audio button. (The rest of these steps show a FaceTime video call, but a FaceTime audio-only is very similar to voice calls described earlier in this chapter.)

3 Tap the contact's FaceTime video button. The iPhone attempts to make a FaceTime connection. You hear the FaceTime "chirping" and see status information on the screen while the call is attempted. When the connection is complete, you hear a different tone and see the other person in the large window and a preview of what he is seeing (whatever your iPhone's front-side camera is pointing at—mostly likely your face) in the small window. If the person you are trying to FaceTime with isn't available for FaceTime for some reason (perhaps he doesn't have a FaceTime-capable device or is not connected to the Internet), you see a message saying that the person you are calling is unavailable for FaceTime and the call terminates.

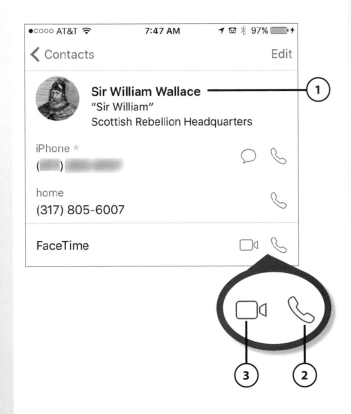

Playing Favorites

If you've set a FaceTime contact as a favorite, you can open the Phone app, tap Favorites, and tap the FaceTime favorite to start the FaceTime session.

(**4**) After the call is accepted, manage the call as described in the "Managing FaceTime Calls" task.

Transforming a Call

You can transform a voice call into a FaceTime session by tapping the FaceTime button on the Call screen. When you transform a call into a FaceTime session, the minutes no longer count against the minutes in your calling plan because all communication happens over the Wi-Fi network or your cellular data plan if you enabled that option and aren't connected to a Wi-Fi network. (The voice call you started from automatically terminates when the switch is made.)

Preview window

4

Other Ways to FaceTime

To use the FaceTime app to start a call, tap the FaceTime icon on the Home screen. Tap the Video tab to make a video call or the Audio tab to make an audio-only call. Tap the Add (+) button to use your contacts to start the call. You can also enter a name, email address, or phone number in the bar at the top of the screen (if you haven't made or received any FaceTime calls before, you won't see the tabs until you make your first call). Tap a person on the Recents list to place a FaceTime call to that person. Once you've connected, you manage the FaceTime session as described in the rest of this chapter.

You can also place a FaceTime call using Siri by activating Siri and saying "FaceTime *name*" where *name* is the name of the person with whom you want to FaceTime. If there are multiple options for that contact, you must tell Siri which you want to use. After you've made a selection, Siri starts the FaceTime call.

And for yet another option, you can open the SIRI SUGGESTIONS screen, tap the icon for the person you want to FaceTime with, and then tap the FaceTime icon shaped like a video camera to make a FaceTime video call, or tap the FaceTime icon that is shaped like a phone receiver to make an audio-only FaceTime call.

Receiving FaceTime Calls

When someone tries to FaceTime with you, you see the incoming FaceTime request screen message showing who is trying to connect with you and the image you are currently broadcasting. Tap Accept to accept the request and start the FaceTime session. Manage the FaceTime call as described in the "Managing FaceTime Calls" task.

Tap Remind Me to decline the FaceTime request and create a reminder or Message to decline the request and send a message. These options work just as they do for a voice call (you have the same custom message options). You can also press the Sleep/Wake button to decline the request.

However you decline the FaceTime request, the person trying to call you receives a message that you're not available (and a message if you choose that option). She can't tell whether there is a technical issue or if you simply declined to take the call.

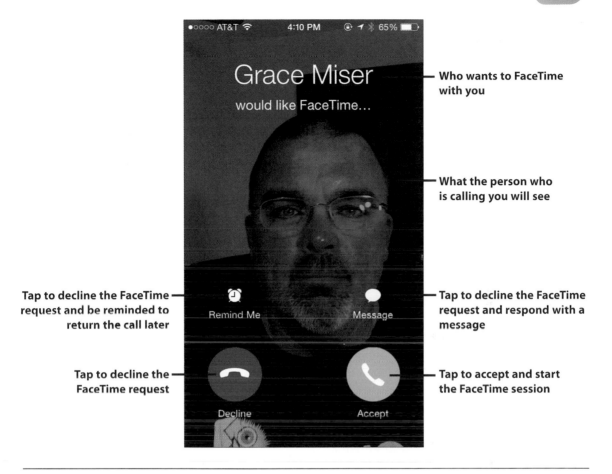

Who wants to FaceTime with you

What the person who is calling you will see

Tap to decline the FaceTime request and be reminded to return the call later

Tap to decline the FaceTime request and respond with a message

Tap to decline the FaceTime request

Tap to accept and start the FaceTime session

Tracking FaceTime Calls

FaceTime calls are tracked just as voice calls are. Open the FaceTime app and tap Video to see recent video FaceTime calls or Audio to see recent audio FaceTime calls. On the recents lists, FaceTime calls are marked with the video camera icon. FaceTime audio-only calls are marked with a telephone receiver icon. FaceTime calls that didn't go through are in red and are treated as missed calls. You can do the same tasks with recent FaceTime calls that you can with recent voice calls.

Managing FaceTime Calls

During a FaceTime call (regardless of who placed the call initially), you can do the following:

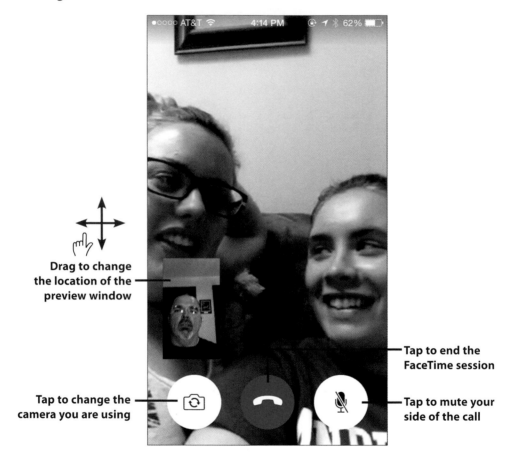

Drag to change the location of the preview window

Tap to end the FaceTime session

Tap to change the camera you are using

Tap to mute your side of the call

- Drag the preview window, which shows the image that the other person is seeing, around the screen to change its location. It "snaps" into place in the closest corner when you lift your finger up.

- Move your iPhone and change the angle you are holding it to change the images you are broadcasting to the other person. Use the preview window to see what the other person is seeing.

- Tap Mute to mute your side of the conversation. Your audio is muted and you see the Mute icon in the preview window. Video continues to be broadcast so the other person can still see you.

The other person is seeing what the backside camera is showing

Tap to change the camera you are using

- To use the camera on the backside of the iPhone, tap the Change Camera button. The other person now sees whatever you have the camera on the back of the iPhone pointed at. If the other person changes her camera, you see what her backside camera is pointing at.

- After a few moments, the controls disappear. Tap the screen to make them reappear.

- Rotate your iPhone to change the orientation to horizontal. This affects what the other person sees (as reflected in your preview), but you continue to see the other person in her iPhone's current orientation.

- Tap the receiver button to end the FaceTime call.

Tap the screen to make the controls reappear

FaceTime works in landscape orientation, too

Preview shows the landscape orientation

FaceTime Break

Just like when you are in a voice call, you can move into and use other apps (if your provider's technology supports this functionality). You see the green FaceTime in progress bar at the top of the screen. The audio part of the session continues, but the other person sees a still image with a camera icon and the word "Paused." As soon as you move back into the FaceTime session, the video resumes. Likewise, if the other person moves out of the FaceTime app, you'll see the Paused icon.

Tap to configure email settings

Tap to use email

In this chapter, you explore all the email functionality that your iPhone has to offer. Topics include the following:

→ Getting started
→ Setting Mail app preferences
→ Working with email
→ Managing email

9

Sending, Receiving, and Managing Email

For most of us, email is an important way we communicate with others. Fortunately, your iPhone has great email tools so you can work with email no matter where you are. Of course, you need to be connected to the Internet through a Wi-Fi or cellular data connection to send or receive email—although you can still read downloaded messages, reply to messages, and compose messages when you aren't connected.

Getting Started

You send and receive email through an email account. There are many sources for email accounts, such as your Internet service provider, iCloud, and Google (Gmail). One thing to keep in mind is that email isn't sent between devices, such as a computer to an iPhone. Rather, all email flows through an email server. It moves from the server onto each device, such as an iPhone or a computer. This means you can have the same email messages on more than one device at a time. You can determine how often email is moved from the server onto your iPhone.

Before you can start using an iPhone for email, you have to configure the email accounts you want to access with it. The iPhone supports many kinds of email accounts, including iCloud, Gmail, and others. Setting up the most common types of email accounts is covered in Chapter 3, "Setting Up and Using iCloud and Other Online Accounts," so if you haven't done that already, go back to that chapter and get your accounts set up. Then, come back here to start using those accounts for email.

You can have multiple email accounts configured on your iPhone at the same time, such as an iCloud account and a Google account. If you only have one email account on your iPhone, some of the screens you see on your iPhone might look a bit different than those in this chapter. The information contained in this chapter still applies; it's just that some of the screens you see are slightly different than those shown here.

Setting Mail App Preferences

There are a number of Mail-specific options you can configure using the Settings app. Following is an example showing how to configure an automatic signature that is added to the end of new emails you create so that you don't have to type it. You can configure other Mail settings using similar steps and the descriptions of the Mail settings in the table that follows these steps.

To configure your automatic email signature, perform the following steps:

1. Tap Settings on the Home screen.

2. Swipe up the screen.

3. Tap Mail, Contacts, Calendars.

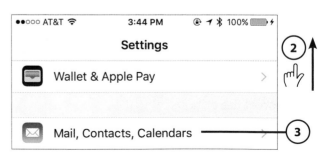

4 Swipe up the screen until you see the Signature option.

5 Tap Signature. A signature is just any text that you want to automatically appear at the end of every email that you send.

6 To use the same signature for email you send from any account, tap All Accounts; to use a different signature for each account, tap Per Account. If you selected All Accounts, you see one signature box. If you selected Per Account, you see a signature box for each account.

7 Tap in the signature box you want to change.

8 Replace the current text with the signature you want to use.

9 If you selected the Per Account option in step 6, repeat steps 7 and 8 to create a signature for each account.

10 Tap Mail. When you create a new email message (how to do this is covered later in "Sending Email"), the signature is automatically added to the end of new messages. You can change the other Mail settings using a similar pattern and the description of the options in the following table.

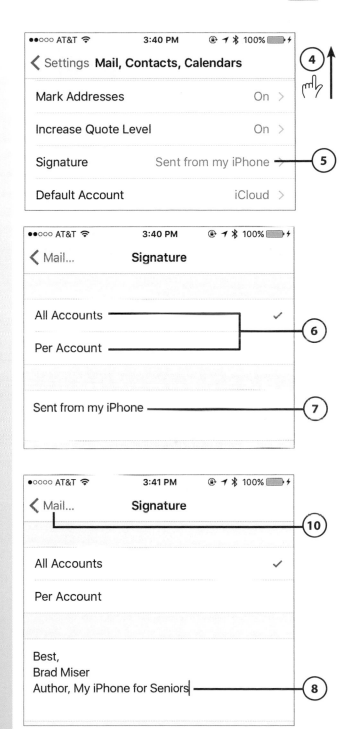

No Signatures, Please

If you don't want any text automatically appended to your messages, choose the All Accounts option and then delete all the text in the signature box.

Mail and Related Settings

Section Setting	Description
Mail, Contacts, Calendars	
ACCOUNTS	
Email accounts	You can configure the accounts used in the Mail app to determine which account can receive or send email on your iPhone (see Chapter 3 for details).
No Section	
Fetch New Data	Determines when new email is downloaded to your iPhone (see Chapter 3 for a complete explanation of the options).
MAIL	
Preview	Determines the number of lines you want to display for each email when you view the Inbox and in other locations, such as alerts. This preview enables you to get the gist of an email without opening it. More lines give you more of the message, but take up more space on the screen.
Show To/Cc Label	Slide the switch to on (green) to always see the To and Cc labels in email headers. (With this disabled, you can still view this information for an email by tapping Details on a message screen.)

Section Setting	Description
Swipe Options	Change what happens when you swipe to the left or right on email when you are viewing an Inbox. You can set the Swipe Right motion to be None, Mark as Read, Flag, Move Message, or Archive. When you swipe all the way to the right on a message, the action you configure for the Swipe Right is performed. When you do a partial swipe, you see a button that you can tap to perform the action. You can set the Swipe Left motion to be None, Mark as Read, Flag, or Move Message. When you do a partial swipe to the left, you see the More button, which leads to a menu of actions, and the option you configure for the Left Swipe setting. When you do a full swipe to the left, a message is deleted. Note that you can't have the same option configured for both directions.
Flag Style	Determines how messages you flag are marked; you can choose a colored circle or a flag icon. Flagging messages marks messages that you want to know are important or that need your attention.
Ask Before Deleting	When this switch is on (green), you're prompted to confirm when you delete or archive messages. When this switch is off (white), deleting or archiving messages happens without the confirmation prompt.
Load Remote Images	When this switch is on (green), images in HTML email messages are displayed automatically. When this switch is off (white), you have to manually load images in a message. (If you receive a lot of spam, you should turn this off so that you won't see images in which you might not be interested.)

Section Setting	Description
Organize By Thread	When this switch is on (green), messages in a conversation are grouped together as a "thread" on one screen. This makes it easier to read all the messages in a thread. When this switch is off (white), messages are listed individually. (You learn more about working with threads in the "Working with Email" task later in this chapter.)
Always Bcc Myself	When this switch is on (green), you receive a blind copy of each email you send; this means that you receive the message, but you are hidden on the list of recipients. When this switch is off (white), you don't receive a blind copy.
Mark Addresses	This feature highlights addresses in red that are not from domains that you specify. You enter the domains (everything after the @ in email addresses, such as icloud.com) from which you do not want addresses to be marked (highlighted in red) when you create email. You can add multiple domains to the list by separating them with commas. All addresses from domains not listed will be marked in red. To disable this feature, delete all the domains from the list.
Increase Quote Level	When this option is enabled (green), the text of an email you are replying to or forwarding (quoted content) is automatically indented. Generally, you should leave this enabled so it is easier for the recipients to tell when you have added text to an email, versus what is from the previous email messages' quoted content.
Signature	Signatures are text that is automatically added to the bottom of new email messages that you create. For example, you might want your name and email address added to every email you create.
Default Account	Determines which email account is the default one used when you send an email (this setting isn't shown if you only have one email account). You can override the default email account for an email you are sending by choosing one of your other email addresses in the From field.

Section Setting	Description
Display & Brightness	
Text Size	Changes the size of text in all apps that support Dynamic Type (Mail does). Drag the slider to the right to make text larger or to the left to make it smaller.
Bold Text	Changes text to be bold when the Bold Text switch is set to on (green).

More on Marking Addresses

When you configure at least one address on the Mark Addresses screen, all addresses except those from domains listed on the Mark Addresses screen are in red text on the New Message screen. This is useful to prevent accidental email going to places where you don't want it to go. For example, you might want to leave domains associated with a club off this list so that whenever you send email to addresses associated with that club, the addresses appear in red to remind you to pay close attention to the messages you are sending.

Email Notifications and Sounds

If you want to be alerted whenever new email is received and when email you create is sent, be sure to configure notifications for the Mail app. These include whether unread messages are shown in the Notification Center, the type of alerts, whether the badge appears on the Mail icon, whether the preview is shown, the alert sound, and whether new messages are shown on the Lock screen. For a detailed explanation of configuring notifications, refer to Chapter 5, "Customizing How Your iPhone Looks and Sounds."

Working with Email

The iPhone's Mail app offers lots of great features and is ideally suited for working with email on your iPhone. The Mail app offers a consolidated Inbox, so you can view email from all your accounts at the same time. Also, the Mail app organizes your email into threads, which makes following a conversation convenient.

You've got email

When you move to a Home screen, you see the number of new email messages you have in the badge on the Mail app's icon (assuming you haven't disabled this); tap the icon to move to the app. Even if you don't have any new email, the Mail icon still leads you to the Mail app. Other ways Mail notifies you of new messages include by displaying alerts and the new mail sound. (You determine which of these options is used for each email account by configuring its notifications as explained in the "Email Notifications and Sounds" note.)

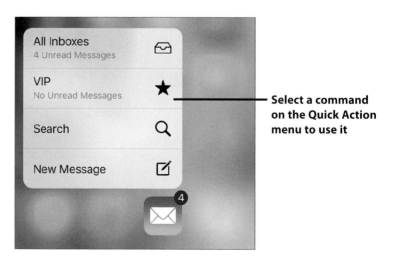

Select a command on the Quick Action menu to use it

New! If you are using an iPhone 6s or 6s Plus, you can press on the Mail icon to open the Quick Actions menu and choose an action you want to perform. For example, you can start a new email message by selecting New Message or move directly to your VIP email by selecting VIP.

About Assumptions

The steps and figures in this section assume you have more than one email account configured and are actively receiving email from those accounts on your iPhone. If you have only one email account active, your Mailboxes screen contains that account's folders instead of mailboxes from multiple accounts and the Accounts sections that appear in these figures and steps. Similarly, if you disable the Organize by Thread setting, you won't see messages in threads as these figures show. Instead, you work with each message individually.

The Mail app enables you to receive and read email for all the email accounts configured on your iPhone. The Mailboxes screen is the top-level screen in the app and is organized into two sections.

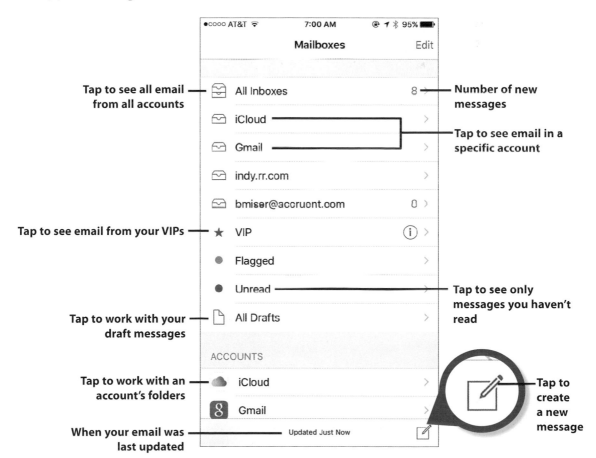

The Inboxes section shows the Inbox for each account along with folders for email from people designated as VIPs (more on this later), your unread messages, and your draft messages (you've started but haven't sent yet). Next to each Inbox or folder the number of new emails in that Inbox or folder is shown. (A new message is simply one you haven't viewed yet.) At the top of the section is All Inboxes, which shows the total number of new messages to all accounts; when you tap this, the integrated Inbox containing email from all your accounts is displayed.

The Accounts section shows each email account with another counter for new messages. The difference between these sections is that the Inbox options take you to just the Inbox for one or all of your accounts, whereas the Account options take you to all the folders under each account.

Receiving and Reading Email

To read email you have received, perform the following steps:

1. On the Home screen, tap Mail. Mail opens. (If the Mailboxes screen isn't showing, tap the back button in the upper-left corner of the screen until you reach the Mailboxes screen.)

2. To read messages, tap the Inbox that contains messages you want to read, or tap All Inboxes to see the messages from all your email accounts. Various icons indicate the status of each message, if it is part of a thread, if it has attachments, if it is from a VIP, etc.

3. Swipe up or down the screen to browse the messages. You can read the preview of each message to get an idea of its contents.

4. If a message you are interested in is in a thread, tap it. You can tell a message is part of a thread by double right-facing arrows along the right side of the screen—single messages have only one arrow. (If the message you want to read isn't part of a thread, skip to step 6.) A thread is a group of emails that are related to the same subject. For example, if someone sends an email to you saying how wonderful the *My iPhone* book is, and you reply with a message saying how much you agree, those two messages are grouped into one thread. Other messages with the same subject are also placed in the thread.

5. Swipe up or down the screen to browse the messages in the thread.

6. To read a message (whether in a thread or not), tap it. As soon as you open a message, it's marked as read and the new mail counter reduces by one. You see the message screen with the address information at the top, including whom the message is from and to whom it was sent. Under that

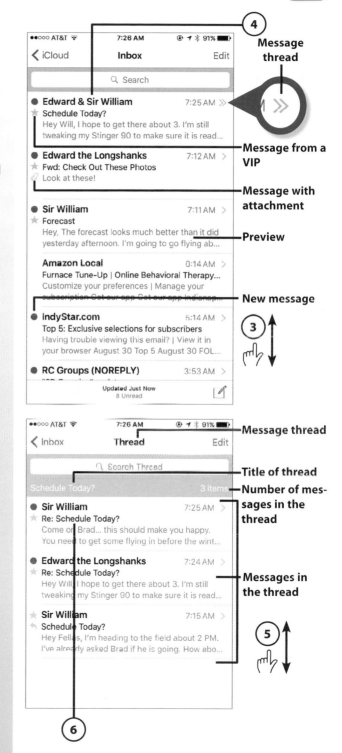

the message's subject along with time and date it was sent are displayed. Below that is the body of the message. If the message has an attachment, or is a reply to another message, the attachment or quoted text appears toward the bottom of the screen.

(7) Swipe up and down the screen to read the entire message.

(8) If the message contains an attachment, swipe up the screen to get to the end of the message. If an attachment hasn't been downloaded yet, it starts to download automatically unless it is a large file. If the attachment hasn't been downloaded yet, which is indicated by the text "Tap to Download" in the attachment icon, tap it to download it into the message. When an attachment finishes downloading, its icon changes to represent the type of file it is. If the icon remains generic, it might be of a type the iPhone can't display and you would need to open it on a computer or other device.

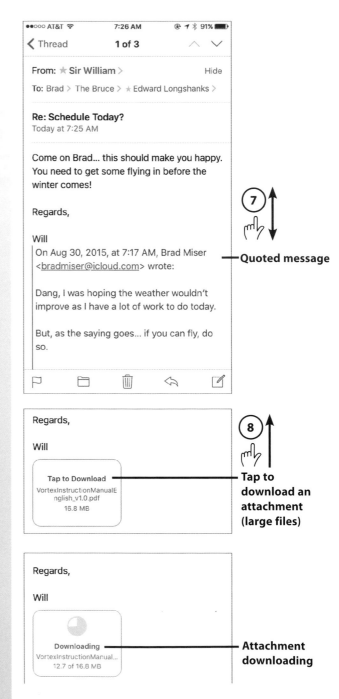

7 — Quoted message

8 — Tap to download an attachment (large files)

Attachment downloading

9 Tap the attachment icon to view it.

10 Scroll the document by swiping up, down, left, or right on the screen.

11 Unpinch or double-tap to zoom in.

12 Pinch or double-tap to zoom out.

13 To see the available actions for the attachment, tap the Share button.

Standard Motions Apply

You can use the standard finger motions on email messages, such as unpinching or tapping to zoom, swiping directions to scroll, and so on. You can also rotate the phone to change the orientation of messages from vertical to horizontal; this makes it easier to type.

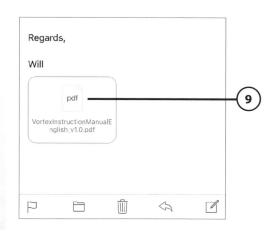

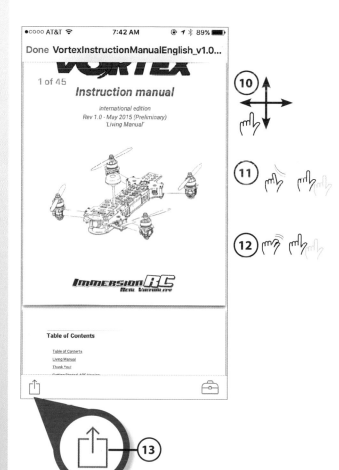

(14) Swipe to the left or right to see all the available options.

(15) Tap the action you want to take, such as opening the attachment in a different app, printing it, or sharing it with a text message. Tap Cancel to return to the attachment if you don't want to do any of these. If you open the attachment in a different app, work with the attachment in that app. To return to the email, tap the Back to Mail link in the top-left corner of the screen.

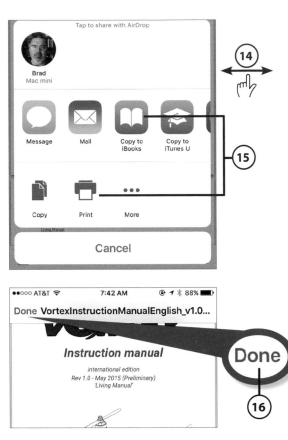

(16) Tap Done (depending on the type of attachment you were viewing, you might tap the back button instead).

(17) To view information for an email address, such as who sent the message, tap it. The Info screen appears. You see the person's email address along with actions you might want to perform, such as placing a call or FaceTime invitation.

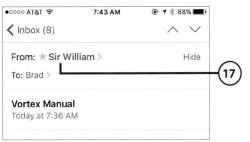

18 Tap Message to return to the message.

19 To read the next message in the current Inbox, tap the down arrow.

20 To move to a previous message in the current Inbox, tap the up arrow.

21 To move back to see the entire Inbox, tap Inbox.

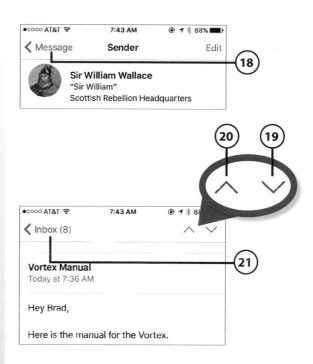

Two Other Ways to Open New Email

You can view a preview of email messages in notifications you receive and tap the notification to get to the full message. You can also use Siri to get and read new email.

Receiving and Reading Email on an iPhone 6 Plus or 6s Plus

The iPhone 6 Plus' and 6s Plus' larger screen provides some additional functionality that is unique to those models. You can access this functionality by holding the iPhone 6 Plus or 6s Plus horizontally when you use the Mail app.

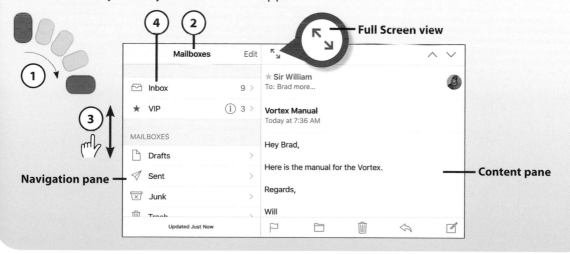

(1) Open the Mail app and hold the iPhone so it is oriented horizontally. The mail window splits into two panes. On the left is the Navigation pane, where you can move to and select items you want to view. When you select something in the left pane, it appears in the Content pane on the right, which shows the email message you were most recently reading.

(2) In the left pane, navigate to the Mailboxes screen by tapping the back button located in the upper-left corner of the pane until the button disappears.

(3) Swipe up or down the Navigation pane to browse the mailboxes and accounts available to you. Notice that the two panes are independent. When you browse the left pane, the right pane doesn't change.

(4) Tap the mailbox or account whose contents you want to view.

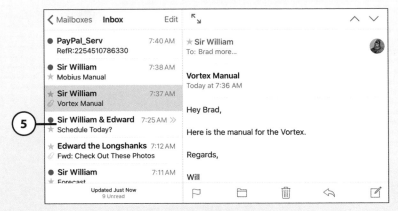

(5) Tap the message or thread that you want to read. If you tap a message, its content appears in the right pane and you can skip to step 8.

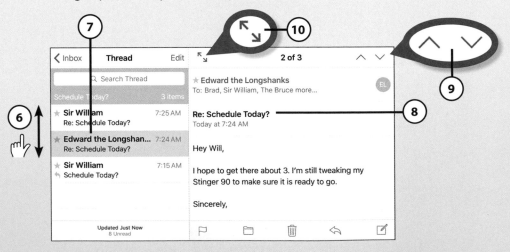

(**6**) Swipe up and down the messages to browse all of them in the thread.

(**7**) Tap the message you want to read. It appears in the Content pane.

(**8**) Read the message.

(**9**) Use the other tools to work with it; these work just like they do on other models and when you hold the iPhone 6 Plus or 6s Plus vertically. For example, tap the up arrow to move to the previous message in the current Inbox.

(**10**) To read the message in full screen, tap the Full Screen View button. The Content pane uses the entire screen.

(**11**) Work with the message.

(**12**) When you're done, tap the back button, which is labeled with the name of the mailbox or folder containing the message you are reading. The screen splits into two panes again.

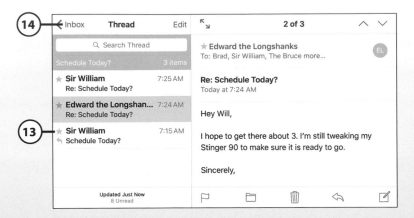

(13) Select and read other messages.

(14) When you're done, tap the back button, which is labeled with the name of the mailbox or folder whose contents you are browsing.

Using 3D Touch for Email (iPhone 6s and 6s Plus)

New! You can use the 3D Touch feature on an iPhone 6s or 6s Plus for email as follows:

(1) Browse a list of email messages.

(2) Tap and hold on an email in which you are interested. A Peek of that email appears.

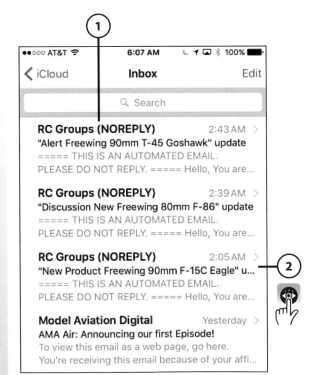

3 Review the preview of the email that appears in the Peek.

4 To open the email so you can read all of it, press down slightly harder until it pops open and use the steps in the earlier task to read it (skip the rest of these steps).

5 To see actions you can perform on the email, swipe up on the Peek.

6 Tap the action you want to perform, such as Reply, to reply to the email.

RC Groups
To: bradm3@me.com more...   RG

"New Product Freewing 90mm F-15C Eagle" update
Today at 2:05 AM

===== THIS IS AN AUTOMATED EMAIL. PLEASE DO NOT REPLY. =====

Hello,

You are subscribed to the thread "Freewing 90mm F-15C Eagle" by Alpha.MotionRC, there have been 35 posts to this thread, the last poster was lpcustom73.
http://www.rcgroups.com/forums/showthread.php?t=2489654

These following posts were made to the thread:
****

These following posts were made to the thread:
****

Reply

Forward

Mark...

Notify Me...

Move Message...

>>>Go Further

MORE ON RECEIVING AND READING EMAIL

Check out these additional pointers for working with email you receive:

- If more messages are available than are downloaded, tap the Load More Messages link. The additional messages download to the inbox you are viewing.

- You can change the amount of detail you see at the top of the message screen by tapping More to show all of the detail, such as the entire list of recipients, or Hide to collapse that information.

- If a message includes a photo, Mail displays the photo in the body of the email message if it can. You can zoom in or out and scroll to view it just as you can for photos in other apps.

- If you tap a PDF attachment in a message and the iBooks app is installed on your iPhone, you might be prompted to select Quick Look or Open in iBooks. If you select Open in iBooks, the document opens in the iBooks app where you can read it using the powerful features it offers for reading ebooks and other documents.

- Some emails, especially HTML messages, are large and don't immediately download in their entirety. When you open a message that hasn't been fully downloaded, you see a message stating that this is the case. Tap the link to download the rest of the message.

- If you have other apps with which an attachment is compatible, you can open the attachment in that app. For example, if you have Pages installed on your iPhone and are viewing a Word document attachment, you can tap the Share button and tap Open in Pages to open the document in the Pages app. You can get the same options by tapping and holding down on the attachment's icon in the body of a message until the Action menu appears.

Sending Email

You can send email from any of your accounts. Follow these steps for a basic walk-through of composing and sending a new email message:

1 Tap the Compose button at the bottom of any Mail screen (if you are using an iPhone 6s or 6s Plus, you can press down on the Mail app's icon and choose New Message to create a new email from a Home page). A new email message containing your signature is created.

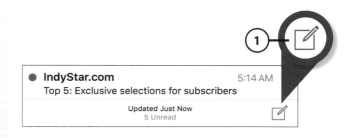

2 Tap the To field and type in the first recipient's email address. As you type, Mail attempts to find matching addresses in your Contacts list, or in emails you've sent or received, and displays the matches it finds. To select one of those addresses, tap it. Mail enters the rest of the address for you. Or, just keep typing information until the address is complete.

3 To address the email using your Contacts app, tap the Add button.

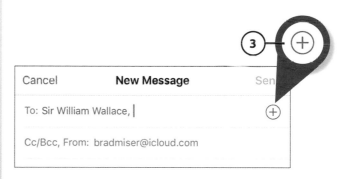

Have Multiple Email Accounts?

If you have more than one email account, it's important to know from which account you are sending a new message. If you tap the Compose button while you are on the Mailboxes screen or the Inboxes screen, the From address is the one for the account you set as your default; otherwise, the From address is the email account associated with the Inbox you are in.

4 Use the Contacts app to find and select the contact to whom you want to address the message. (Refer to Chapter 7 for the details about working with contacts.) When you tap a contact who has only one email address, that address is pasted into the To field and you return to the New Message window. When you tap a contact with more than one email address, you move to the Info screen, which shows all available addresses; tap the address to which you want to send the message.

5 Repeat steps 2–4 to add other recipients to the message.

6 Tap the Cc/Bcc, From line. The Cc and Bcc lines expand.

7 Follow the same procedures from steps 2–4 to add recipients to the Cc field.

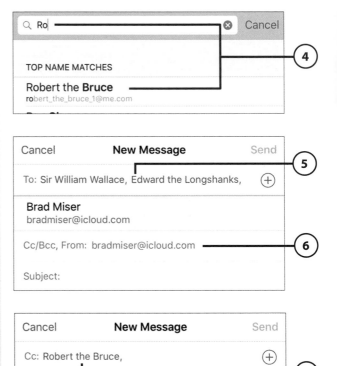

Removing Addresses
To remove an address, tap it so it is highlighted in a darker shade of blue; then tap the Delete button on the iPhone's keyboard.

(8) Follow the same procedures from steps 2–4 to add recipients to the Bcc field. (The difference is that other recipients do not see those listed on the Bcc line.)

(9) If the correct account is shown, skip to step 11; to change the account from which the email is sent, tap the From field. The account wheel appears at the bottom of the screen.

(10) Swipe up or down the wheel until the From address you want to use is shown between the lines.

(11) Tap in the Subject line. The account selection wheel closes.

(12) Type the subject of the message.

(13) If you want to be notified when someone replies to the message you are creating, tap the bell; if not, skip to step 16.

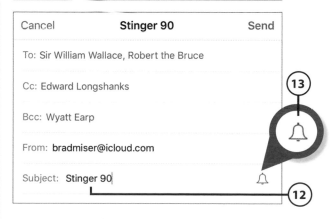

(14) Tap Notify Me. When someone replies to the message, you are notified.

(15) If you don't see the body of the message, swipe up the screen and it appears.

(16) Tap in the body of the message, and type the message above your signature. Mail uses the iOS's text tools, attempts to correct spelling, provides Predictive Text, and makes suggestions to complete words. (Refer to Chapter 1, "Getting Started with Your iPhone," for the details of working with text.)

(17) To make the keyboard larger, rotate the iPhone so that it is horizontal.

(18) When you finish the message, tap Send. The progress of the send process is shown at the bottom of the screen; when the message has been sent, you hear the send mail sound you configured, which confirms that the message has been sent.

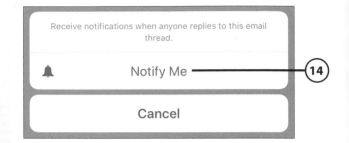

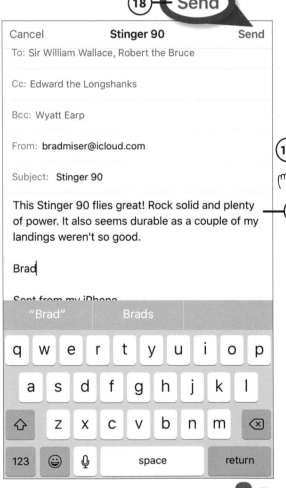

Write Now, Send Later

If you want to save a message you are creating without sending it, tap Cancel. A prompt appears; select Save Draft to save the message; if you don't want the message, tap Delete Draft instead. When you want to work on a draft message again, tap and hold down the Compose button. After a moment, you see your most recent draft messages; select the draft message you want to work on. You can make changes to the message and then send it or save it as a draft again. (You can also move into the Drafts folder to select and work with draft messages; moving to this folder is covered later in this chapter.)

Using Mail's Suggested Recipients

New! As you create messages, Mail suggests recipients based on the new message's current recipients. For example, if you regularly send emails to the same group of people, when you add two or more people from that group, Mail suggests others you may want to include. As you add others to the message, Mail continues suggesting recipients based on the current recipient list. You can use these suggestions to quickly add more recipients to a new message.

(1) Create a new message.

(2) Add at least two recipients. Just below the To line, Mail suggests additional recipients for the new message based on other messages you have created.

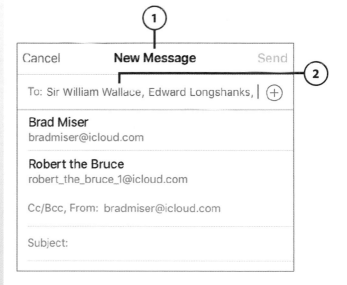

3 Tap the additional recipients you want to add to the new message. As you select these recipients, Mail keeps making suggestions and new people appear in the gray bars.

4 When you're done adding To recipients, tap in the next field you want to complete and continue creating the new message.

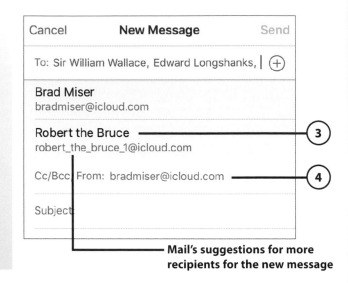

Mail's suggestions for more recipients for the new message

Replying to Email

Email is all about communication, and Mail makes it simple to reply to messages.

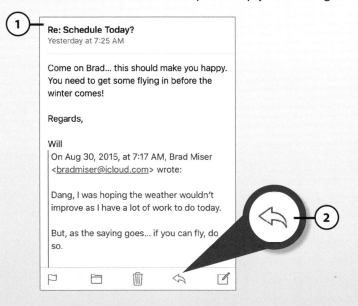

1 Open the message you want to reply to.

2 Tap the Share button.

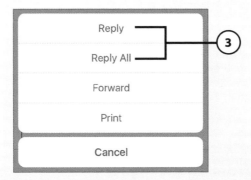

(3) Tap Reply to reply to only the sender or, if there was more than one recipient, tap Reply All to reply to everyone who received the original message. The Re: screen appears showing a new message. Mail pastes the contents of the original message at the bottom of the body of the new message below your signature. The original content is in blue and is marked with a vertical line along the left side of the screen.

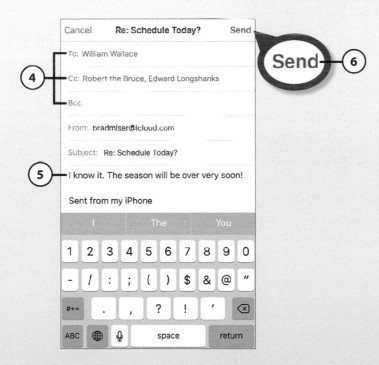

(4) Use the message tools to add or change the To, Cc, or Bcc recipients.

(5) Write your response.

(6) Tap Send. Mail sends your reply.

Including a Photo or Video in a Message

To add a photo or video to a message, tap twice in the body. Swipe to the left on the resulting toolbar (if you don't see it immediately) until you see the Insert Photo or Video command, and then tap it. Use the Photos app (see Chapter 14, "Working with Photos and Video You Take with Your iPhone," for information about this app) to move to and select the photo or video you want to attach. Tap Choose. The photo or video you selected is attached to the message.

Sending Email from All the Right Places

You can send email from a number of places on your iPhone. For example, you can share a photo with someone by viewing the photo, tapping the Share button, and then tapping Mail. Or you can tap a contact's email address to send an email from your contacts list. For yet another example, you can share a YouTube video. In all cases, the iPhone uses Mail to create a new message that includes the appropriate content, such as a photo or link; you use Mail's tools to complete and send the email.

Print from Your iPhone

If you need to print a message, tap the Share button and tap Print. To learn about printing from your iPhone, refer to Chapter 1.

Forwarding Email

When you receive an email you think others should see, you can forward it to them.

(1) Read the message you want to forward.

(2) If you want to include only part of the current content in the message you forward, tap where you want the forwarded content to start. This is useful (and considerate!) when only a part of the message applies to the people to whom you are forwarding it. If you want to forward the entire content, skip to step 4.

(**3**) Use the text selection tools to select the content you want to include in your forwarded message.

(**4**) Tap the Share button.

(**5**) Tap Forward.

(**6**) If the message includes attachments, tap Include at the prompt if you also want to forward the attachments, or tap Don't Include if you don't want them included. The Forward screen appears. Mail pastes the contents of the message that you selected, or the entire content if you didn't select anything, at the bottom of the message below your signature. It you included attachments, they are added to the new message as well.

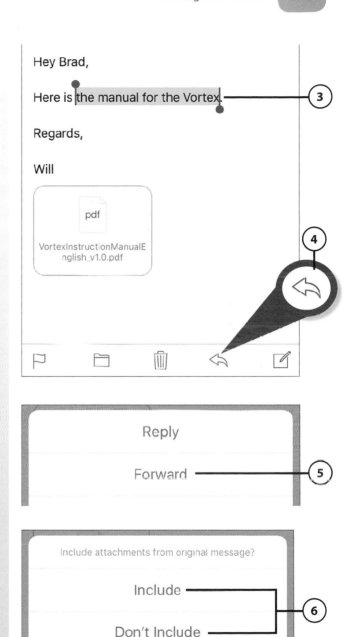

(7) Address the forwarded message using the same tools you use when you create a new message.

(8) Type your commentary about the message above your signature.

(9) Tap Send. Mail forwards the message.

Large Messages

Some emails, especially HTML messages, are so large that they don't immediately download in their entirety. When you forward a message whose content or attachments haven't fully downloaded, Mail prompts you to download the "missing" content before forwarding. If you choose not to download the content or attachments, Mail forwards only the downloaded part of the message.

Managing Email

Following are some ways you can manage your email. You can check for new messages, see the status of messages, delete messages, and organize messages using the folders associated with your email accounts.

Checking for New Email

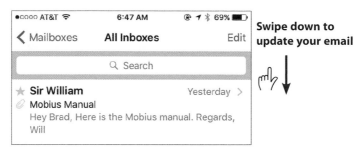

Swipe down to update your email

To manually retrieve messages, swipe down from the top of any Inbox or the Mailboxes screen. The screen "stretches" down and when you lift your finger, the Mail app checks for and downloads new messages.

Mail also retrieves messages whenever you move into the app or into any Inbox or all your Inboxes. Of course, it also retrieves messages according to the Fetch New Data option you selected (refer to Chapter 3).

How many unread messages you have in the current Inbox

When your email was last updated

The bottom of the Mailboxes or Inbox screen always shows when email was most recently downloaded to your iPhone; on the bottom of Inbox screens, you also see the number of new email messages (if there are any unread messages).

Understanding the Status of Email

When you view an Inbox or a message thread, you see icons next to each message to indicate its status (except for messages that you've read but not done anything else with, which aren't marked with any icon).

When the message is replied to, you receive a notification ──

Message you've flagged ──

Message with attachments ──

Message from a VIP ──

Message to which you've replied ──

Message you've forwarded ──

Unread message ──

Managing Email from the Message Screen

Tap to delete a message

To delete a message while reading it, tap the Trash button. If you enabled the warning preference, confirm the deletion and the message is deleted. If you disabled the confirmation prompt, the message is deleted immediately.

Dumpster Diving

As long as an account's trash hasn't been emptied, you can work with a message you've deleted by moving to the account's screen and opening its Trash folder.

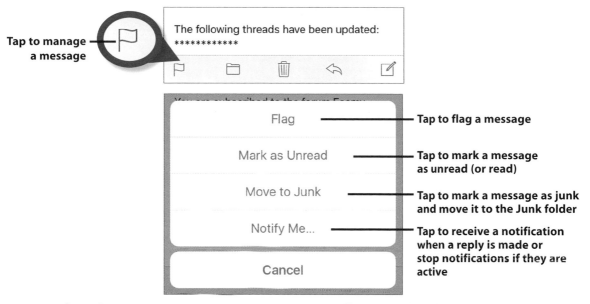

Tap to manage a message

The following threads have been updated:
****

Flag ————————— **Tap to flag a message**

Mark as Unread ————— **Tap to mark a message as unread (or read)**

Move to Junk ————— **Tap to mark a message as junk and move it to the Junk folder**

Notify Me... ————— **Tap to receive a notification when a reply is made or stop notifications if they are active**

Cancel

To take other action on a message you are reading, tap the Flag icon. On the menu that opens, you can do the following:

- Tap Flag to flag the message or Unflag to unflag it.
- Tap Mark as Unread or Mark as Read to change its read status.
- Tap Move to Junk to mark the message as junk and move it to the Junk folder.
- Tap Notify Me to receive a notification when there is a reply to the message or Stop Notifying to remove the notification.

Where Has My Email Gone?

When you send an email to the Archive folder, it isn't deleted. To access messages you've archived, tap the back button in the upper-left corner of the screen until you get to the Mailboxes screen. Tap the account to which email you've archived was sent. Then tap the Archive folder.

Managing Email from an Inbox

Previously in this chapter, you saw the settings options for swipe actions for email. You can use those to configure how right and left swipes affect your email from an Inbox screen, such as flagging a message with a left swipe. (Depending on the choices you set for the swipe preferences, the results you see when you swipe might be different than shown here.)

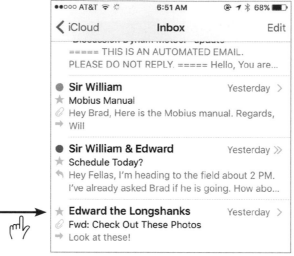

Tap to mark a message as read (or unread) —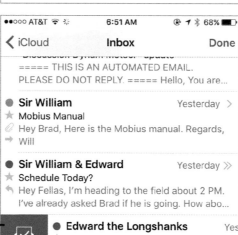

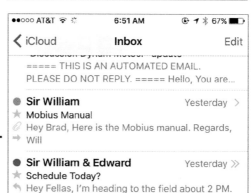

Swipe to the right on a message to change its read status. If the message has been read, you can reset its status to unread or if it hasn't been read, you can mark it as read.

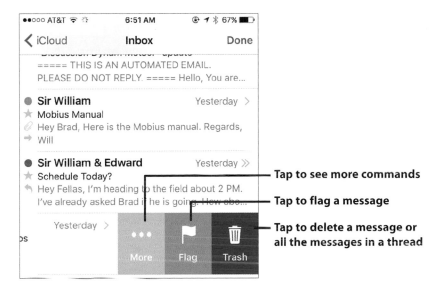

Tap to see more commands

Tap to flag a message

Tap to delete a message or all the messages in a thread

Swipe to the left on a message to see several options. Tap Trash to delete the message or messages, if you swiped on a thread (the number of messages that will be deleted is shown in parentheses). Tap Flag to flag the message or Unflag to remove the flag. Tap More to open a menu of additional commands.

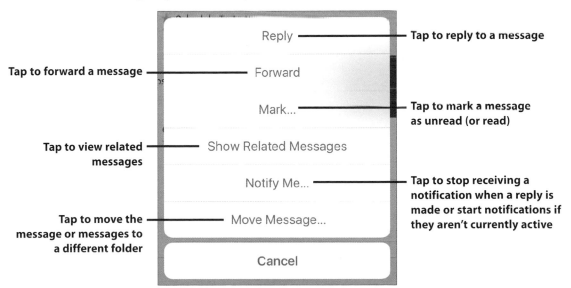

Tap to reply to a message

Tap to forward a message

Tap to mark a message as unread (or read)

Tap to view related messages

Tap to stop receiving a notification when a reply is made or start notifications if they aren't currently active

Tap to move the message or messages to a different folder

When you tap More, you see other commands for actions you can take on the message. These include:

- Tap Reply to reply to a message.

- Tap Forward to forward a message.

- Tap Mark as Unread or Mark as Read to change its read status.

- Tap Show Related Messages to show messages related to the one on which you swiped.

- Tap Notify Me to receive a notification when there is a reply to the message or Stop Notifying to remove the notification.

- Tap Move Messages to move one or more messages to a different folder.

No Stop Swiping to Delete

If you quickly swipe all the way to the left on a message on an Inbox screen, the message is deleted in one fell swoop.

Managing Multiple Emails at the Same Time

You can also manage email by selecting multiple messages on an Inbox screen, which is more efficient because you can take action on multiple messages at the same time.

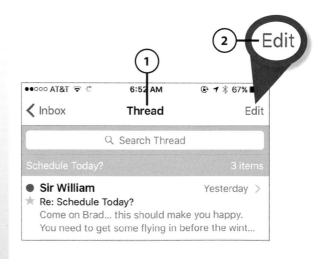

(1) Move to an Inbox screen showing messages you want to manage.

(2) Tap Edit. A selection circle appears next to each message, and actions appear at the bottom of the screen.

(3) Select the message(s) you want to manage by tapping their selection circles. As you select each message, its selection circle is marked with a check mark. At the top of the screen, you see how many messages you have selected.

When you use an iPhone 6 Plus or 6s Plus in the horizontal orientation, you see the selection screen on the left and a preview of what you have selected in the right pane. Even though it looks a bit different, it works in the same way.

(4) To delete the selected messages, tap Trash. Mail deletes the selected messages and exits Edit mode. (If you enabled the warning prompt, you have to confirm the deletion.)

(5) To change the status of the selected messages, tap Mark.

Selected message

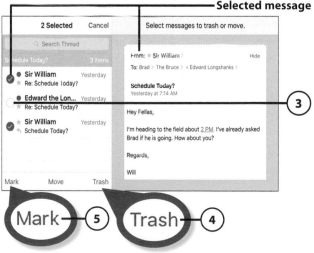

Selected message

6 Tap the action you want to take on the selected messages. You return to the Inbox screen and exit Edit mode.

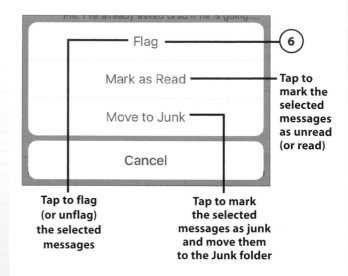

Flag — **6**

Mark as Read — **Tap to mark the selected messages as unread (or read)**

Move to Junk

Cancel

Tap to flag (or unflag) the selected messages

Tap to mark the selected messages as junk and move them to the Junk folder

Organizing Email from the Message Screen

You can have various folders to organize email, and you can move messages among these folders. For example, you can recover a message from the Trash by moving it from the Trash folder back to the Inbox.

1 Open a message you want to move to a different folder.

2 Tap the Mailboxes button. The Mailboxes screen appears. At the top of this screen is the message you are moving. Under that are the mailboxes available under the current account.

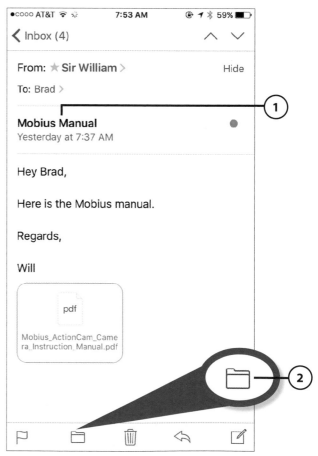

oooo AT&T 7:53 AM 59%

‹ Inbox (4)

From: ★ Sir William › Hide

To: Brad ›

— **1**

Mobius Manual
Yesterday at 7:37 AM

Hey Brad,

Here is the Mobius manual.

Regards,

Will

pdf

Mobius_ActionCam_Came
ra_Instruction_Manual.pdf

— **2**

3 Swipe up and down the screen to browse the mailboxes available in the current account.

4 Tap the mailbox to which you want to move the message. The message moves to that mailbox, and you move to the next message in the list you were viewing.

Makin' Mailboxes

You can create a new mailbox to organize your email. Move to the Mailboxes screen and tap the account under which you want to create a new mailbox. Tap Edit, and then tap New Mailbox. Type the name of the new mailbox. Tap the Mailbox Location and then choose where you want the new mailbox located (for example, you can place the new mailbox inside an existing one). Tap Save. You can then store messages in the new mailbox.

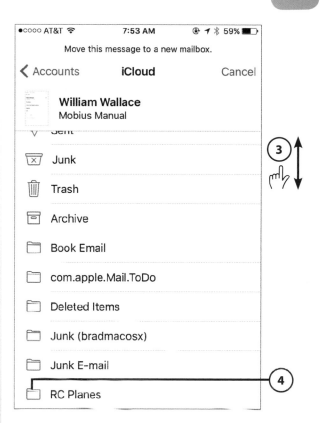

Organizing Email from the Inbox

Like deleting messages, organizing email from the Inbox can be made more efficient because you can move multiple messages at the same time.

1. Move to an Inbox screen showing messages you want to move to a folder.

2. Tap Edit. A selection circle appears next to each message. Actions appear at the bottom of the screen.

3. Select the messages you want to move by tapping their selection circles. As you select each message, its selection circle is marked with a check mark.

4. Tap Move.

5. Swipe up and down the screen to browse the mailboxes available in the current account.

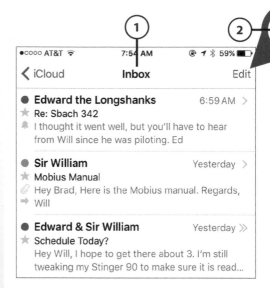

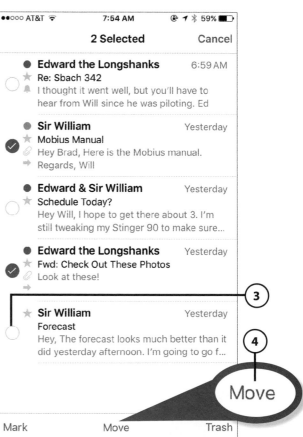

6 Tap the mailbox to which you want to move the selected messages. They are moved into that folder, and you return to the previous screen, which is no longer in Edit mode.

Picking at Threads
When you select a thread, you select all the messages in that thread. Whatever action you select is taken on all the thread's messages at the same time.

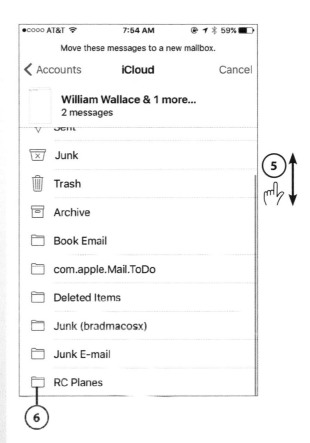

Viewing Messages in a Mailbox

You can open a mailbox within an account to work with the message it contains. For example, you might want to open the Trash mailbox to recover a deleted message.

1. Move to the Mailboxes screen.

2. If necessary, swipe up the screen to see the ACCOUNTS section.

3. Tap the account containing the folders and messages you want to view. You see all of that account's mailboxes and folders.

4. Tap the folder or mailbox containing the messages you want to view. You see the messages it contains.

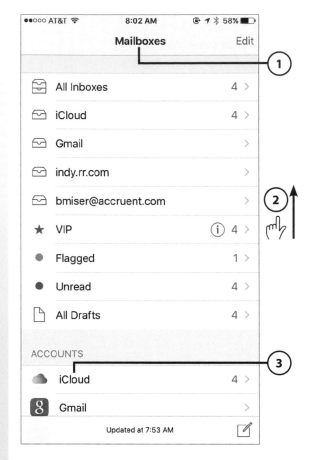

5 Tap a message or thread to view it. (If you want to move messages, such as to recover messages that are in the Trash, see "Organizing Email from the Inbox.")

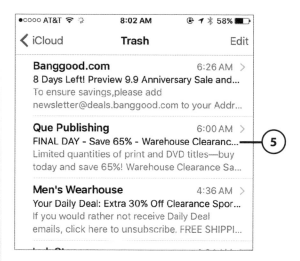

Changing Mailboxes

You can change the mailboxes that appear on the Mailboxes screen. Move to the Mailboxes screen and tap Edit. To cause a mailbox to appear, tap it so that it has a check mark in its circle. To hide a mailbox, tap its check mark so that it just shows an empty circle. For example, you can show the Attachments mailbox to make messages with attachments easier to get to. Drag the Order button for mailboxes up or down the screen to change the order in which mailboxes appear. Tap Add Mailbox to add a mailbox not shown to the list. Tap Done to save your changes.

Saving Images Attached to Email

Email is a great way to share photos. When you receive a message that includes photos, you can save them on your iPhone.

1 Move to the message screen of an email that contains one or more photos or images.

2 Tap the Share button.

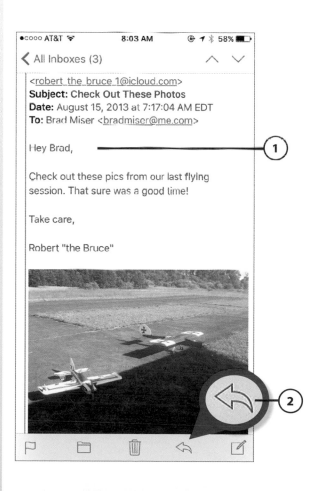

③ Tap Save *X* Images, where *X* is
the number of images attached
to the message. (If there is only
one image, the command is just
Save Image.) The images are
saved in the Photos app on your
iPhone.

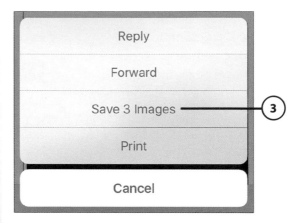

Searching Your Email

As you accumulate email, you might
want to find specific messages.
For example, suppose you want to
retrieve an email message that was
sent to a specific person, but you
can't remember where you stored it.
Mail's Search tool can help you find
messages like this quite easily.

① Move to the screen you want
to search, such as an account's
Inbox or a folder's screen.

② Swipe down to move to the top
of the screen.

③ Tap in the Search tool.

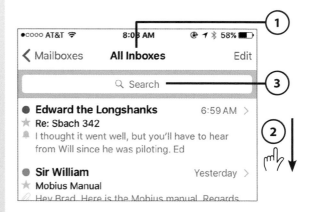

(4) Enter the text for which you want to search. As you type, Mail makes suggestions about what you might be searching for. These appear in different sections based on the type of search Mail thinks you are doing, such as People, Subjects, and more.

(5) To use one of Mail's suggestions to search, such as a person, tap their name; or continue typing your search term and when you are done, tap Search. Mail searches for messages based on your search criterion and you see the results.

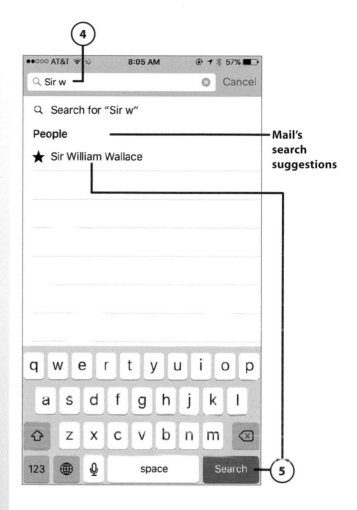

Mail's search suggestions

6. Work with the messages you found, such as tapping a message to read it. Tap the back button in the upper-left corner of the screen to return to the search results.

7. To clear a search and exit Search mode, tap Cancel.

8. To clear a search but remain in Search mode, tap the Clear button.

When you use an iPhone 6 Plus or 6s Plus horizontally, searching is even better, because you can select a found message in the search results in the right pane and read it in the right pane.

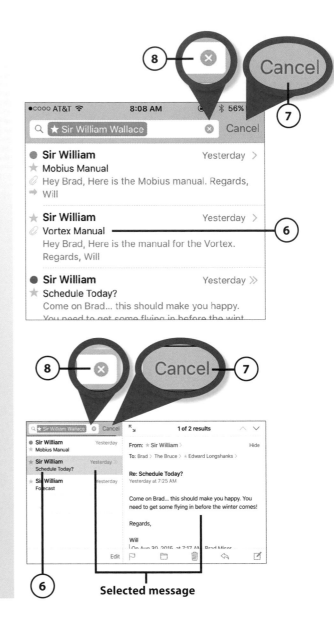

Selected message

Working with VIPs

The VIP feature enables you to indicate specific people as your VIPs. When a VIP send you email, it is marked with a star icon and goes into the special VIP mailbox so you access these important messages easily. You can also create specific notifications for VIPs, such as a unique sound when you receive email from a VIP (see Chapter 5).

Designating VIPs

To designate someone as a VIP, perform the following steps:

1 View information about the person you want to be a VIP by tapping his name in the From or Cc fields as you learned earlier in the chapter.

2 On the Info screen, tap Add to VIP. The person is designated as a VIP and any email from that person receives the VIP treatment.

Accessing VIP Email

To work with VIP email, do the following:

1 Move to the Mailboxes screen.

2 Tap VIP.

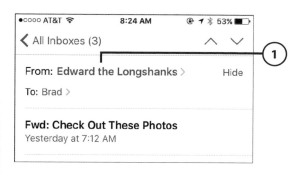

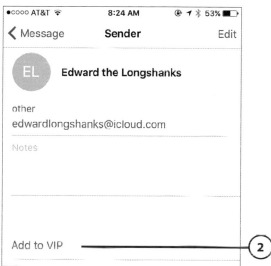

3. Work with the VIP messages you see.

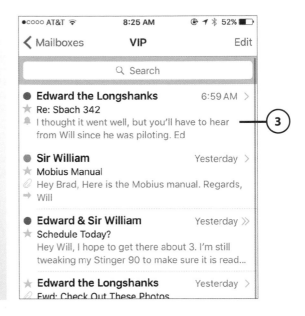

>>>Go Further

MORE ON VIPS

Here are a few more tidbits on VIPs:

- Messages from VIPs are marked with the star icon no matter in which mailbox you see the messages. If you haven't read a VIP message, the star is blue. If you have read it, the star is gray.

- To see the list of your current VIPs, move to the Mailboxes screen and tap the Info button (i) for the VIP mailbox. You see everyone currently designated as a VIP. Tap Add VIP to add more people to the list. Tap VIP Alerts to create special notifications for VIPs.

- To return a VIP to normal status, view his information and tap Remove from VIP.

- If you use an iPhone 6s or 6s Plus, you can jump directly to the VIP folder from the Home screen by tapping and holding the Mail icon and choosing VIP on the resulting menu.

Managing Junk Email

Junk email, also known as spam, is an unfortunate reality of email. No matter what precautions you take, you are going to receive some spam emails. Of course, it is good practice to be careful about where you provide your email address to limit the amount of spam you receive.

Consider using a "sacrificial" email account when you shop, post messages, and in the other places where you're likely to get spammed. If you do get spammed, you can stop using the sacrificial account and create another one to take its place. Or you can delete the sacrificial account from your iPhone and continue to use it on your computer where you likely have better spam tools in place. If you have an iCloud account, you can set up and use email aliases for this purpose.

The Mail app on the iPhone doesn't include any spam or filtering tools. However, if you use an account or an email application on a computer that features a junk mail/spam tool, it acts on mail sent to your iPhone, too. For example, if you configure spam tools for a Gmail account, those tools act on email before it reaches your iPhone. Similarly, if you use the Mail app on a Mac, its rules and junk filter work on email as you receive it; the results of this are also reflected on your iPhone.

To change how you deal with junk email on your iPhone, change the junk email settings for your account online (such as for Gmail) or by changing how an email app on a computer deals with junk mail. The results of these changes are reflected in the Mail app on your iPhone.

Many email accounts, including iCloud and Google, have Junk folders; these folders are available in the Mail app on your iPhone. You can open the Junk folder under an account to see the messages that are placed there. As you saw earlier, you can also move a message to the Junk folder by swiping to the left on it, tapping More, and then tapping Move to Junk.

It's Not All Good

Unfortunately, while you can move email to a Junk folder in the Mail app, this really doesn't do any good, because the Mail app doesn't use that action to be able to mark similar future emails as junk like email apps on computers do. On an iPhone, there's really no difference between moving a message to a Junk folder and deleting it. Because it is faster to delete a message, that is a better way to get rid of junk email than moving it to a Junk folder.

Tap to send and receive text messages, photos, video, and more

Send messages from other apps too, such as to share photos

Tap to configure Messages

In this chapter, you'll explore the texting and messaging functionality your iPhone has to offer. Topics include the following:

→ Getting started
→ Preparing Messages for messaging
→ Sending messages
→ Receiving, reading, and replying to messages
→ Working with messages

10

Sending, Receiving, and Managing Texts and iMessages

You can use the iPhone's Messages app to send, receive, and converse; you can also send and receive images, videos, audio, and links with this app. You can maintain any number of conversations with other people at the same time, and your iPhone lets you know whenever you receive a new message via audible and visible notifications you configure. In addition to conversations with other people, many organizations use text messaging to send important updates, such as airlines communicating flight status changes. You might find messaging to be one of the most used functions of your iPhone.

Getting Started

Texting, also called messaging, is an especially great way to communicate with others when you have something quick you want to say, such as an update on your arrival time. It's much easier to send a quick text, "I'll be there in 10 minutes," than it is to make a phone call or send an email. Texting/messaging is designed for relatively short messages. It is also a great way to share photos and videos quickly and easily. And if you communicate with younger people, you might find they tend to respond quite well since texting is a primary form of communication for them.

There are two types of messages that you can send with and receive on your iPhone using the Messages app.

The Messages app can send and receive text messages via your cell network based on telephone numbers. Using this option, you can send text messages to and receive messages from anyone who has a cell phone capable of text messaging.

You can also use the iMessage function within the Messages app to send and receive messages via an email account, to and from other iOS devices (using iOS 5 or newer), or Macs (running OS X Lion or newer). This is especially useful when your cell phone account has a limit on the number of texts you can send via your cell account; when you use iMessage for texting, there is no limit on the amount of data you can send when you are connected to the Internet using a Wi-Fi network and so you incur no additional costs for your messages. This is also really useful because you can send messages to, and receive messages from, iPod touch, iPad, Apple Watch, and Mac users. The limitations to iMessage are that it only works on those supported devices, and the people with whom you are messaging have to set up iMessage on their device (as you'll see shortly, this isn't difficult).

You don't need to be overly concerned about which type is which because the Messages app makes it clear which type a message is by color and text. It uses iMessage when available and automatically uses cellular texting when it isn't possible to use iMessage.

You can configure iMessage on multiple devices, such as an iPhone and an iPad. This means you have the same iMessages on each device. So, you can start a conversation on your iPhone, and then continue it on other devices.

Preparing Messages for Messaging

Like most of the apps described in this book, there are settings for the Messages app you can configure to choose how the app works for you. For example, you can configure iMessage so you can communicate via email addresses, configure how standard text messages are managed, and so on. You can also choose to block messages from specific people.

Setting Your Text and iMessage Preferences

Perform the following steps to set up Messages on your iPhone:

(1) Move to the Settings app and tap Messages.

(2) Set the iMessage switch to on (green).

(3) Tap Use your Apple ID for iMessage.

Already Signed In to an Apple ID?

If you have already signed into an Apple ID for Messages, you can start with step 5 to configure the settings being used for your messages. If you want to change the Apple ID currently being used for iMessage, tap Send & Receive, tap the Apple ID shown at the top of the iMessage screen, and then tap Sign Out. You can then use these steps to sign into a different Apple ID for Messages.

(4) Type your Apple ID and associated password, and then tap Sign In.

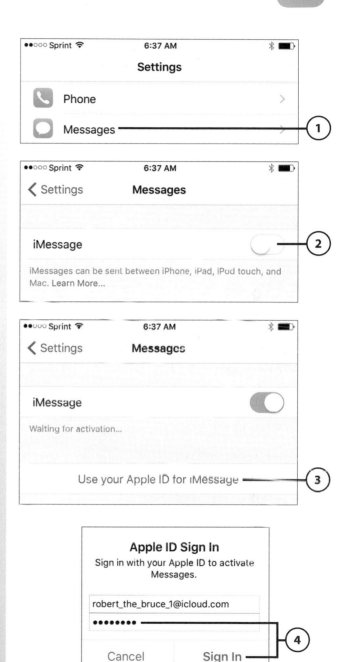

(5) Tap Text Messaging Forwarding; if you don't see this option, your cell phone carrier doesn't support it and you can skip to step 11.

(6) Set the switch to on (green) for a device on which you want to be able to receive and send text messages using your iPhone's cell phone function (this doesn't impact messages sent via iMessages). A code appears on the device for which you turned on the switch in step 6 (in this case, Brad's Mac Mini).

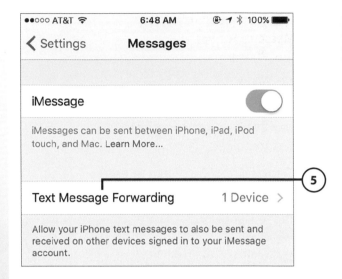

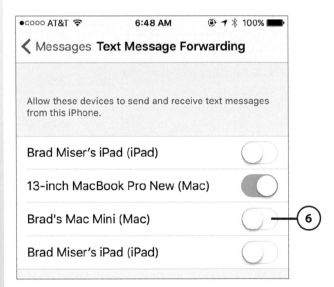

7 Type the code into the Text Message Forwarding box on the iPhone.

8 Tap Allow.

9 Repeat steps 6 through 8 to enable other devices to receive text messages via your iPhone's cell phone function.

10 Tap Messages.

11 To notify others when you read their messages, slide the Send Read Receipts switch to on (green). Be aware that receipts apply only to iMessages (not texts sent over a cellular network).

12 To send texts via your cellular network when iMessage is unavailable, slide the Send as SMS switch to on (green). If your cellular account has a limit on the number of texts you can send, you might want to leave this set to off (white) so you use only iMessage when you are texting. If your account has unlimited texting, you should set this to on (green).

13 Tap Send & Receive. At the top of the iMessage screen, you see the Apple ID via which you'll send and receive iMessages. On the rest of the screen are the phone number and email addresses that can be used with the Messages app.

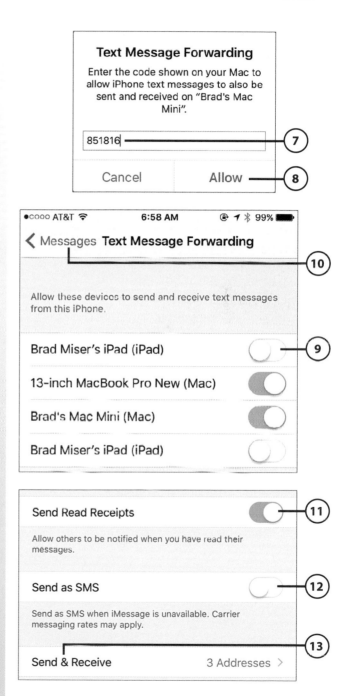

(14) To prevent an email address from being available for messages, tap it so it doesn't have a check mark; to enable an address so it can be used for messages, tap it so it does have a check mark.

(15) Tap the phone number or email address you want to use by default when you start a new text conversation. Each number or email address becomes a separate conversation in the Messages app so choose the number or address you want to use most frequently to start new conversations.

(16) Tap Messages.

(17) Swipe up the screen so you see the SMS/MMS section.

(18) If you don't want to allow photos and videos to be included in messages sent via your phone's cellular network, set the MMS Messaging switch to off (white). You might want to disable this option if your provider charges more for these types of messages—or if you simply don't want to deal with anything but text in your cellular texting messages.

(19) To keep messages you send to a group of people organized by the group, set the Group

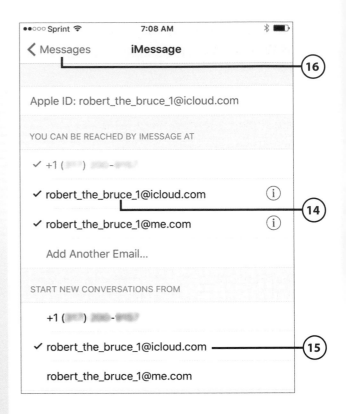

Messaging switch to on (green). When enabled, replies you receive to messages you send to groups (meaning more than one person on a single message) are shown on a group message screen where each reply from anyone in the group is included on the same screen. If this is off (white), when someone replies to a message sent to a group, the message is separated out as if the original message was just to that person. (The steps in this chapter assume Group Messaging is on.)

(20) To add a subject field to your messages, set the Show Subject Field switch to on (green). This is not commonly used, and the steps in this chapter assume this setting is off.

(21) To display the number of characters you've written compared to the number allowed (such as 59/160), set the Character Count switch to on (green). This is not commonly used, and the steps in this chapter assume this setting is off.

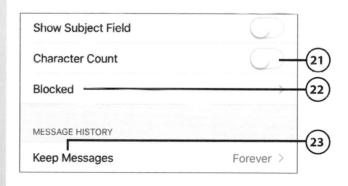

(22) Use the Blocked option to block people from texting you (see the next task).

(23) Tap Keep Messages.

(24) Tap the length of time for which you want to keep messages.

(25) If you tapped something other than Forever in Step 24, tap Delete. The messages on your iPhone older than the length of time you selected in step 24 are deleted.

(26) Tap Messages.

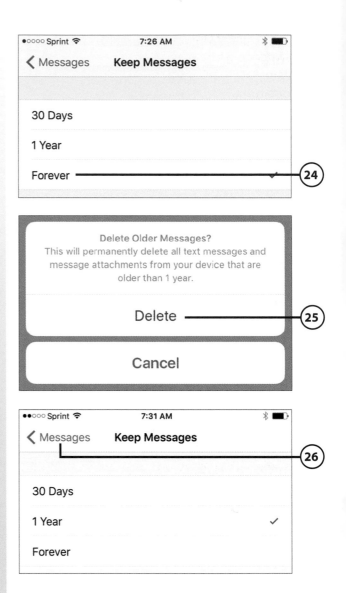

27 Set the Filter Unknown Senders switch to on (green) if you want messages from people or organizations not in the Contacts app to be put on a separate list. Notifications for those messages are also disabled. This can be useful if you receive a lot of messages from people you don't know and don't want to be annoyed by notifications about those messages.

28 Tap Expire in the AUDIO MESSAGES section.

29 Tap Never if you want to keep audio messages until you delete them or After 2 Minutes to have them deleted after two minutes. If you selected After 2 Minutes, audio messages are automatically deleted two minutes after you listen to them. This is good because audio messages require a lot of storage space and deleting them keeps that space available for other things.

30 Tap Messages.

31 If you want to be able to listen to audio messages by lifting the phone to your ear, set the Raise to Listen switch to on (green). If you set this to off (white), you need to manually start audio messages by tapping the Play button.

32 Tap Expire in the VIDEO MESSAGES section.

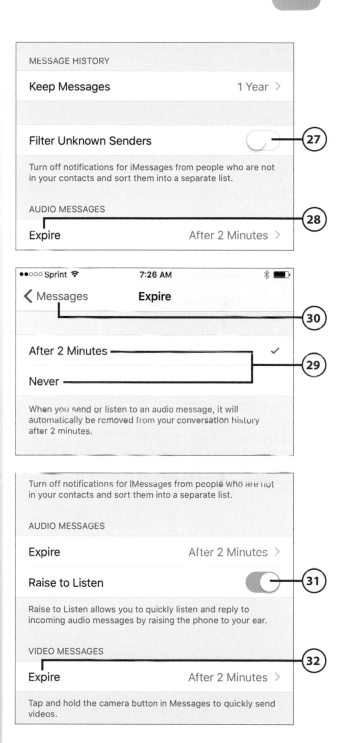

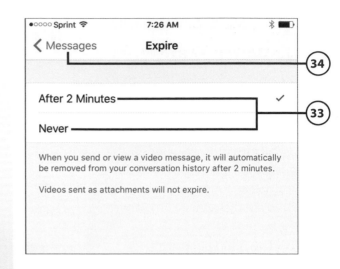

(33) Tap Never if you want video messages included in an iMessage to be kept on your phone or After 2 Minutes to have them automatically deleted after two minutes. Video messages can take up a lot of storage space so it's usually a good idea to choose After 2 Minutes.

(34) Tap Messages. You're ready to send and receive messages.

Avoiding Scam Email

When you enable email addresses for iMessage, the resulting confirmation message should only contain a link you click to verify the address you provided. If you receive an email asking for your Apple ID or other identifying information, this is not from Apple and you should delete it without responding to it.

Audio and Video Messages

There are two types of audio and video messages you can send via the Messages app. Instant audio and video messages are included as part of the message itself. Audio and videos can also be attached to messages. The Expire settings only affect instant audio or video messages. Audio or videos that are attached to messages are not deleted automatically.

Blocking People from Messaging or Texting You

To block a phone number or email address from sending you a message, you need to have a contact configured with that information. Refer to Chapter 7, "Managing Contacts," for the steps to create contacts. Creating a contact from a message you receive is especially useful for this purpose. When you start receiving messages from someone you want to block, use a message to create a contact. Then use the following steps to block that contact from sending messages to you:

1. Move to the Messages screen in the Settings app.
2. Swipe up the Messages screen.
3. Tap Blocked.
4. Tap Add New.
5. Use the Contacts app to find and tap the contact you want to block. (Note that contacts without email addresses or phone numbers that don't have the potential to send messages to you are grayed out and cannot be selected.) You return to the Blocked screen and see the contact on your Blocked list. Any messages from the contact, as long as they come from an email address or phone number included in his contact information, won't be sent to your iPhone.

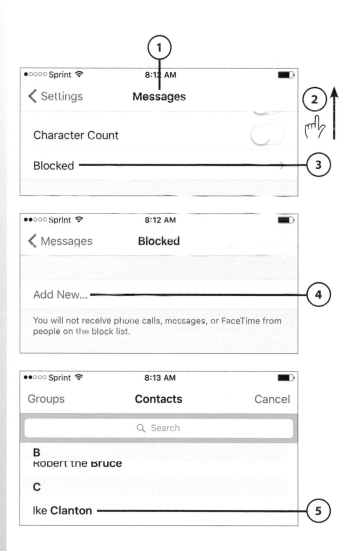

⑥ Repeat steps 4 and 5 to block other addresses or phone numbers for the person you are blocking or to block other people.

>>>Go Further

MORE ON MESSAGES CONFIGURATION

Following are a couple more Messages configuration tidbits for your consideration:

• You can configure the notifications the Messages app uses to communicate with you. You can configure the alert styles (none, banners, or alerts), badges on the icon to show you the number of new messages, sounds and vibrations when you receive messages, and so on. Messages also supports repeated alerts, which by default is to send you two notifications for each message you receive but don't read. Configuring notifications is explained in detail in Chapter 5, "Customizing How Your iPhone Looks and Sounds."

• To unblock someone so you can receive messages from them again, move to the Messages screen in the Settings app, tap Blocked, swipe to the left across the contact you want to unblock, and tap Unblock.

Sending Messages

You can use the Messages app to send messages to people using a cell phone number (as long as the device receiving it can receive text messages) or an email address that has been registered for iMessage. If the recipient has both a cell number and iMessage-enabled email address, the Messages app assumes you want to use iMessage for the message.

When you send a message to more than one person, and at least one of those people can use only the cellular network, all the messages are sent via the cellular network and not as an iMessage.

Whether messages are sent via a cellular network or iMessage isn't terribly important, but there are some differences. If your cellular account has a limit on the number of texts you can send, you should use iMessage when you can because those messages won't count against your limit. Also, when you use iMessage, you don't have to worry about a limit on the number of characters in a message. When you send a message via a cellular network, your messages might be limited to 160 characters.

Creating and Sending Messages

You can send text messages by entering a number or email address manually or by selecting a contact from your contacts list.

1. On the Home screen, tap Messages.

2. Tap New Message (if you don't see this, tap the back button in the upper-left corner of the screen until you do). If you haven't used the Messages app before, you skip this step and move directly to the compose message screen in the next step.

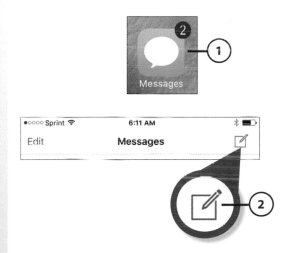

(3) Type the recipient's name, email address, or phone number. As you type, the app attempts to match what you type with a saved contact or to someone you have messaged with before and shows you a list of suggested recipients. You see phone numbers or email addresses for each recipient on the list. Phone numbers or addresses in blue indicate the recipient is registered for iMessages and your message will be sent via that means. When you see a phone number in green, the message will be sent as a text message over the cellular network. If a number or email address is gray, you haven't sent any messages to it yet; you can tap it to attempt to send a message. You also see groups you have previously messaged.

(4) Tap the phone number, email address, or group to which you want to send the message. The recipients' names are inserted into the To field. Or, if the information you want to use doesn't appear, just type the complete phone number, including area code, or email address.

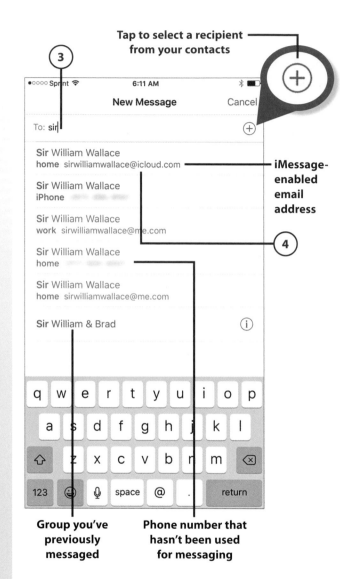

Tap to select a recipient from your contacts

iMessage-enabled email address

Group you've previously messaged

Phone number that hasn't been used for messaging

Straight to the Source
You can tap the Add button (+) in the To field to use the Contacts app to select a contact to whom you want to address the message.

Go to the Group
You can tap the Info button (i) next to a group on the suggested recipients list to see the people that are part of that group.

5 If you want to send the message to more than one recipient, tap in the space between the current recipient and the + button and use steps 3 and 4 to enter additional recipients.

Change Your Mind?
To remove a contact or phone number from the To box, tap it once so it becomes highlighted in blue and then tap the Delete key on the keyboard.

6 Tap in the Message bar, which is labeled iMessage, if you entered iMessage addresses; or Text Message, if you entered a phone number. The cursor moves into the Message bar and you are ready to type your message.

•●ooo Sprint 🛜   6:11 AM   ✳ ■▷

New iMessage   Cancel

To: Sir William Wallace, Brad Miser,   ⊕   5

iMessage   6

⑦ Type the message you want to send in the Message bar.

⑧ Tap Send, which is blue if you are sending the message via iMessage or green if you are sending it via the cellular network. The Send status bar appears as the message is sent; when the process is complete, you hear the message sent sound and the status bar disappears.

If the message is addressed to iMessage recipients, your message appears in a blue bubble in a section labeled iMessage. If the person to whom you sent the message enabled his read receipt setting, you see when he reads your message.

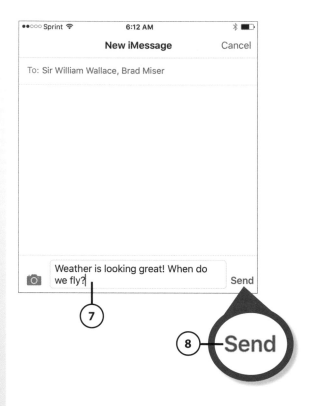

⑦

⑧ **Send**

Recipients of the message

Message sent to more than one person

This message has been sent via iMessage

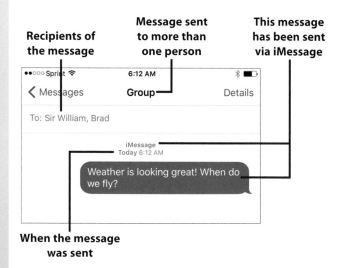

When the message was sent

If you sent the message via the cellular network instead of iMessage, you see your message in a green bubble in a section labeled Text Message.

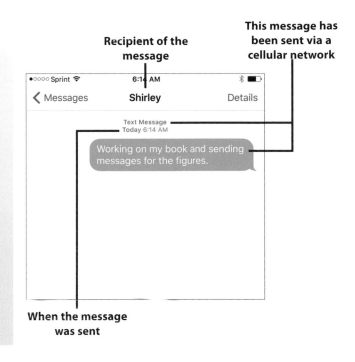

Recipient of the message

This message has been sent via a cellular network

When the message was sent

>>>Go Further
TEXT ON

Following are some additional points to help you take your texting to the next level (where is the next level, anyway?):

- **iMessage or Cell**—If the recipient has an iOS device or Mac that has been enabled for iMessage, text messages are sent via iMessage when possible even if you choose the recipient's phone number.

- **No Group Messaging**—When you address a message to more than one person with Group Messaging disabled, it is sent to each person but becomes a separate conversation from that point on. If one or more of the recipients replies to the message, only you see the responses. In other words, replies to your messages are sent only to you, not to all the people to whom you sent the original message.

- **Larger Keyboard**—Like other areas where you type, you can rotate the iPhone to be horizontal where the keyboard is larger as is each key. This can make texting easier, faster, and more accurate.

- **Recents**—When you enter To information for a new message, included on the list of potential recipients are people being suggested to you. When a suggested recipient has an info button (i), tap that button, tap Ignore Contact, and then tap Ignore at the prompt to prevent that person from being suggested in the future.

Receiving, Reading, and Replying to Messages

Text messaging is about communication so when you send messages, you expect to receive responses. People can also send new messages to you. The Messages app keeps messages grouped as a conversation consisting of messages you send and replies you receive to the same person or group of people.

Receiving Messages

Message alert notification on the Lock screen

Swipe to the right on the notification to move into the Messages app to read the entire message

When you aren't currently using the Messages screen in the Messages app and receive a new message (as a new conversation or as a new message in an ongoing conversation), you see, hear, and feel the notifications you have configured for the Messages app. (Refer to Chapter 5 to configure your message notifications.)

If you are on the Messages screen in the Messages app when a new message comes in, you hear and feel the new message notification sound and/or vibration, but a notification alert box does not appear. The conversation containing a new message is marked with a blue circle.

Tap a message to move into the Messages app

Your new messages

Swipe down to open the Notification Center and tap the Notifications tab to see your messages

You can also access your new messages using the Notification Center. Swipe down from the top of the screen to open the Notification Center and tap the Notifications tab. In the Messages section, you see the new messages with the newest message being at the top of the screen and older messages shown toward the bottom. You can swipe up and down the screen to browse the messages or tap a message to read it in the Messages app.

Speaking of Texting

Using Siri to hear and speak text messages is extremely useful. Check out Chapter 12, "Working with Siri," for examples showing how you can take advantage of this great feature.

Reading Messages

Tap an alert to read a new message in the Messages app

You can get to new messages you receive by doing any of the following:

- Tap a banner alert notification from Messages. You move into the message's conversation in the Messages app.

Conversations with new messages are marked with a blue dot

Tap a conversation with a new message to read the new message

- Open the Messages app and tap the conversation containing a new message; these conversations appear at the top of the Messages list and are marked with a blue circle. The conversation opens and you see the new message.

You can read new messages in alert notifications

- Read a message in its alert notification.
- Swipe to the right on a message notification when it appears on the Lock screen.
- Open the Notifications tab of the Notification Center and tap a message.
- If you receive a new message in a conversation that you are currently viewing, you immediately see the new message.

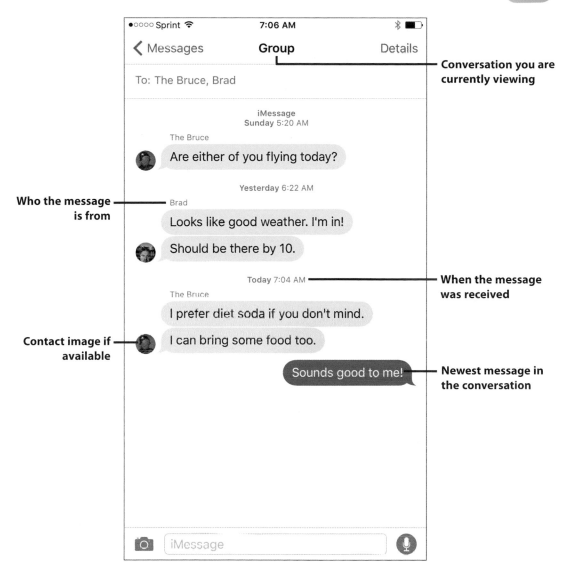

Conversation you are currently viewing

Who the message is from

When the message was received

Contact image if available

Newest message in the conversation

However you get to a message, you see the new message in either an existing conversation or a new conversation. The newest messages appear at the bottom of the screen. You can swipe up and down the screen to see all of the messages in the conversation. As you move up the screen, you move back in time.

Messages sent to you are on the left side of the screen and appear in a gray bubble. Just above the bubble is the name of the person sending the message; if you have an image for the contact, that image appears next to the bubble. The color of your bubbles indicates how the message is sent: blue indicates an iMessage and green indicates a cellular message.

Viewing Images or Video You Receive in Messages

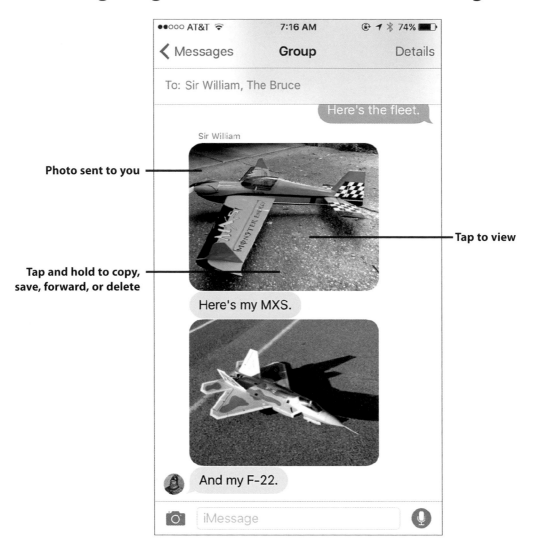

Photo sent to you

Tap and hold to copy, save, forward, or delete

Tap to view

When you receive a photo or video as an attachment, it appears in a thumbnail along with the accompanying message (video can also be embedded in a message as you'll see shortly).

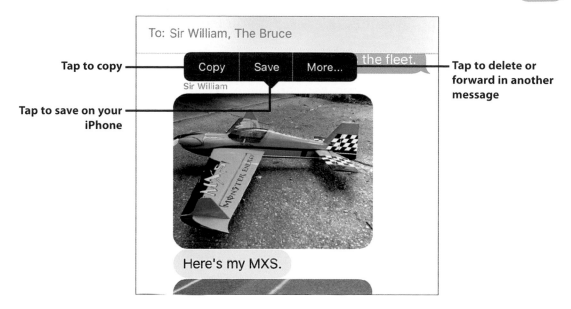

Tap to copy —— Copy   Save   More...   —— **Tap to delete or forward in another message**

Tap to save on your iPhone ——

To copy the photo or video and paste it into another app, tap and hold on it; when the Copy command appears, tap it. To save the image on your iPhone, tap and hold on it until the menu appears; then, tap Save. To forward it to someone else, tap and hold on the image. On the resulting menu, tap More. Tap the Share button located in the bottom-right corner of the screen. Complete the New Message that appears to send the photo along with a message. To delete the photo, tap and hold on the image. On the resulting menu, tap More. Then tap the Trash button.

Tap to return to the conversation —— Done   3 of 4   —— **Number of photos in the conversation**

Tap to share

Tap to bring up a list of recent photos in the conversation

Swipe to see other photos or videos in the conversation

To view a photo or video attachment, tap it. You see the photo or video at a larger size.

If there is more than one photo or video in the conversation, you see the number of them at the top of the screen. You can swipe to the left or right to move through the photos in the conversation. You can rotate the phone, zoom, and swipe around the photo just like viewing photos in the Photos app. You can watch a video in the same way, too.

Tap the List button to see a list of the recent photos in the conversation (this only appears if there is more than one photo in the conversation). Tap a photo on the list to view it.

Tap the Share button to share the photo with others via a message, email, tweet, Facebook, and so on. (When you hold an iPhone 6 Plus or 6s Plus horizontally, all the buttons are at the top of the screen.)

To move back to the conversation, tap Done.

Listening to Audio in Messages You Receive in Messages

Messages can include embedded audio that is recorded and added to a conversation so you can hear it (you learn how to send your own audio shortly).

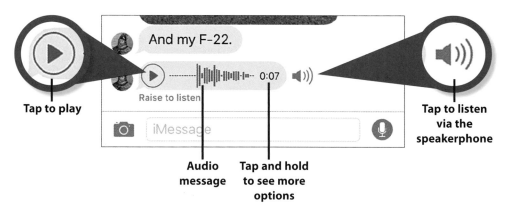

Tap to play

Raise to listen

Audio message

Tap and hold to see more options

Tap to listen via the speakerphone

When you receive an audio message, you can tap the Play button to play it or if you enabled the Raise to Listen option, lift the phone to your ear and the message plays automatically. Tap the Speaker icon to hear the message via the iPhone's speakerphone.

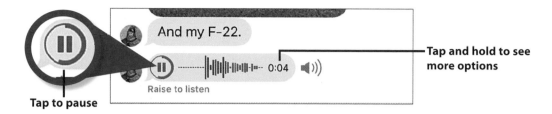

Tap and hold to see more options

Raise to listen

Tap to pause

While the message is playing you see its status along with the Pause button that you can tap to pause it. After the message finishes, you see a message saying that it expires in 2 minutes or 1 year, depending on your settings. That message is quickly replaced by Keep.

Tap to show Trash button so you can delete the audio

Speakerphone is on

Tap to save the audio message

Raise to talk   Keep

Tap Keep if you want to save the message on your phone. (Keep disappears indicating the audio is saved.) To delete a message you have kept, tap and hold on it until you see More. Tap More, and then tap the Trash icon. (If you have chosen the setting to have the audio messages expire in 2 minutes in the Settings app, then you can just let it expire rather than deleting it. See, "Setting Your Text and iMessage Preferences," earlier in this chapter.)

Kept Audio Messages

When one or more of the recipients of an audio message that you sent keeps it, a status message is added to the conversation on your phone. So, you know who keeps audio messages you have sent. And, others know when you keep their messages, too.

Watching Video in Messages You Receive in Messages

Messages can include embedded video that is recorded and added to a conversation so you can watch it.

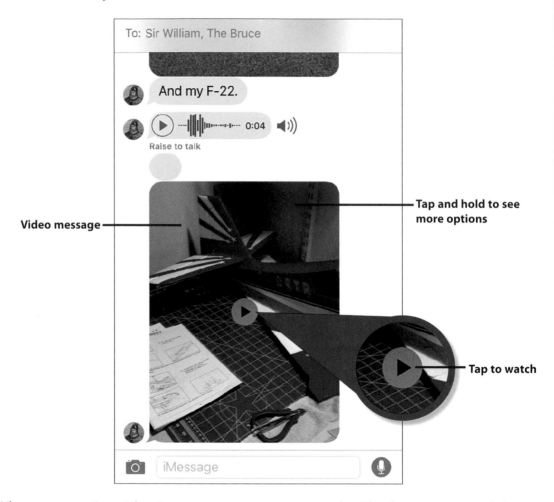

To: Sir William, The Bruce

And my F-22.

0:04
Raise to talk

Video message

Tap and hold to see more options

Tap to watch

iMessage

When you receive video in a message, you can tap the Play button to watch it. The video plays. Tap it to stop the playback.

Assuming you left the Expire setting for videos at After 2 Minutes, the video is deleted automatically after two minutes. Like an audio message, you see a brief message saying when the video will be deleted that is replaced by the Keep button. To keep the video in the conversation, tap Keep.

Video is playing

Tap to stop the video

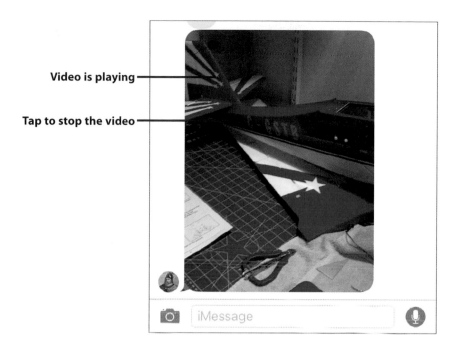

Tap to save the video

Tap to be able to delete the video

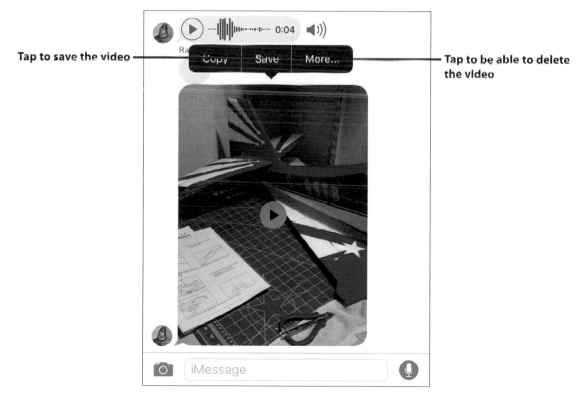

To save a video message on your phone, tap and hold on it until the menu appears, and then tap Save. It is saved in the Photos app (see Chapter 14, "Working with Photos and Video You Take with Your iPhone," for information about using the Photos app).

If you want to delete a video before it expires—or if you have the Expire setting on the Never option—tap and hold on the video to open the menu, and then tap More. Tap the Trash icon and tap Delete Message at the prompt.

Replying to Messages from the Messages App

To reply to a message, read the message and do the following:

(1) Read, watch, or listen to the most recent message.

(2) Tap in the Message bar.

(3) Type your reply or use the Dictation feature to speak your reply (this is translated to text unlike recording and embedding an audio message).

(4) Tap Send. The message is sent, and your message is added to the conversation. Messages you send are on the right side of the screen in a blue bubble if they were sent via iMessage or a green bubble if they were sent via the cellular network.

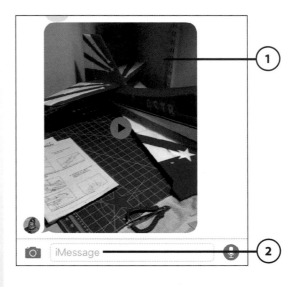

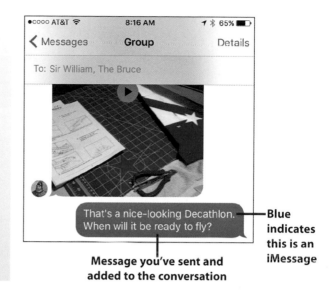

Message you've sent and
added to the conversation

Blue indicates this is an iMessage

More Tricks of the Messaging Trade

My Acquisitions Editor Extraordinaire pointed out that when people have cellular data turned off, they can't receive messages. You don't see a warning in this case; you can only tell the message wasn't delivered because the "Delivered" status doesn't appear under the message. The message is delivered as soon as the other person's phone is connected to the Internet again, and its status is updated accordingly on your phone. Also, when an iMessage can't be delivered, you can tap and hold on it; then tap Send as Text Message. The app tries to send the message via SMS instead of iMessage.

Replying to Messages from a Banner Alert

If you have banner alerts configured for your messages, you can reply directly from the alert:

1 Swipe down on the center of the banner alert notification. The reply box opens.

(2) Type your reply.

(3) Tap Send. Your message is added to the conversation.

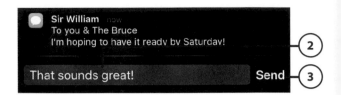

Using Quick Actions to Send Messages (iPhone 6s and 6s Plus)

New! You can use the Quick Actions feature on an iPhone 6s or 6s Plus with the Messages app as follows:

(1) Press on the Messages icon. The Quick Actions menu appears.

(2) Select the person to whom you want to send a message or select New Message to send a new message to someone not shown on the list. If you choose a person, you move into an existing conversation with that person or a new conversation is started. If you choose New Message, you move to the New Message screen.

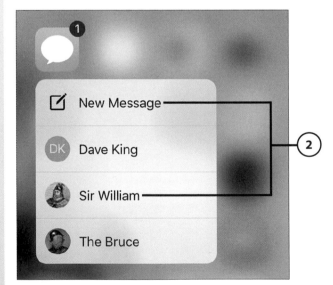

(**3**) Complete and send the message.

The iMessage Will Be With You…Always

Messages that are sent with iMessage move with you from device to device, so they appear on every device configured to use your iMessage account. Because of this, you can start a conversation on your iPhone while you are on the move and pick it up on your iPad or Mac later.

Working with Messages

As you send and receive messages, the interaction you have with each person or group becomes a separate conversation; a conversation consists of all the messages that have gone back and forth. You manage your conversations from the Messages screen.

Multiple Conversations with the Same People

The Messages app manages conversations based on the phone number or email address associated with the messages in that conversation rather than the people (contacts) involved in the conversation. So, you may have multiple conversations with the same person if that person used a different means, such as a phone number and an email address, to send messages to you.

Receiving and Reading Messages on an iPhone 6 Plus or 6s Plus

The iPhone 6 Plus' and 6s Plus' larger screen provides some additional functionality that is unique to those models. You can access this by holding the iPhone 6 Plus or 6s Plus horizontally when you use the Messages app.

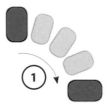

1. Open the Messages app and hold the iPhone so it is oriented horizontally. The window splits into two panes. On the left is the Navigation pane, where you can move to and select conversations you want to view. When you select a conversation in the left pane, its messages appear in the Content pane on the right.

2. Swipe up or down the Navigation pane to browse the conversations available to you. Notice that the two panes are independent.

3. Tap the conversation containing messages you want to read. The messages in that conversation appear in the Content pane on the right.

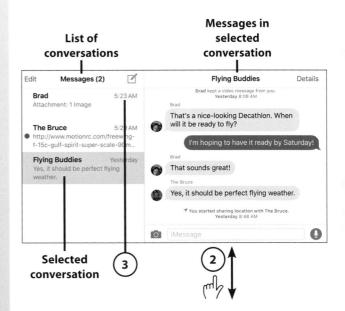

List of conversations

Messages in selected conversation

Selected conversation

(4) Swipe up and down the Content pane to read the messages in the conversation.

(5) Listen to embedded audio, watch embedded video, or work with attachments just like when you hold the iPhone vertically.

(6) To add a message to the conversation, tap in the send bar, type your message, and tap Send. Of course, you can embed audio or video, attach photos or video, or send your location just as you can when using Messages when you hold the iPhone vertically.

(7) To work with the conversation's details, tap Details.

(8) To change conversations, tap the conversation you want to view.

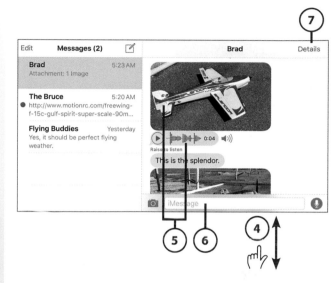

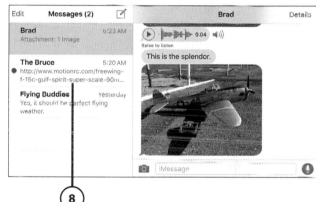

Using 3D Touch for Messages (iPhone 6s and 6s Plus)

New! You can use the 3D Touch feature on an iPhone 6s or 6s Plus with the Messages app as follows:

(1) Browse your messages.

(2) Tap and hold on a message in which you are interested. A Peek of that message appears.

(3) Review the preview of the message that appears in the Peek.

(4) To open the message so you can read the conversation of which it is a part, press down slightly harder until it pops open and use the steps in the earlier task to read it (skip the rest of these steps).

(5) To see actions you can perform on the message, swipe up on the Peek.

(6) Tap the action you want to perform, such as Ok, to reply to the current message with "Ok." If you tap the Custom command, you can create a custom reply to the message as you can when you view the conversation.

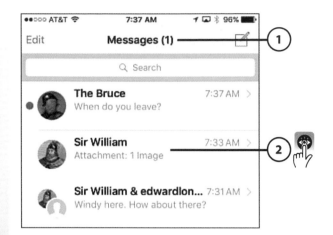

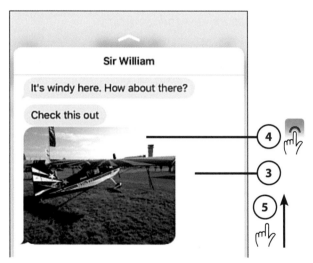

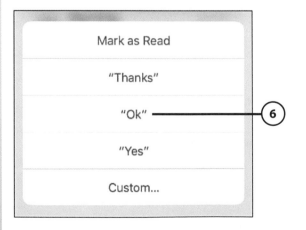

Adding Images and Video to Conversations

You can include any image, photo, or video stored on your iPhone in a text conversation, or you can take a photo or video to include in a message. This is a great way to share photos and videos.

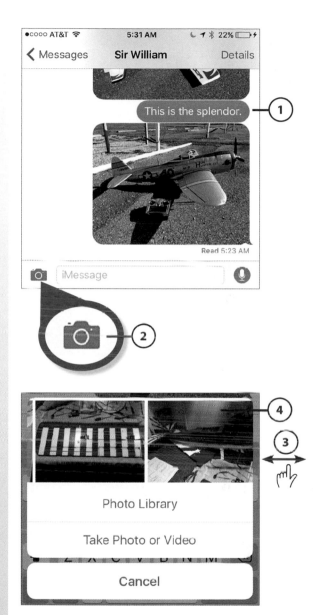

(1) Move into the conversation with the person to whom you want to send a photo, or start a new conversation with that person.

(2) Tap the Camera button. A dialog appears that allows you to add photos or videos in three ways. Perform steps 3 through 6 to send a photo you've recently taken. Perform steps 7 through 11 to send any photo or video stored on your iPhone. Start with step 12 to take a new photo or video and send it.

(3) If you have taken the photo recently, swipe to the left or right on the thumbnails you see above Photo Library to view the photos available to send.

(4) Tap the photo you want to send. The photo is enlarged and marked with a check mark to show it is selected.

Limitations, Limitations

Not all cell carriers support MMS messages (the type that can contain images and video), and the size of messages can be limited. Check with your carrier for more information about what is supported and whether there are additional charges for using MMS messages. If you're using iMessage, you don't have this potential limit and are always able to include images and video in your texts. Also be sure your recipient can receive MMS messages before sending one.

(5) To send more photos, swipe to the left and right on the photo to browse the others, and then tap the photos you want to send.

(6) To send the photos without comment, tap Send *X* Photos, where *X* is the number of photos you selected; the photos send and you go back to the conversation and can skip the rest of these steps. To send the photos and make a comment about them, tap Add Comment; the photos are added to the conversation and you are ready to type your comment; skip to step 16.

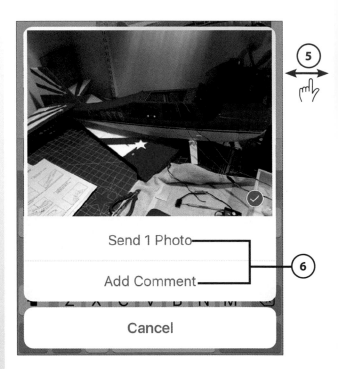

(7) Tap Photo Library.

(8) Browse the source containing the photos you want to send. (For more information about viewing sources of photos, see Chapter 14.)

(9) Swipe up or down the screen until you see the photo you want to send.

(10) Tap the photo you want to send.

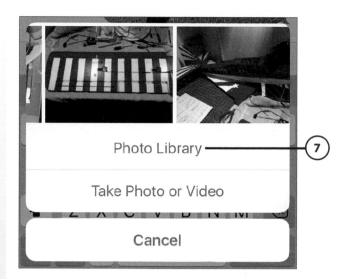

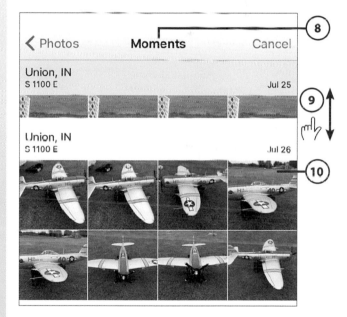

11 Tap Choose. You move back to the conversation and see the image in the Send box; move to step 16.

12 Tap Take Photo or Video.

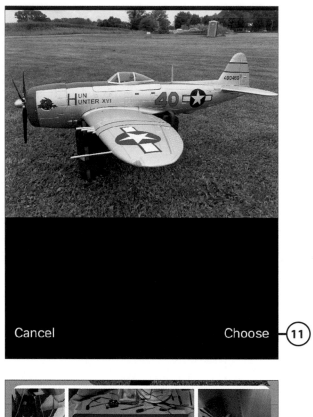

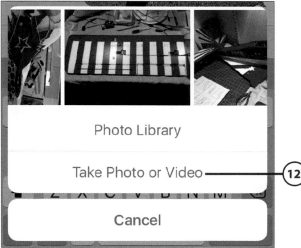

13 Choose VIDEO to take video or PHOTO to take a photo.

14 Take the photo or video you want to send. (For more information about taking photos or videos, see Chapter 14.)

15 Tap Use Photo or Use Video or tap Retake to redo the photo or video you are sending.

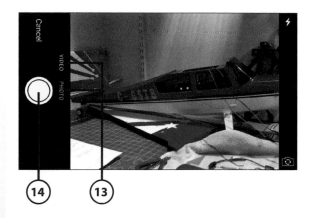

(16) Type the message you want to send with the photo or video; if you want to just send the photo or video, skip this step.

(17) Tap Send. The message, and photo or video, is sent.

This Isn't Houston, but There Is a Problem

If a message you try to send is undeliverable or has some other problem, it is marked with an exclamation point inside a red circle. Tap that icon and tap Try Again to attempt to resend the message.

Sharing with Messages

You can share all sorts of information via Messages from many apps, such as Safari, Contacts, Maps, and so on. From the app containing the information you want to share, tap the Share button. Then tap Messages. The information with which you are working is added to a new message. Use the Messages app to complete and send the message.

Adding Audio Recordings to Conversations

In a previous task you learned how to listen to embedded audio messages. Here's how to send your own embedded audio messages:

(1) Move to the conversation to which you want to add an audio message, or start a new conversation.

(2) Tap and hold on the Microphone at the right edge of the screen (not the one on the keyboard). Recording starts.

(3) Speak your message; keep your finger touching the screen while you speak.

(4) When you are done recording, take your finger off the screen.

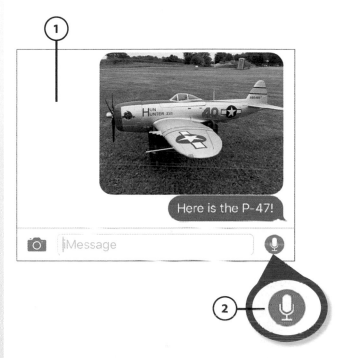

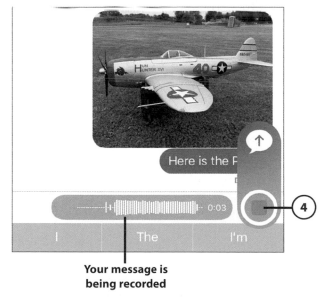

Your message is being recorded

5 To replay your message, tap the Play button.

6 To delete your message, tap Delete (x).

7 To send the message, tap the upward-facing arrow. The audio message is added to the conversation and the recipients are able to listen to it.

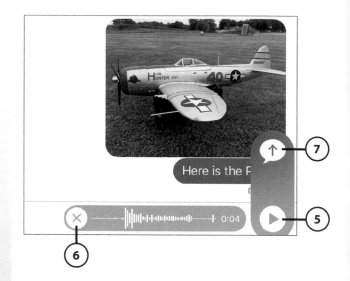

Embedded vs. Attachments

When you record audio or video for a message, it is embedded in the message. When you use the steps in "Adding Images and Video to Conversations," the images or video are attachments to the conversation. You can view or watch these similarly, but attachments are not affected by the Expire settings, and you can do more actions with attachments than you can with embedded items, such as forwarding to others and viewing all the attachments to a conversation.

Adding Video and Photos to Conversations

Here's how to add embedded video and photos to your conversations:

1. Move to the conversation to which you want to add video or photos, or start a new conversation.

2. Tap and hold the Camera icon until the video and photo tool appears and the Messages screen is replaced by the camera screen.

3. If you don't want to take a "selfie" video or photo, tap the Switch Camera button to change to the backside camera.

4. Adjust the image to what you want it to be when you start the video or take the photo.

5. To take a photo, tap the white Shutter button. The photo is taken and added to the conversation; skip to step 8.

6. To take a video, tap the red Record button. The video starts recording.

7. When you're done recording, tap the Stop button. The video is added to the message.

8. To send the photo or video, add your commentary and tap the Send button. The photo or video is added to the conversation and the recipients are able to view it.

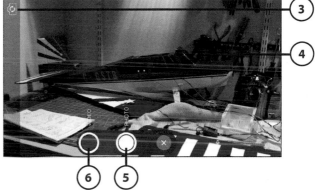

Adding Locations to Conversations

Location information can be available for the participants in a conversation. You can add your location information to a conversation as follows:

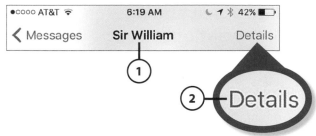

(1) Move to the conversation to which you want to add your location information.

(2) Tap Details.

(3) To share your current location as a snapshot, tap Send My Current Location. Your current location is captured and sent to the recipients of the message.

Current Locations

When a current location is added to a conversation, it is static, meaning it is only the location at that point in time. It appears as a map thumbnail in the conversation. Recipients can tap it to zoom in on the location, and then tap Directions to Here to generate directions from their location to the one sent as the current location.

---

(4) To dynamically share your location so that it updates as you move around, tap Share My Location.

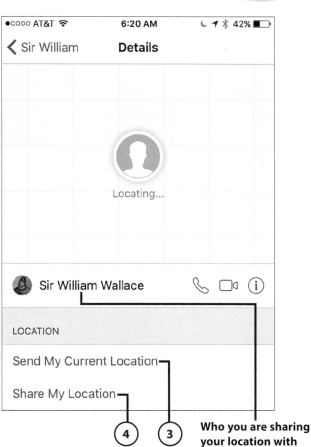

5 Tap how long you want your location information to be shared.

6 Tap Use to share your location or Not Now if you change your mind and don't want to share it. If you choose Use, your location is shared with the participants in the conversation and can be viewed on the Details screen on their devices. A notification that you are sharing your location is added to the conversation.

7 To stop sharing your location, tap Stop Sharing My Location. If you selected to share it for one hour or until the end of the day, location sharing stops automatically at the time you selected.

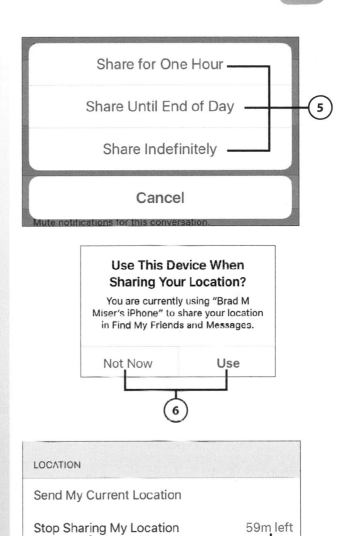

Time until your location information expires

Browsing Attachments to Conversations

As photos and videos are added to a conversation, they are collected so you can browse and view them at any time:

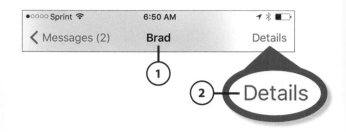

1. Move to the conversation in which you want to browse attachments.

2. Tap Details.

3. Swipe up until you see the ATTACHMENTS section.

4. Swipe up and down on the attachments until you see one you want to view.

5. Tap the attachment you want to view.

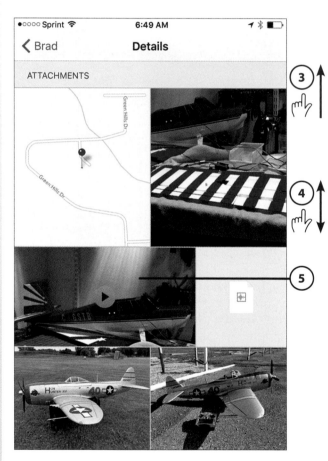

(**6**) View the attachment, such as watching a video.

(**7**) Tap the attachment.

(**8**) Tap the List button to see a list of all the attachments; tap an attachment to view it.

(**9**) Tap the Share button to share the attachment via Messages, email, and so on or to save it to your iPhone, add it to a contact, or take one of other available actions on it.

(**10**) Tap Done to return to the Details screen.

Stop Bugging Me!

You can disable notifications for a specific conversation by moving to its Details screen and setting the Do Not Disturb switch to on (green). You no longer are notified when new messages arrive in that conversation. Set the switch to off (white) to have notifications resume.

Deleting Messages and Conversations

Old text conversations never die, nor do they fade away. All the messages you receive from a person or that involve the same group of people stay in the conversation. Over time, you can build up a lot of messages in one conversation, and you can end up with lots of conversations. (If you set the Keep Messages setting to be 30 Days or 1 Year, messages older than the time you set are deleted automatically.)

Long Conversation?

When a conversation gets very long, the Messages app won't display all its messages. It keeps the more current messages visible on the conversation screen. To see earlier messages, swipe down on the screen to move to the top and tap Load Earlier Messages.

When a conversation gets too long or if you just want to remove specific messages from a conversation, take these steps:

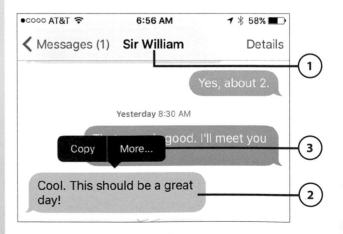

1. Move to a conversation containing an abundance of messages.

2. Tap and hold on a message you want to delete.

3. Tap More. The message on which you tapped is marked with a check mark to show it is selected.

Delete Them All!

To delete the whole conversation, instead of performing step 4, tap Delete All, which appears in the upper-left corner of the screen. Tap Delete Conversation. The conversation and all its messages are deleted.

4 Tap other messages you want to delete. They are marked with a check mark to show you have selected them.

5 Tap the Trash icon.

6 Tap Delete X Messages, where X is the number of messages you have selected. The messages are deleted and you return to the conversation.

Pass It On

If you want to send one or more messages to someone else, perform steps 1–3. Tap the Forward button that appears in the lower-right corner of the screen. A new message is created and the messages you selected are pasted into it. Select or enter the recipients to whom you want to send the messages, and tap Send.

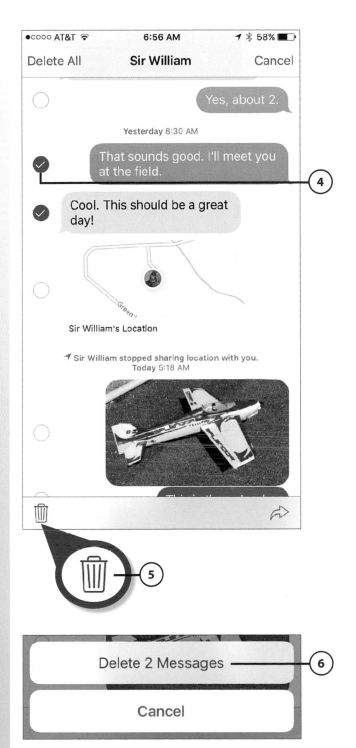

Deleting Conversations

If a conversation's time has come, you can delete it.

① Move to the Messages screen.

② Swipe to the left on the conversation you want to delete.

③ Tap Delete. The conversation and all the messages it contains are deleted.

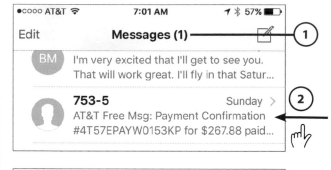

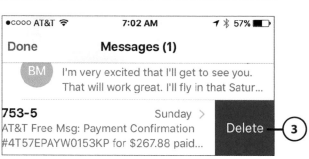

>>>Go Further

TEXTING LINGO

People frequently use shorthand when they text. Here is some of the more common shorthand you might see. This list is extremely short, but there are many websites dedicated to providing this type of information if you are interested. One that boasts of being the largest list of text message acronyms is www.netlingo.com/acronyms.php.

- FWIW—For What It's Worth
- LOL—Laughing Out Loud
- ROTFL—Rolling On the Floor Laughing
- CU—See You (later)
- PO—Peace Out
- IMHO—In My Humble Opinion
- TY—Thank You
- RU—Are You
- BRB—Be Right Back
- CM—Call Me
- DND—Do Not Disturb

- EOM—End of Message
- FSR—For Some Reason
- G2G—Got to Go
- IDK—I Don't Know
- IKR—I Know, Right?
- ILU—I Love You
- NM or NVM—Never Mind
- OMG—Oh My God
- OTP—On the Phone
- P911—Parent Alert
- PLZ—Please

Go here to figure out where and when you're supposed to be

Tap here to use your iPhone as a clock

Use this app to remind yourself of…anything

Tap here to configure your date, time, and reminder preferences

In this chapter, you explore all the calendar, time, date, and reminder functionality your iPhone has to offer. Topics include the following:

→ Getting started
→ Setting calendar, reminder, date, and time preferences
→ Working with calendars
→ Working with reminders
→ Working with the clock

Managing Calendars, Reminders, and Clocks

When it comes to time, your iPhone is definitely your friend. Using the iPhone's Calendar app, you can view calendars that have been synchronized among all your devices, such as computers and iPads, using an online account, such as iCloud or Google. You can also make changes to your calendars on your iPhone and they sync with your other devices so you have consistent information no matter which device you happen to be using at any time. The Reminders app ensures you don't forget tasks or anything else you want to remember. You can use the Clock app to set alarms, use as a stopwatch, and as a timer.

Getting Started

This chapter includes three different apps, because they are all related to managing your time.

The Calendar app does what it sounds like: it allows you to manage one or more calendars. This app has lots of features designed to help you work with multiple calendars and accounts, manage events that other people are invited to, and more. You don't have to use all these features, and you might just want to use its basic functionality, such as to record doctor appointments, dinner reservations, and similar events for which it is important to know the time and date (and be reminded when those times and dates are approaching).

The Reminders app can remind you about things you need to do at a specific time or it can be used to capture lists that don't have any specific time, such as things you need to buy the next time you go to a specific store.

The Clock app provides lots of very useful time functions, including an alarm, timer, and stopwatch.

Setting Calendar, Reminder, Date, and Time Preferences

There are a number of calendar, reminder, date, and time options you can config-ure using the Settings app. Following is an example showing how to determine how many months of events are available in the Calendar app on your iPhone. You can configure other calendar, reminder, date, and time settings using similar steps and the descriptions of the settings in the table that follows these steps.

To configure how far back in time calendars on your iPhone go, perform the following steps:

(1) Tap Settings on the Home screen.

(2) Swipe up the screen.

(3) Tap Mail, Contacts, Calendars.

(4) Swipe up the screen until you see the CALENDARS section.

(5) Tap Sync.

(6) Tap the amount of time you would like to see on your calendars. For example, to show events as far back as three months, tap Events 3 Months Back.

(7) Tap Mail. The Calendar app shows events as far back in time as you selected in step 6. You can change the other calendar, time, date, and reminder settings using a similar pattern and the description of the options in the following table.

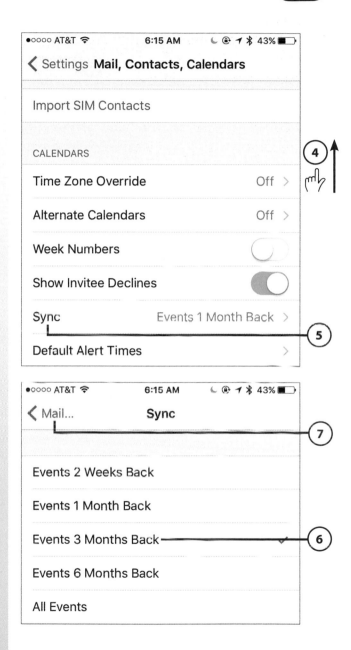

Calendar, Reminder, and Time Settings

Setting	Description
Mail, Contacts, Calendars	
CALENDARS	
Time Zone Override	When disabled, the time for events is based on your current time zone. When enabled, the time zone for events on the calendars is overridden with the time zone for a city you select. This is useful if you always want event times to be based on a specific time zone.
Alternate Calendars	You can choose among different types of calendars, such as Chinese or Hebrew.
Week Numbers	When on (green), week numbers appear on your calendars in the Month view.
Show Invitee Declines	When on (green) and someone declines a meeting, they are shown on the Invitee list as having declined. When off (white), they are removed from the list.
Sync	Determines how far back events are synced onto your calendars. You can choose 2 weeks, 1 month, 3 months, 6 months, or all events.
Default Alert Times	Determines the default alert times for birthdays, events, and all-day events. When you set the Time To Leave switch to on (green), the Calendar app can use your travel time to configure an event's alert.
Start Week On	Determines the first day of the week.
Default Calendar	Determines which calendar is used for new events by default (you can override this setting for any events you create).
Events Found in Mail	When on (green) and the Mail app detects event information in an email, it presents a prompt that enables you to add the event to a calendar.

Setting	Description
General	
Date & Time	
24-Hour Time	Causes the iPhone to display 24-hour instead of 12-hour time.
Set Automatically	When on (green), the iPhone sets the time and date automatically based on the current network it is using. When off (white), you can manually set the time zone, time, and date.
Time Zone	When Set Automatically is turned off, you can use this to manually set the time zone you are in.
Date, Time	When Set Automatically is turned off, you can use this to manually set the date and time.
Reminders	
Sync	Determines how far back reminders are synced onto your calendars. You can choose 2 weeks, 1 month, 3 months, 6 months, or all reminders.
Default List	Determines which reminder list new reminders are placed on when you create them. You can override this for any new reminder you create.

Notifications

The Calendar and Reminders apps can communicate with you in various ways, such as displaying alerts or banners when something happens that you might want to know about; for example, you can be alerted with a banner when you receive an invitation to an event. Configuring notifications for these apps will make them even more valuable. The information you need to configure notifications is explained in the section called "Setting Up Notifications and the Notification Center" in Chapter 5, "Customizing How Your iPhone Looks and Sounds."

Working with Calendars

The Calendar app helps you manage your calendars; you'll notice I wrote *calendars* rather than *calendar*. That's because you can have multiple calendars in the app at the same time. To use the most cliché example, you might have a calendar for work and one for your personal life. Or, you might want a calendar for your travel plans, and then share that calendar with people who care about your location.

In most cases, you start by adding existing calendar information from an iCloud, Google, or similar account. From there, you can use the Calendar app to view your calendars, add or change events, and much more. Any changes you make in the Calendar app are automatically made in all the locations that use calendars from the same account.

The best option for storing your calendar information is an online account (such as iCloud or Google) because you can easily access your calendar information from many devices, and your calendars are kept in sync automatically. To learn how to configure an online account for calendar information, refer to Chapter 3, "Setting Up and Using iCloud and Other Online Accounts."

Viewing Calendars and Events

You use the Calendar app to view and work with your calendars, and you can choose how you view them, such as by month, week, or day.

 — **The badge indicates how many invitations to events you have received**

To get into your calendars, move to the Home screen and tap the Calendar app (which shows the current day and date in its icon and a badge, if you have at least one new invitation). The most recent screen you were viewing appears.

There are three viewing modes you use in the app. The mode in which you'll spend most of your time is the one that displays your calendars in various views, such as showing a month, week, or day. Another mode is the Calendars tool that enables you to choose and edit the calendar information that is displayed. The third mode is your Inbox, which you use to work with event invitations you receive.

Configuring Calendars

To configure the calendar information you see in the app, perform the following steps:

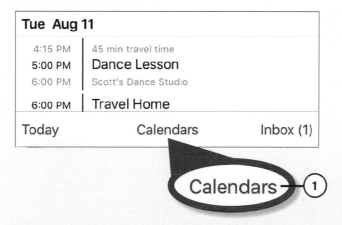

1 If you only have one calendar, skip to step 2. Tap Calendars to see all of your synced calendars. If you don't see this at the bottom of the screen, you are already on the Calendars screen (look for "Calendars" at the top of the screen).

The Calendars screen displays the calendars available, organized by the account from which they come, such as ICLOUD or GMAIL. By default, all your calendars are displayed, which is indicated by the check marks next to the calendars' names. Any calendars that don't have a check mark next to their names are not displayed when you view your calendar.

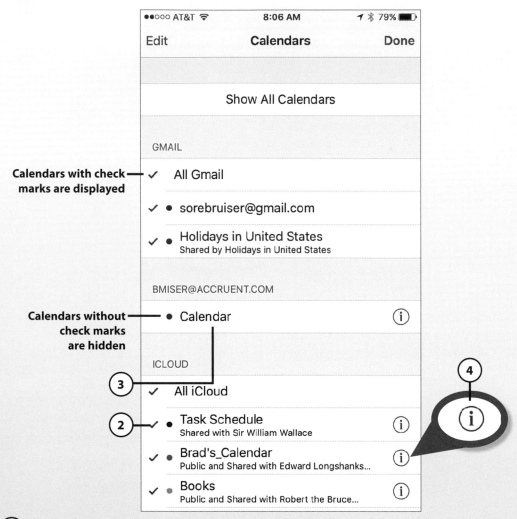

Calendars with check marks are displayed

Calendars without check marks are hidden

(2) Tap a calendar with a check mark to hide it. The check mark disappears and the calendar is hidden. (The calendar is still there, you just won't see it when you are viewing your calendars.)

(3) To show a calendar again, tap its name. It is marked with a check mark and appears when you are viewing calendars.

(4) Tap the Info button to see or change a calendar's information settings. Not all types of calendars support this function, and those that do can offer different settings. The following steps show an iCloud calendar; if you are working with a calendar of a different type, such as an Exchange calendar, you might not have all or the same options as those shown here. In any case, the steps to make changes are similar across all available types of calendars.

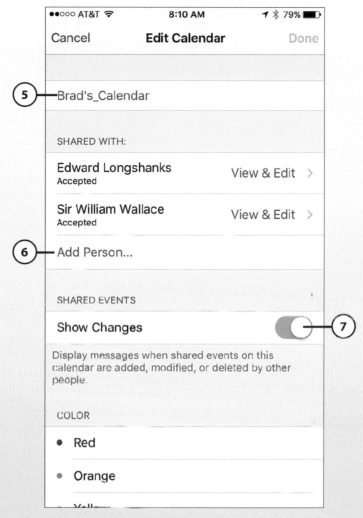

(5) Change the name of the calendar by tapping it and then making changes on the keyboard; when you're done making changes, swipe down the screen to close the keyboard.

(6) To share the calendar with someone, tap Add Person, enter the email address of the person with whom you are sharing it, and tap Add. (Sharing calendars is explained in more detail later in this chapter.)

(7) If the calendar is shared and you don't want to be notified when shared events are changed, added, or deleted, set the Show Changes switch to off (white). When this switch is enabled and a change is made to a shared calendar, you receive notifications about the changes that were made. If the calendar is not shared, you won't see this switch.

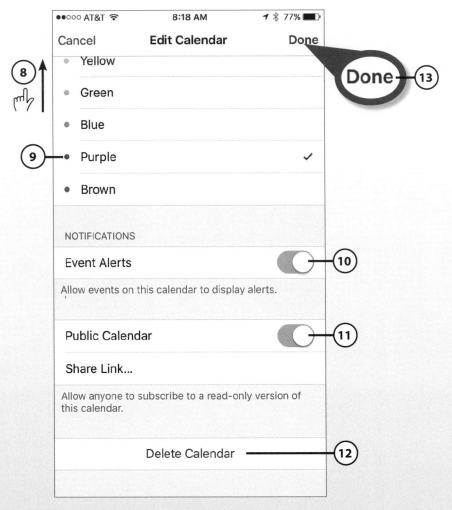

8 Swipe up the screen.

9 Tap the color you want events on the calendar to appear in.

10 If you want alerts to be enabled (active) for the calendar, set the Event Alerts switch to on (green). (Not all types of calendars support this setting.)

11 To make the calendar public so that others can subscribe to a read-only version of it, set the Public Calendar switch to on (green), tap Share Link, and then use the resulting Share tools to invite others to subscribe to the calendar (more on this later in this chapter).

12 To remove the calendar entirely (instead of hiding it from view), tap Delete Calendar and then tap Delete Calendar at the prompt. The calendar and all its events are deleted. (It's usually better just to hide a calendar as described in step 2 so you don't lose its information.)

13 Assuming that you didn't delete the calendar, tap Done.

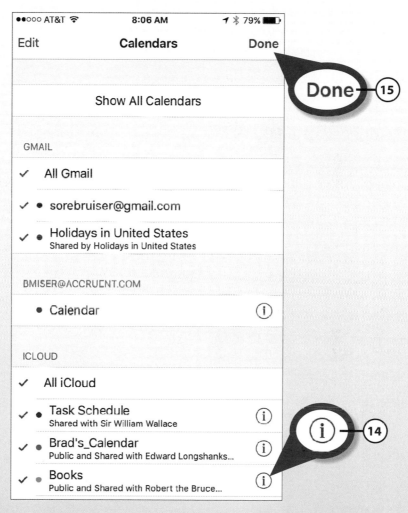

14 Edit other calendars as needed.

15 Tap Done. The app moves into viewing mode, and the calendars you enabled are displayed.

>>>Go Further
ALL OR NOTHING

You can make all your calendars visible by tapping the Show All Calendars button at the top of the screen; tap Hide All Calendars to do the opposite. After all the calendars are shown or hidden, you can tap individual calendars to show or hide them. You can show all the calendars from the same account by tapping the All command at the top of each account's calendar list, such as All iCloud to show all your iCloud calendars. Tap this again to hide all the account's calendars.

Navigating Calendars

The Calendar app uses a hierarchy of detail to display your calendars. The lowest level of detail, but longest timeframe displayed, is the year view. Next is the month view, which shows more detail but covers a shorter timeframe. This is followed by the week/day view; showing the highest level of detail is the event view.

Viewing Calendars

You can view your calendars from the year level all the way down to the day/week view. It's easy to move among the levels to get to the time period you want to see. Here's how:

1. Starting at the year view, swipe up and down until you see the year in which you are interested. (If you aren't in the year view, keep tapping the back button located in the upper-left corner of the screen until the back button disappears.)

2. Tap the month in which you are interested. The days in that month display, and days with events are marked with a dot.

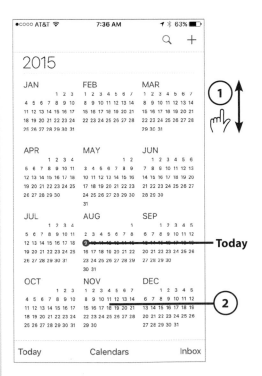

3 Swipe up and down the screen to view different months.

4 To see the detail for a date, tap it. There are two ways to view the daily details: the Calendar view or the List view. Steps 5 through 8 show the Calendar view, while steps 9 though 11 show the List view. Each of these views has benefits and as you can see, it is easy to switch between them.

Today Is the Day

To quickly move to the current day, tap Today, located at the bottom of the screen.

5 To see the Calendar view, ensure the List button is not selected (isn't highlighted). On the resulting screen are the days of the week you are viewing. The date in focus is highlighted with a red circle for when that day is today and a black circle for any other day. Below this area is the detail for the selected day showing the events on that day.

6 Swipe to the left or right on the dates or date being displayed to change the date for which detailed information is being shown.

7 Swipe up or down on the date detail to browse all its events.

8 Tap an event to view its detail and skip to step 12.

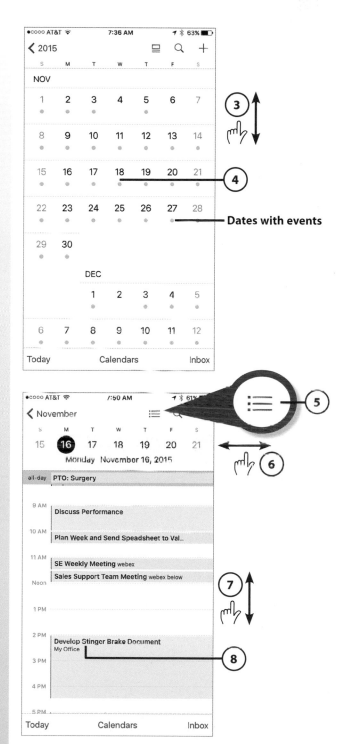

Dates with events

9 To see the events in List view, tap the List button so it is highlighted.

10 Swipe up and down to see the events for each day.

11 Tap on an event to view its detail.

12 Swipe up and down the screen to see all of the event's information.

13 Read information about the event.

14 Tap the Calendar or Alert fields to change these settings.

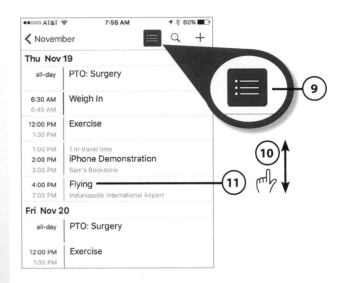

(15) Tap attachments to view them.

(16) Tap any links to move to information related to the event.

(17) Read notes associated with the event.

(18) See the event's location on a map.

(19) Tap the date to move back to the week/day view.

Red Line

The red line stretching horizontally across the screen indicates the current time, which is shown at the left end of that line.

(20) Tap the back button (labeled with the month you are viewing) to move back to the month view.

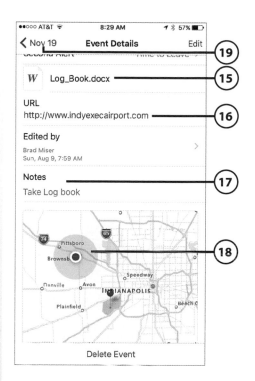

●●○○○ AT&T 🅢   8:29 AM   ⬤ ❋ 57% ■⬝

❮ Nov 19   **Event Details**   Edit — **(19)**

W Log_Book.docx — **(15)**

URL
http://www.indyexecairport.com — **(16)**

Edited by
Brad Miser   ❯
Sun, Aug 9, 7:59 AM

Notes — **(17)**
Take Log book

— **(18)**

Delete Event

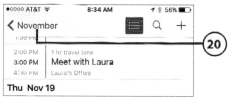

●○○○○ AT&T 🅢   8:34 AM   ⬤ ❋ 56% ■⬝

❮ November   🔲 🔍 ＋

— **(20)**

2:00 PM | 1 hr travel time
3:00 PM | **Meet with Laura**
4:30 PM | Laura's Office

Thu Nov 19

(21) To view your calendars in the multiday view, rotate your iPhone so it is horizontal. You can do this while in the week/day view or the month view.

(22) Swipe left or right to change the dates being displayed.

(23) Swipe up or down to change the time of day being displayed.

(24) Tap an event to see its detail.

Using 3D Touch for Events (iPhone 6s and 6s Plus Only)

New! You can use the 3D Touch feature on an iPhone 6s or 6s Plus with the Calendar app as follows:

(1) Browse events, such as when you use the List view.

(2) Tap and hold on an event in which you are interested. A Peek of that event appears.

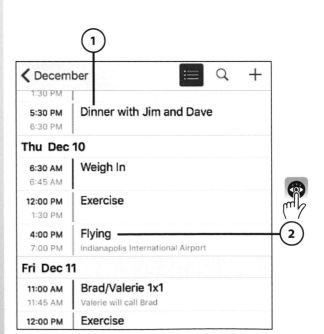

3 Review the preview of the event that appears in the Peek.

4 To open the event so you can see all of its detail, press down slightly harder until it pops open and use the steps in the earlier task to work with it (skip the rest of these steps).

5 To see actions you can perform on the event, swipe up on the Peek.

6 Tap the action you want to perform, such as Delete Event, to delete the event from your calendar.

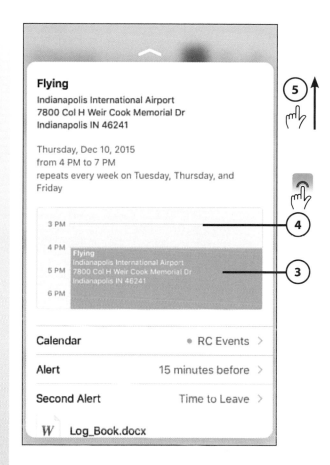

Adding Events to a Calendar

There are a number of ways you can add events to your calendar. You can create an event in an app on a computer, website, or other device and sync that event onto the iPhone through an online account. You can also manually create events in the Calendar app on the iPhone. Your events can include a lot of detail; you can choose to just create the basic information on your iPhone while you are on the move and complete it later from a computer or other device, or you can fill in all the details directly in the Calendar app.

(1) Tap the Add button, which appears in the upper-right corner of any of the views when your phone is vertical (except when you are viewing an event's details). The initial date information is taken from the date currently being displayed, so you can save a little time if you view the date of the event before tapping the Add button.

(2) Tap in the Title field and type the title of the event.

(3) Tap the Location bar and type the location of the event; if you allowed the app to use Location Services, you're prompted to find and select a location; if not, just type the location and skip to step 6.

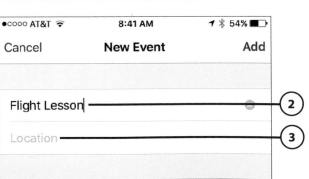

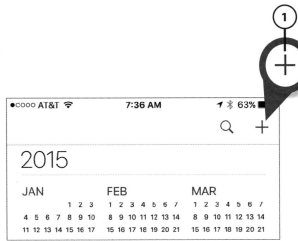

Location Prompt

The first time you create an event, you might be prompted to allow the Calendar app to access your location information. When you allow the app to use Location Services, you can search for and select event locations. The app can use this information to include an estimate of travel time for the event and to display events on a map when you view their detail.

(4) Type the location in the Search bar. Sites that meet your search are shown below.

(5) Tap the location for the event.

(6) To set the event to last all day, set the All-day switch to the on position (green); when you select the All-day option, you provide only the start and end dates (you don't input times). To set a specific start and end time, leave this in the off (white) position; you'll set both the dates and times as described in the following steps.

(7) To set a timeframe for the event, tap Starts. The date and time tool appears.

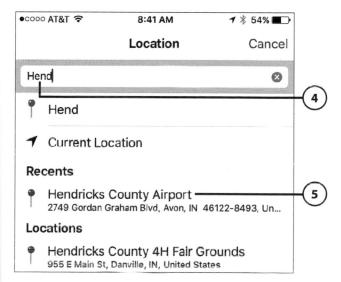

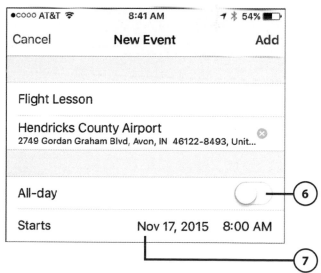

Your Results May Vary

The fields and options available when you create a new event are based on the calendar with which the event is associated. For example, an iCloud calendar offers different options than a Google calendar does. If you aren't creating an event on your default calendar, it's a good idea to associate the event with a calendar before you fill in its details (to do that, perform step 31 before you do step 2).

8 Swipe up or down on the date wheel until the date on which the event starts appears in the center.

9 Swipe up or down on the hour wheel until the event's starting hour is shown.

10 Scroll and select the starting minute in the same way.

11 Swipe up or down on the hour wheel to select AM or PM.

12 If you want to associate the event with a specific time zone, tap Time Zone; if not, don't tap it and skip to step 14.

13 Search for and select the time zone with which the event should be associated.

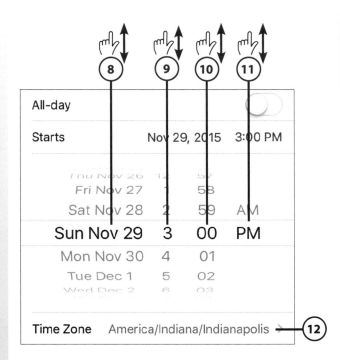

No Changes?

When you change a selection on most of the screens you see, you automatically return to the previous screen. If you don't make a change, you can return to the previous screen by tapping the back button that always appears in the upper-left corner of the screen (it can have different labels depending on the context of the current screen).

(14) Tap Ends.

(15) Use the date and time tool to set the ending date and time (if applicable) for the event; these work the same way as for the start date and time.

(16) Tap Ends. The date and time tool closes.

(17) To make the event repeat, tap Repeat and follow steps 18–23. (For a nonrepeating event, skip to step 24.)

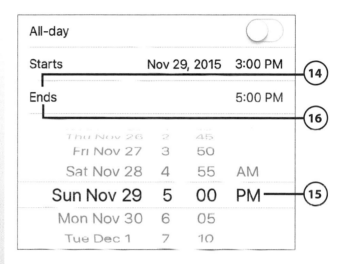

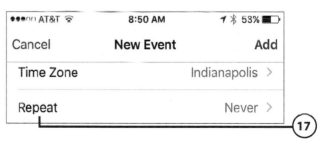

18 Tap the frequency with which you want the event repeated, such as Every Day, Every Week, and so on; if you want to use a repeat cycle not shown, tap Custom and create the frequency with which you want the event to repeat.

19 Tap End Repeat to set a time at which the event stops repeating.

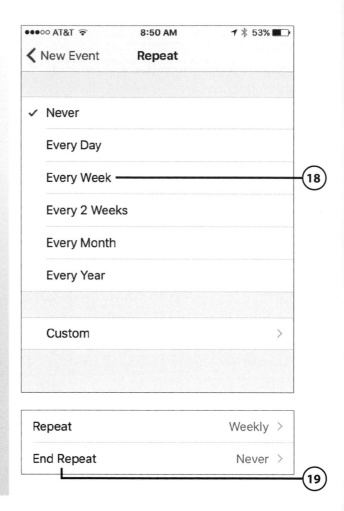

Custom Repeat

To configure a custom repeat cycle for an event, such as the first Monday of every month, tap Custom on the Repeat screen. Then use the Frequency (Monthly for the example) and Every (for example, On the first Monday) settings to configure the repeat cycle. Tap Repeat to return to the Repeat screen, and then New Event to get back to the event you are creating.

20 To have the event always repeat, tap Never and skip to step 23.

21 To set an end to the repetition, tap On Date.

22 Use the date tool to set the date for the last repeated event.

23 Tap New Event.

24 To configure travel time for the event, tap Travel Time; if you don't want to configure this, skip to step 31.

25 Set the Travel Time switch to on (green).

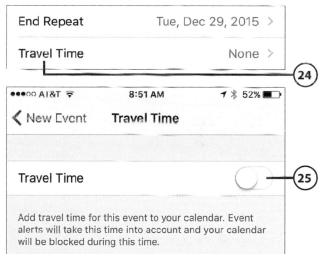

(26) To manually add a travel time to the event, tap it and skip to step 30.

(27) To build a travel time based on a starting location, tap Starting Location.

No Change Needed

If you don't make a change to one of the settings, such as on the Repeat screen, you need to tap the New Event link to get back to the New Event screen.

---

(28) To use your current location as the starting point, tap Current Location. Alternatively, use the Search tool to find a starting location, and then tap it to select that location.

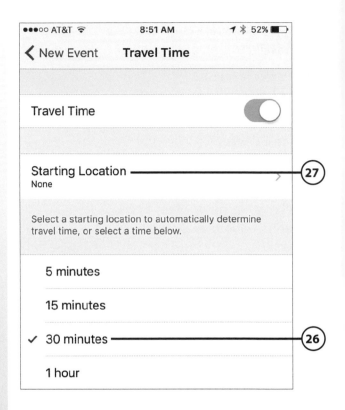

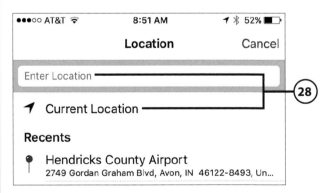

(29) Tap the method you will use to travel to the location.

(30) Tap New Event.

(31) To change the calendar with which the event is associated, tap Calendar (to leave the current calendar selected, skip to step 33).

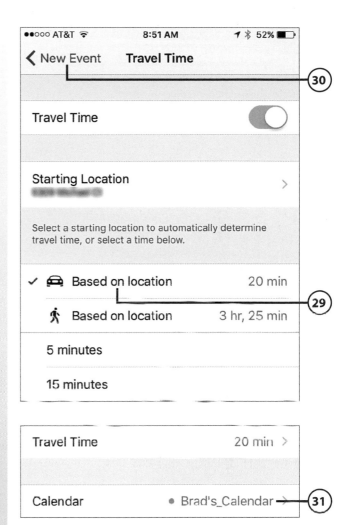

●●○○○ AT&T 🛜   8:51 AM   ⬀ ✳ 52% 🔋

❮ New Event   **Travel Time** — (30)

Travel Time   ⬤

Starting Location   ❯

Select a starting location to automatically determine travel time, or select a time below.

✓ 🚗 Based on location   20 min — (29)

🚶 Based on location   3 hr, 25 min

5 minutes

15 minutes

Travel Time   20 min ❯

Calendar   ● Brad's_Calendar ➔ (31)

32 Tap the calendar with which the event should be associated.

33 To invite others to the event, tap Invitees; if you don't want to invite someone else, skip to step 38.

34 Enter the email addresses for each person you want to invite; as you type, the app tries to identify people who match what you are typing. You can tap a person to add him to the event. You can also use the Add button to choose people from your Contacts.

35 Repeat step 34 until you've added everyone you want to invite.

36 Tap Done. You move to the Invitees screen and see those whom you invited.

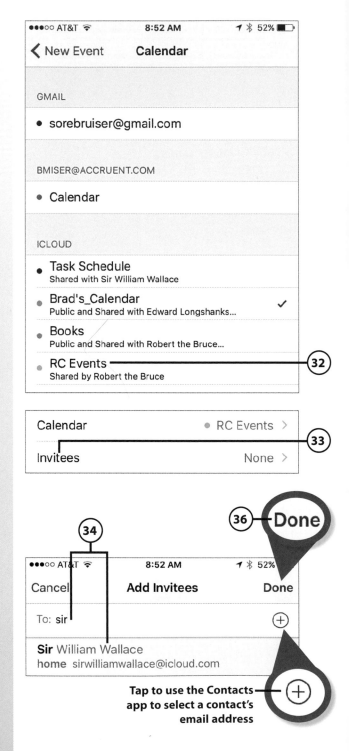

Tap to use the Contacts app to select a contact's email address

37) Tap New Event.

38) To set an alert for the event that is different than the default, tap Alert; if you want to use the default alert, skip to step 40.

39) Tap when you want to see an alert for the event.

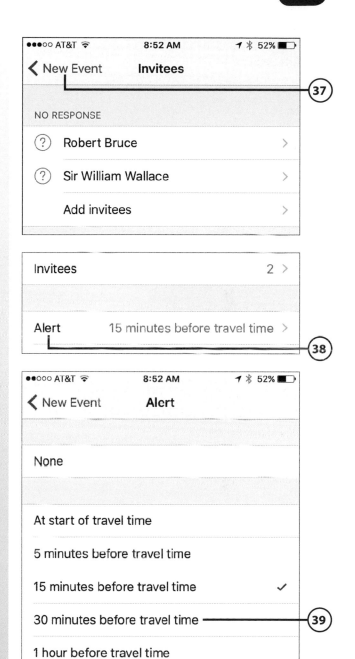

40 To set a second alert that is different than the default, tap Second Alert; to use the default, skip to step 42.

41 Tap when you want to see a second alert for the event. If you have included travel time in the event, the At start of travel time option is useful because it alerts you when your journey should begin.

42 To indicate your availability during this event, tap Show As.

43 Tap the availability status you want to indicate during the event.

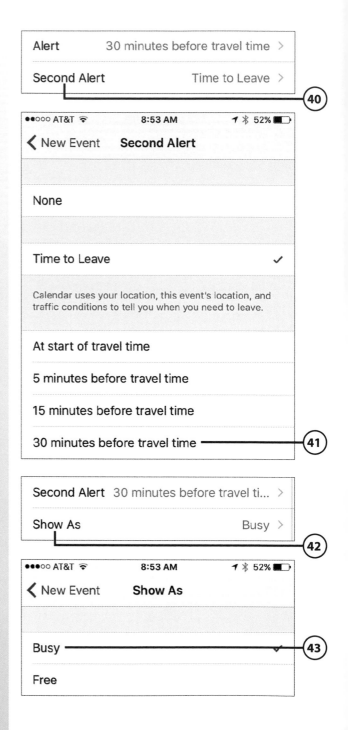

44 To enter a URL associated with the event, tap in the URL field.

45 Type the URL.

46 Tap Done.

47 Tap Notes and type information you want to associate with the event.

48 Tap Add. The event is added to the calendar you selected, and invitations are sent to its invitees. Alerts trigger according to the event's settings.

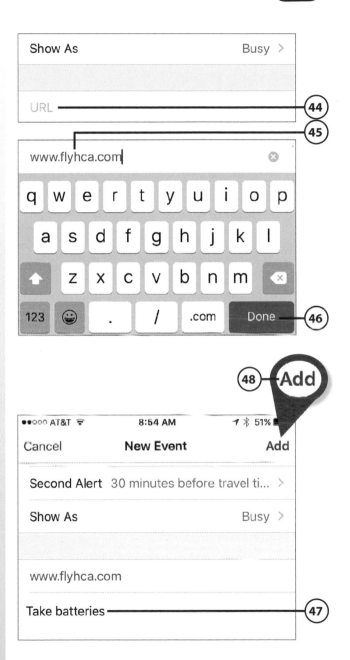

New event on the calendar

A Better Way to Create Events

Adding a lot of detail to an event in the Calendar app can be challenging. One effective and easy way to create events is to start with Siri. You can activate Siri and say something like "Create meeting with William Wallace in my office on November 15 at 10 AM." Siri creates the event with as much detail as you provided (and might prompt you to provide additional information, such as which email address to use to send invitations). When you get to a computer or iPad, edit the event to add more information, such as website links. When your calendar is updated on the iPhone, via syncing, the additional detail for the event appears in the Calendar app, too. (See Chapter 12, "Working with Siri," for detailed information about using Siri.)

Using Quick Actions with the Calendar App (iPhone 6s and 6s Plus Only)

You can use the Quick Actions feature on an iPhone 6s or 6s Plus with the Calendar app as follows:

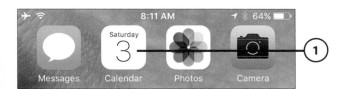

1. Press on the Calendar icon. The Quick Actions menu appears.

2. To add a new event, choose Add Event and use the steps in the previous task to create the event.

3. To view an event, choose the event you want to see. You move to the event and can see all of its information.

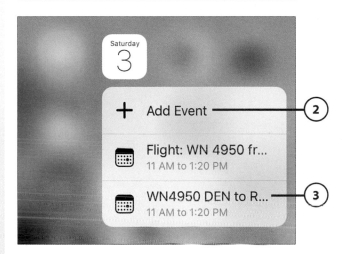

Searching Calendars

You can search for events to locate specific ones quickly and easily. Here's how:

1. Tap the Search tool. A list of all your events displays.

2. Tap in the Search box.

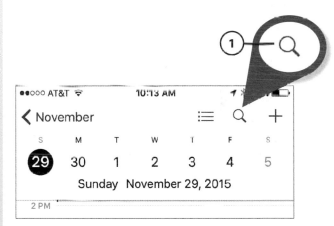

3 Type your search term. The events shown below the Search bar are those that contain your search term.

4 Swipe up or down the list to review the results.

5 Tap an event to see its detail.

6 Swipe up or down the event's screen to review its information.

7 Tap Back to return to the results.

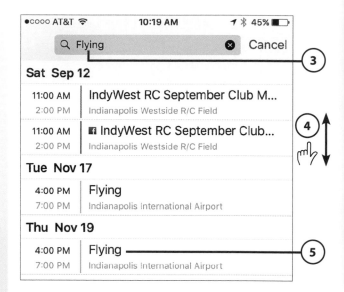

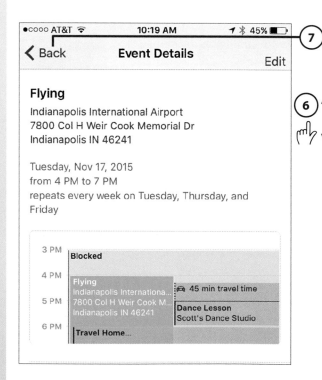

8 Continue reviewing the results until you get the information for which you were searching.

9 Tap Cancel to exit the search mode or the Clear button (x) to clear the search but remain in search mode.

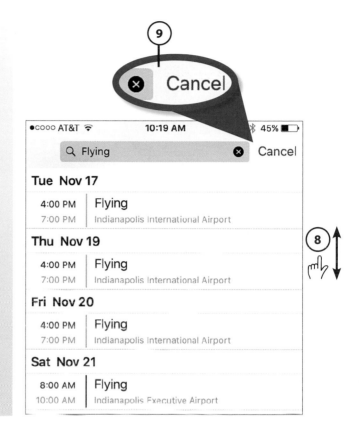

Managing Calendars and Events

Following are some more points about the Calendar app you might find helpful:

- You can also use the List view when you are viewing the calendar in month view. Tap the List button (just to the left of the Search button). The list opens at the bottom of the screen and shows the events on the day currently selected (indicated in the black circle unless the day selected is today in which case the circle is red).

- You can see today's events at any time by swiping down from the top of the screen to open the Notification Center. On the Today tab is a summary of your events for the day; your next event is shown just under the date at the top of the screen. Swipe up and down on the Calendar section to see the entire day's events.

Swipe down to open the Notification Center

Swipe to see your events

Alert style event notification

Banner style event notification

- When an event's alarm goes off, an onscreen notification appears (according to the notification settings for the Calendar app) and the calendar event sound you've selected plays. When an alert notification appears, the event's title, location (if one is set), and time appear. You have to take some action. You can tap Close to dismiss the alert or tap Options to see additional choices. On the Options dialog box, tap Snooze to snooze the alarm, View Event to see its details, or Close to dismiss the alarm. When a banner notification appears, you see the event's name and location. You can tap the event to view its details or ignore it and it moves off the screen after a few moments. You can also swipe up from the bottom of the notification to manually close it.

- Siri is useful for working with calendars, especially for creating events. See Chapter 12 for detailed information about using Siri.

Working with Reminders

Tap to see what you want to be reminded about

The badge indicates how many items you are currently being reminded of

The Reminders app does just what it sounds like it does, which is to remind you about things. The things it reminds you about are up to you; these might be to-do items/tasks, thoughts you want to be reminded to follow up on later, or anything else you can think of. Reminders are also useful for lists of things you need to get or want to remember to think about later. Just as you can have multiple calendars to manage your events, you can have multiple lists for your reminders.

Reminder lists

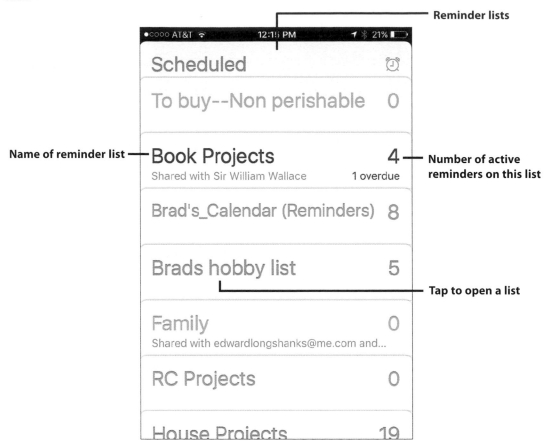

Name of reminder list — Book Projects

Number of active reminders on this list

Tap to open a list

Open the Reminders app by tapping its icon on the Home screen. Tap the list you want to view. If a list is already open, swipe down the screen to view the area showing all the reminder lists.

Reminder list — **Book Projects**

Shared with Sir William Wallace

4 — **Number of active reminders on this list**

Edit

!!! Finish Ch 11
Today, 12:15 PM

Finish Ch 6 — **Reminders**
8/11/15, 1:00 PM

Call William

Complete radio button — Call Robert
Tomorrow, 8:00 AM

+

Show Completed

Tap to move back to the list of reminder lists

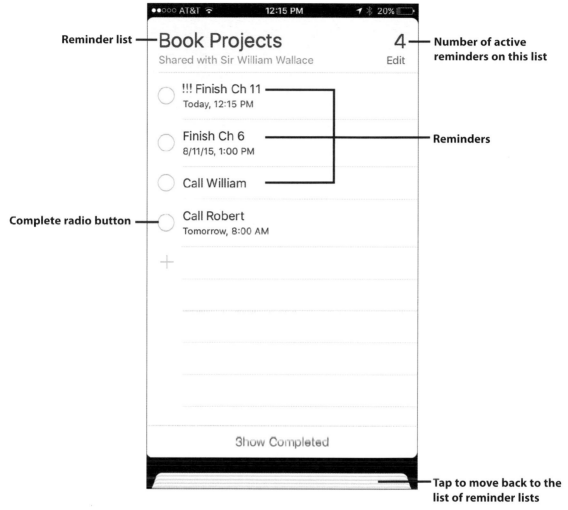

You can see how easily you can move between the list of reminder lists and a specific reminder list. There are a couple of other views you can use, too (as you learn in a bit), but you'll likely spend most of your time on these two.

Creating Reminders

You can manually create reminders by performing the following steps:

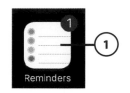

1. Tap the Reminders icon on the Home screen.

2. If you see a reminder list instead of the list of reminder lists, skip this step. If you see the list of your reminder lists, tap the list on which you want to create a new reminder.

3. Tap in an open reminder space that contains the +. The keyboard appears.

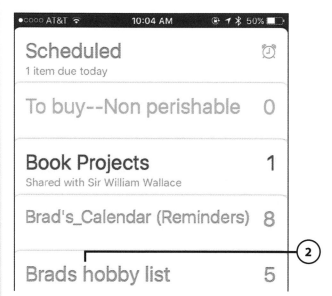

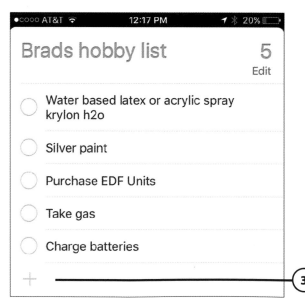

4 Type the reminder.

5 To create more reminders, tap the return button on the keyboard.

6 Create the next reminder.

7 Repeat steps 5 and 6 until you've created all the reminders you want.

8 Tap Done. You can stop here if you only want basic information in the reminder, which is just the reminder's text (the app won't actually remind you unless you configure the reminder for a specific date and time). Continue these steps to fully configure a reminder.

9 Tap the reminder you want to configure for an alert.

10 Tap the Info button.

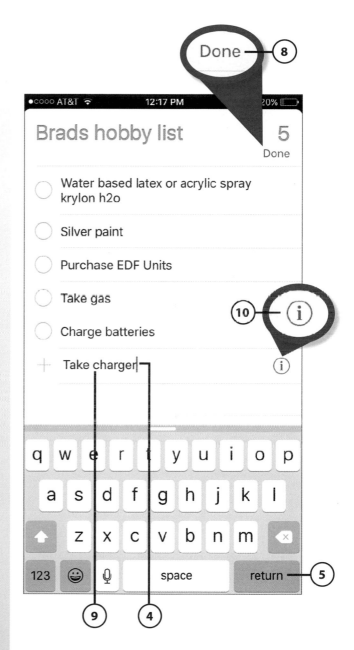

(11) Slide the Remind me on a day switch to on (green) to set a specific date and time on which you want to be reminded; if you don't want the reminder to be time based, skip to step 16 instead.

(12) Tap Alarm to open the date and time tool.

(13) Use the date and time tool to set a time for the reminder; these work by scrolling to the desired day and time, just like when you create an event (see "Adding Events to a Calendar," earlier in this chapter).

(14) To have the reminder repeated, tap Repeat, and on the resulting screen tap the repeat interval. This also works just like it does when you create an event.

(15) If you configured the reminder to repeat, tap End Repeat (this appears only when you have set a reminder to repeat). Use the tools on the End Repeat screen to set the end of the repeating event, and tap Done (this works just like setting the Repeat).

(16) Slide the Remind me at a location switch to on (green) to set the reminder to be activated based on you leaving or arriving at a location; if you don't want to set this, skip to step 20.

(17) Tap Location.

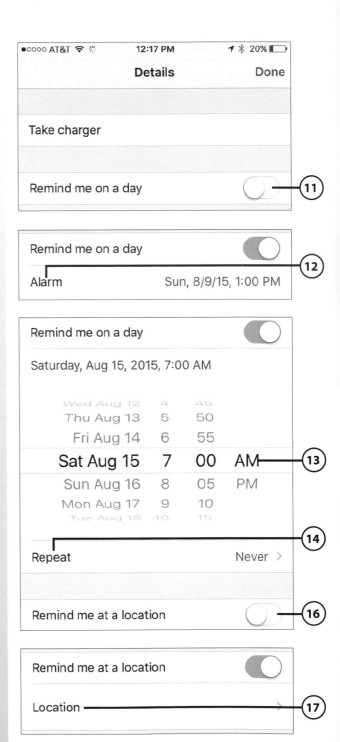

Location Services Required

If you haven't enabled Location Services on your iPhone, and for the Reminders app specifically, you're prompted to do so the first time you enable the Remind me at a location feature. You only have to do this the first time or after you disable the required Location Services.

(18) Tap Current Location, tap one of the addresses that appear on the list, or enter an address to associate the reminder with one of those locations, and then select it on the list.

(19) Tap When I Arrive to be reminded when you arrive at the location you selected, or tap When I Leave to be reminded when you leave the location you selected.

(20) Drag the circle to be larger or smaller to change the distance from the location at which the reminder is triggered. As you drag, the distance appears.

(21) Tap Details.

Location and Time Interactions

If you set both a date/time reminder and a location reminder, you're reminded at the earliest event, such as the time passing or the change in location you set.

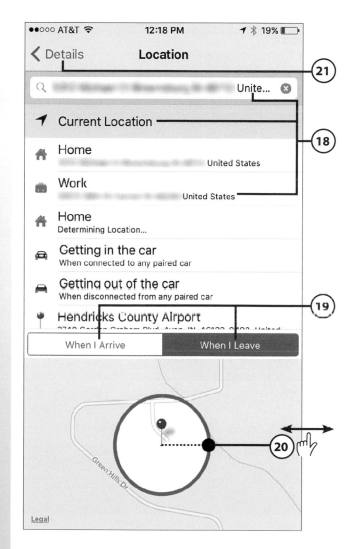

(22) Tap the priority you want to associate with the reminder.

(23) Tap List.

(24) Tap the list on which you want to store the reminder (reminder lists are organized by the accounts from which they come).

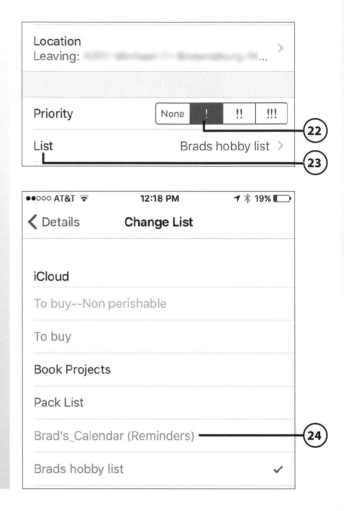

It's Not All Good

It Turns Out that Priorities Really Don't Matter

Note that the priority rating is just a visual indication of the reminder's importance. Currently, there are no automatic actions that happen based on priority, such as the reminder list for a given day being sorted by priority by default or getting automatic alerts for high priority items. Hopefully, the priority setting will become more useful in future versions of the iOS software.

(25) Tap Notes.

(26) Type notes you want to associate with the reminder.

(27) Tap Done. The reminder is complete and you return to the reminder list, where you see the reminder you created including the alert time and location and notes.

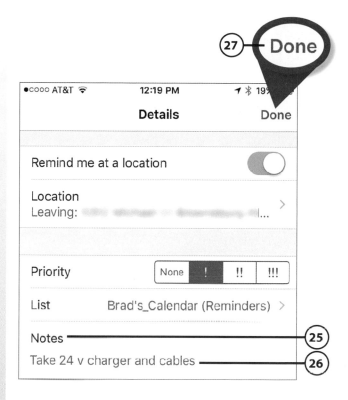

The Ultimate Assistant

Siri can handle reminders really well. Activate Siri and say something like "Remind me to take batteries to the field at 10 A.M. today." Siri creates the reminder for you. You can move to it in the Reminders app to add more detail if you want, but using Siri makes creating reminders really fast and easy. See Chapter 12 for more on Siri.

Organizing Reminders with Lists

You can keep multiple lists of reminders for different purposes. Following are some tips to help you with your lists:

- The title of the current list is shown at the top of the list screen.

- To move between your lists, swipe down on the list title at the top of the screen. The list of your lists appears. Tap the list you want to view; the list and the reminders it contains appear.

Reminder list —

Swipe down
to change
lists

Tap to search
for reminders

Tap the list you
want to view

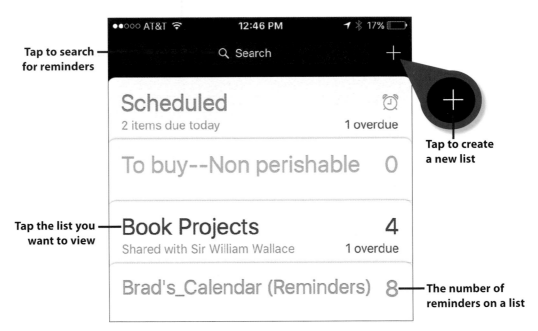

Tap to create
a new list

The number of
reminders on a list

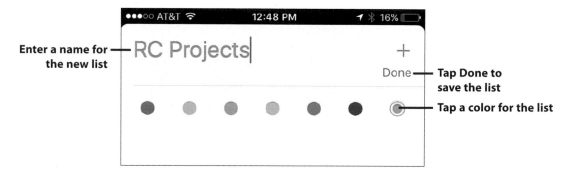

Enter a name for —— the new list

Done —— Tap Done to save the list

Tap a color for the list

- To create a new list, tap the Add button (+), and then tap List at the prompt. Type the new list's name. Tap the color you want to associate with the list, and then tap Done. You can then assign reminders to the new list.

- To change a list, move to its screen and tap Edit. Change the list's name and tap color to change the list's color. Tap Done to save your changes.

- You can share reminder lists just like sharing calendars. Tap Edit while viewing a list, and then tap Sharing. Tap Add person, configure the people with whom you want to share the list, and then tap Add. Tap Done. After the people you invite accept the invitation, they see the list in the Reminders app on their device.

- If you enable Family Sharing, a list called "Family" is created automatically and shared with everyone on your Family Sharing list. Family Sharing is covered in "Using Family Share to Share your iTunes Store Content," In Chapter 6, "Downloading Apps, Music, Movies, TV Shows, and More onto Your iPhone."

- To delete a list, tap Edit while viewing that list. Tap Delete List and confirm this is what you want to do at the prompt. The list and all the reminders it contains are deleted.

Managing Reminders

When you have reminders set up, you can manage them using some of the tips in the following list:

- When a reminder's Remind Me time or location event occurs, you see an alert according to the notification setting for the Reminders app. If it is a banner, you can tap it to view the reminder's details or ignore it. If it is an alert, you must dismiss it or view the reminder's details.

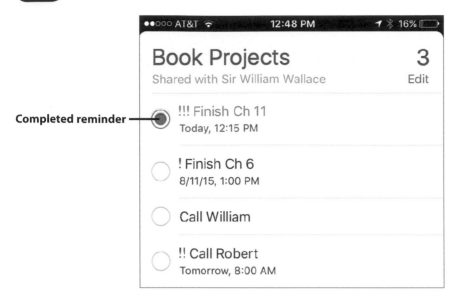

Completed reminder

• To mark a reminder as complete, tap its radio button. The next time you move back to the list, the reminder doesn't appear (it is moved onto your Completed list).

• To see your completed reminders, tap Show Completed, located at the bottom of the screen. All the reminders on the list appear. Those whose radio buttons are filled with the list's color are complete. Tap Hide Completed, also located at the bottom of the screen, to show only active reminders again.

• To see your reminders organized by date instead of by list, move to the Lists screen and tap the Scheduled list (which is marked with the alarm clock icon). The Scheduled list shows your reminders based on the time and date with which they are associated. Swipe down on the word "Scheduled" to return to the List screen.

• To change or delete a reminder, tap it. Edit its text if needed. Tap the Information button to change its other details. Tap Done when you've made all the changes you want to make.

• To search for reminders, move to the list of reminder lists, swipe down to open the Search bar, and type your search term in the Search bar. As you type, reminders that match your search term are shown. Tap a reminder to view it.

• To delete a reminder, swipe across it to the left and tap Delete.

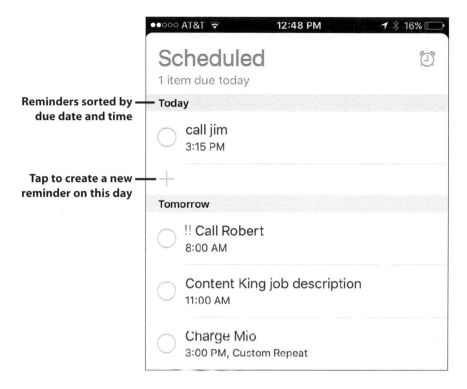

Reminders sorted by due date and time —

Tap to create a new reminder on this day —

Working with the Clock

Using the Clock app, you can configure alarms, use a stopwatch, and count time down with the timer.

Telling Time

Your iPhone is also handy for knowing what time it is. The time is displayed at the top of many screens (although it is hidden when an app uses the full screen or when an app's controls are hidden). It also appears on the Lock screen. To get the time quickly while your iPhone is locked, just press the Home or Sleep/Wake button. The Lock screen appears and displays the time and date.

Setting and Using Alarms

Your iPhone is a handy alarm clock on which you can set and manage multiple alarms.

(1) On the Home screen, tap Clock.

(2) Tap Alarm. You see the currently set alarms, listed by their times, with the earlier alarms toward the top of the screen. Next to each alarm, you see its status switch. When the switch is off (white), the alarm is disabled. When it is on (green), the alarm is active.

(3) To add an alarm, tap the Add button (+).

4 Swipe on the hour, minute, and AM/PM bars to set the time you want the alarm to activate.

5 To configure the alarm to repeat, tap Repeat; to set a one-time alarm, skip to step 9.

6 Tap the day of the week on which you want the alarm to repeat. It is marked with a check mark.

7 Repeat step 6 as many times as you need; however, the most frequently an alarm can repeat is once per day. Of course, you can create multiple alarms for the same day.

8 Tap Back.

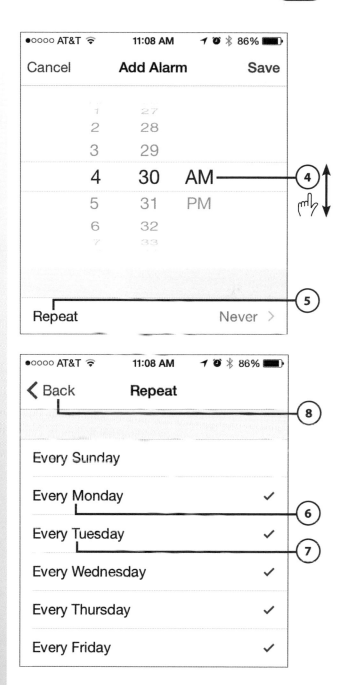

(9) To name the alarm, tap Label. The label is what appears on the screen when the alarm activates, so you might want to give it a meaningful title. (To leave the default label, which is "Alarm," skip to step 13.)

How iPhone Alarms Are Like Those on Bedside Clocks

You can't set an alarm for a specific date; they are set only by day of the week, just like a bedside alarm clock. To set an alarm for a specific date, configure an event using the Calendar app and associate an alarm with that event. Or, you can set a reminder as another way to be notified at a specific time and date.

(10) To remove the current label, tap the Clear button (x).

(11) Type a label for the alarm.

(12) Tap Back.

(13) To choose the alarm sound, tap Sound.

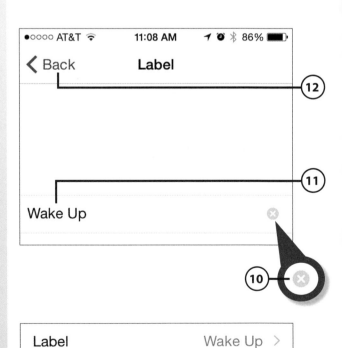

Silent Alarm

If you select the None sound, you won't hear anything when the alarm goes off, but a visual alarm displays.

(14) Browse the list of available sounds.

(15) Tap the sound you want to use for the alarm. You hear the sound, and it is marked with a check mark.

(16) After you select the sound you want to use, tap Back.

(17) To disable the Snooze function, set the Snooze switch to off (white). When the alarm sounds and you dismiss it, it won't appear again. With Snooze set to on (green), you can tap Snooze to dismiss the alarm, and it returns at 10-minute increments until you dismiss it.

(18) Tap Save. You return to the Alarm screen, which now shows the new alarm you set. When the appointed time arrives, the alarm sounds and displays on the screen (or just displays on the screen if it is a silent alarm).

World Clock

On the World Clock tab, you can configure clocks to display the times in different time zones around the world. Tap the Add button (+) and use the Search tool to find and tap a city in the time zone in which you are interested. A clock for that city is added to the World Clock screen and you see the current time there. You can add multiple clocks to see the time in many times zones at once.

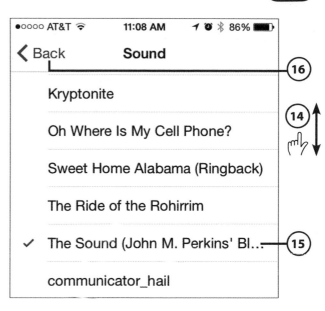

Managing Alarms

As you work with alarms, keep the following in mind:

Tap to change an alarm —

At least one alarm is active

Tap to disable an alarm

Tap to enable an alarm

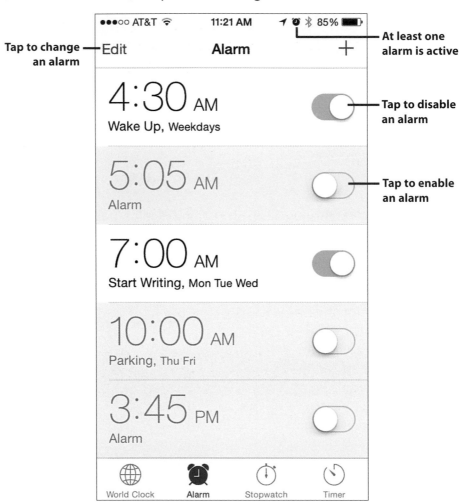

- When at least one alarm is active, you see the Alarm Clock icon in the upper-right corner of the screen next to the Battery icon.

- You can enable or disable alarms by tapping their switches. Alarms showing green in their switches are enabled and sound when the time comes. Those with white are disabled and are ignored until you enable them.

- To change an alarm, tap Edit, and then tap the alarm you want to change. You can change it using the same tools as when you create a new alarm. Tap Save when you're done making changes.

- To delete an alarm, tap Edit and then tap the Lock button (-) for the alarm you want to delete. Then tap Delete. Tap Done when you are done deleting alarms.

- When an alarm triggers, you see an alert and hear the sound associated with it. If the alarm is snooze-enabled, tap Snooze to dismiss it; it returns in 10 minutes. To dismiss the alarm completely, tap OK. You can also dismiss an alarm by pressing the Sleep/Wake button.

Not Dismissed So Easily

When you dismiss an alarm, it isn't deleted, but its status is set to off (unless it is set to repeat, in which case, it remains active and goes off at the next appointed time). To reenable the alarm, move to the Alarm screen and tap its switch. It turns on, and the alarm activates at the next appropriate time.

Using the Stopwatch

You can use the Stopwatch tab to record times for various things, such as walking laps.

1. On the Home screen, tap Clock.

2. Tap Stopwatch.

3. Tap the Start button to start the count.

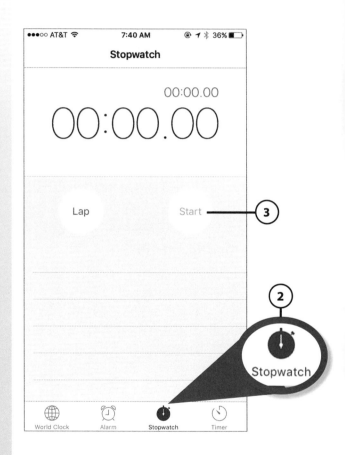

(4) Tap Lap to set lap times. As you set lap times, they are recorded on a list on the app's screen along with the lap number.

(5) Tap Stop to stop the stopwatch.

(6) To start over, tap Reset.

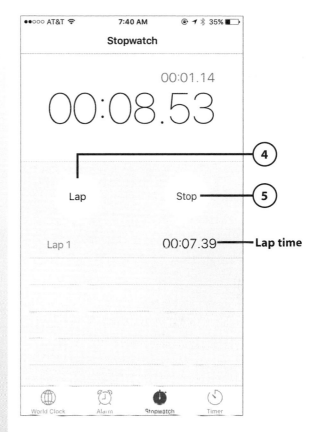

Using the Timer

The Timer is a handy way to count down from a starting time and see and hear an alarm when that time expires. Here's how to use it:

1. On the Home screen, tap Clock.

2. Tap Timer.

3. Use the hour and minute wheels to set the amount of time you want for the countdown.

4. Tap When Timer Ends.

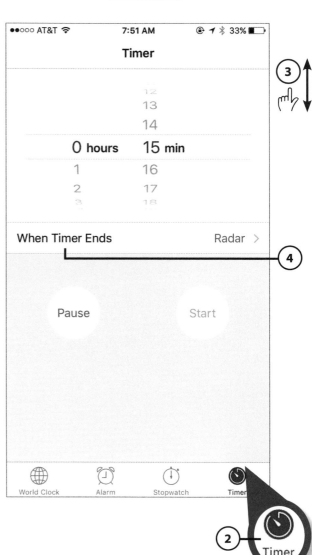

(5) Tap the sound you want to play when the timer expires.

(6) Tap Set.

(7) Tap Start. The timer begins counting down.

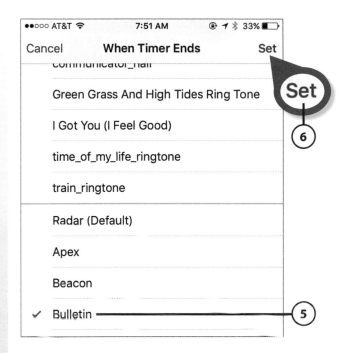

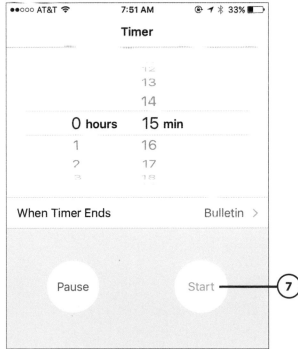

8 To pause the timer, tap Pause (tap Resume to restart it).

9 To cancel the timer before it finishes, tap Cancel. Otherwise, when the time you selected passes, you hear the end sound you selected in step 5 and see an onscreen message informing you that the time has expired.

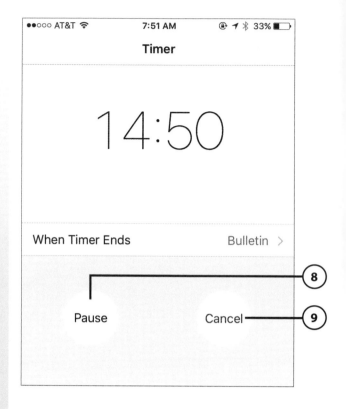

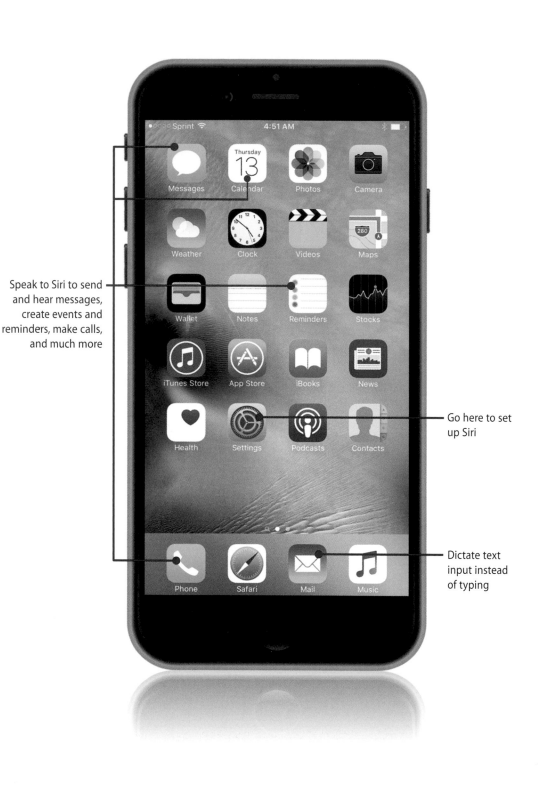

Speak to Siri to send and hear messages, create events and reminders, make calls, and much more

Go here to set up Siri

Dictate text input instead of typing

In this chapter, you'll learn about all the great things you can do with your iPhone by speaking to it. Topics include the following:

→ Getting started
→ Setting up Siri
→ Understanding Siri's personality
→ Learning how to use Siri by example
→ Getting suggestions from Siri

12

Working with Siri

Siri is Apple's name for the iPhone's and iPad's voice recognition feature. This technology enables your iPhone to "listen" to words you speak so that you can issue commands just by saying them, such as "Send text message to Sam," and the iPhone accomplishes the tasks you speak. This technology also enables the iPhone to take dictation; for example, you can speak words that you want to send in a text or email instead of typing them on the keyboard.

Getting Started

Siri gives you the ability to talk to your iPhone to control it and to dictate text. Siri also works with lots of iPhone apps—this feature enables you to accomplish many tasks by speaking instead of using your fingers on the iPhone's screen. For example, you can hear, create, and send text messages; reply to emails; make phone and FaceTime calls; create and manage events and reminders; and much more. Using dictation, you can speak text into any supported app instead of typing. The SIRI SUGGESTIONS page presents people you communicate with, apps you use, and news you might be interested in so you do tasks very easily and quickly. The Siri Search bar is amazingly powerful and you can get to all sorts of information from one quick query.

In fact, Siri does so many things, it's impossible to list them all in a short chapter like this one; you should give Siri a try for the tasks you perform and to get the information you need, and in many cases, Siri can handle what you want to do.

One particularly good thing about Siri is that you don't have to train it to work with your voice; you can speak to it normally and Siri does a great job understanding what you say. Also, you don't have to use any specific kind of phrases to have Siri do your bidding. Simply talk to Siri like you talk to people (well, you probably won't be ordering other people around like you do Siri, but you get the idea).

Because Siri works so well and quickly, you might not realize that your iPhone has to be connected to the Internet for Siri and dictation to work. That's because the words you speak are sent over the Internet, transcribed into text, and then sent back to your iPhone. If your iPhone isn't connected to the Internet, this can't happen, and if you try to use it, Siri reports that it can't complete its tasks. Because your iPhone is likely to be connected to the Internet most of the time (via Wi-Fi or a cellular network), this really isn't much of a limitation—but it is one of which you need to be aware.

Siri doesn't take much to set up either; most of the time, you don't need to do the steps in the next task as Siri is set up by default when you first turn on your iPhone. If you haven't made any changes to the Siri settings, skip ahead to "Understanding Siri's Personality." If you have made changes to Siri's settings, or just want to understand its options, proceed to the next section.

Just start speaking to your phone and be prepared to be amazed by how well it listens! You'll find many examples in this chapter to get you going with specific tasks; from there, you can explore to learn what else Siri can do for you.

Setting Up Siri

There are several settings that impact how Siri works. In most cases, you can leave these settings in their default positions (including those you selected the first time your turned your iPhone on) and start using Siri right away (beginning with "Understanding Siri's Personality" later in this chapter).

If you decide you want to make changes to Siri's settings, you can use the following example steps that show you how to change the voice that Siri uses to speak to you along with the subsequent table that provides a description of the other Siri options available to you.

To change the voice Siri uses to speak to you, perform the following steps:

(1) Tap Settings on the Home screen.

(2) Swipe up the screen.

(3) Tap General.

(4) Tap Siri.

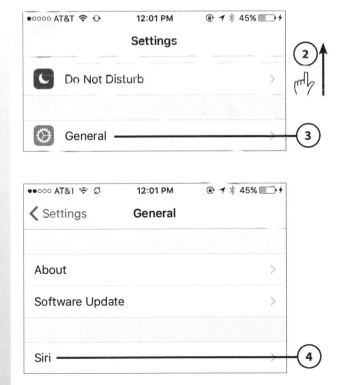

5. Tap Siri Voice.

6. Tap the accent you want Siri to use (the options you see depend on the language currently selected).

7. Tap the gender of the voice you want Siri to use (the options you see depend on the language currently selected).

8. Tap Siri. Siri uses the voice you selected to speak to you. You can change the Siri settings using a similar pattern and the description of the options in the following table.

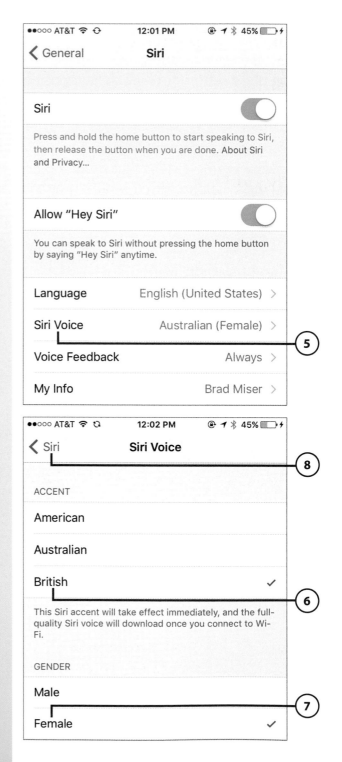

Siri Settings

Section Setting	Description
General	
Siri	
Siri	When on (green), Siri is ready to do your bidding. When off (white), Siri is disabled.
Allow "Hey Siri"	When this switch is on (green), you can activate Siri by saying, "Hey Siri" (along with the other options). The first time you turned your iPhone on, you were prompted to speak the phrases Siri uses to recognize when you want its attention. When this switch is off (white), you can only activate Siri with the other options. If you turn this off and then back on, you're prompted to re-train Siri to recognize you saying "Hey Siri." So, if speaking the phrase doesn't work too well for you, try doing this to re-train Siri to recognize the activation phrase.
Language	Set the language you want Siri to use to speak to you.
Siri Voice	Choose the accent and gender of the voice that Siri uses to speak to you (the options you see depend on the language you have selected).
Voice Feedback	Choose when Siri provides verbal feedback as it works for you. When Always On is selected, Siri provides verbal feedback at all times. If you want to control Siri's voice feedback with the ring (Mute) switch, choose Control with Ring Switch. If you only want voice feedback when you are operating in handsfree mode, such as when you are using the iPhone's EarPods or a Bluetooth headset, tap Handsfree Only. Regardless of this setting, you always see Siri's feedback on the screen.
My Info	Choose your contact information in the Contacts app, which Siri uses to address you by name, take you to your home address, etc.

Section Setting	Description
General	
Keyboard	
Enable Dictation	When on (green), you can tap the Microphone key on the keyboard to dictate text. When off (white), the Microphone key is hidden and you can't dictate text.
Cellular	
Cellular Data	When Cellular Data is on (green), your iPhone can access its cellular data network to connect to the Internet. This must be turned on for Siri to work when you aren't connected to the Internet via a Wi-Fi network.

Understanding Siri's Personality

Siri's personality is pretty simple because it follows a consistent pattern when you use it, and it always prompts you for input and direction when needed.

If Siri is already active, tap the Microphone icon at the bottom of the screen. If not, activate Siri using one of the following methods:

- Pressing and holding the Touch ID/Home button until the Siri screen appears and you feel the phone vibrate.

- Pressing and holding the center part of the buttons on the EarPods until the Siri screen appears and you hear the Siri tone.

- Saying "Hey Siri" (if you've enabled this setting) until the Siri screen appears and you hear the Siri tone.

This puts Siri in "listening" mode and the "What can I help you with?" text appears along with a line at the bottom of the screen that shows when Siri is hearing you. This screen indicates Siri is ready for your command. If you don't speak within a second or two, Siri starts prompting you for a request and presents examples of what you can do.

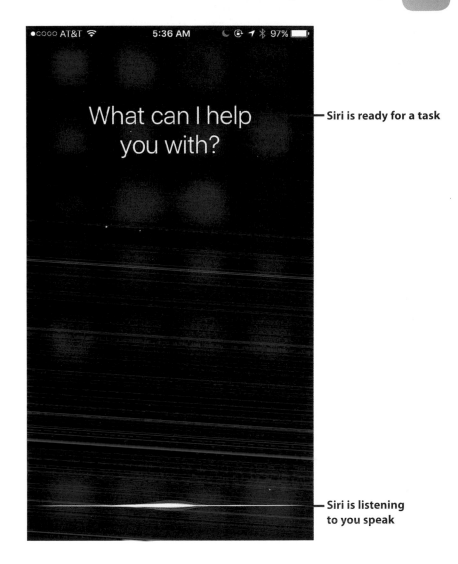

Siri is ready for a task

Siri is listening
to you speak

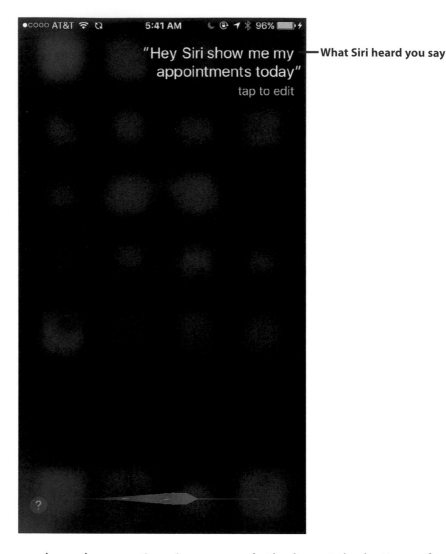

What Siri heard you say

Speak your command or ask a question. As you speak, the line at the bottom of the screen oscillates to show you that Siri is hearing your input, and Siri displays what it is hearing you say at the top of the screen. When you stop speaking, Siri goes into processing mode.

After Siri interprets what you've said, it provides two kinds of feedback to confirm what it heard: it displays what it heard on the screen and provides audible feedback to you (unless it's disabled through the settings you learned about earlier). Siri then tries to do what it thinks you've asked and shows you the outcome.

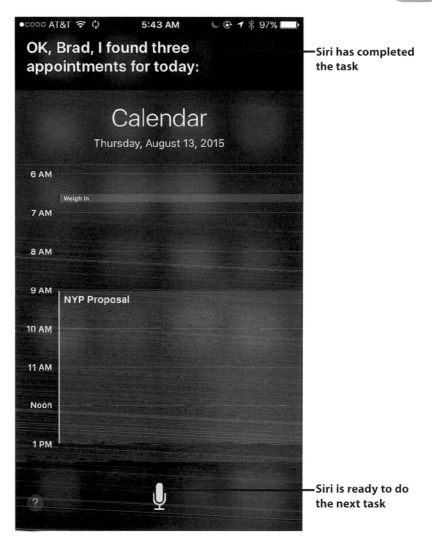

●oooo AT&T 📶 ◌   5:43 AM   🌙 © ✈ ✲ 97% 🔋▶

OK, Brad, I found three appointments for today: ——Siri has completed the task

Calendar

Thursday, August 13, 2015

6 AM

Weigh In

7 AM

8 AM

9 AM

NYP Proposal

10 AM

11 AM

Noon

1 PM

——Siri is ready to do the next task

If it needs more input from you, you're prompted to provide it and Siri moves into "listening" mode automatically. If Siri asks you to confirm what it is doing or to make a selection, do so. Siri completes the action and displays what it has done; it also audibly confirms the result (again unless audible feedback is disabled as described earlier). If you want Siri to do more for you, tap the Microphone icon at the bottom of the screen and speak your command. If you want to work with the object Siri created for you in its associated app, tap the object Siri presents.

Also, how Siri interacts with you can depend on how it was activated. For example, if you started the interaction using the verbal "Hey Siri" option, Siri assumes you want to interact verbally and may respond with other options than you would see or hear when you activate Siri manually. When you ask Siri to show you your appointments for the day in this mode, you see the summary, but then Siri asks if you want to hear the details; if you say yes, Siri reads each event to you. When you activate Siri by using the Touch ID/Home button with the same request, Siri stops after showing you the summary.

When you're done with Siri, you can lock the iPhone or tap the Touch ID/Home button to move back to the Home screen or to the app you were using.

Siri uses this pattern for all the tasks it does, but often Siri needs to get more information from you, such as when there are multiple contacts that match the command you've given. Siri prompts you for what it needs to complete the work. Generally, the more specific you make your initial command, the fewer steps you have to work through to complete it. For example, if you say "Meet Will at the park," Siri may require several prompts to get you to tell it who Will is and what time you want to meet him at the park. If you say "Meet William Wallace at the park on 10/17 at 10 am," Siri will likely be able to complete the task in one step.

The best way to learn how and when Siri can help you is to try it—a lot. You find a number of examples in the rest of this chapter to get started.

Following are some other Siri tidbits:

- If Siri doesn't automatically quit "listen" mode after you've finished speaking, tap the oscillating line.

- If you are having trouble with Siri understanding commands, speak a bit more slowly and make sure you firmly enunciate and end your words.

- Don't pause too long between words or sentences because Siri interprets pauses of a certain length to mean that you are done speaking and goes into processing mode.

- If Siri doesn't understand what you want, or if you ask it a general question, it will often perform a web search for you. Siri takes what it thinks you are looking for and does a search. You then see the results page for the search Siri performed and you might have to manually open and read the results by tapping the listing you want to see. It opens in the Safari app. In some cases, Siri reads the results to you.

- When Siri presents information to you on the screen, you can often tap that information to move into the app with which it is associated. For example, when you tap an event that Siri has created, you move into the Calendar app where you can add more detail using that app's tools.

- When Siri needs direction from you, it presents your options on the screen, such as Yes, Cancel, Confirm, lists of names, and so on. You can speak these items or tap them to select them.

- Siri is very useful for some tasks, such as creating reminders, responding to text messages, and so on, but not so useful for others, such as inputting search criteria, because it can take longer to use Siri than to just type your input.

- Siri is not so good at editing text you dictate. In many cases, your only option is to replace the text you've dictated.

- To use Siri effectively, you should experiment with it by trying to say different commands or similar commands in different ways. Saying "Meet with Wyatt Earp at 10am on 11/3 in my office" requires fewer steps than saying "Meet with Wyatt Earp" because you've given Siri all the information it needs to complete the task.

- When Siri can't complete a task that it thinks it should be able to do, it usually responds with the "I can't connect to the network right now," or "Sorry, I don't know what you mean." This indicates that your iPhone isn't connected to the Internet, the Siri server is not responding, or Siri just isn't able to complete the command for some other reason. If your iPhone is connected to the Internet, try the command again.

- When Siri can't complete a task that it knows it can't do, it will respond by telling you so. Occasionally, you can get Siri to complete the task by rephrasing it, but typically you have to use an app directly to get it done.

- If you have a passcode set to protect your iPhone's data (which you should), Siri might not be able to complete some tasks because the phone is locked. If that happens, simply unlock your phone and continue with what you were doing.

- Siri is really good at retrieving all sorts of information for you. This can include schedules, weather, directions, unit conversions, etc. When you need something, try Siri first, as trying it is really the best way to learn how Siri can work for you.

Learning How to Use Siri by Example

As mentioned earlier in this chapter, the best way to learn about Siri is to use it. Following are a number of tasks for which Siri is really helpful. Try these to get some experience with Siri and then explore on your own to make Siri work at its best for you.

Using Siri to Make Voice Calls

You can use Siri to make calls by speaking. This is especially useful when you are using your iPhone in handsfree mode.

(1) Activate Siri (such as by pressing and holding the Touch ID/Home button).

(2) Say "Call *name numberlabel*," where *name* is the person you want to call and *numberlabel* is the label of the specific number you want to call, such as Home, Work, iPhone, and so on. Siri identifies the contact you named. If the contact has only one number or you were specific about which number you want to call, Siri places the call and you move into the Phone app. If you weren't specific about the number you want to call (you simply said "Call *name*") and the person has multiple numbers, Siri lists the numbers available and asks you which number to use.

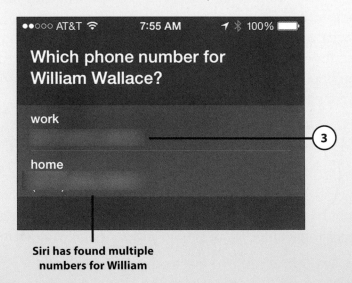

Siri has found multiple numbers for William

(3) Speak the label for the number you want to call, or tap it. Siri dials the number for you and you move to the Phone app as if you had dialed the number yourself.

Placing FaceTime Calls

You can also use Siri to make FaceTime calls by saying "FaceTime *name*."

Composing New Email with Siri

To create email with Siri, do the following:

(1) Activate Siri.

(2) Say "Send email to *name*," where *name* is the person you want to email. Siri creates a new email addressed to the name you spoke. (If the recipient has more than one email address, Siri prompts you to choose the address you want to use.)

3. Speak the subject of the email. Siri inserts the subject, and then prompts you for the body of the message.

More Than One Recipient?

To send an email to more than one recipient, say "and" between each name as in, "Send email to William Wallace and Edward Longshanks." Siri adds each address before and after the "and."

4. Speak the body of the email. As you speak, you can include punctuation; for example, to end a sentence, say the word "period" or to end a question, say the words "question mark." When Siri completes the email, it displays the message on the screen and prompts you to send it.

5. Say "send" to send the email or "cancel" to delete it. If you say "send," Siri sends the message, confirms it will be sent, and plays the sent mail sound when it is.

Replying to Emails with Siri

You can also use Siri to speak replies to emails you've read. Here's how:

1. Open the message to which you want to reply.

2. Activate Siri.

(3) Say "reply to this email." Siri prompts you for what you want your reply to say.

(4) Complete and send the reply; this works just like when you create a new message.

>>>Go Further
DOING MORE IN EMAIL WITH SIRI

Following are some other ways to use Siri for email:

- If you tell Siri to "Read email," Siri tells you how many emails are in your Inboxes and starts reading the time and date of the most recent email message followed by the subject and sender of the message. Siri then does the same for the next email until it has read a number of them. When it gets to the last message it reads, it prompts you to ask if you want to hear the entire list. On the screen, Siri lists the emails; you can tap an email message to read it yourself.

- Siri can read the content of email messages to you when you speak commands that tell it which email you want it to read, such as "Read most recent email" or "Read last email from William Wallace." Siri reads the entire message to you.

- To edit an email Siri created, say "Change." Siri prompts you to change the subject, change the message, cancel it, or send it. If you choose one of the change options, you can replace the subject or the body of the message. To change just some of the subject or body or to change the recipients, tap the message and edit it in the Mail app.

>>>Go Further

- You can start a new and completely blank email by saying "New email." Siri prompts you for the recipients, subject, and body.

- You can address a new email and add the subject with one statement, such as "Send email to William Wallace about flying."

- You can retrieve your email at any time by activating Siri and saying "Check email." Siri checks for new email and then announces how many emails you have received since the oldest message in your Inboxes was received. If you don't have any new email messages, Siri announces how many email messages are currently in your inboxes.

- You can determine if you have emails from a specific person by asking something like, "Any email from William Wallace?" Siri's reply includes the number of emails in your Inboxes from William and displays them on the screen. Tap an email to read it.

- You can forward an email you are reading by saying "Forward this email" and then following Siri's lead to complete the process.

Having Messages Read to You

The Messages app is among the best to use with Siri because you can speak just about any task you would normally do with messages. Especially useful is Siri's ability to read new messages to you. When you receive new text messages, do the following to have Siri read them to you:

(1) When you receive a text notification, activate Siri.

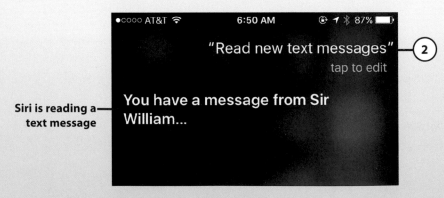

Siri is reading a text message

(**2**) Speak the command "Read new text messages." Siri reads all the new text messages you've received, announcing the sender before reading each message. You have the option to reply (covered in the next task) or have Siri read the message again.

Siri reads each new message in turn until it has read all of them and then announces, "That's it" to let you know it has read all of them.

Siri only reads new text messages to you when you aren't on the Messages screen. If you've already read all your messages and you aren't in the Messages app, when you speak the command "Read text messages," Siri tells you that you have no new messages.

Reading Old Messages

To read an old message, move back to the conversation containing the message you want to hear. Activate Siri and say the command "Read text message." Siri reads the most recent text message to you.

Replying to Messages with Siri

You can also use Siri to speak replies to messages you've received. Here's how:

(**1**) Listen to a message.

(**2**) At the prompt, say "Reply." Siri prepares a reply to the message.

3. Speak your reply. Siri displays your reply.

4. At the prompt, say "Send" to send it, "Cancel" to delete it, or "Change" to replace it. If you tell Siri that you want to send the message, Siri sends it and then confirms that it was sent.

Sending New Messages with Siri

To send a new message to someone, do the following:

1. Activate Siri.

2. Say "Send text to *name*," where *name* is the person you want to text. Siri confirms your command and prepares to hear your text message.

(3) Speak your message. Siri listens and then prepares your message.

(4) If you want to send the message, say "Send." Siri sends the message.

>>>Go Further

DOING MORE MESSAGING WITH SIRI

Following are some other ways to use Siri with messaging:

- If you say "Change" after you have created a new message, Siri prompts you to replace the message with a different one. If you say "Review" after creating a new message, Siri reads your message back to you. If you say "Cancel," Siri stops the process and deletes the message.

- To send a text message to more than one recipient, say "and" between each name; as in, "Send text to William Wallace and Edward Longshanks."

- You can speak punctuation, such as "period" or "question mark" to add it to your message.

- You can tap buttons that Siri presents on the screen, such as Send or Cancel, to take those actions on the message you are working on.

- Messages you receive or send via Siri are stored in the Messages app just like messages you receive or send by tapping and typing.

- You can dictate into a text message you start in the Messages app (you learn about dictating later in this chapter).

Using Siri to Create Events

Siri is useful for capturing meetings and other events you want to add to your calendars. To create an event by speaking, do the following steps:

(1) Activate Siri.

2 Speak the event you want to create. There are a number of variations in what you can say. Examples include "Set up a meeting with William Wallace on Friday at 10 am," "Doctor appt on Thursday at 1 pm," and so on. If you have any conflicts with the event you are setting up, Siri lets you know about them.

3 Say "Confirm" if you don't have any conflicts or "Yes" if you do and you still want to have the appointment confirmed; you can also tap Confirm. Siri adds the event to your calendar. Say "Cancel" to cancel the event.

4 To add more information to an event Siri has created for you, tap it on the confirmation screen. You move into the Calendar app and can edit the event just like events you create within that app.

Invitees

If you include the name of someone for whom you have an email address, Siri automatically sends invitations. If you include a name that matches more than one contact, Siri prompts you to choose the contact you want to invite. If the name doesn't match a contact, Siri enters the name but doesn't send an invitation.

Using Siri to Create Reminders

Using Siri to create reminders is one of the more useful things you can do with Siri, assuming you find reminders useful of course. Here's how:

1. Activate Siri.

2. Speak the reminder you want to create. Examples include "Remind me to buy the A-10 at Motion RC," "Remind me to finish Chapter 10 at 10 a.m. on Saturday," "Remind me to buy milk when I leave work," and so on. Siri provides a confirmation of what you asked. If you didn't mention a time or date when you want to be reminded, Siri prompts you to provide the details of when you want to be reminded.

3. Speak the date and time when you want to be reminded. If you included a date and time in your original reminder request, you skip this step. Unlike some of the other tasks, Siri creates the reminder without confirming it with you.

4. If you don't want to keep the reminder, activate Siri and say "Remove."

5. To add detail to the reminder, tap it. You move into the Reminders app and can add more information to the reminder, as you can when you create one manually.

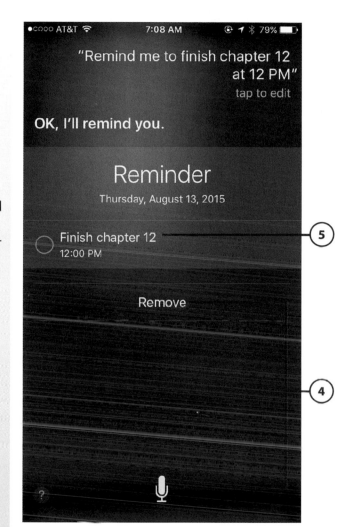

>>>Go Further

GOING FURTHER WITH SIRI TO MANAGE TIME

Following are some other ways to use Siri with the Calendar, Reminders, and Clock apps:

- You can change events with Siri, too. For example, if you have a meeting at 3 p.m., you can move it by saying something like "Move my 3 pm meeting to Friday at 6 pm."

- You can get information about your events with Siri by saying things such as "Show me today's appointments," "Do I have meetings on November 3?," "What time is my first appointment tomorrow?," "What are my appointments tomorrow?," and so on. Siri tells you about the events and shows you what they are on the screen. You can tap any event to view it in the Calendar app.

- You can speak to your iPhone to set alarms. Tell Siri what you want and when you want the alarm to be set. For example, you can say something like "New alarm *alarmname* 6 am tomorrow," where *alarmname* is the label of the alarm. Siri sets an alarm to go off at that time and gives it the label you speak. It displays the alarm on the screen along with a status button so you can turn it off if you change your mind. You don't have to label alarms, and you can just say something like "Set alarm 6 am tomorrow." However, a label can be useful to issue other commands. For example, if an alarm has a name, you can turn off an alarm by saying "Turn off *alarmname*." Any alarms you create with Siri can be managed just like alarms you create directly in the Clock app.

- To set a countdown timer, tell Siri to "Set timer for x minutes," where x is a number of minutes (you can do the same to set a timer for seconds or hours, too). You can also reset the time, pause it, and so on by speaking.

- You can get information about time by asking questions, such as "What time is it?," "What is the date?," and so on. You can add location information to the time information, too, as in "What time is it in London, England?"

- Tapping any confirmation Siri displays takes you back into the related app. For example, if you tap a clock that results from your asking what time it is, you can tap that clock to move into the Clock app. If you ask about your schedule today, you can tap any of the events Siri presents to move back into the Calendar app to work with them.

- When you use Siri to create events and reminders, they are created on your default calendar (events) or reminder list (reminders).

Using Siri to Get Information

Siri is a great way to get information about lots of different topics in many different areas. You can ask Siri for information about subjects, places in your area, unit conversion (such as inches to centimeters), and so on. Just try speaking what you want to learn to best get the information you need. Here's an example looking for pizza places in my area:

(**1**) Activate Siri.

(**2**) Say something like, "Show me pizza restaurants close to me." Siri presents a list of results that match your query and even provides a summary of reviews at the top of the screen. (You must have Location Services enabled for this to work.)

If you like pizza (or just about anything else), Siri can help you find it.

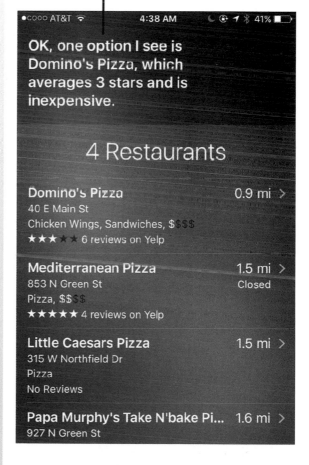

●cooo AT&T 🔊   4:38 AM   ◖ ⊛ ✈ ⁂ 41% ▭

OK, one option I see is Domino's Pizza, which averages 3 stars and is inexpensive.

4 Restaurants

Domino's Pizza   0.9 mi >
40 E Main St
Chicken Wings, Sandwiches, $$$$
★★★☆☆ 6 reviews on Yelp

Mediterranean Pizza   1.5 mi >
853 N Green St   Closed
Pizza, $$$$
★★★★★ 4 reviews on Yelp

Little Caesars Pizza   1.5 mi >
315 W Northfield Dr
Pizza
No Reviews

Papa Murphy's Take N'bake Pi... 1.6 mi >
927 N Green St

Siri is also useful for getting information about topics. Siri responds by conducting a web search and showing you the result. For example, suppose you want to learn about William Wallace. Activate Siri and say, "Tell me about William Wallace." Siri responds with information about your topic. You can have Siri read the information by activating Siri and saying "Read." Siri reads the results (this doesn't always work; it works best when the results are presented via Wikipedia or something similar).

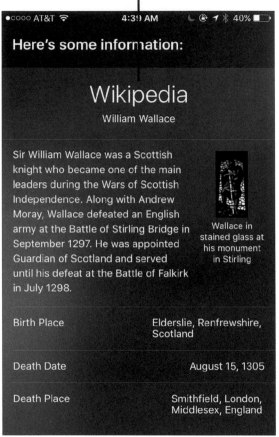

Want to learn about something? Just ask Siri.

Using Siri to Play Music

You can also play music by telling Siri which music you want to hear.

1. Activate Siri.

2. Tell Siri the music you want to hear. There are a number of variations in what you can say. Examples include "Play album Time of My Life," "Play song Gone by Switchfoot," "Play playlist Jon McLaughlin," and so on. Siri provides a confirmation of what you asked and begins playing the music.

3 To move into the Music app to control the music with your fingers, tap Open Music.

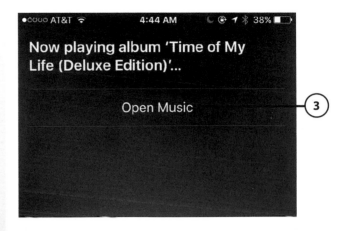

Using Siri to Get Directions

With Siri, it's easy to get directions—you don't even have to stop at a gas station to ask.

1 Activate Siri.

2 Speak something like "Show me directions from Indianapolis Motor Speedway to Lucas Oil Stadium." If you don't include the "from" part, Siri assumes you want directions from your current location (as in "Show me directions to Lucas Oil Stadium").

3 If Siri needs you to confirm one or more of the locations, tap the correct one. Siri uses the Maps app to generate directions.

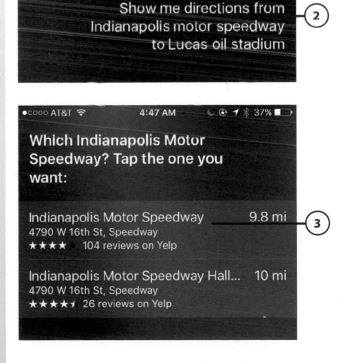

4 To start turn-by-turn instructions, tap Start.

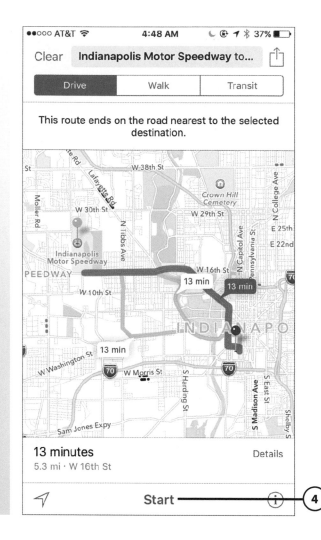

It's Not All Good

Voice commands to Siri work very well, but they aren't perfect. Make sure you confirm your commands by listening to the feedback Siri provides when it repeats them or reviewing the feedback Siri provides on the screen. Sometimes, a spoken command can have unexpected results, which can include making a phone call to someone in the Contacts app. If you don't catch such a mistake before the call is started, you might be surprised to hear someone answering your call instead of hearing music you intended to play. You can put Siri in listening mode by tapping the Microphone button, and then saying "no" or "stop" to stop Siri should a verbal command go awry.

Using Dictation to Speak Text Instead of Typing

You can use the iPhone's dictation capability to speak text into any app, such as Mail, Messages, and so on. In fact, any time you see the Microphone button on the keyboard, dictation is available to you. Here's how this works:

(1) In the app you are using, put the cursor where you want the text you will dictate to start. For example, if you are creating an email, tap in the body.

(2) Tap the Microphone key on the virtual keyboard.

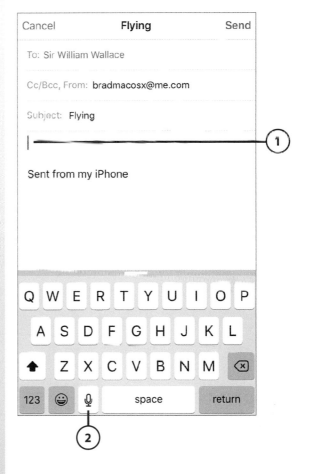

(3) Speak the text you want to add. For instance, when you create a new message, you can speak punctuation, but in this mode, you can create a new paragraph by saying "new paragraph." While you are speaking, you see the line that oscillates as you speak and the text you are speaking at the location of the cursor.

(4) Tap Done when you finish your dictation. The Dictation box closes, and the keyboard reappears. The text you spoke is part of the message. From there, you can edit it just like text you've typed.

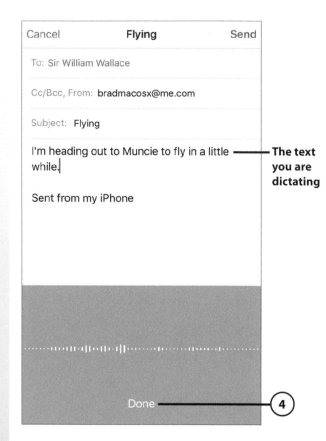

The text you are dictating

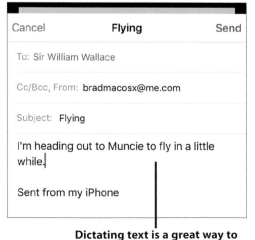

Dictating text is a great way to write without having to type

Using Siri to Open Apps

As you accumulate apps on your iPhone, it can take several taps and swipes to get to a specific app, such as one that is stored in a folder that isn't on the page of the Home screen you are viewing. With Siri, you can open any app on your phone with a simple command.

(1) Activate Siri.

(2) Say "Open *appname*," where *appname* is the name of the app you want to open. Siri opens the app for you and you move to the last screen in that app you were using.

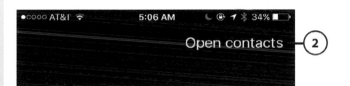

Getting Suggestions from Siri

New! This chapter has focused on speaking to Siri and having it perform your command, but Siri has a few more tricks ups it digital sleeve. In addition to its amazing ability to respond to your voice, Siri also provides the very useful SIRI SUGGESTIONS screen. This screen shows you the people you've interacted with recently and makes it easy to contact them again. It also shows apps you have used recently. In the NEARBY section, you see locations that might of interest to you based on your current location. At the bottom of the screen, you see news that might be of interest to you.

No Siri Suggestions?

If you don't see the SIRI SUGGESTIONS screen, open the Settings app, tap General, tap Spotlight Search, and set the Siri Suggestions switch to on (green).

Tap to perform a search

Tap to dictate a search

Tap to work with a contact

Swipe all the way to the right to open the SIRI SUGGESTIONS screen

Tap to open an app

Tap to see nearby locations

Tap to show more

Swipe up and down to read news stories

To access Siri suggestions, move to the Home screen and swipe all the way to the right. The SIRI SUGGESTIONS screen appears. On this screen you can do the following:

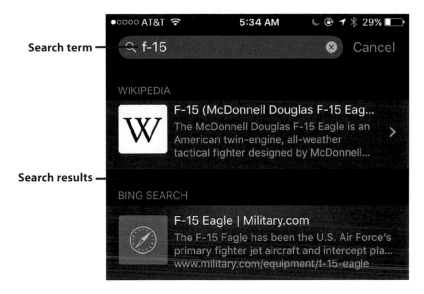

Search term —

Search results —

- Tap in the Search bar to type a search or tap the Microphone to dictate a search. Siri presents the results of the search to you based on the source of information, such as Wikipedia, a web search, YouTube, etc. You can tap a result to move to it. You can also tap the commands at the bottom of the screen, such as Search App Store, to search in other places.

- Tap Show More to expand any of the sections you see, such as SIRI SUGGESTIONS. The section opens so you see more of its information.

Tap to see the contact's information

Tap to communicate with the contact

- Tap a contact to reveal options you can use to communicate with her via a phone call, message, or FaceTime; tap the Info button (i) to move to the contact's information in the Contacts app.

- Tap an app you've used recently to return to it.

- Tap a category of location shown in the NEARBY section to move to the Maps app and see a list of places of that type. You can use the Maps app to quickly get directions to a specific location.

- Swipe up and down in the NEWS section to browse news stories. Tap a story to read its detail in the News app.

Tap to configure Safari

Tap to have the World Wide Web in the palm of your hand

In this chapter, you explore the amazing web browsing functionality your iPhone has to offer. Topics include the following:

→ Getting Started
→ Setting Safari preferences
→ Visiting websites
→ Viewing websites
→ Working with multiple websites at the same time
→ Searching the Web
→ Saving and organizing bookmarks
→ Using 3D Touch with Safari
→ Completing forms on the Web
→ Signing into websites automatically

Surfing the Web

The Web has become an integral part of most of our lives. It is often the first step to search for information, make plans (such as travel arrangements), conduct financial transactions, shop, and so much more. Safari on the IPhone puts the entire Web in the palm of your hand. Safari is a full-featured web browser; anything you can do on a website in a browser on a computer can be done with Safari on your iPhone.

Getting Started

The World Wide Web, more commonly called the Web, is a great resource for finding information, making travel arrangements, keeping up with the news, and just about anything else you want to do. Following are some of the more common terms you encounter as you use the Web:

- **Web page**—This is a collection of information (text and graphics) that is available on the Web. A web page is what you look at when you use the Web.

- **Website**—This is a collection of web pages that "go together." For example, most companies and other organizations have websites that contain information they use to help their customers or members, provide services, market and sell their products and services, and so on. A website organizes the web pages it contains and provides the structure you use to move among them.

- **Web browser**—This is the software you use to view web pages. There are many different web browsers available. Examples include Safari, Google Chrome, Internet Explorer, and Firefox. They all allow you to view and interact with web pages, and each has its own set of features. Some are available on just about every device there is, such as Safari and Google Chrome, while some are limited to certain devices, such as Internet Explorer that only runs on Windows computers.

- **Safari**—This is the default web browser on your iPhone; it is also the default web browser on Mac computers. You can download and install it on Windows computers, too.

- **URL**—A Uniform Resource Locator (URL) is a web page's or website's "address" on the Web. URLs allow you to direct your web browser to specific locations on the Web. Most URLs you deal with consist of text, such as www.apple.com or www.aarp.org. Some URLs are more complicated because they take you to specific web pages instead of a website. An example of this is: www.aarp.org/health, which takes you to the Health web page on the AARP website. You seldom have to type URLs because you usually access web pages by tapping on links or using a bookmark, but it's good to know what they are and how to use them.

- **Link**—A link is a photo or other graphic, text, or other object that has a URL attached to it. When you tap a link, you move to the URL and open the web page associated with it. Most text links are formatted with a color so you can distinguish them from regular text.

- **Bookmark**—This is a saved location on the Web. When you visit a web page or website, you can save its URL as a bookmark so you can return to it with a just a few taps instead of typing its URL. Safari allows you to save and organize your bookmarks on your iPhone.

- **Search engine or search page**—The Web contains virtually unlimited information on every topic under the sun. You can use a search engine/page to search for information in which you are interested. There are a number of search engines available, with Google being the most popular. You access a search engine through a web browser. Safari uses Google by default, but you can use any search engine you'd like, such as yahoo.com.

Setting Safari Preferences

The Safari web browser app on your iPhone is set up to work as soon as you turn your iPhone on and connect it to the Internet. You don't have to change anything in its settings, as explained in this section, until you want to change the way Safari works. I recommend you skip ahead to "Visiting Websites" and get started browsing the Web on your iPhone. If you want to change how Safari works after you've started using it, you can come back to this section to make changes.

To make changes to Safari's settings, you can use the following example steps that show you how to change what happens when you tap and hold on a link on a web page along with the subsequent table that provides a description of the other Safari settings.

To change how web pages open when you tap and hold on a link, perform the following steps:

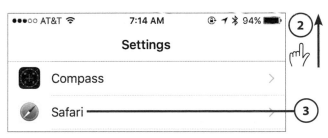

1. Tap Settings on the Home screen.

2. Swipe up the screen.

3. Tap Safari.

④ Swipe up the screen.

⑤ Tap Open Links.

⑥ Tap In New Tab to have the web pages you are opening appear in a new tab. (You learn about Safari tabs in "Opening New Pages in a New Tab").

⑦ Tap In Background to have web pages you are opening open in the background. (You learn about Safari tabs in "Opening New Pages in the Background").

⑧ Tap Safari. When you tap and hold on a link, the resulting web page opens according to the option you selected in step 6 or 7. You can change other Safari settings using a similar pattern and the description of the options in the following table.

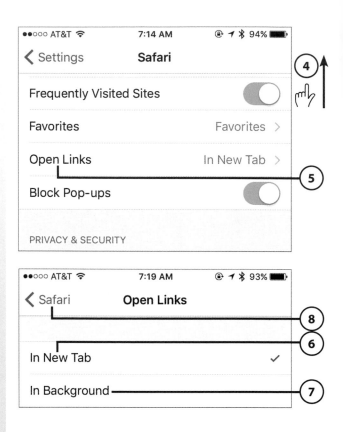

Safari Settings

Section Setting	Description
SEARCH	
Search Engine	Enables you to choose your default search tool; the options are Google (default), Yahoo, Bing, or DuckDuckGo.
Search Engine Suggestions	When this switch is on (green), Safari asks your default search engine for suggestions related to what you type in the Address/Search bar. This makes search easier because you can type your search term in the Address/Search bar instead of first moving to the search web page.

Section Setting	Description
Safari Suggestions	When this switch is on (green), Safari makes suggestions related to what you type in the Address/Search bar. This makes search easier because you can type your search term in the bar instead of first moving to the search web page.
Quick Website Search	When this switch is on (green), you can perform a search at a specific website by typing its name before your search term. For example, you can type "wiki william wallace" in the Address/Search box and the first section of the results will be entries in the Wikipedia related to William Wallace; this saves you the steps of moving to the search engine results, and then tapping the articles you want to read because you can do this directly from the Search screen instead.
Preload Top Hit	When this switch is on (green), the sites you move to or find more frequently are loaded while you search, making accessing them faster.
GENERAL	
Passwords	When you tap this setting and confirm your security (with Touch ID or a passcode), you see the list of passwords stored on your iPhone. Tap a password to see its details or edit it. Swipe to the left on a password, and then tap Delete to remove it.
Autofill	These settings enable you to automatically log in to websites and to quickly complete forms on the Web by automatically filling in key information for you. Set the Use Contact Info switch to on (green), and then tap your contact information in the Contacts app. You can determine what data is saved on your iPhone by setting the following switches on (green) or off (white): Names and Passwords or Credit Cards. Tap Saved Credit Cards to view or change existing credit card information or to add new credit cards to Safari.

Section Setting	Description
Frequently Visited Sites	When this switch is on (green) and you move into the Address/Search bar, Safari shows a section of sites that you visit frequently, making them easier to return to.
Favorites	Use this option to choose the folder of bookmarks for sites that you use most frequently. The bookmarks in the folder you select appear at the top of the screen when you move into the Address/Search bar, making them fast and easy to use.
Open Links	This tells Safari the option you want to see when you tap and hold a link on a current web page to open a new web page. The In New Tab option causes Safari to open and immediately take you to a new tab displaying the web page with which a link is associated. The In Background option causes Safari to open pages in the background for links you tap so you can view them later.
Block Pop-ups	Some websites won't work properly with pop-ups blocked, so you can use this setting to temporarily enable pop-ups by sliding the switch to off (white). When the Block Pop-ups switch is on (green), pop-ups are blocked.
PRIVACY & SECURITY	
Do Not Track	To enable private browsing, which means Safari doesn't track and keep a list of the sites you visit, set the Do Not Track switch to on (green). With this setting on, you won't be able to use the History list to return to sites you visited.

Section Setting	Description
Block Cookies	Enables you to choose the kind of cookies you want to allow to be stored on your iPhone. The Always Block option blocks all cookies. The Allow from Current Website Only setting allows cookies only from the website you are currently viewing to be stored on your phone. Allow from Websites I Visit blocks cookies from sites you didn't visit directly. This is the setting I recommend you choose because it enables websites you visit to store information on your iPhone while blocking cookies from sites you didn't visit. The Always Allow option accepts all cookies (not recommended).
Fraudulent Website Warning	If you don't want Safari to warn you when you visit websites that appear to be fraudulent, set the Fraudulent Website Warning switch to off (white).
Clear History and Website Data	When you tap this command and confirm it by tapping Clear History and Data at the prompt, Safari removes the websites you have visited from your history list. The list starts over, so the next site you visit is added to your history list again—unless you have enabled private browsing. It also removes all cookies and other website data that have been stored on your iPhone.
READING LIST	
Use Cellular Data	The Reading list enables you to store web pages on your iPhone for offline reading. If you want to allow pages to be saved to your iPhone when you are using its cellular data connection, slide the Use Cellular Data switch to the on (green) position. When it is off (white) you can only use this feature when connected to Wi-Fi.
Advanced	
Website Data	Website Data displays the amount of data associated with websites you have visited; swipe up on the screen and tap Remove All Website Data to clear this data.

Section Setting	Description
JavaScript	Set this switch to off (white) to disable JavaScript functionality (however, some sites won't work properly without JavaScript).
Web Inspector	This switch controls a feature that is used by website developers to see how their sites work on an iPhone.

Making Cookies

Cookies are data that websites store on the device you use to browse them. Cookies can contain data about you, such as areas you last visited or things in which you are interested. Cookies are typically used to direct you back to these areas or point you to related areas. Most of the time, cookies are harmless and can even be helpful to you, at least from legitimate sites you intentionally visit.

Visiting Websites

If you've used a web browser on a computer before, using Safari on an iPhone is a familiar experience. If you've not used a web browser before, don't worry because using Safari on an iPhone is simple and intuitive.

Syncing Bookmarks

Using iCloud, you can synchronize your Internet Explorer favorites or Safari bookmarks on a Windows PC—or Safari bookmarks on a Mac—to your iPhone so you have the same set of bookmarks available on your phone that you do on your computer and other devices, and vice versa (refer to Chapter 3, "Setting Up and Using iCloud and Other Online Accounts"). You should enable iCloud's Safari switch before you start browsing on your iPhone so you avoid typing URLs or recreating bookmarks. When you enable Safari syncing via iCloud, you can also view tabs open in Safari on other devices, such as a Mac or an iPad.

Using Bookmarks to Move to Websites

Using bookmarks you've synced via iCloud onto your iPhone makes it easy to get to websites that are of interest to you. You can also create bookmarks on your iPhone (you learn how later in this chapter) and use them just like bookmarks you've synced onto the iPhone.

Safari

(**1**) On the iPhone Home screen, tap Safari.

(**2**) Tap the Bookmarks button

Back to the Bookmarks

The most recent Bookmarks screen is retained when you move away from Bookmarks and then come back. Each time you open your Bookmarks, you're at the same place you were when you left it.

(**3**) Tap the Bookmarks tab (the open book) if it isn't selected already. (If you don't see this tab, tap the back button in the upper-left corner of the screen until you do.)

(**4**) Swipe up or down the list of bookmarks to browse the bookmarks and other folders of bookmarks available to you.

(**5**) To move to a bookmark, skip to step 10; to open a folder of bookmarks, tap it.

Your Favorites bookmark folder

Folder containing bookmarks   Bookmark

6 Swipe up or down the folder's screen to browse the folders and bookmarks it contains.

7 You can tap a folder to see the bookmarks it contains.

Change Your Mind?

If you decide not to visit a bookmark, tap Done. You return to the page you were previously viewing.

8 To return to a previous screen, tap the back button in the upper-left corner of the screen, which is labeled with the name of the folder you previously visited (the parent folder); this disappears when you are at the top-level Bookmarks screen

9 Repeat steps 5–8 until you see a bookmark you want to visit.

10 Tap the bookmark you want to visit. Safari moves to that website.

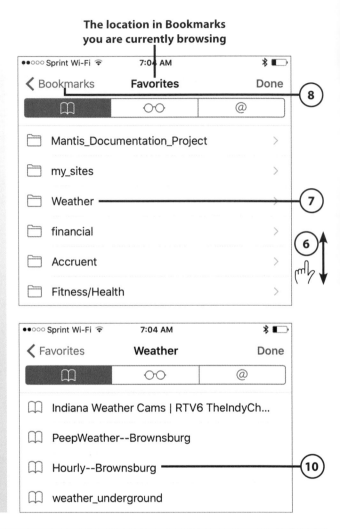

The location in Bookmarks you are currently browsing

Playing Favorites

You might see two Favorites folders on the Bookmarks screen. The folder marked with a star is the folder you designated, using the Safari settings described previously in this chapter, as the place to store Favorites on your iPhone. If you use Safari on a computer, you can also configure bookmarks and folders of bookmarks on its Bookmarks bar. When these bookmarks are synced from your computer to the iPhone, they might be stored in a folder of bookmarks also called Favorites and shown with the standard folder icon. If you set this synced folder in your iPhone's Safari settings to also be its Favorites folder, you won't have to deal with this potentially confusing situation of having two Favorites folders.

(11) Use the information in the section "Viewing Websites" later in this chapter to get information on viewing the web page.

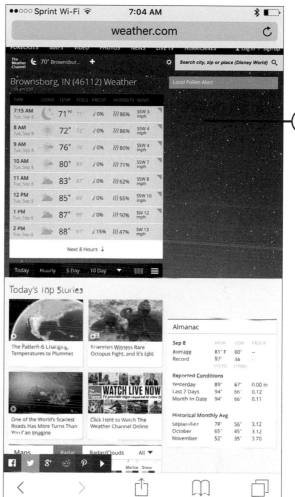

iPhone Web Pages

Some websites have been specially formatted for mobile devices. These typically have less complex information on each page, so they load faster. When you move to a site like this, you might be redirected to the mobile version automatically, or you might be prompted to choose which version of the site you want to visit. On the mobile version, there is typically a link that takes you to the "regular" version, too. (It's sometimes called the Desktop, Full, or Classic version.) Sometimes the version formatted for handheld devices offers less information or fewer tools than the regular version. Because Safari is a full-featured browser, you can use either version.

Using Your Favorites to Move to Websites

Using the Safari settings described earlier, you can designate a folder of bookmarks as your Favorites. You can get to the folders and bookmarks in your Favorites folder more quickly and easily than navigating to it as described in the previous section. Here's how to use your Favorites:

① On the Home screen, tap Safari. (If you are in Safari and have the Bookmarks screen open, tap Done to close it.)

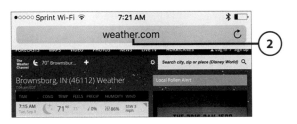

② Tap in the Address/Search bar (if you don't see the Address/Search bar, tap at the top of the screen to show it). Just below the Address/Search bar are your Favorites (bookmarks and folders of bookmarks). The keyboard opens at the bottom of the screen.

③ Swipe up and down on your Favorites. The keyboard closes to give you more room to browse.

More Commands

At the top of the Favorites screen, you might see two more commands. Tap Add to Favorites to add a bookmark to the current site to your Favorites folder. Tap Request Desktop Site if you are currently viewing the mobile version of a site and want to see the "full" version; you move to that version after you tap the command.

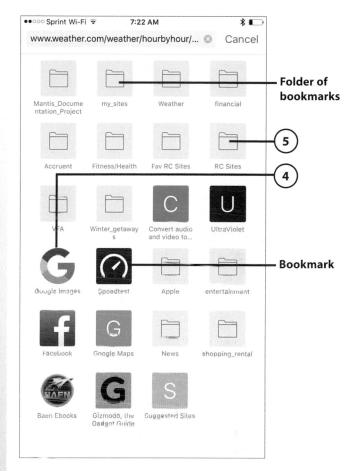

Folder of bookmarks

Bookmark

(4) To move to a bookmark, tap it and skip to step 8.

(5) To move into a folder, tap it.

(6) Continue browsing your Favorites until you find the bookmark you want to use. Like using the Bookmarks screen, you can tap a folder to move into it, tap a bookmark to move to its website, or tap the back button to move to the previous screen.

(7) Tap the bookmark for the site you want to visit.

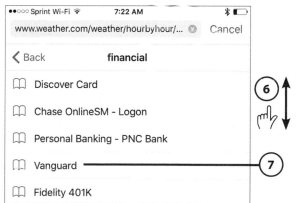

(8) Use the information in the section "Viewing Websites" later in this chapter to view the web page.

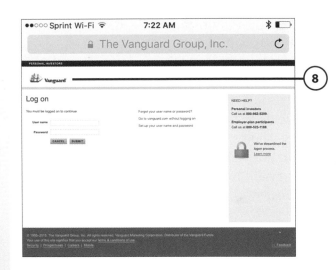

Typing URLs to Move to Websites

A Uniform Resource Locator (URL) is the Internet address of a web page. URLs can be relatively simple, such as www.apple.com, or they can be quite long and convoluted. The good news is that by using bookmarks, you can save a URL in Safari so you can get back to it using its bookmark (as you learned in the previous two tasks) and thus avoid typing URLs. To use a URL to move to a website, do the following:

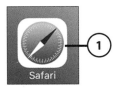

(1) On the Home screen, tap Safari. (If you are in Safari and have the Bookmarks screen open, tap Done to close it.)

(2) Tap in the Address/Search bar (if you don't see the Address/Search bar, tap at the top of the screen). The URL of the current page becomes highlighted, or if you haven't visited a page, the Address/Search bar is empty.

(3) If an address appears in the Address/Search bar, tap the clear button (x) to remove it.

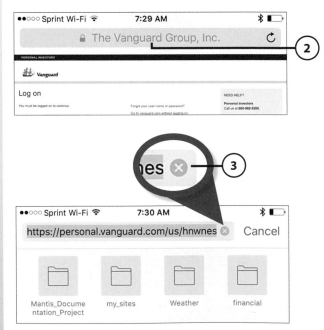

(4) Type the URL you want to visit. If it starts with www (which almost all URLs do), you don't have to type "www." As you type, Safari attempts to match what you are typing to a site you have visited previously and completes the URL for you if it can. Just below the Address/Search bar, Safari presents a list of sites that might be what you are looking for, organized into groups, such as Suggested Websites.

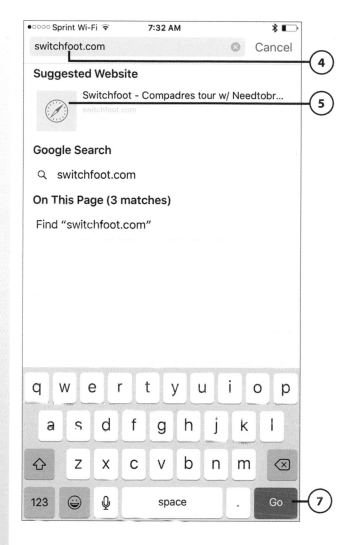

Shortcut for Typing URLs

URLs include a top-level domain code that represents the type of site (theoretically anyway) that URL leads to. Common examples are .com (commercial sites), and .edu (educational sites). To quickly enter a URL's code, tap and hold the period key to see a menu from which you can select other options, such as .net, or .edu. Select the code you want on the keyboard, and it is entered in the Address/Search bar.

(5) If one of the sites shown is the one you want to visit, tap it. You move to that web page; skip to step 8.

(6) If Safari doesn't find a match, continue typing until you enter the entire URL.

(7) Tap Go. You move to the web page.

8) Use the information in the section "Viewing Websites" to view the web page.

Using Your Browsing History to Move to Websites

As you move about the Web, Safari tracks the sites you visit and builds a history list (unless you enabled the Do Not Track option, in which case this doesn't happen and you can't use History to return to previous sites). You can use your browsing history list to return to sites you've visited.

1) Tap the Bookmarks button.

2) If you aren't on the Bookmarks screen, tap the back button until you move to the Bookmarks screen.

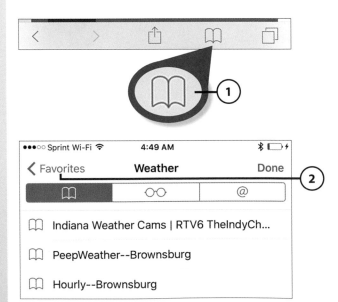

(3) If necessary, swipe down the Bookmarks page until you see the History folder.

(4) Tap History.

(5) Swipe up and down the page to browse all the sites you've visited. The more recent sites appear at the top of the screen; the further you move down the screen, the further back in time you go. Earlier sites are collected in folders for various times, such as This Morning, or Monday Afternoon.

(6) Tap the site you want to visit. The site opens and you can use the information in the section "Viewing Websites" to view the web page.

Erasing the Past

To clear your browsing history, tap the Clear button at the bottom of the History screen. At the prompt, tap the timeframe that you want to clear; the options are The last hour, Today, Today & Yesterday, or All history. Your browsing history for the period of time you selected is erased. (Don't you wish it was this easy to erase the past in real life?)

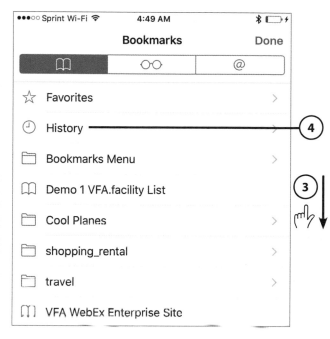

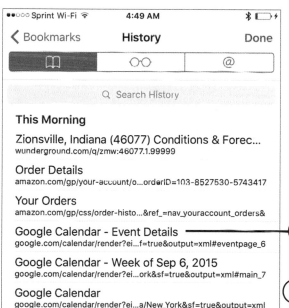

Viewing Websites

Even though your iPhone is a small device, you'll be amazed at how well it displays web pages designed for larger screens.

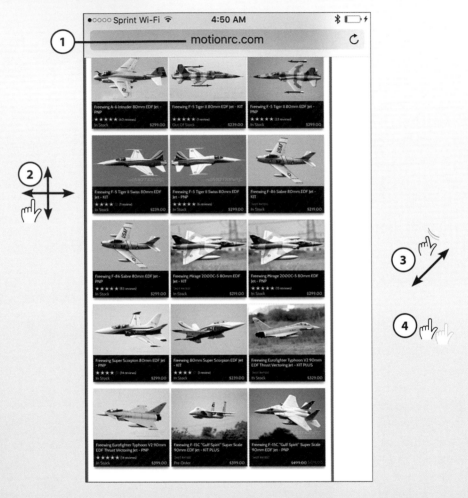

① Use Safari to move to a web page as described in the previous tasks.

Where Did the URL Go?

When you first move to a URL, you see that URL in the Address/Search bar. After you work with a site, the URL is replaced with the high-level domain name for the site (such as sitename.com, sitename.edu, etc.). To see the full URL again, tap the Address/Search bar.

2 To browse around a web page, swipe your finger right or left, or up or down.

3 To zoom in manually, unpinch your fingers.

4 To zoom in automatically, tap your finger on the screen twice.

5

6

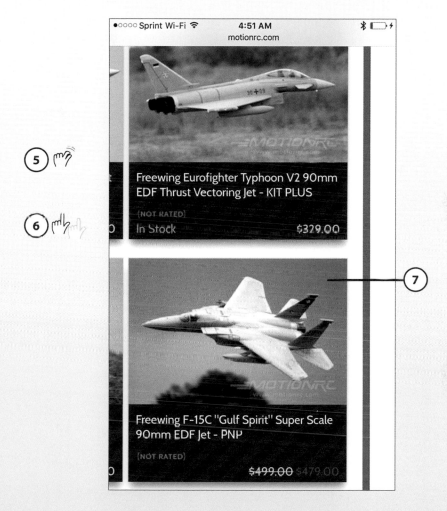

5 To zoom out manually, pinch your fingers.

6 To zoom on a column or a figure, tap it twice.

7 To move to a link, tap it once. Links can come in many forms including text (most text that is a link is in color and underlined), or graphics. The web page to which the link points opens and replaces the page currently being displayed.

Do More with Links

To see options for a link, tap and hold your finger down for a second or so. When you lift your finger, a menu appears. Tap Open to open the page to replace the current page at which the link points (this is the same as tapping a link once). Tap Open in Background to open the page in a new Safari window that opens in the background, or tap Open in New Tab to open the new page in a new tab. The command that appears depends on the Open Links Safari setting. Tap Add to Reading List to add the page to your Reading List. If the link is an image, tap Save Image to save the image on your phone. Tap Copy to copy the link's URL so that you can paste it elsewhere, such as in an email message. Tap Cancel to return to the current page and take no action.

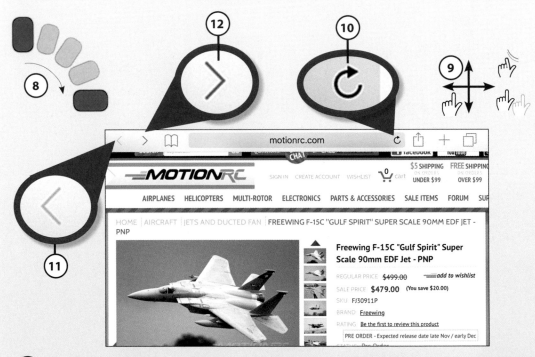

8. To view the web page in landscape orientation, rotate the iPhone so that it is horizontal.

9. Scroll, zoom in, and zoom out on the page to read it, as described in steps 2–7.

10. To refresh a page, tap Refresh. (Note: while a page is loading, this is the "x" button; tap it to stop the rest of the page from loading.)

11. To move to a previous page you've visited, tap the back button (left-facing arrow).

12. To move to a subsequent page, tap the forward button (right-facing arrow).

13 As you move around, the Address/Search bar at the top of the page and the toolbar at the bottom of the page are hidden automatically; to show them again, tap the top or bottom of the screen (on the iPhone 6 and 6s Plus, tap the top of the screen when the phone is horizontal).

Different Phones, Different Look

The type of iPhone you are using to browse the Web affects how pages look and where controls are located. For example, when you use an iPhone 5s, you see black at the top and bottom of the screen while you see white there on an iPhone 6. Also, when you rotate an iPhone 5s, the tools are at the top and bottom of the screen, while on an iPhone 6, the controls are all at the top of the screen.

Working with Multiple Websites at the Same Time

When you move to a web page by using a bookmark, typing a URL, or tapping a link on the current web page, the new web page replaces the current one. However, you can also open and work with multiple web pages at the same time so that a new web page doesn't replace the current one.

When you work with multiple web pages, each open page appears in its own tab. You can use the tab view to easily move to and manage your open web pages. You can also close open tabs, and you can even open web pages that are open on other devices on which your iCloud account has been configured and Safari syncing enabled.

Tapping Without Holding

When you tap, but don't hold down a link on a web page, the web page to which the link points opens and replaces the current web page—no new tab is created. When you tap and hold a link, the behavior is determined by the setting you chose in the preferences as covered in a task earlier in this chapter ("Setting Safari Preferences").

Opening New Pages in the Background

If you enabled the In Background option for the Open Links preference, you can open new web pages by doing the following:

1 Tap and hold on the link you want to open in the background.

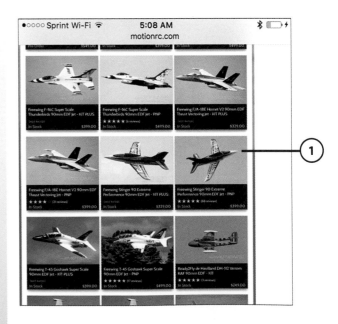

2 Tap Open in Background. The page to which the link points opens. The only result you see is the page "jumping" down to the Tab Manager button in the lower-right corner of the screen.

3 Continue opening pages in the background; see "Using Tab View to Manage Open Web Pages" to learn how to use the tab view to move to pages that are open in the background.

Opening New Pages in a New Tab

If you enabled the In New Tab option for the Open Links preference, you can open new pages by doing the following:

1 Tap and hold on the link you want to open in a new tab.

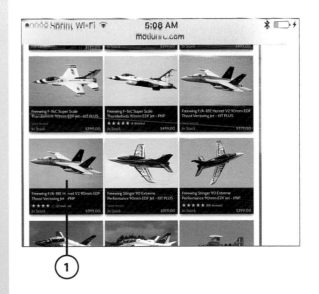

2 Tap Open in New Tab. A new tab opens and displays the page to which the link points. The web page from which you started moves into the background.

3 Continue opening pages; see "Using Tab View to Manage Open Web Pages" to learn how to use the tab view to manage your open pages.

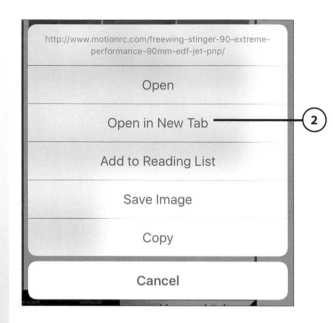

Just Open It

If you tap the Open command on the menu in step 2 of the previous tasks, the new web page replaces the one you were viewing on the current tab. This is the same as just tapping a link on the page rather than tapping and holding on it.

Using Tab View to Manage Open Web Pages

As you open new pages, whether in the background or not, new tabs are opened. Safari's tab view enables you to view and work with your open pages/tabs. Here's how:

1 Tap the tab view button. Each open page appears on its own tab.

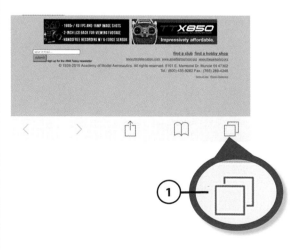

(2) Swipe up or down on the open tabs to browse them.

(3) Tap a tab/page to move into it. The page opens and fills the Safari window.

(4) Work with the web page.

(5) Tap the tab view button.

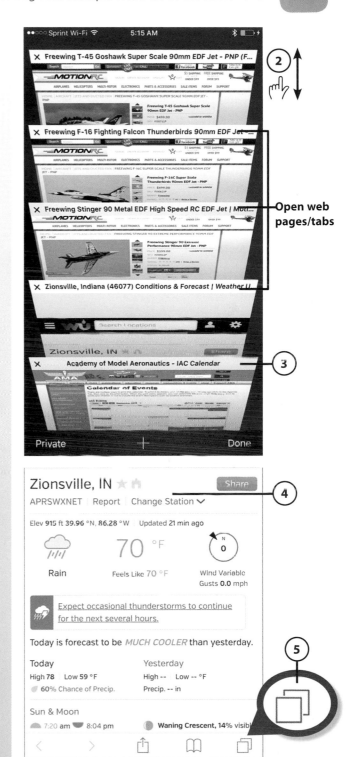

Open web pages/tabs

6. To close a tab, click its close button or swipe to the left on the tab you want to close. That page/tab closes.

7. To open a new tab, tap the Add button (+) to create a new tab that shows your Favorites screen; navigate to a new page in that tab using the tools you've already learned in other tasks (tapping bookmarks, or typing a URL).

8. To close the tab view, tap Done. The tab view closes, and the page you were most recently viewing is shown.

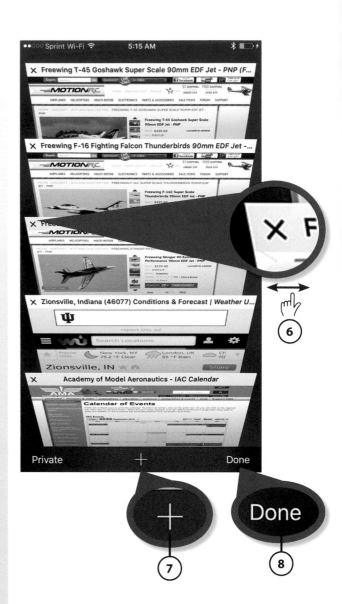

Tabs Are Independent

Each tab is independent. So, when you are working with a tab and use the back/forward buttons to move among its pages, you are just moving among the pages open under that tab. Pages open in other tabs are not affected.

Keep Private Things Private

If you aren't browsing in Private mode and tap the Private button at the bottom of the tab view, Safari moves into Private mode and stops tracking the sites you visit. Tap the button again to return to the previous state. If you are browsing in Private mode, tapping the Private button shows or hides the tabs in the tab view.

Searching the Web

In the first task of this chapter, you learned that you can set Safari to search the Web using Google, Yahoo!, Bing, or DuckDuckGo. No matter which search engine you chose, you search the Web in the same way.

(1) Tap in the Address/Search bar. The keyboard appears along with your Favorites.

(2) If there is any text in the Address/Search bar, tap the clear button.

(3) Type your search word(s). As you type, Safari attempts to find a search that matches what you typed. The list of suggestions is organized in sections, which depend on what you are searching for and the search options you configured through Safari settings. One section, labeled with the search engine you are using (such as Google Search), contains the search results from that source. Other sections can include Bookmarks and History, or Apps (from the App Store). At the bottom of the list is the On This Page section, which shows the terms that match your search on the page you are browsing.

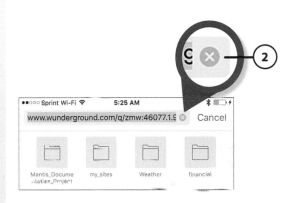

Quick Website Search

If you enabled the Quick Website Search feature, you can include the site you want to search in the Address/Search bar, such as "Wiki F-15." When you do this, the results from the site you entered appear at the top of the list and you can access them directly by tapping the information that appears (as opposed to having to move to the search engine site first as in these steps).

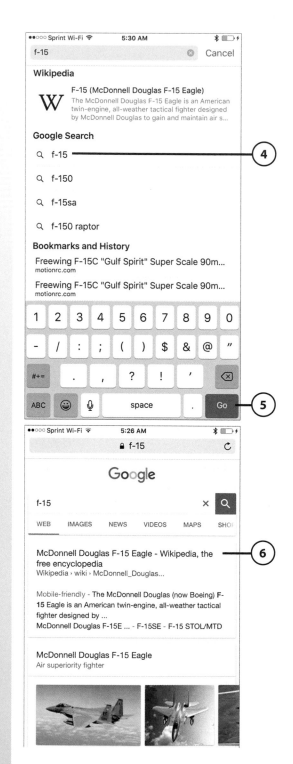

(4) To perform the search using one of the suggestions provided, tap the suggestion you want to use. The search is performed and you can skip to step 6.

(5) If none of the suggestions are what you want, keep typing until you have entered the entire search term, and then tap Go. The search engine you use performs the search and displays the results on the search results page.

(6) Use the search results page to view the results of your search. These pages work just like other web pages. You can zoom, scroll, and tap links to explore results.

Searching on a Web Page

To search for words or phrases on a web page you are viewing, perform these steps, except in step 4, tap the word or phrase for which you want to search in the On This Page section (you may have to swipe up the screen to see this section). You return to the page you are browsing and each occurrence of your search term on the page is highlighted.

Saving and Organizing Bookmarks

In addition to moving bookmarks from iCloud onto your iPhone, you can save new bookmarks directly in your iPhone (they are synced onto other devices, too). You can also organize bookmarks on your iPhone to make them easier and faster to access.

Creating Bookmarks

When you want to make it easy to return to a website, create a bookmark. Do the following to create a new bookmark:

1. Move to a web page for which you want to save a bookmark.
2. Tap the Share button.

(3) Tap Add Bookmark. The Add Bookmark screen appears.

(4) Edit the bookmark's name as needed, or tap the Clear button (x) to erase the current name, and then type the new name of the bookmark. The titles of some web pages are quite long, so it's a good idea to shorten them so the bookmark's name is easier to read on the iPhone's screen and you can fit more bookmarks on the screen.

(5) Tap LOCATION. The LOCATION section expands and you see all of the folders of bookmarks on your phone. The folder that is currently selected is marked with a check mark.

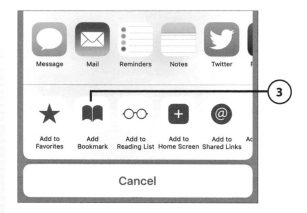

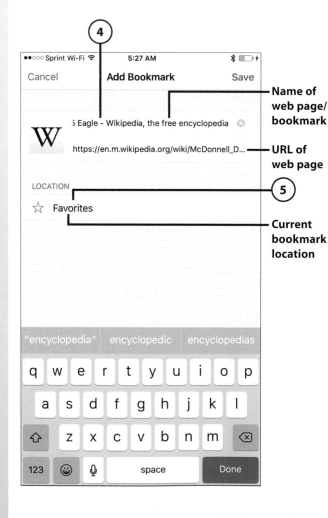

Name of web page/ bookmark

URL of web page

Current bookmark location

6 Swipe up and down the screen to find the folder in which you want to place the new bookmark. You can choose any folder on the screen; folders are indented when they are contained within other folders.

7 To choose a folder in which to store the new bookmark, tap it. You return to the Add Bookmark screen, which shows the location you selected.

8 Tap Save. The bookmark is created and saved in the location you specified. You can use the bookmark to return to the website at any time.

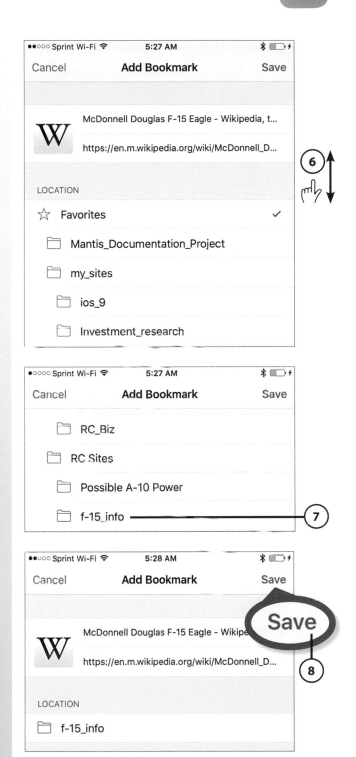

It's Not All Good

Unfortunately, bookmarks that you create on the iPhone are useful on the computer to which they are synced only if you use Internet Explorer or Safari (Windows PC) or Safari (Mac). If you use Firefox, Chrome, or another web browser, the bookmarks moved onto the computer from the iPhone are of little value to you because they appear in only one of the supported browsers (Internet Explorer or Safari). You can make them available in other browsers, but that requires going through extra gyrations, which can negate the value of syncing.

Organizing Bookmarks

You've seen how bookmarks can be contained in folders, which is a good thing because you're likely to have a lot of them. You can change the names and locations of your existing bookmarks and folders as follows:

1. Move to the Bookmarks screen showing the bookmarks and folders you want to change. (You can't move among the Bookmarks screens while you are in Edit mode so you need to start at the location where the items you want to change are located.)

2. Tap Edit. Unlock buttons appear next to the folders and bookmarks you can change; some folders, such as the History folder, can't be changed. The order icons also appear on the right side of the screen, again only for folders or bookmarks you can change.

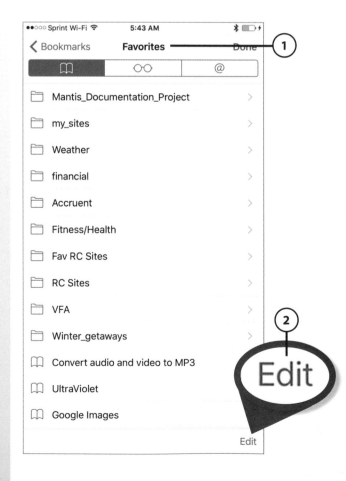

3 Touch the order icon next to the bookmark or folder you want to move and drag it up or down the screen to change the order in which it appears on the screen. When you drag a folder or bookmark between other items, they slide apart to make room for the folder or bookmark you are dragging. The order of the items in the list is the order in which they appear on the Bookmarks screen.

4 To change the name or location of a folder, tap it.

Can't Move?

If you have only one bookmark you've added, you can't move them around as described here because Safari won't let you "disturb" the default bookmarks and folders (such as Favorites and History). You can only delete default bookmarks.

5 Change the name in the name bar.

6 To change the location of the folder, tap the Location bar, which shows the folder's current location.

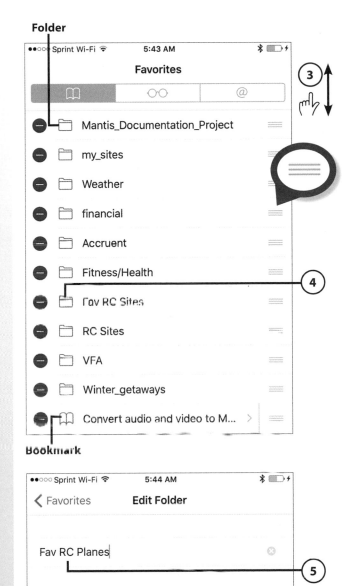

Folder

Bookmark

7 Swipe up and down the list of folders until you see the folder in which you want to place the folder you are working with.

8 Tap the folder into which you want to move the folder you are editing.

9 Tap the back button. You move back to the prior Bookmarks screen, which reflects any changes you made.

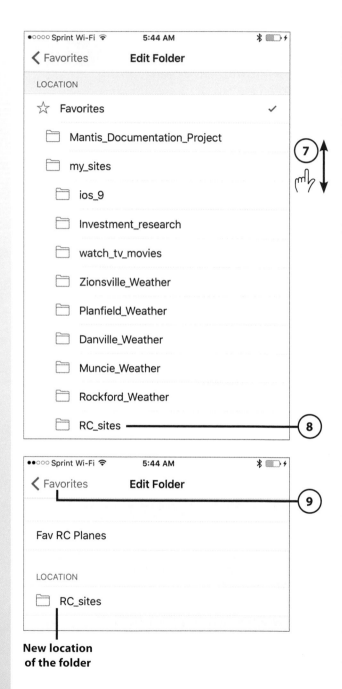

New location of the folder

10 Tap a bookmark you want to change.

Editing a Bookmark

If the bookmark you want to change isn't on the Bookmarks screen you are currently viewing, tap Done to exit Edit mode. Then open the folder containing the bookmark you want to change and tap Edit. You are able to change the bookmark.

11 Change the bookmark's name in the name bar.

12 If you want to change a bookmark's URL, tap the URL bar and make changes to the current URL. For example, you might want to change it to have the bookmark point to a site's home page rather than the page you are viewing.

13 To change the location of the folder or bookmark, tap the Location bar and follow steps 7 and 8.

14 Tap Done. You move back to the previous screen, and any changes you made—such as changing the name or location of a bookmark—are reflected.

Can't Change?

You can't change default book-marks, you can only delete them.

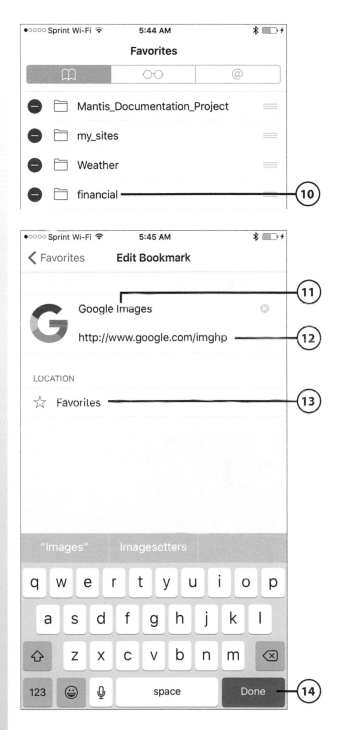

(15) To create a new folder, tap New Folder.

(16) Enter the name of the folder.

(17) Follow steps 6–8 to choose the location in which you want to save the new folder.

(18) Tap Done. The new folder is created in the location you selected. You can place folders and bookmarks into it by using the Location bar to navigate to it.

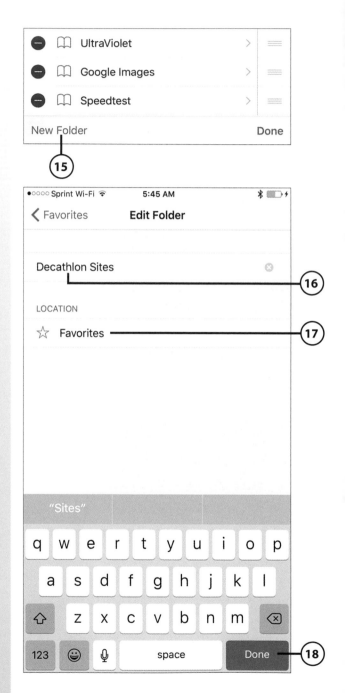

19 Tap Done. Your changes are saved and you exit Edit mode.

Browsing Both Ways

As you browse, make sure you try both the horizontal and vertical orientations. Safari sometimes offers different features in the two orientations on different models. For example, when you open the Bookmarks screen and rotate an iPhone 6 Plus or 6s Plus, the screen is divided into two panes. On the left is the Bookmarks pane you are viewing while the right pane shows the web page you were browsing. If you tap a bookmark, the web page in the right pane becomes the page at which the bookmark points.

Deleting Bookmarks or Folders of Bookmarks

You can get rid of bookmarks or folders of bookmarks you don't want any more by deleting them:

1 Move to the screen containing the folder or bookmark you want to delete.

2 Swipe to the left on the folder or bookmark you want to delete.

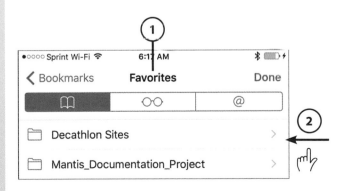

③ Tap Delete. The folder or bookmark is deleted. Note that when you delete a folder, all the bookmarks it contains are deleted, too.

Creating Bookmarks on the Home Screen

You can add a bookmark icon to a Home screen so that you can visit a web page from there; this handy trick saves you several navigation moves that would be required to move into Safari and type the URL or use a bookmark to get to the page you want to see.

① Use Safari to move to a web page to which you want to have easy access from the Home screen.

② Tap the Share button.

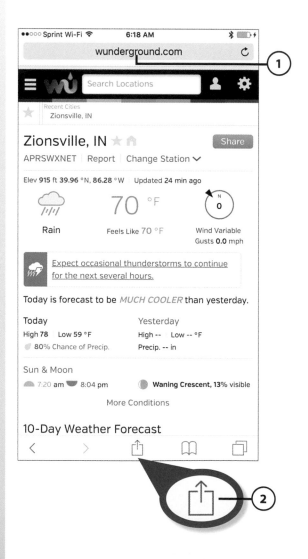

(3) Tap Add to Home Screen.

(4) If needed, edit the name of the icon that will appear on the Home screen. The default name is the name of the web page. It's best to edit it to a shorter name because it has a small amount of room on its icon on the Home screen.

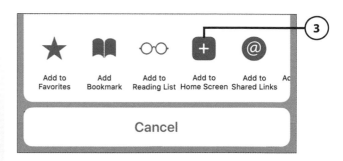

(5) Tap Add. You move to the Home screen and see the icon you added (it is added to the last page of your Home screen). You can return to the site at any time by tapping this button.

Location Is Everything

You can organize the buttons on the pages of the Home screen so that you can place your web page buttons in convenient locations, and you can create folders on your Home screens to keep your web page icons neat and tidy there, too. Refer to Chapter 5, "Customizing How Your iPhone Looks and Sounds," for details.

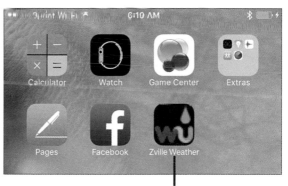

Tap to open
the web page

Using 3D Touch with Safari (iPhone 6s and iPhone 6s Plus Only)

New! Like other default iPhone apps, Safari supports 3D Touch, which you can use in a couple of ways.

Perform a Peek to see the Quick Actions menu

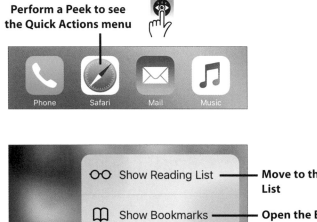

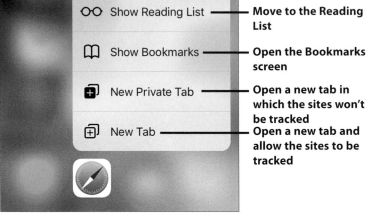

Show Reading List ——— **Move to the Reading List**

Show Bookmarks ——— **Open the Bookmarks screen**

New Private Tab ——— **Open a new tab in which the sites won't be tracked**

New Tab ——— **Open a new tab and allow the sites to be tracked**

When you press on the Safari app's icon, you see the Quick Actions menu. You can select from among its options to quickly perform actions in Safari. For example, choose New Tab to open a new tab in which you can navigate to a web page, or choose Show Bookmarks to jump to the Bookmarks page.

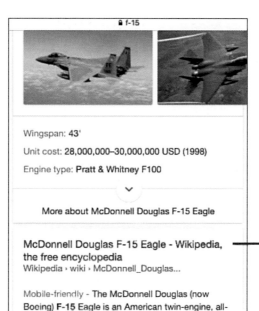

Perform a Peek on links you are browsing

When you see this, you can swipe up the screen to see options

Perform a Pop to open the web page

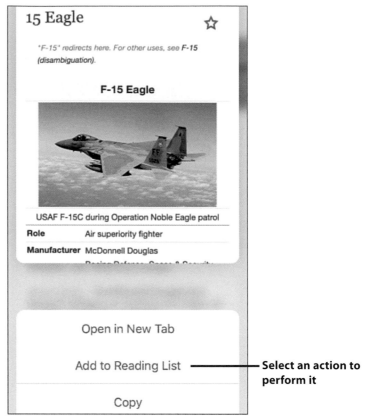

Select an action to perform it

When you are browsing links, such as when you have performed a search, or your bookmarks, press on a link or a bookmark in which you are interested to perform a Peek on it. In the Peek window, you see the web page for the link or web page on which you peeked. If you continue to press on the Peek, it pops open so you can view the web page in Safari. When you perform a Peek on some screens, such as the links resulting from a search, you see an upward-facing arrow at the top of the screen; this indicates you can swipe up the screen to reveal a menu of commands. Tap a command to perform it. For example, tap Open in New Tab to open the web page in a new tab in Safari.

Completing Forms on the Web

Just like web browsers on a computer, you often have to complete forms on your iPhone, such as to log in to your account on a website or request information about something. You can manually enter information or use AutoFill to have Safari add the information for you. (AutoFill must be enabled using Safari settings, as described at the beginning of this chapter.)

Manually Completing Forms

To manually fill in a form, do the following:

(1) Open Safari and move to a website containing a form.

(2) Zoom in on the fields you need to complete.

(3) Tap in a field. If you tapped a text field, the keyboard appears.

(4) Enter the information in the field. (If the site suggests information you want to enter, just tap it to enter it. You might have to tap Done to temporarily hide the keyboard to see all the suggestions. If a suggestion isn't the information you want to enter, just keep typing.)

(5) Tap the next button. If there isn't another field on the form, this button is disabled, so skip this step. If it is enabled, you move to the next field on the form.

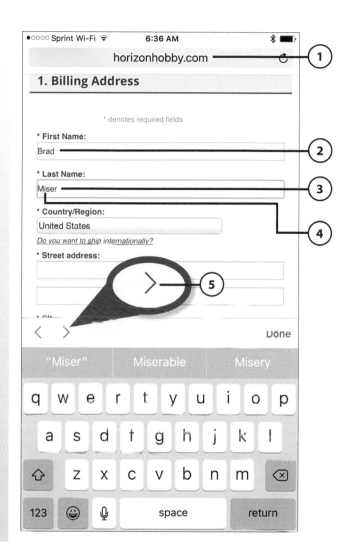

Selecting Data

You can select, instead of type, some types of information. For example, when you are entering an address, you usually choose a state or province from a list. And you often choose dates rather than typing them. When you see a downward-facing arrow in a field, tap it to choose that information or just move into a field that you select like any other. The selection tool replaces the keyboard at the bottom of the screen. Swipe on the wheels or use the other tools in this area to select the data you want to enter.

6 Repeat steps 4 and 5 to complete all the fields on the form.

7 Tap Done. If it's open, the keyboard closes and you move back to the web page.

8 Tap Next, Continue, Submit, Go, Login, or whatever button is provided to send the form's information to the website.

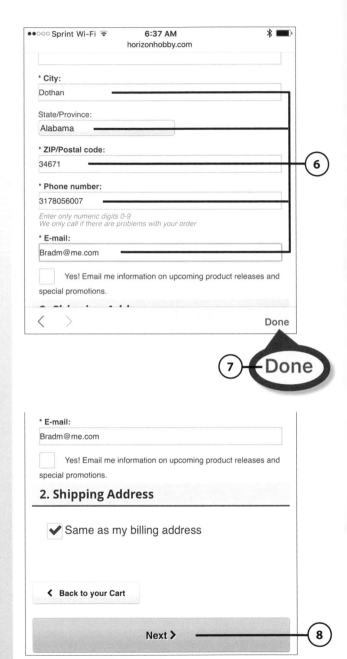

Using AutoFill to Complete Forms

AutoFill makes completing forms faster and easier because Safari can enter information for you with the tap of a button.

(1) Open Safari and move to a website containing a form. Zoom in on the fields you need to complete, and tap in a field. If you tapped a text field, the keyboard appears.

(2) Tap AutoFill. Safari fills in any fields it can, based on the information you designate when you configure AutoFill to use your contact information. Any fields that Safari completes are highlighted in yellow.

(3) Use the steps shown in the preceding task to review all the fields and to type in what AutoFill wasn't able to complete or edit those that AutoFill completed but that need to be changed.

AutoFillin'

For AutoFill to work, it must be enabled in the Safari settings as described at the beginning of the chapter. If the data AutoFill enters is not correct, use the Safari settings to choose your correct contact info.

Signing In to Websites Automatically

If you enable Safari to remember usernames and passwords, it can enter this information for you automatically. When Safari encounters a site for which it recognizes and can save login information, you are prompted to allow Safari to save that information. This doesn't work with all sites; if you aren't prompted to allow Safari to save login information, you can't use this feature with that site. When saved, this information can be entered for you automatically.

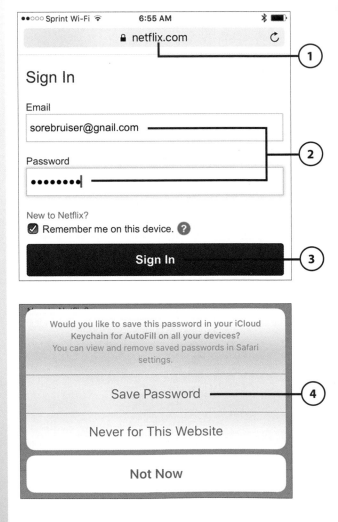

(1) Move to a web page that requires you to log in to an account.

(2) Enter your account's username and password.

(3) Tap the button to log in to your account, such as Continue, Sign In, Submit, Login, and such. You are prompted to save the login information.

(4) To save the information, tap Save Password. The next time you move to the login page, your username and password are entered for you automatically. Tap Never for This Website if you don't want the information to be saved and you don't want to be prompted again. Tap Not Now if you don't want the information saved but do want to be prompted again later to save it.

>>>Go Further

LETTING SAFARI CREATE PASSWORDS FOR YOU

If you have enabled the Names and Passwords setting, Safari can create passwords for you. Go to a website that requires you to create a password, such as when you register for a new account. When you tap in a field that Safari recognizes as requiring a password, tap Suggest Password. Safari presents a password for you; most of these are not easy to remember, but that doesn't matter because it is saved for you automatically so you won't have to enter it manually. If you want to use the recommended password, tap Use Suggested Password; Safari enters the password in the password and verify password fields. When syncing is enabled, the password is stored on the synced devices, too, so you are able to sign in from those devices just as easily.

View, edit, and share photos, slideshows, and video

Take photos and video

Configure photo and camera settings

In this chapter, you'll explore all the photo and video functionality that your iPhone has to offer. Topics include the following:

→ Getting started
→ Setting your Photos & Camera preferences
→ Taking photos and video with your iPhone
→ Viewing, editing, and working with photos on your iPhone
→ Viewing, editing, and working with video on your iPhone
→ Using AirPlay to view photos and videos on a TV
→ Using iCloud with your photos

Working with Photos and Video You Take with Your iPhone

The iPhone's cameras and Camera app capture high quality photos and video. Because you'll likely have your iPhone with you at all times, it's handy to capture photos with it whenever and wherever you are. And, you can capture video just as easily.

Whether you've taken photos and video on your iPhone or added them from another source, the Photos app enables you to edit, view, organize, and share your photos. You'll likely find that taking and working with photos and videos are among the most useful things your iPhone can do.

Getting Started

An iPhone has lots of capabilities when it comes to taking and working with photos and videos. In fact, there are so many capabilities they can seem overwhelming. The good news is that you can do basic things such as taking photos or videos very simply and learn to use the more advanced features, such as editing and sharing your photos, over time.

Each generation of iPhone has had different photo and video capabilities and features. The current versions sport high-quality cameras, and in fact, there is a camera on each side of the iPhone. Current generations also have a flash; the ability to zoom; take burst, panoramic, and time-lapse photos; and other features you expect from a quality digital camera. The iPhone 6s and 6s Plus models can also take Live Photos, which capture a small amount of video along with the photo.

The iPhone's photo and video capabilities and features are probably the largest area of differences between the various models. Because the iPhone 6s and iPhone 6s Plus are the most advanced models, they are the focus of this chapter. If you have a different model, some of the tasks described might not be applicable to you, or some of the details in this chapter might be different than what you see on your iPhone.

Additionally, the iPhone's photo and video capabilities have been increasingly tied into iCloud. For example, you can store your entire photo library under your iCloud account; this offers many benefits including backing up all your photos, making it easy to access your photos from any device, and being able to quickly share your photos with others. Therefore, I've assumed you are using iCloud and have configured it to work with photos as described in Chapter 3, "Setting Up and Using iCloud and Other Online Accounts." Like differences in iPhone camera capabilities, if you don't use iCloud with your photos, some of the information in this chapter doesn't apply to you and what you see on your phone might look different than what you see in this chapter.

Setting Your Photos & Camera Preferences

You can use the iPhone's cameras and Photo app "out of the box" without making any changes to the related settings. However, you might want to make some changes to these settings as you learn more about this part of your iPhone.

To make changes to Photos & Camera settings, you can use the following example steps that show you how to change the quality (and thus file size) of the video you take with your iPhone along with the subsequent table that provides a description of the other Photos & Camera settings.

To change the quality and file size of video you take, perform the following steps:

(**1**) Tap Settings on the Home screen.

(**2**) Swipe up the screen.

(**3**) Tap Photos & Camera.

(**4**) Swipe up the screen.

(**5**) Tap Record Video.

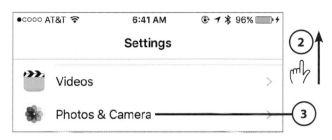

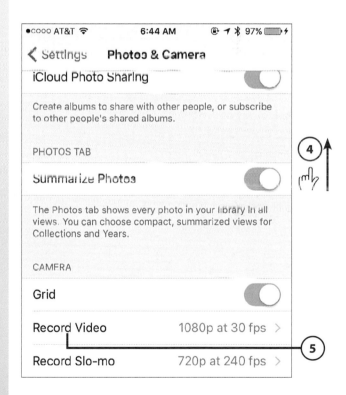

(6) Tap the option you want to use for your videos; the options you see depend on the model of iPhone you are using. This example shows the options on an iPhone 6s.

The first part of the option is the resolution (the amount of detail) of the images in the video, such as 720p HD or 1080p HD (the p stands for progressive scan while the HD stands for High Definition in case you were wondering). The higher the resolution, the better quality the image will be and the larger the file size is; the larger the file size is, the more storage space each video takes up on your iPhone.

The second part of the option is the frame rate of the video (in fps or frames per second). The faster the frame rate, the smoother the resulting video plays. Like resolution, video captured with higher frame rates is better and the corresponding files are larger.

In most cases, the 1080p HD at 30 fps is a good choice because the resulting video has very good quality without the file sizes being too large. If space on your iPhone is hard to come by, choose a lower resolution and frame rate. If quality is the most important factor to you, choose a higher resolution and frame rate.

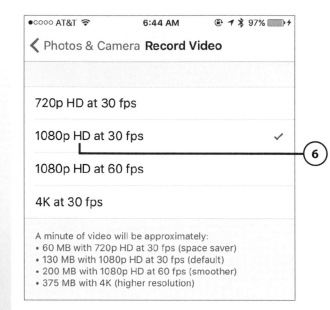

7 Tap Photos & Camera. When you take video, it is captured with the options you selected in step 6. You can change other Photos & Camera settings using a similar pattern and the description of the options in the following table.

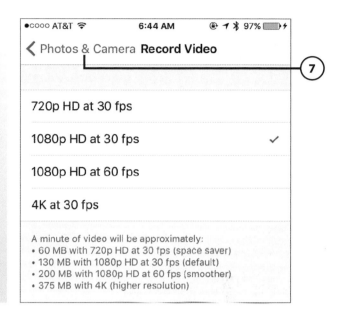

●○○○ AT&T 📶	6:44 AM	@ ✈ ⁂ 97% ▭▸⚡
⟨ Photos & Camera **Record Video**		

720p HD at 30 fps

1080p HD at 30 fps   ✓

1080p HD at 60 fps

4K at 30 fps

A minute of video will be approximately:
• 60 MB with 720p HD at 30 fps (space saver)
• 130 MB with 1080p HD at 30 fps (default)
• 200 MB with 1080p HD at 60 fps (smoother)
• 375 MB with 4K (higher resolution)

Photos & Camera Settings

Section Setting	Description
iCloud Photo Library	When enabled, all your photos are stored in iCloud so that you can access them from multiple devices. Additionally, this ensures that your photos are backed up in the event something happens to your iPhone. I recommend you enable this option to protect your photos, even if you only use your iPhone for photos and video. The only downside is that photos can require large amounts of storage, and so you might need to upgrade your iCloud storage space at some point to store all of your photos there.
Optimize iPhone Storage	If you select this option, only versions of your photos that are optimized for the iPhone are stored on your phone; this saves space so that you can keep more photos and videos on your iPhone while providing images with quality perfect for displaying on the iPhone's screen. Full resolution photos are uploaded to iCloud so you can still use them with devices that are capable of displaying them in all their glory.

Section Setting	Description
Download and Keep Originals	This option downloads full resolution versions of your photos and videos on your iPhone. They consume more space than optimized versions, and you aren't likely to be able to tell the difference when viewing them on your iPhone, so Optimize iPhone Storage is the better option.
Upload to My Photo Stream	When enabled, all your photos are automatically uploaded to your iCloud Photo Stream when you are connected to the Internet with Wi-Fi. New photos are also downloaded from iCloud to your iPhone and other devices.
Upload Burst Photos	Later in this chapter, you learn about Burst photos, which are a series of photos taken rapidly. This setting determines if all of the photos in a burst are uploaded to iCloud or only photos you tag as favorites are uploaded. Because burst photos can take up a lot of space, it's usually better to leave this disabled; when you select favorite photos in a burst series, only those photos are uploaded.
iCloud Photo Sharing	When enabled, you can share your photos with others and subscribe to other people's Photo Streams to share their photos.
PHOTOS TAB	
Summarize Photos	When this switch is on (green), you see thumbnails for only some of the photos in a collection and the timeframe of each group is larger. If you set this to off (white), you see a thumbnail of every photo in your collections, which takes up much more screen space and you have to scroll more to move among your collections. This setting impacts how you see Collections view and Years view only.
CAMERA	
Grid	When this switch is on, you see a grid on the screen when you are taking photos with the Camera app. This grid can help you align the subject of your photos in the image you are capturing.

Section Setting	Description
Record Video	Use the options under this menu to determine how video is recorded. The options available depend on the model of iPhone you have. You can choose from among different combinations of resolution and frame rate. Higher resolution and frame rates mean better quality video, but also larger files (see the task prior to this table).
Record Slo-mo	The selections under this menu determine the resolution and frame rate for slow-motion video. Like regular video, the higher the resolution and frame rate, the better quality the resulting video is and the file sizes are larger.
HDR (High Dynamic Range)	
Keep Normal Photo	When this switch is on (green) the HDR (you'll learn more about this in a later sidebar) and the normal version of photos are stored. When this switch is off (white), only the HDR version of the photo is stored.

Taking Photos and Video with Your iPhone

You use the Camera app to take photos and video with your iPhone. This app has a number of controls and features. Some features are easy to spot while others aren't so obvious. By the end of this section, you'll know how to use these features to take great photos and video with your iPhone.

The general process for capturing photos or video is:

(1) Choose the type of photo or video you want to capture.

(2) Set the options for the type of photo or video you selected.

(3) Take the photos or video.

(4) View and edit the photos or video you captured.

The information you need to accomplish the steps in this process is provided in tables and tasks throughout this chapter.

Type of photo or video being taken

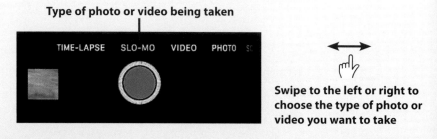

Swipe to the left or right to choose the type of photo or video you want to take

The first step is to choose the type of photo or video that you want to capture. You do this by swiping to the left or right (up or down if you are holding the iPhone horizontally) on the selection bar located near the large shutter button on the Camera app's screen. The option shown in yellow at the center of the screen is the current type of photo or video you will capture. The options available in the Camera app are explained in the following table.

Types of Photo and Video iPhones Can Capture

Type of Photo or Video	Description
TIME-LAPSE	This captures a video with compressed time so that the time displayed in the video occurs much more rapidly than "real time." This is what is often used to show a process that takes a long time, such as a plant growing, in just a few seconds.
SLO-MO	This takes slow motion video so that you can slow down something that happens quickly.
VIDEO	The VIDEO option captures video at a real-time speed. The steps to take video are provided in the task "Taking Video," later in this chapter.
PHOTO	The PHOTO tool captures still photos (or Live Photos on iPhone 6s or 6s Plus only). Step-by-step instructions showing how to use this option are provided in the task "Taking Photos," later in this chapter.
SQUARE	Takes "square" photos in which the height and width are the same.
PANO	This one takes panoramic photos that enable you to capture very wide images. An example of capturing a panoramic photo is provided in the task "Taking Panoramic Photos," later in this chapter.

When you choose the type of photo or video you want to take, there are quite a few options you can select (the options available to you depend on the specific model of iPhone you are using). When you select options, the icons you see on the screen change to reflect your selection. For example, when you choose a self-timed photo, the Self-Timer icon changes to show the time delay you have selected. And, not all options are available at the same time. For example, you can't set the flash and HDR to on at the same time because you can't take HDR images with the flash.

The following table describes the icons and tools available on the Camera app's screen. (Remember that the specific icons and tools you see depend on the type of photo or video you are capturing and the model of iPhone you are using.)

Photo and Video Options and Icons

Icon	Description
⚡	**Flash**. When you tap this icon, you see a menu with the flash options, which are Auto (the app uses the flash when required), On (flash is always used), or Off (flash is never used). Tap the option you want to use and the menu closes. When the flash is set to on, the icon is yellow.
⚡	**Flash Being Used**. When this icon appears on the screen, it indicates the flash will be used when taking a photo or video.
HDR	**High Dynamic Range (HDR)**. Tap this to set the HDR options. You learn more about HDR in the "More on Taking Photos and Video" Go Further sidebar later in this chapter. The options are Auto, On, or Off. When the flash is set to on, this is disabled and you see a line through the HDR icon because you can't use the flash with HDR images.
◎	**Live Photo on**. When enabled, you take Live Photos (see the "Live Photos" note following this table) and the Live Photos icon is yellow. To turn Live Photos off, tap this icon. This is on 6s and 6s Plus models, only.
◎	**Live Photo off**. When disabled, you take static photos and the Live icon is white. To turn Live Photos on, tap this icon. This is on 6s and 6s Plus models, only.
⏲	**Self-timer**. When you tap this icon, a menu appears on which you can choose a 3- or 10-second delay for photos. When you choose a delay, the icon is replaced with one showing the delay you set.
📷	**Change Camera**. When you tap this icon, you toggle between the back side and front side camera (front camera is typically used for selfies).

Icon	Description
	Shutter. This button changes based on the type of photo or video you are taking. For example, when you are taking a photo, this button is white as shown. When you take a video, it becomes red. It looks a bit different for other types as well, such as TIME-LAPSE. Regardless of what the button looks like, its function is the same. Tap it to start the process, such as to take a photo or start capturing video. If applicable, tap it again to stop the process, such as stopping video capture. To take burst photos, you tap and hold it to capture the burst.
	Filter. When you tap this button, a palette of filters appears. You can tap a filter to apply it to the photo or video you are capturing. For example, you can apply the Instant filter to make a photo look like it was taken on an old instant camera. When you apply a filter, you see the image with the filter applied. Generally, it's better to apply filters after you take a photo so that you have an original, unfiltered version of the photo (this is covered in the task "Applying Filters to Photos" later in this chapter).
	Filter applied. When the Filter icon is in color, you know a filter is currently applied. Tap the icon, and then tap the None option in the center of the screen to remove the filter.
00:00:08	**Timer**. When you capture video, the timer shows the elapsed time of the video you are capturing.
	Focus/exposure box. When you frame an image, the camera uses a specific part of the image to set the focus, exposure, and other attributes. The yellow box that appears on the screen indicates the focus/exposure area. You can manually set the location of this box by tapping on the part of the image that you want the app to use to set the image's attributes. The box moves to the area on which you tapped and sets the attributes of the image based on that area.

Icon	Description
	Exposure slider. When you tap in an image you are framing, the focus/exposure box appears. If you tap on this box, you see the exposure slider. Drag the sun up to increase the exposure or down to decrease it. The image changes as you move the slider so you can see its impact immediately.
AE/AF LOCK	**AE/AF Lock**. When you tap an image to set the location of the focus/exposure box and keep your finger on the screen after a second or so, the focus and exposure becomes locked based on the area you selected. This icon indicates that the exposure and focus are locked so you can move the camera without changing the focus or exposure that will be used when you capture the image. Tap the screen to release the lock and refocus on another area.
	Faces Found. When your iPhone detects faces, it puts this box around them and identifies the area as a face. You can use faces to organize photos by applying names to the faces in your photos.
	Zoom Slider. You can unpinch on an image to zoom in or pinch on an image to zoom out. When you do, the Zoom slider appears on the screen. This indicates the relative level of zoom you are applying. You can also drag the slider toward the - to zoom out or drag it toward the + to zoom in to change the level of zoom you are using.

And Now a Few Words on Live Photos (iPhone 6s and 6s Plus)

The iPhone 6s and 6s Plus can capture Live Photos. A Live Photo is a static image, but it also has a few of what Apple calls "moments" of video around the static image that you take. To capture a Live Photo, you set the Live function to be on (the icon is yellow) and take the photo as you normally would. When you are viewing a Live Photo you have taken, tap and hold on the photo to see the motion associated with that photo. When you aren't tapping and holding on a Live Photo, it looks like any other photo you've taken.

Taking Photos

You can use the Camera app to capture photos, like so:

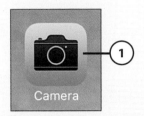

(1) On the Home screen, tap Camera.

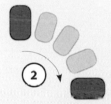

(2) To capture a horizontal photo, rotate your iPhone so that it's horizontal; of course, you can use either orientation to take photos just as you can with any other camera.

(3) Swipe up or down (right or left if the phone is vertical) on the selection bar until PHOTO is in the center and in yellow.

(4) If you want to change the camera you are using, tap the Change Camera button. When you change the camera, the image briefly freezes, and then the view changes to the other camera. On some iPhone models, the front camera (the one facing you when you look at the screen) has fewer features than the back camera. For example, you can't zoom when using the front camera.

(5) Set the Flash, HDR, Live, and Self-timer options you want to use for the photo; see the previous table for an explanation of these options you can use and how they work.

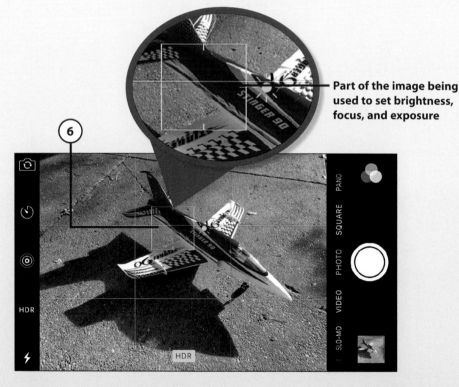

Part of the image being used to set brightness, focus, and exposure

(6) Frame the image by moving and adjusting the iPhone's distance and angle to the object you are photographing; if you have the Grid turned on, you can use its lines to help you frame the image the way you want it. When you stop moving the phone, the Camera app indicates the part of the image that is used to set focus, brightness, and exposure with the yellow box. If this is the most important part of the image, you are good to go. If not, you can set this point manually by tapping where you want the focus to be (see step 9).

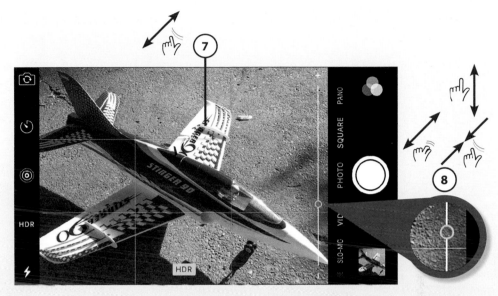

(7) To zoom in, unpinch on the image. The camera zooms in on the subject and the Zoom slider appears.

(8) Unpinch on the image or drag the slider toward the + to zoom in or pinch on the image or drag the slider toward the – to zoom out to change the level of zoom until it's what you want to use.

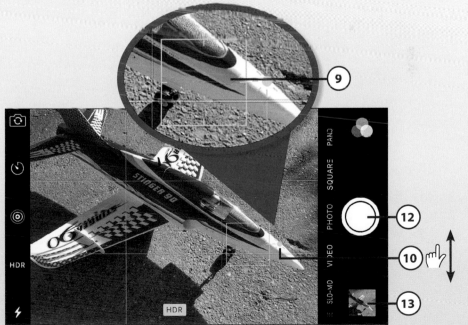

(9) Tap the screen to manually set the area of the image to be used for setting the focus and exposure. The yellow focus box appears where you tapped.

(10) To change the exposure, swipe up on the sun icon to increase the brightness or down to decrease it.

(11) Continue making adjustments in the framing of the image, the zoom, focus point, and brightness until it is the image you want to take.

(12) Tap the Shutter button on the screen, or either Volume button on the side of the iPhone. The Photo app captures the photo, and the shutter closes briefly while the photo is recorded. When the shutter opens again, you're ready to take the next photo.

(13) To see the photo you most recently captured, tap the Thumbnail button to view it.

(14) Use the photo-viewing tools to view the photo (see "Viewing, Editing, and Working with Photos on Your iPhone" later in this chapter for the details).

(15) To delete a photo, tap the Trash icon, and then tap Delete Photo.

(16) To Edit the photo, tap the Edit button and use the resulting editing tools to make changes to it (see "Viewing, Editing, and Working with Photos on Your iPhone" later in this chapter for the details).

(17) Tap Done. You move back into the Camera app, and can take more photos.

Taking Panoramic Photos

The Camera app can take panoramic photos by capturing a series of images as you pan the camera across a scene, and then "stitching" those images together into one panoramic image. To take a panoramic photo, perform the following steps:

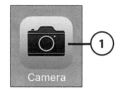

The shaded bar indicates the total possible area that can be included in the image

Current position in the image

(1) Open the Camera app.

(2) Swipe on the selection bar until PANO is selected. On the screen, you see a bar representing the entire image that contains a smaller box representing the current part of the image that will be captured.

(3) Tap the Shutter button. The app begins capturing the image.

4 Slowly sweep the iPhone to the right while keeping the arrow centered on the line on the screen (if you move the phone too fast, you see a message on the screen telling you to slow down). The better you keep the tip of the arrow aligned with the line, the more consistent the centerline of the resulting image will be.

5 When you've moved to the "end" of the image you are capturing or the limit of what you can capture in the photo, tap the Shutter button and the process stops. You move back to the starting point and the panoramic photo is created. You can tap the image's thumbnail to view, delete, or edit it as described in the previous task.

As you move the iPhone from the start of the image to the end, keep the arrow centered on the line

Taking Video

You can capture video as easily as you can still images. Here's how.

1 Move into the Camera app.

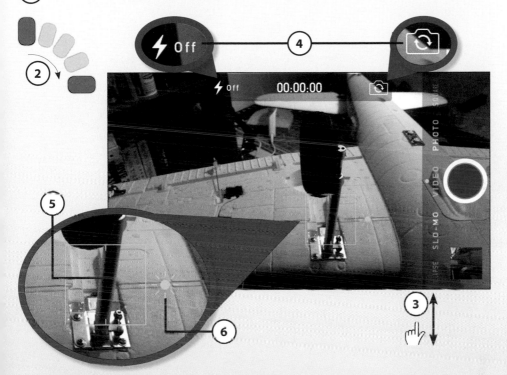

2 To capture horizontal video, rotate the iPhone so that it's horizontal; of course, you can use either orientation to take video just as you can with any other video camera.

3 Swipe on the selection bar until VIDEO is selected.

4 Choose the camera on the back of the iPhone or the one facing you, configure the flash, or zoom in, just like setting up a still image. (The Self-timer, grid, and HDR mode are not available when taking video.)

5 Tap on the screen where you want to focus.

6 If needed, adjust the exposure by sliding the sun icon up or down.

7 To start recording, tap the Shutter button. You hear the start/stop recording tone and the app starts capturing video; you see the timer on the screen showing how long you've been recording.

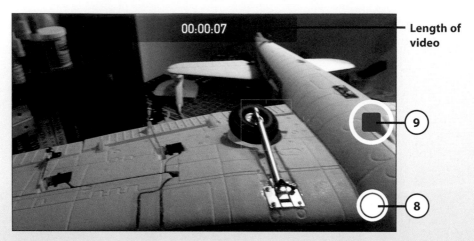

00:00:07 — **Length of video**

(8) To take still images while you take video, tap the white Shutter button.

(9) To stop recording, tap the red Shutter button again. Also, like still images, you can then tap the video's thumbnail to preview it. You can use the Photos app's video tools to view or edit the clip. (See "Viewing, Editing, and Working with Video on Your iPhone" later in this chapter for the details.)

Taking Photos and Video from the Lock Screen

Because it is likely to be with you constantly, your iPhone is a great camera of opportunity. You can use its Quick Access feature to quickly take photos when your iPhone is asleep/locked. Here's how:

(1) When the iPhone is locked, press the Touch ID/Home button. The Lock screen appears.

(2) Swipe up on the camera icon. The Camera app opens. (If you don't swipe far enough up the screen, the Lock screen "drops" down again. Swipe almost all the way up the screen to open the Camera app. It also opens more easily if you give the icon a quick flick up.)

(3) Use the Camera app to take the photo or video as described in the previous tasks. You can only view the most recent photos or videos you captured from within the Camera app. Move to the Photos app to see more.

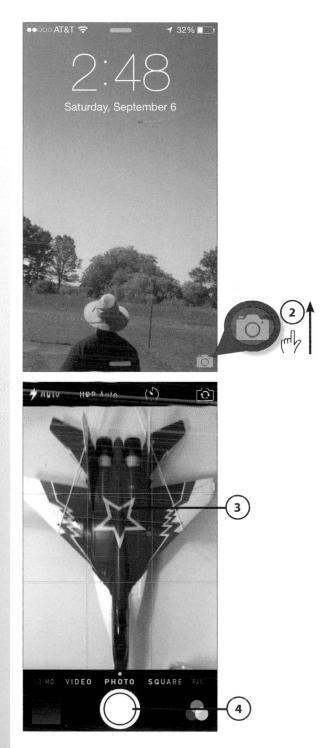

Taking Photos and Video from the Control Center

You can get to the camera quickly using the Control Center, too.

1. Swipe up from the bottom of the screen to open the Control Center.

2. Tap the Camera button. The Camera app opens.

3. Use the Camera app to take photos or video as you've learned in the previous tasks.

Taking Photos with Quick Actions (iPhone 6s, 6s Plus Only)

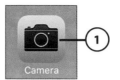

New! On an iPhone 6s or 6s Plus, the Quick Access menu offers a selection of photos and video commands that you can choose right from a Home screen.

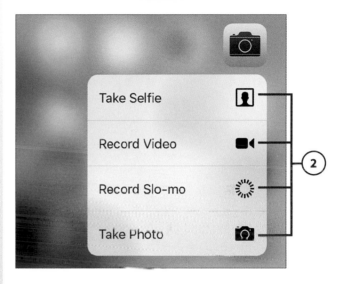

1. Tap and hold on the Camera icon until the Quick Actions menu opens.

2. Tap the type of photo or video you want to take. The Camera app opens and is set up for the type you selected.

3. Use the Camera app to capture the photo or video.

>>>Go Further

MORE ON TAKING PHOTOS AND VIDEO

The Photos app enables you to do all sorts of interesting and fun things with photos and video. Following are some additional pointers that help you make the most of this great app:

- **Set Once**. You only need to set the Flash, HDR, and other options when you want to change the current settings because these settings are retained even after you move out of the Camera app and back into it.

- **HDR**. The High Dynamic Range (HDR) feature causes the iPhone to take three shots of each image with each shot having a different exposure level. It then combines the three images into one higher-quality image. HDR works best for photos that don't have motion and where there is good lighting. (You can't use the iPhone's flash with HDR images.) Also, HDR photos take longer to capture.

When the Keep Normal Photo switch in the Photos & Camera Settings is on, you see two versions of each HDR photo in the Photos app: One is the HDR version, and the other is the normal version. If you prefer the HDR versions, set the Keep Normal Photo switch to off so that your photos don't use as much space on your iPhone, and you don't have twice as many photos to deal with.

- **Location.** The first time you use the Camera app, you are prompted to decide whether or not you allow it to use Location Services. If you allow the Camera app to use Location Services, the app uses the iPhone's GPS to tag the location where photos and video were captured. Some apps can use this information, such as the Photos app on your iPhone, to locate your photos on maps, find photos by their locations, and so on.

- **Sensitivity.** The iPhone's camera is sensitive to movement, so if your hand moves while you are taking a photo, it's likely to be blurry. Sometimes, part of the image will be in focus while part of it isn't, so be sure to check the view before you capture a photo. This is especially true when you zoom in. If you are getting blurry photos, the problem is probably your hand moving while you are taking them. Of course, since it's digital, you can take as many photos as you need to get it right; you'll want to delete the rejects (you learn how later) periodically, so you don't have to waste storage room or clutter up the Photos app with them.

- **Burst Photos.** When you press and hold on the Shutter button while taking photos, a series of images are captured rapidly and you see a counter showing the number being taken. When you release the Shutter button, a burst photo is created; the burst photo contains all of the images you captured, but appears as a single image in the Photos app. You can review the images in the burst and choose to keep only the images you want to save (this task is covered later in this chapter).

- **Self-timer.** When you set the Self-timer option, you choose either a 3- or 10-second delay between when you tap the Shutter button and when the image is captured. Like the other settings, the Self-timer is persistent so you need to turn it off again when you want to stop using it.

- **Self-timer and Burst.** If you set the timer, and then tap and hold on the Shutter button for a second or so, a burst of ten photos is captured when the timer expires.

- **Slow-motion Video.** You can also take slow-motion video. Choose SLO-MO on the selection bar. Set up the shot and take the video as you do with normal speed video. When you play it back, the video plays in slow motion except for the very beginning and ending. (The speed of the video is determined by the Record Slo-mo setting, described earlier.)

- **Time-lapse Video**. When you choose the TIME-LAPSE option, you can set the focus and exposure level and choose the camera you want to use. You record the video just like "real time" video. When you play it back, the video plays back rapidly so you seemingly compress time.

- **Screenshots**. You can take screenshots of your iPhone's screen by pressing and holding the Home and Sleep/Wake buttons at the same time. The screen flashes white and the shutter sound plays to indicate the screen has been captured. The resulting image is stored in the Recently Added album. You can view the screen captures you take, email them, send them via Messages, or other tasks as you can with photos you take with the iPhone's camera.

Viewing, Editing, and Working with Photos on Your iPhone

After you've loaded your iPhone with photos, you can use the Photos app to view them individually and as slideshows. You can also edit your photos and use them in a number of tasks, such as sharing your photos via AirDrop or email.

Finding Photos to Work With by Browsing

The first step in viewing, editing, or doing other tasks with photos is finding the photos you want to work with. When you open the Photos app, you see three ways to access your photos: Photos, Shared, and Albums. You can browse these sources to find photos in which you are interested.

The Photos source organizes your photos with groupings of photos by date and location. The top level is Years, which shows your photos grouped by the year in which they were taken. You can then "drill down" into a year where you find collections, under which photos are organized by location and date ranges, which are determined according to the time, date, and location information on your photos. When you tap one of these collections, you drill down and see moments, which show you the detail of a collection. At the moment level, you see and can work with the individual photos in the collection.

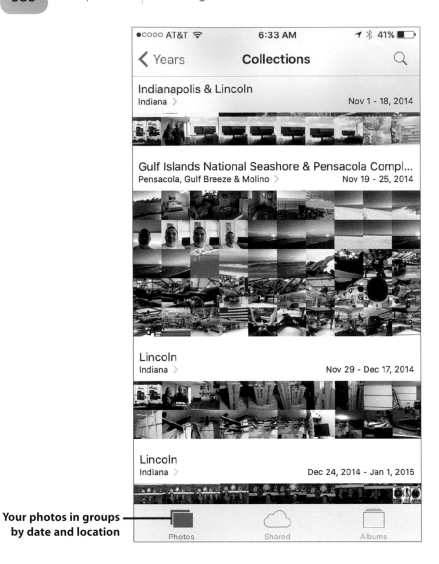

Your photos in groups by date and location

Shared shows photos you are sharing with other people and photos other people are sharing with you. For each group of photos being shared, you see the name of the group and who is sharing it (you, for photos you are sharing, or the name of the person sharing with you). When you tap a shared group, you see the photos it contains and can work with them. (Working with photo sharing is covered in detail in "Using iCloud with Your Photos" later in this chapter.)

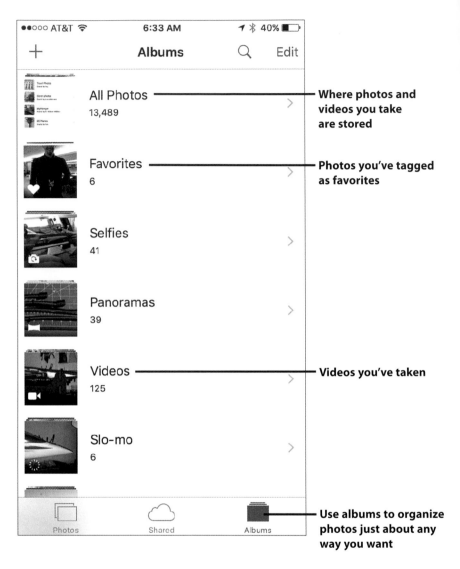

Albums allow you to organize your photos in a number of ways. Following are some of the albums or types of albums you might see:

- **All Photos or Camera Roll**. When you see the All Photos album, you have the iCloud Photo Library enabled so that you can use this album to see all the photos in your library. When this is not enabled, you see Camera Roll instead. In either situation, this album contains photos and videos you've taken with the iPhone's camera or saved from other apps, such as attachments to email in Mail.

- **Favorites**. This folder contains images you have tagged as a favorite by tapping their Heart button.

- **Selfies**. Photos you take with the front-facing camera are stored here.

- **Panoramas**, **Videos, Slo-mo, Time-lapse, Bursts, and Screenshots**. These folders contain photos and videos of the types for which they are named. For example, to get to the videos you have taken, open the Videos album.

- **Albums you create**. Later in this chapter, you learn how to create albums for your photos. Albums that you've created on your iPhone are indicated by just having the name you give them.

Your Albums May Vary

Some apps, such as Instagram, might add their own albums to the Albums tab.

While each of these sources looks a bit different, the steps to browse them to find the photos you want to work with are similar for all three sources; this example shows using the Photos source to browse for photos:

(1) On the Home screen, tap Photos.

(**2**) Tap Photos. On the Years screen, you see photos collected by the year in which they were taken. Next to the year, you see a summary of the various locations where the photos were taken.

Start at the Beginning

If the title at the top of the screen isn't "Years," tap the back button located in the upper-left corner of the screen until it is.

(**3**) Swipe up and down the screen to browse all the years.

(**4**) Tap the thumbnails in the year that contains photos you want to work with. You move to the Collections screen that groups the selected year's photos based on locations and time periods.

Straight to the Map

If you want to jump directly to the map view of a group of photos, tap the heading for the period in which you are interested instead of the thumbnails it contains.

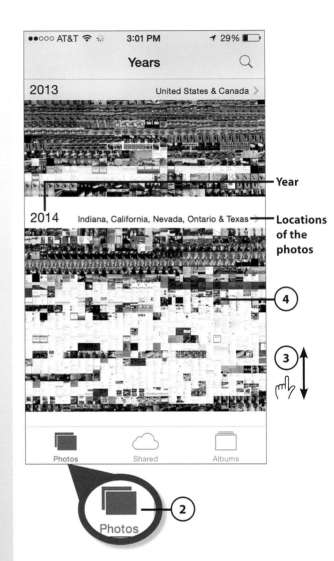

5 Swipe up and down the screen to browse all the collections in the year you selected.

6 Tap the collection that contains photos you want to see. Doing so opens the Moments screen, which breaks out the photos in the collection by location and date.

7 Swipe up and down the screen to browse all the moments in the collection you selected.

8 To see the photos in the moment based on their location, tap the moment's heading. You see a map with photos collected at the various locations.

No Map Required

If you don't want to see photos in a moment shown on the map, just tap any photo in a moment to start browsing that moment's photos.

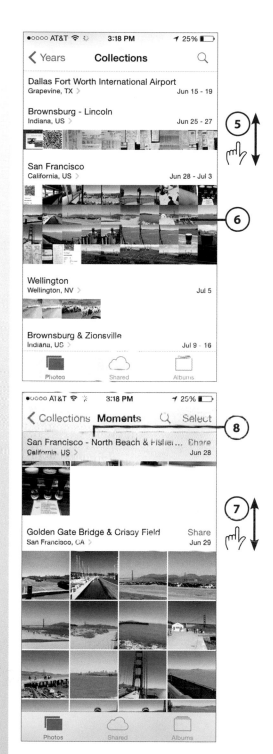

9 Zoom in by unpinching your fingers on the map to get more detail. As you zoom, the locations of photos become more specific.

10 Tap the location that contains photos you want to see. You see a thumbnail of each photo at that location.

11 You're ready to view the photos in the group and can move to the next task.

Go Back

You can move back to the screens from where you came by tapping the back button, which is always located in the upper-left corner of the screen; this button is named with the screen it takes you back to. To choose a different source, you might have to tap the back button several times as the Photos, Shared, and Albums buttons at the bottom of the screen are only visible on the opening screen of the Photos app.

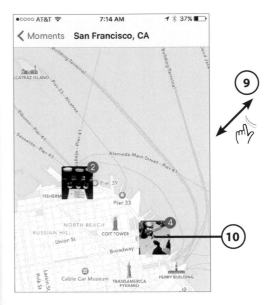

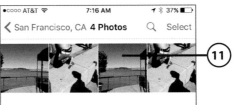

Finding Photos to Work With by Searching

Browsing photos can be a fun way to find photos, but at times you might want to get to specific photos more quickly. You can use the Search tool to get to photos quickly.

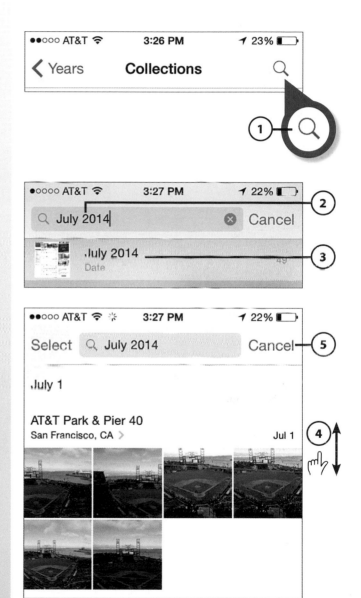

1. Continuing in the Photos app, tap the magnifying glass.

2. Type your search term. This can be any information associated with your photos, such as a date or location. As you type, collections of photos that match your search criteria are listed under the Search bar. The more specific you make your search term, the smaller the set of photos that will be found.

3. Tap the results you want to explore.

4. Browse the results to find the photo you want.

5. Tap Cancel to clear the search.

Using 3D Touch with Photos (iPhone 6s, 6s Plus Only)

New! You can use 3D Touch to preview and open photos as follows:

1. Browse a collection of photos in the Photos app.

2. Tap and hold on a photo in which you are interested. A Peek of that photo appears.

3. To open the photo, press down slightly harder until it pops open and use the steps in the previous task to view it (if you pop the photo open, skip the rest of these steps).

4. To see actions you can perform on the photo preview, swipe up the image.

(5) Tap the action you want to perform, such as Favorite, to tag the photo as a favorite.

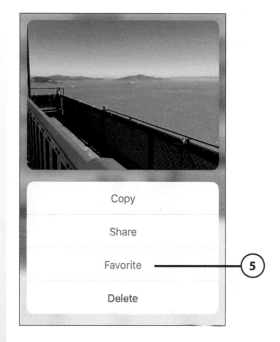

Viewing Photos in Slideshows

You can view photos in slideshows as the following steps demonstrate:

(1) Using the skills you learned in the previous task, select and view the photo in a group of photos that you want to be the first one in the slideshow.

(2) Tap the Share button.

It's Not All Good

When you select a photo and tap the Share button, the app indicates that one photo is selected, which is true. However, when you play the slideshow, all the photos in the group are shown. The one you selected is just the first one displayed. This is a bit confusing, but as it appears to have no bearing on what plays in the slideshow, you can safely ignore the information about how many photos are selected. If you want to choose the photos that are shown, create an album containing only those photos and view that in a slideshow instead.

(3) Tap Slideshow. The slideshow begins to play.

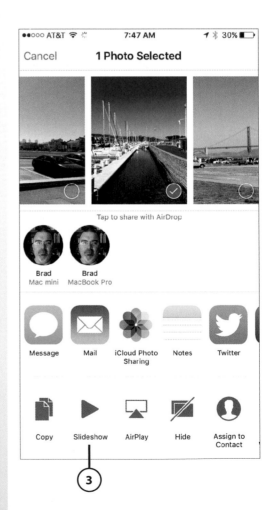

4 You can watch the slideshow with the current options, in which case, skip to step 14, or if you want to configure slideshow options, tap the screen.

5 Tap Options.

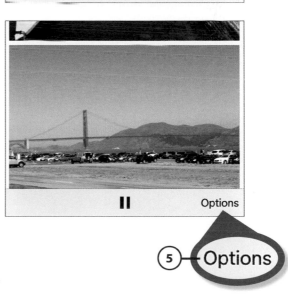

6 Tap Theme. The theme determines how the images are displayed on the screen.

7 Tap the theme you want to use in the slideshow.

8 Tap Music.

9 Tap the theme music you want to use or tap iTunes Music and then use the Select Music tool to choose the music you want to play during the slideshow.

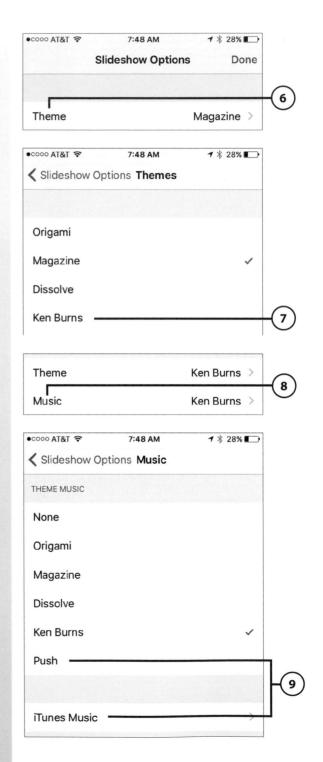

(10) To have the slideshow repeat until you stop it manually, set the Repeat switch to on (green).

(11) Drag the slider to the left to slow down the speed of the slideshow or to the right to increase it.

(12) Tap Done. You return to the slideshow, and it plays with the options you selected.

(13) To hide the controls, tap the screen.

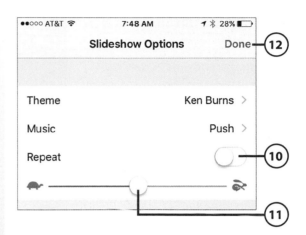

(14) To stop the show before it finishes, tap the screen.

(15) To pause the show, tap the Play/Pause button.

(16) To exit the slideshow, tap Done.

Working with Burst Mode Photos

When you use the Burst mode to take photos, the Camera app rapidly takes a series of photos. (Typically, you use Burst mode to capture motion, where the action is happening too quickly to be able to frame and take individual photos.) You can review the photos taken in Burst mode and save any you want to keep as favorites; your favorites become separate photos just like those you take one at a time. Here's how:

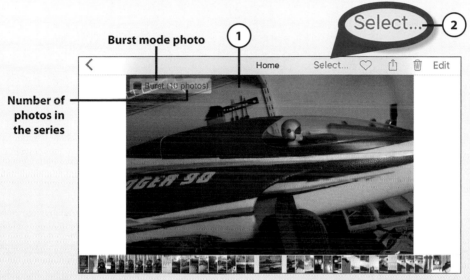

1. View a Burst mode photo. Burst mode photos are indicated by the word Burst and the number of photos in the burst. (You can see all of the burst photos on your phone by opening the Bursts album.)

2. Tap Select. The burst is expanded. At the bottom of the screen, you see thumbnails for the photos in the burst. At the top part of the screen, you see thumbnails of the photos; the photo in the center of the previews is marked with a downward-facing arrow. Photos marked with a dot are "suggested photos," meaning the best ones in the series according to the Photos app.

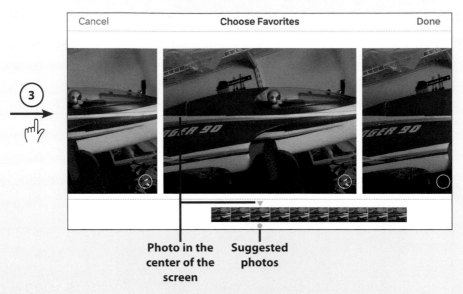

Photo in the center of the screen **Suggested photos**

(3) Swipe all the way to the right to move to the first photo in the series; swiping on the thumbnails at the bottom flips through them faster.

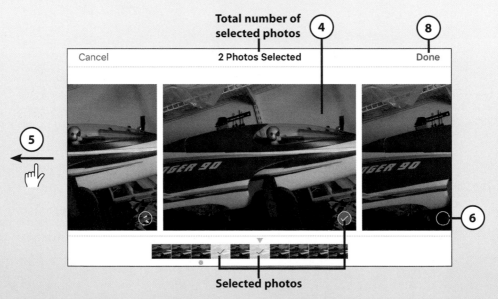

Total number of selected photos

Selected photos

(4) Tap a photo that you want to save. It is marked with a check mark.

(5) Swipe to the left to move through the series.

(6) Tap each photo you want to save.

(7) Continue reviewing and selecting photos until you've gone through the entire series.

(8) Tap Done.

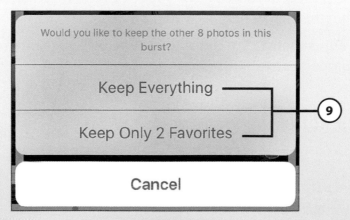

(9) Tap Keep Only X Favorites, where X is the number of photos you selected or tap Keep Everything to keep all the photos in the burst. Each photo you keep becomes a separate, individual photo; you can work with these just like photos you take individually.

Burst Mode Photos and Uploads to the Cloud

If the Upload Burst Photos switch is set to off, burst photos are not uploaded to the cloud until you go through the steps to select and save photos from a burst. The photos you selected to keep are then uploaded to the cloud just like individual photos you take.

Editing Photos

Even though the iPhone has great photo-taking capabilities, not all the photos you take are perfect from the start. Fortunately, you can use the Photos app to edit your photos. The following tools are available to you:

- **Enhance.** This tool attempts to automatically adjust the colors and other properties of the photos to make them better.

- **Straighten, rotate, and crop.** You can rotate your photos to change their orientation and crop out the parts of photos you don't want to keep. You can also have the Photos app do this with the tap of a button.

- **Filters.** You can apply different filters to your photos for artistic or other purposes.

- **Remove red-eye.** This one helps you remove that certain demon-possessed look from the eyes of people in your photos.

- **Smart adjustments.** You can adjust the light, color, and even the black and white properties of your photos.

Enhancing Photos

To improve the quality of a photo, use the Enhance tool.

1. View the image you want to enhance.

2. Tap Edit.

3. Tap the Enhance button. The image is enhanced and the Enhance button turns blue.

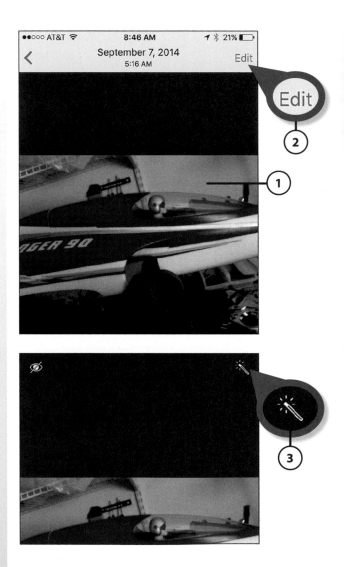

(4) If you don't like the enhancements, tap the Enhance button again to remove the enhancements.

(5) To save the enhanced image, tap Done.

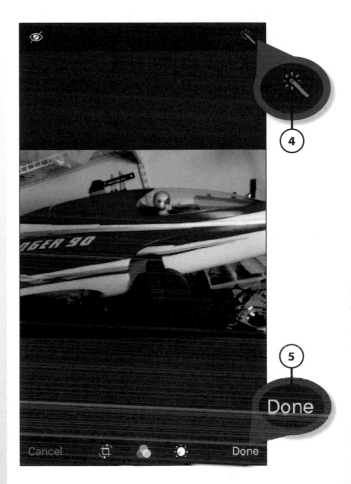

Straightening, Rotating, and Cropping Photos

To change the orientation of a photo, use the Rotate tool.

1. View the image you want to rotate.

2. Tap Edit.

3. Tap the Crop button. The Photos app attempts to straighten and crop the photo automatically.

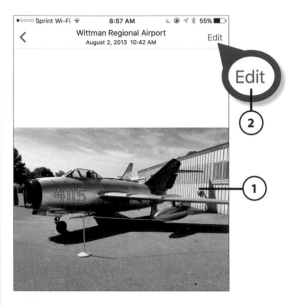

(4) If you are satisfied with how the photo is straightened and cropped, tap Done and skip the rest of these steps. If not, continue to the next step.

(5) To undo the automatic straighten and crop, tap RESET.

(6) To rotate the image, tap the Rotate button. Each time you tap this button, the image rotates 90 degrees.

(7) To straighten the image, drag the triangle to the left or right to rotate the image.

(8) When the image is straightened, remove your finger. The dial shows how much you've rotated the image.

(9) To crop the image proportionally, tap the Constrain button; to crop the image without staying to a specific proportion, skip to step 11.

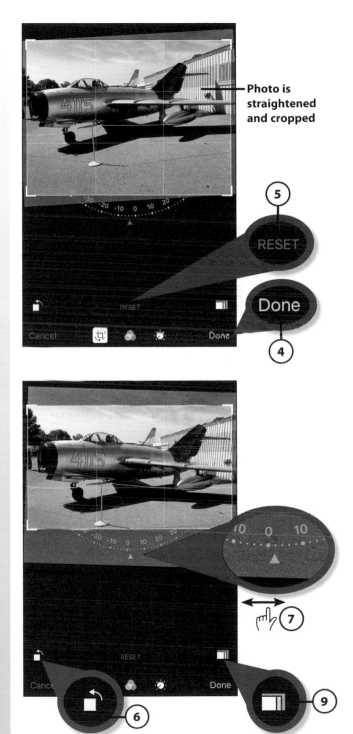

Photo is straightened and cropped

10 Tap the proportion with which you want to crop the image. You use this to configure the image for how you intend to display it. For example, if you want to display it on a 16:9 TV, you might want to constrain the cropping to that proportion so the image matches the display device.

11 Drag the corners of the crop box until the part of the image you want to keep is shown in the box.

12 Drag on the image to move it around inside the crop box.

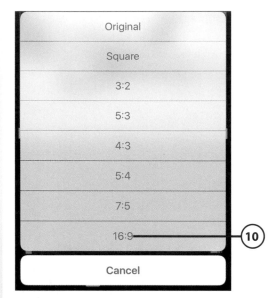

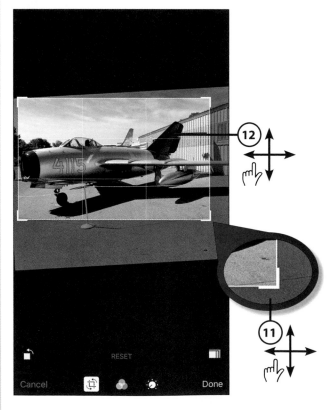

13 When the image is cropped and positioned as you want it to be, tap Done. The edited image is saved.

More on Straightening and Cropping Photos

To undo changes you've made, tap the RESET button and the photo returns to the state it was in before you started editing it. To have the app automatically straighten and crop the photo again, tap AUTO. To exit the Edit mode without saving your changes, tap Cancel.

Applying Filters to Photos

To apply filters to photos, do the following:

1 View the image to which you want to apply filters.

2 Tap Edit.

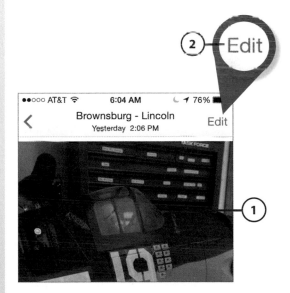

(3) Tap the Filters button. The palette of filters appears.

(4) Swipe to the left or right on the palette to browse all of the filters.

(5) Tap the filter you want to apply. The filter is applied to the image and you see a preview of the image as it will be with the filter; the filter currently applied is highlighted with a blue box. Keep trying filters until the image is what you want it to be.

(6) Tap Done. The photo with the filter applied is saved.

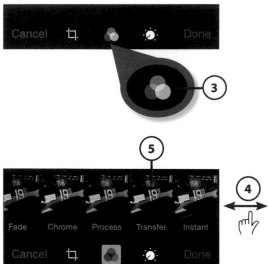

Undoing What You've Done

To restore a photo to its unedited state, tap Revert, which appears when you edit a photo that you previously edited and saved. At the prompt, tap Revert to Original and the photo is restored to its "like new" condition.

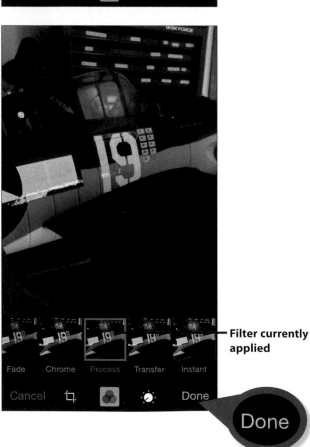

Filter currently applied

Removing Red-Eye from Photos

When you edit a photo with people in it, the Red-eye tool becomes available (if no faces are recognized, this tool is hidden). To remove red-eye, perform the following steps:

1. View an image with people that have red-eye.

2. Tap Edit.

3. Tap the Red-eye button.

(4) Zoom in on the eyes from which you want to remove red-eye.

(5) Tap each eye containing red-eye. The red in the eyes you tap is removed.

(6) Repeat steps 4 and 5 until you've removed all the red-eye.

(7) Tap Done.

Making Smart Adjustments to Photos

You can edit your photos using the Photos app's Smart Adjustment tools. Using these tools, you can change various characteristics related to light, color, and black and white aspects of your photos.

1. View the image you want to adjust.

2. Tap Edit.

3. Tap the Smart Adjust button.

4. Tap the area you want to adjust, such as Color.

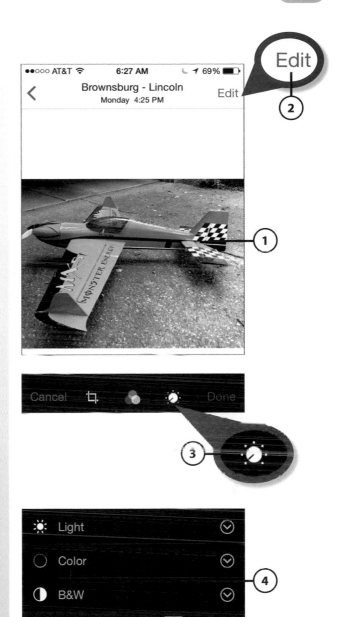

Get Straight to the Point

To jump directly to a specific aspect of the area you are adjusting, tap the downward-facing arrow along the right side of the screen. On the resulting menu, tap the aspect you want to adjust. For example, if you open this menu for Color, you tap Saturation, Contrast, or Cast to adjust those factors.

5 Swipe to the left or right to change the level of the parameter you are adjusting. As you make changes, you see the results of the change on the image.

6 When you're done adjusting the first attribute you selected, tap the List button.

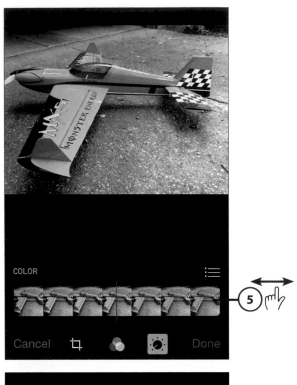

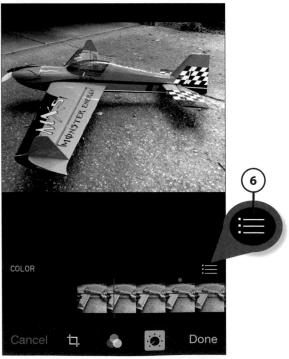

(7) Tap one of the options under the attribute you are already working with to adjust it; or tap the downward-facing arrow under one of the other attributes, and then tap the characteristic you want to change.

(8) Swipe to the left or right to change the level of the parameter you are adjusting. As you make changes, you see the results of the change on the image.

(9) Repeat steps 6 through 8 until you've made all the adjustments you want to make.

(10) Tap Done to save the adjusted image.

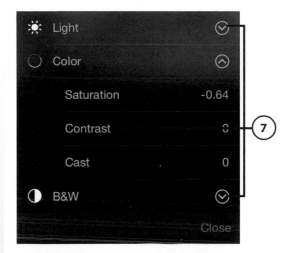

Working with Photos

Once you have photos on your iPhone, there are a lot of things you can do with them, including:

- Emailing one or more photos to one or more people (see the next task).
- Sending a photo via a text message (see Chapter 10, "Sending, Receiving, and Managing Texts and iMessages").
- Sharing photos via AirDrop.
- Sharing photos with others via Photo Stream (covered later in this chapter).
- Posting your photos on your Facebook wall or timeline.
- Assigning photos to contacts (see Chapter 7, "Managing Contacts").
- Using photos as wallpaper (see Chapter 4, "Configuring an iPhone to Suit Your Preferences").
- Sharing photos via tweets.
- Printing photos (see Chapter 1, "Getting Started with Your iPhone").
- Deleting photos (covered later).
- Organizing photos in albums (also covered later).

Copy 'Em

If you select one or more photos and tap the Copy button, the images you selected are copied to the iPhone's clipboard. You can then move into another application and paste them in.

You'll easily be able to accomplish any actions on your own that are not covered in detail here once you've performed a couple of those that are demonstrated in the following tasks.

Individual versus Groups

Some actions are only available when you are working with an individual photo. For example, you can send only a single photo via Twitter whereas you can email multiple photos at the same time. Any commands that aren't applicable to the photos that are selected won't appear on the screen.

Sharing Photos via Email

You can email photos via iPhone's Mail application starting from the Photos app.

(1) View the source containing one or more images that you want to share.

(2) Tap Select.

(3) Select the photos you want to send by tapping them. When you tap a photo, it is marked with a check mark to show you that it is selected.

(4) Tap the Share button.

Too Many?

If the photos you have selected are too much for email, the Mail button won't appear. You need to select fewer photos to attach to the email message.

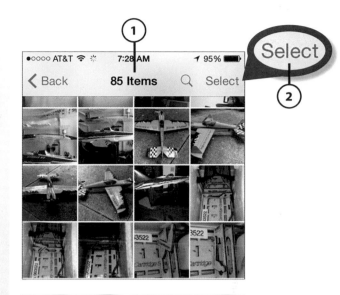

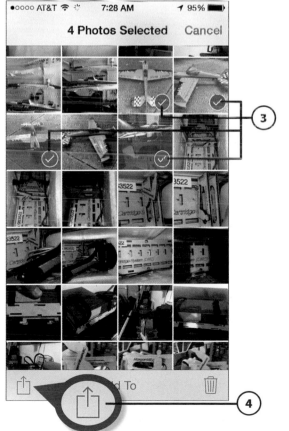

(5) Tap Mail. A new email message is created, and the photos are added as attachments.

(6) Use the email tools to address the email, add a subject, type the body, and send it. (See Chapter 9, "Sending, Receiving, and Managing Email," for detailed information about using your iPhone's email tools.)

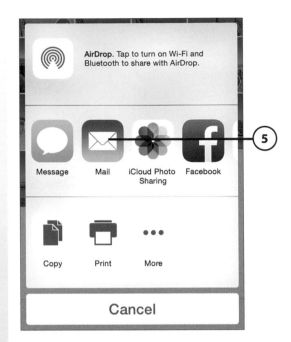

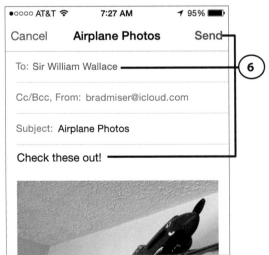

7 Tap the size of the images you want to send. Choosing a smaller size makes the files smaller and reduces the quality of the photos. You should generally try to keep the size of emails to 5MB or less to ensure the message makes it to the recipient. (Some email servers block larger messages.) After you send the email, you move back to the photos you were browsing.

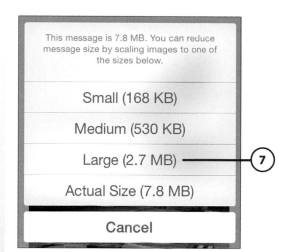

This message is 7.8 MB. You can reduce message size by scaling images to one of the sizes below.

Small (168 KB)

Medium (530 KB)

Large (2.7 MB) **7**

Actual Size (7.8 MB)

Cancel

Images from Email

As you learned in Chapter 9, when you save images attached to email that you receive, they are stored in the All Photos or Camera Roll photo album just like photos you take with your iPhone.

Organizing Photos in a New Album

You can create photo albums and store photos in them to keep your photos organized.

To create a new album, perform these steps:

1. Move to the Albums screen by tapping Albums on the toolbar.

2. Tap the Add button (+).

3. Type the name of the new album.

4. Tap Save. You're prompted to select photos to add to the new album.

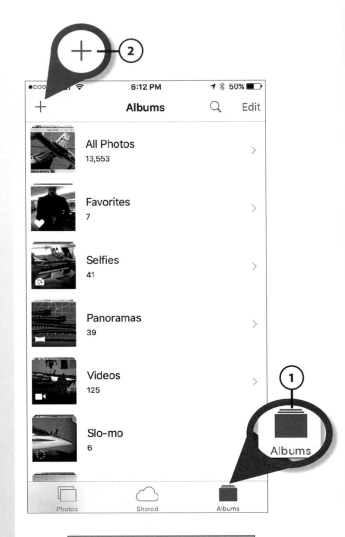

(5) Move to the source of the photos you want to add to the new album.

(6) Swipe up and down to browse the source and tap the photos you want to add to the album. They are marked with a check mark to show that they are selected. The number of photos selected is shown at the top of the screen.

(7) Tap Done. The photos are added to the new album and you move back to the Albums screen. The new album is shown on the list, and you can work with it just like the other albums you see.

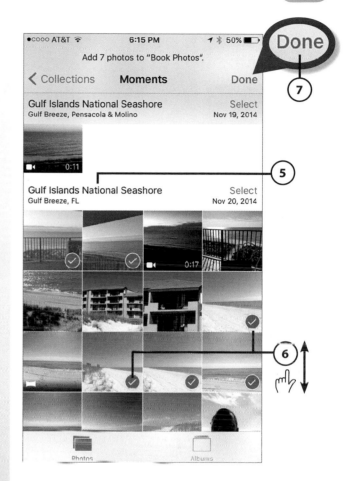

Playing Favorites

To mark any photo or video as a favorite, tap the Heart button. It fills in with blue to show you that the item you are viewing is a favorite. Favorites are automatically collected in the Favorites album so this is an easy way to collect photos and videos you want to be able to easily find again without having to create a new album or even put them in an album. You can unmark a photo or video as a favorite by tapping the Heart button again.

Adding Photos to an Existing Album

To add photos to an existing album, follow these steps:

1. Move to the source containing the photos you want to add to an album.

2. Tap Select.

3. Tap the photos you want to add to the album.

4. Tap Add To. You move to the Albums screen.

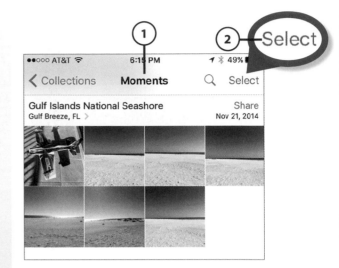

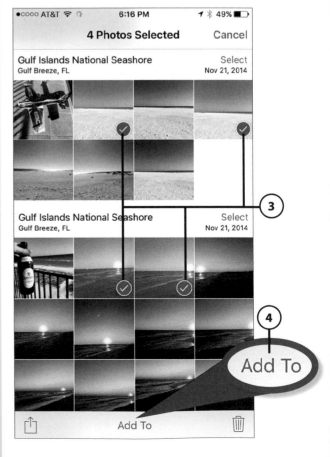

(**5**) Swipe up and down the list to find the album to which you want to add the photos.

(**6**) Tap the album (if an album is grayed out and you can't tap it, that album was not created on the iPhone and so you can't change its contents). The selected photos are added to the album.

More Album Fun

You can change the order in which albums are listed on the Albums screen. Move to the Albums screen and tap Edit. Tap the Unlock button next to the albums you want to move, and then drag albums up or down by their List buttons. Likewise, you can delete an album that you created in the Photos app. Move to the Albums screen and tap Edit. Tap the Unlock button for the album you want to delete, tap Delete, and then tap Delete Album. When you're done making changes to your Albums, tap Done. To remove a photo from an album, view the photo, tap the Trash button, and then tap Remove from Album. Photos you remove from an album remain in the Recently Added album and in your library; they are only deleted from the album.

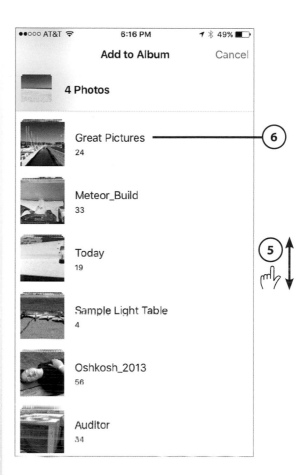

Deleting Photos

You can delete photos and videos that you don't want to keep on your iPhone. If you use the iCloud Photo Library, deleting the photos from your phone also deletes them from your photo library and from all the other devices using your library. So, make sure you really don't want photos any more before you delete them.

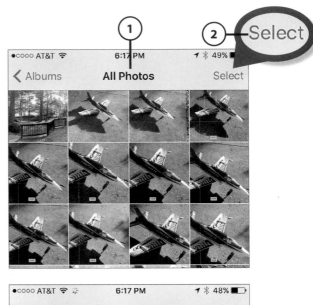

(1) Open the source containing photos you want to delete.

(2) Tap Select.

(3) Tap the photos you want to delete. Each item you select is marked with a check mark.

(4) Tap the Trash button.

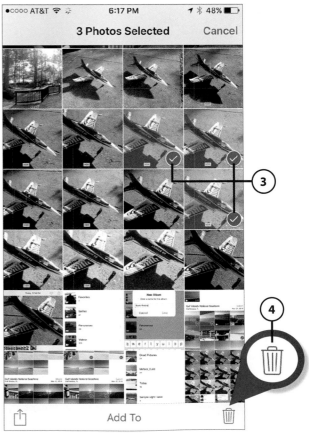

(5) Tap Delete *X* Photos, where
X is the number of photos
you selected. The photos you
selected are deleted.

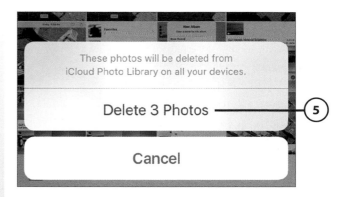

Deleting Individual Photos

You can delete individual photos
that you are viewing by tapping
the Trash button, and then tapping
Delete Photo.

Viewing, Editing, and Working with Video on Your iPhone

As shown previously in this chapter, you can capture video clips with your
iPhone. Once captured, you can view clips on your iPhone, edit them, and
share them.

Finding and Watching Videos

Watching videos you've captured
with your iPhone is simple.

(1) Move to the Albums screen.

(2) Tap the Videos album. Video
clips have a camera icon and
running time at the bottom of
their icons.

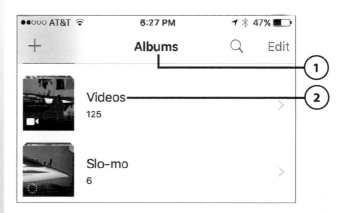

(3) Swipe up and down the screen to browse your videos.

(4) Tap the video you want to watch.

(5) Rotate the phone to change its orientation if necessary.

(6) Tap Play. The video plays. After a few moments, the toolbars disappear.

(7) Tap the video. The toolbars reappear.

Deleting Video

To remove a video clip from your iPhone, view it, tap the Trash button, and then tap Delete Video at the prompt.

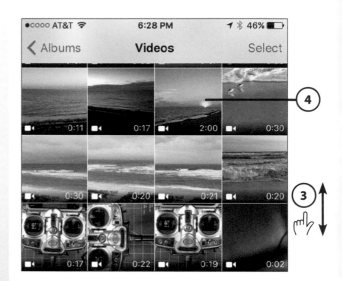

8 To pause the video, tap the Pause button.

9 To jump to a specific point in a video, swipe to the left or right on the thumbnails at the bottom of the screen. When you swipe to the left, you move ahead in the video; when you swipe to the right, you move back in the video.

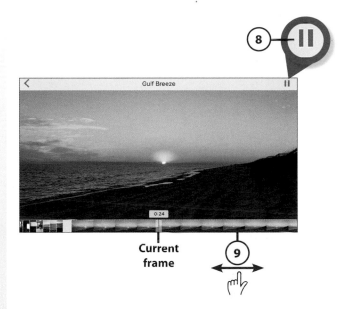

Current frame

Watching Slow-Motion and Time-Lapse Video

Watching slow-motion video is just like watching regular speed video except after a few frames, the video slows down until a few frames before the end at which point it speeds up again. Watching time-lapse is similar except the video plays faster instead of slower than real time.

Editing Video

You can trim a video clip to remove unwanted parts. Here's how you do it:

1 View the video you want to edit.

2 Tap Edit. If the video isn't stored on your phone, it is downloaded. When that process is complete, you can edit it.

3 Drag the left trim marker to where you want the edited clip to start; the trim marker is the left-facing arrow at the left end of the timeline. If you hold your finger in one place for a few seconds, the thumbnails expand so your placement of the crop marker can be more precise. As soon as you move the trim marker, the part of the clip that is inside the selection is highlighted in the yellow box; the Trim button also appears.

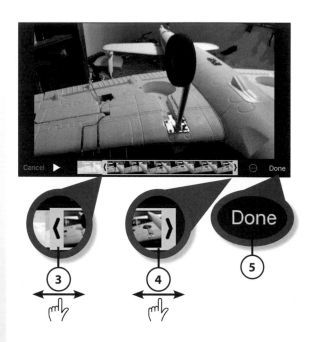

4 Drag the right trim marker to where you want the edited clip to end.

5 Tap Done.

6 Tap Save as New Clip to save the trimmed clip as a new clip or Cancel to leave the clip as it was. When you save it as a new clip, the frames outside the crop markers are removed from the clip and it is added to your library as a new clip.

There's an App for That

For more powerful video editing on your iPhone, download the iMovie app. This app provides a much more powerful video editor. You can use themes to design a video, add music, include titles and photos, and much more.

>>>*Go Further*
SHARING VIDEO

There are lots of ways to share your videos. View the video you want to share. Tap the Share button. Tap Next. Tap how you want to share the video. There are a number of options including Messages, Mail, iCloud, iCloud Photo Sharing, YouTube, Facebook, and Vimeo. Follow the onscreen prompts to complete the sharing process.

Using AirPlay to View Photos and Videos on a TV

Viewing photos and slideshows on the iPhone's screen is good, but seeing them on a big screen is even better. If you have an Apple TV connected to a home theater system, you can stream your photos and videos so that you can see them on your TV and hear their soundtracks via the system's audio components.

After your Apple TV is configured, your iPhone needs to be on the same network as the Apple TV so the two devices can communicate.

To view photos on your TV, do the following:

1. View a photo in the source containing the photos you want to stream.

2. Tap the Share button.

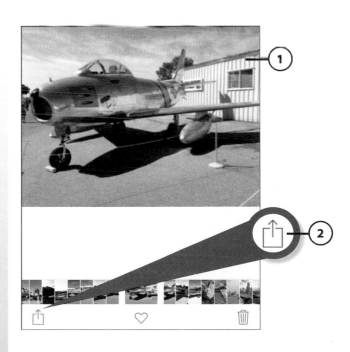

(**3**) Tap AirPlay.

(**4**) Tap Apple TV. The photo is
streamed to the TV and you
return to the photo on the
iPhone; at the top of the screen,
you see a blue bar indicating
you are streaming. You can
swipe to the left or right to
move to the previous or next
photo and use the other
viewing tools you learned about
earlier. You see the same image
on the iPhone and on the TV (at
very different sizes of course!).

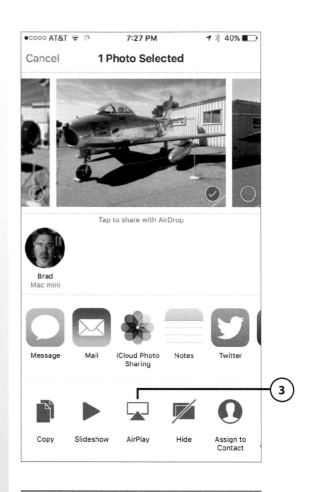

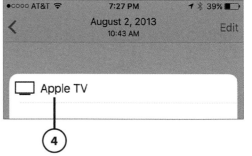

5 To stop streaming, tap the AirPlay button.

6 Tap Turn off AirPlay.

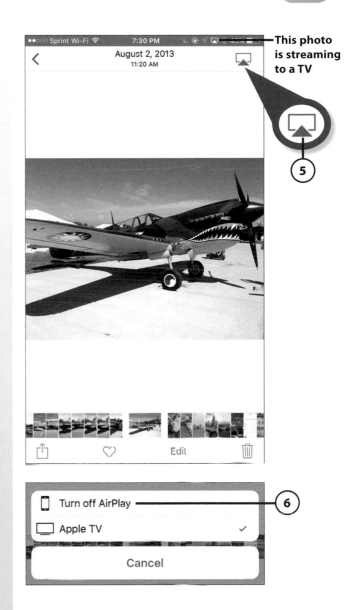

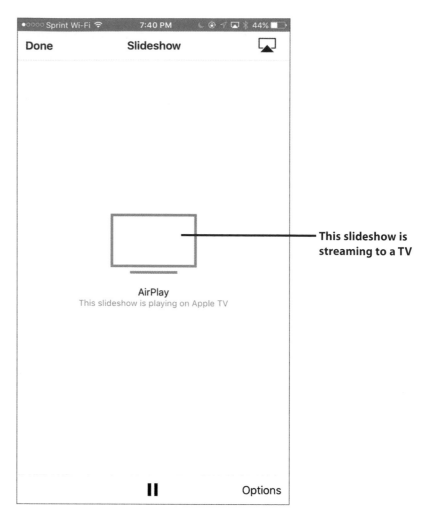

This slideshow is streaming to a TV

Previously in this chapter, you learned how to view photos in a slideshow. You can also stream a slideshow through an Apple TV by tapping the Share button and then tapping Apple TV. Start the slideshow as you learned earlier. You see the images on the TV and hear its music on the audio device connected to the Apple TV. On the iPhone, you see the screen indicating the slideshow is being streamed. To stop the slideshow, tap the Pause button on the iPhone's screen. Exit AirPlay mode by tapping the AirPlay button and then tapping Turn off AirPlay.

Similarly, you can stream videos to an Apple TV using the same process. View the video you want to stream. Tap the Share button and tap AirPlay. Tap Apple TV. The video plays on the device connected to the Apple TV. You can control the video using the controls on the iPhone's screen.

To turn streaming off, open the AirPlay menu and tap iPhone.

Using iCloud with Your Photos

With iCloud, your devices can automatically upload photos to your iCloud account on the Internet. Other devices can automatically download photos from iCloud, so you have your photos available on all your devices at the same time. Using iCloud with your photos has two sides: a sender and receiver. Your iPhone can be both. Photo applications can also access your photos and download them to your computer automatically. Windows PCs can also be configured to automatically download photos from the cloud.

In addition to backing up your photos and having all your photos available to you, you can also share your photos and videos with others and view photos and videos being shared with you.

Sharing Your Photos

You can share your photos with others by creating a shared album. This is a great way to share photos, because others can subscribe to your shared albums to view and work with the photos you share. When you share photos, you can add them to an album that's already being shared or create a new shared album.

To create a new, empty, shared album, do the following:

1. Open the Shared source. You see the iCloud Photo Sharing screen that lists the shared albums in which you are currently participating (as either the person sharing them or subscribed to them).

2. Tap the Add (+) button.

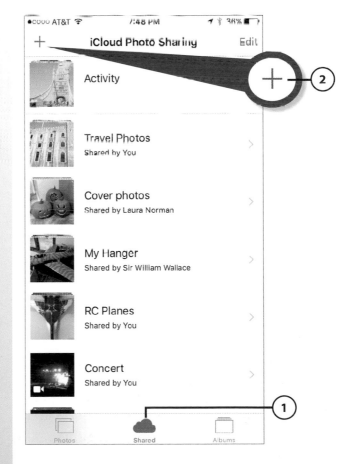

3 Type the title of the new album.

4 Tap Next.

5 Enter or select the email address of the first person with whom you want to share the photos.

6 Add other recipients until you've added everyone you want to access the photos.

7 Tap Create. The shared album is created and is ready for you to add photos. The recipients you included in the new album receive notifications that invite them to join the album.

Cancel   iCloud   Next—**4**

Beach —**3**

For example: "Cars", "Trip to Hawaii" or "Wedding"

Cancel   iCloud   Create

To: sir w   ⊕

home (317) 805-6007

Sir William Wallace —**5**
work sirwilliamwallace@me.com

Sir William Wallace
home sirwilliamwallace@icloud.com

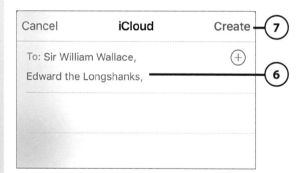

Cancel   iCloud   Create—**7**

To: Sir William Wallace,   ⊕
Edward the Longshanks, —**6**

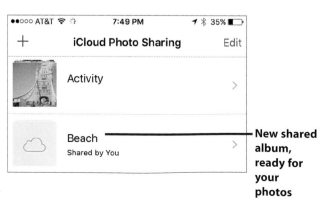

●●○○○ AT&T 🔋 ☼   7:49 PM   ↑ ∗ 35% ▮▭

＋   **iCloud Photo Sharing**   Edit

Activity   ＞

Beach ——— New shared
Shared by You   ＞   album, ready for your photos

Adding Photos to a Shared Album

To add photos to an album you are sharing, perform the following steps:

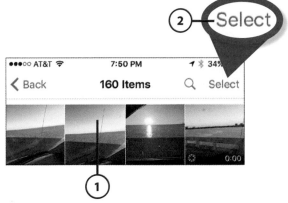

1. Move to the source containing photos you want to add to a shared album.

2. Tap Select.

3. Tap the photos you want to share.

4. Tap the Share button.

5 Tap iCloud Photo Sharing.

6 Enter your commentary about the photos you are sharing. (Note, this commentary is associated only with the first photo.)

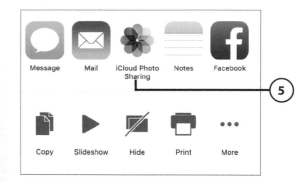

7 Tap Shared Album.

8 Swipe up and down to browse the list of shared albums available.

9 Tap the album to which you want to add the photos.

New Shared Album with Photos

You can create a new shared album with the selected photos by tapping New Shared Album.

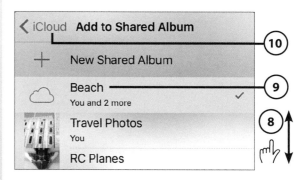

10 Tap iCloud.

11 Tap Post. The photos you selected are added to the shared album. People who are subscribed to the album receive a notification that photos have been added and can view the new photos along with your commentary.

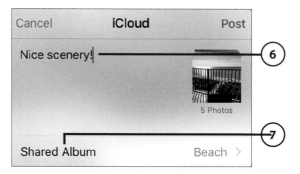

iCloud Account Required

The people with whom you share photos must have an iCloud account.

>>>Go Further

MORE ON iCLOUD PHOTO SHARING

Following are a few more pointers to help you use iCloud photo sharing:

- You can add comments to photos you are sharing. Open the shared album and tap the photo to which you want to add comments. Tap Add a comment. Type your comment and tap Send. People with whom you are sharing the photo receive a notification and can read your comments.

- To add more photos to a shared album, open the album and tap the Add (+) button. Use the resulting screen to select the photos you want to add, include commentary, and post the photos.

- To invite people to join a shared album, open the shared album. Tap the People tab at the bottom of the screen and then tap Invite People. Enter the email addresses of the people you want to invite and tap Add.

- You can configure various aspects of a shared album by opening it and tapping the People tab at the bottom of the screen. You can see the status of people you have invited, determine if the people with whom you are sharing the album can post to it, make the album a public website, determine if notifications are sent, or delete the shared album

- If you have Family Sharing set up (see Chapter 6, "Downloading Apps, Music, Movies, TV Shows, and More onto Your iPhone"), an album called Family is created automatically and shared with everyone in your sharing group automatically. Like other shared albums, you can add photos to this album to share them with your family group. Any photos added to it by the others in your group are shared with you, too.

Working with Photo Albums Shared with You

You can work with albums people share with you as follows:

(1) Tap the notification you received, or tap the Shared source when you see a badge indicating you have activity.

(2) Tap Accept for the shared album you want to join. The shared album becomes available on your Shared tab.

(3) Tap Sharing.

(4) Tap the new shared album.

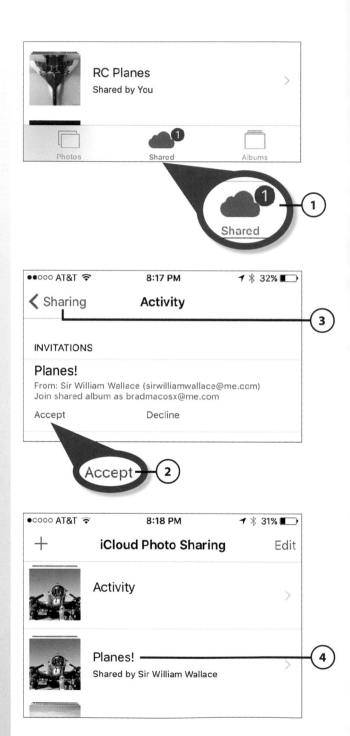

5 Tap a photo in the album.

6 Tap Like to indicate you like the photo.

7 Tap Add a comment. (If you previously liked the photo, you see the number of likes for it instead; tap that number to add a comment.)

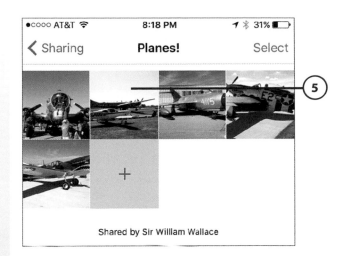

8. Type your comment.

9. Tap Send. Your comments are added to the album.

10. Tap the back button.

11. If allowed, tap the Add (+) button and post your own photos to the album you are sharing. This works just like posting to your own albums.

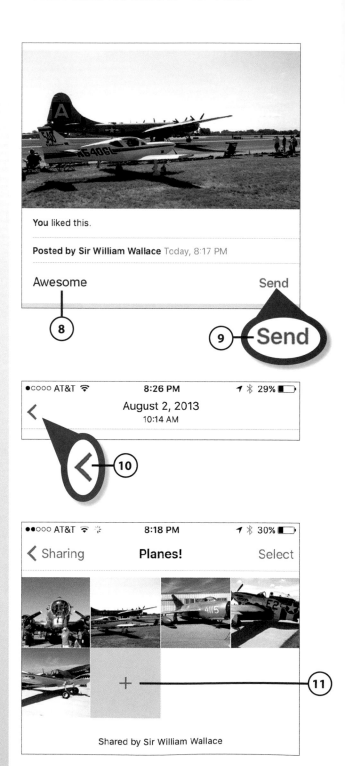

>>>Go Further

MORE ON PHOTOS SHARED WITH YOU

When you share other people's photos, keep the following points in mind:

- You can do most of the tasks with shared photos that you can with your own, such as emailing them, using them as wallpaper, and so on.

- To unsubscribe from an album, move to its People screen and tap Unsubscribe and confirm that is what you want to do. The shared album is removed from your iPhone.

- To see the activity associated with albums being shared with you, and those you are sharing, open the Activity Album on the iCloud Photo Sharing screen. You see new postings to the albums, when someone comments and so on.

Find your way

Manage and use
store cards, credit
cards, and more

Take a library of
reading content
wherever you go

Get the news you
want when you
want it

Keep yourself healthy

Listen to or watch
podcasts

Take phone calls on Macs
and iPads, too

Use Handoff to work
seamlessly across
devices

In this chapter, you learn about some other really useful apps and iPhone functionality. Topics include the following:

→ Getting started
→ Touring other cool iPhone apps
→ Listening to podcasts with the Podcasts app
→ Finding your way with Maps
→ Working with the Wallet app and Apple Pay
→ Managing your health with the Health app
→ Working seamlessly across your devices

Using Other Cool iPhone Apps and Features

In previous chapters, you learned about many of the iPhone's great apps, such as Phone, Mail, Messages, Safari, and Calendar. In this chapter, you learn about a number of other apps you might find useful.

You also learn how to use your iPhone with Macs and iPads. The iOS Handoff feature makes it easy to work on the same things on Macs, iPhones, and iPads. For example, you can start an email on a Mac, and finish the same email on an iPad and your iPhone, too. When a phone call comes in to your iPhone, you can choose to answer it on your Mac, iPad, or Watch.

Getting Started

An iPhone can truly become *your* iPhone over time as you customize it with the apps that you find to be useful for living your daily life, traveling, managing your health, and communicating. The great thing about iPhone apps is that there are so many to choose from, and because many of them are free, you can try lots of apps. Keep and use the ones you like, delete the ones you don't. Over time, you'll develop a group of core apps that you use constantly and a few that you use just occasionally. The rest you can just delete to get rid of them or move them out of the way.

In previous chapters, you learned about many of the core apps that come pre-installed on your iPhone. In this chapter, you learn about a few more of the pre-installed apps and get an overview of a number of apps that you might want to download onto your iPhone so you can give them a try.

Don't be hesitant to try apps. Apple maintains extremely tight control over the apps that make it into the App Store so there's virtually no chance that an app you download and install can put you or your information at any risk. It usually only takes a few minutes using an app to determine if it is useful to you, so you're not risking much of your time either.

Touring Other Cool iPhone Apps

There are many thousands of apps available for the iPhone. Some of these are pre-installed on your iPhone; others you download from the App Store. No matter how they get installed on your iPhone, these apps can be really useful in so many ways.

Touring Other Cool iPhone Apps Already Installed on Your iPhone

The following table provides an overview of a number of other apps (all of which are installed by default) that you might find useful or entertaining:

Other Cool iPhone Apps Installed by Default

	App	Description
	Weather	See high-level weather conditions and a forecast for any number of locations. You can use the default locations, and if you tap the List button in the lower-right corner of the screen, you can add, remove, and organize the locations you want to track. Swipe through the screens to see each area's forecast.
	Videos	Use this app to watch movies, TV shows, and podcasts.
	Notes	Capture different kinds of information, including text notes, lists, photos, maps, and more. You can also draw in the app and attach different types of objects to notes, and then use the Attachment Manager to view them. Using online accounts with the Notes app, such as iCloud, your notes can be available on all your devices.
	Stocks	Use this one to track stocks in which you are interested. You can add any index, stock, or fund as long as you know the symbol for it, and you can even use the application to find a symbol if you don't know it. You can see current performance and view historical performance for various time periods. Rotate the iPhone to see a more in-depth view when you are examining a specific stock. You can see the current "ticker" for the items you are tracking by pulling the Notification Center down by swiping down from the top of the screen.
	iBooks	Access and organize books and PDFs so that you always have something to read. The app enables you to change how the books appear on the screen, such as making the font larger or smaller. iBooks syncs across your devices so that you can read something on your iPhone and then pick it up later at the same spot on an iPad.

	News	Read news from a variety of sources. You can search news and save items of interest to you. You can also choose your favorite news sources so that you can focus more on what you care about and avoid what you don't.
	Music	The Music app enables you to listen to all kinds of music from your own CD collection (when you import it into iTunes on a computer and sync it onto your iPhone), the iTunes Store, iTunes Radio, or Apple Music. You can find detailed information about this app on this book's website (www.quepublishing.com/title/9780789755483).
	Calculator	In portrait orientation, the Calculator is the equivalent of one you would get at the local dollar store. Rotate the iPhone to access scientific calculator options. Access the Calculator quickly by swiping up from the bottom of the screen to open the Control Center; then, tap the Calculator button.
	Watch	Use this app to pair and configure your iPhone with an Apple Watch. Once paired with your iPhone, you can configure how your Watch accesses content from your iPhone's apps such as Mail, Calendar, Messages, Phone, Contacts, Photos, Music, Reminders, and more.
	Compass (Extras folder)	Transform your iPhone into a compass. When you open the app for the first time, you need to calibrate it following the on-screen directions. When that is done, you can see your current location on the analog-looking compass and with precision in degree latitude and longitude. If you swipe to the right, you transform your iPhone into a level that measures on the horizontal planes along with angles. Swipe to the right to get back to the compass.
	Voice Memos (Extras folder)	Record audio notes using the Voice Memos app. Play them back, and through syncing, move them onto your computer. You can record through the iPhone's microphone or via the mic on the earbud headset.

	Find Friends (Extras folder)	See the current location of "friends" who are part of your Family Sharing group or whom you add to the app manually. You can also share your location with others.
	Find iPhone (Extras folder)	Use this app to locate other iPhones, iPads, or Macs that have enabled Find My iPhone using the same iCloud account.
	Flashlight (Control Center)	This app, which is only available on the Control Center, uses your iPhone's flash as a flashlight. It's a very simple app, but also happens to be extremely useful.

Touring Other Cool iPhone Apps You Can Download onto Your iPhone

The following table provides "mini-reviews" of some apps you might find useful, but that aren't installed on your iPhone by default. Fortunately, as you learned in Chapter 6, "Downloading Apps, Music, Movies, TV Shows, and More onto Your iPhone," it is easy to download and install apps from the App Store onto your iPhone.

Other Useful Apps Not Installed by Default

	App	Description
	AARP	You can get information provided by AARP by reading articles and watching videos. You can also get information about your AARP benefits and access your AARP account.
	Airline apps	All the major airlines have apps you can use to make reservations, check flight status, and more. The best of these apps also enable you to check in for flights and provide an electronic boarding pass through the Wallet app.

	AroundMe	Use the app to locate "things" that are around you. You can find hospitals, restaurants, gas stations, hotels, and much more. This app is really useful when you are in a new area because you can quickly find and get to places of interest.
	First Aid	This handy app provides first aid information for a wide variety of situations, including emergencies. It provides examples, and then leads you through how to deal with them in a step-by-step format.
	Foodler	Foodler is a service that collects information about restaurants in a specific area. You can view menus and make orders for delivery in many cases. When you are in a populated area that Foodler services, this app gives you lots of dining choices that you can access quickly and easily.
	GateGuru	This one helps you make airline travel better by providing information about the airports you visit along the way. You can find amenities, see maps, and get flight information.
	TripAdvisor	You can use this handy app to access TripAdvisor services to plan your travel by accessing reviews of hotels, restaurants, and attractions posted by other travelers who use Trip Advisor.
	TripIt	This is a great app if you travel frequently because it consolidates your travel plans in one place. When you book a trip, you email your itinerary to the TripIt address. The details are extracted and a TripIt itinerary is created. The app then tracks the status of flights and other information and it keeps you informed of any changes. For example, if a flight gets delayed, you see a notification and your itinerary is automatically updated.

	Urbanspoon	This app provides information about restaurants and enables you to book reservations in many of them. You can find restaurants by category, such as pizza, or based on reviews or location.
	WebMD	You can use this one to look up symptoms of health problems to help you identify potential causes and treatment. You can also look up medical terms, get information about tests and treatments, and access other medical information.
	Yelp	This is another app you can use to find places of interest to you, including shopping, restaurants, gas stations, and more. You can also get deals at participating organizations and read reviews posted by other Yelp users.

Listening to Podcasts with the Podcasts App

Podcasts are episodic audio or video programs that are available on many, many topics. Using the Podcasts app, you can subscribe to and manage lots of podcasts so that you always have something of interest available to you.

Setting Your Podcast Preferences

Like most apps you've seen in this book, you can set some preferences for the Podcasts app. These preferences, which you access by opening the Settings app and tapping Podcasts on the left side, are described in the following table.

Podcasts Settings

Section Setting	Description
ALLOW PODCASTS TO ACCESS	
Notifications	
Allow Notifications	Set to on (green) if you want the Podcasts app to notify you when new episodes are downloaded or for other events.
Show in Notification Center	When enabled, notifications from the Podcasts app are shown on the Notification Center.
Badge App Icon	When on, this switch causes the number of new episodes to be displayed on the Podcasts icon.
Show on Lock Screen	Set to on (green) if you want podcast notifications to appear on the Lock screen.
Background App Refresh	To allow the Podcasts app to update itself when it is not being used, set this switch to on (green). If the general Background App Refresh setting in the General settings is turned off, this is disabled.
Cellular Data	Set this to off (white) if you have a limited data plan and only want the app to refresh its data when you are using a Wi-Fi network.
PODCASTS SETTINGS	
Sync Podcasts	When enabled, your podcasts sync in the Podcasts app on your iOS devices and in iTunes on computers. You can listen to the same podcasts on any synced device, and you pick up in an episode on one device right where you left off on another.

Section Setting	Description
Only Download on Wi-Fi	This switch determines if podcast episodes can be downloaded to your phone using only Wi-Fi or using Wi-Fi or cellular. With this switch on (green), episodes are only downloaded when your phone is connected to Wi-Fi. With this switch off (white), episodes can be downloaded using Wi-Fi or a cellular connection. The Cellular Data switch controls whether the app can access information, such as determining if new episodes are available, using the cellular connection. This switch controls whether podcasts can be downloaded using the cellular connection or not.
PODCAST DEFAULTS	
Refresh Every	Tap how often you want the Podcasts app to check for, and download, new episodes.
Limit Episodes	Tap how you want the app to keep downloaded episodes. Tap Off if you want to keep all episodes. Tap the number of most recent episodes to limit episodes based on their number.
Download Episodes	Tap the download option you want: Off, if you don't want episodes to be downloaded automatically; Only New, if you want only new episodes to be downloaded automatically; or All Unplayed, if you want all available episodes that you haven't listened to yet to be downloaded automatically.
Delete Played Episodes	If you want the app to automatically delete episodes you have listened to, set the switch to on (green).
ACCESSIBILITY	
Custom Colors	When enabled, a podcast's colors reflect its artwork.

Using the Podcasts App to Subscribe to Podcasts

You can subscribe to podcasts you want to listen to or watch so they are available in the Podcasts app. Here's how to search for podcasts from a specific organization or by topic:

(1) On the Home screen, tap Podcasts.

(2) Tap Search.

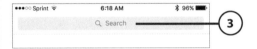

(3) Tap in the Search bar.

(4) Type your search term. As you type, the app presents podcasts related to your search term.

(5) Browse the search results.

(6) Tap the search you want to perform. If none of the searches are what you are looking for, type a more detailed search term and tap Search to see the entire list. The search is performed and you see the results organized into different categories, such as episodes and podcasts. You can use the tabs at the top of the screen to limit the results to one or the other.

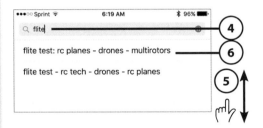

7 Browse the search results.

8 Tap a podcast that you want to explore. You move to the podcast's screen where you see its image, title, and other information. Below the SUBSCRIBE button, you see the podcast's description.

9 Read the description.

10 If the entire description isn't displayed, tap more.

11 To subscribe to the podcast, tap SUBSCRIBE. You are subscribed to the podcast and episodes are downloaded according to the Podcast app's settings (see table earlier in this chapter for settings and their descriptions). For example, if in the Podcast app settings you chose the 1 Month Limit Episodes setting, only the episodes released within the past month are downloaded.

12 Tap My Podcasts. You move back to your podcast library where you see the podcast to which you subscribed and it is ready for you to listen to it.

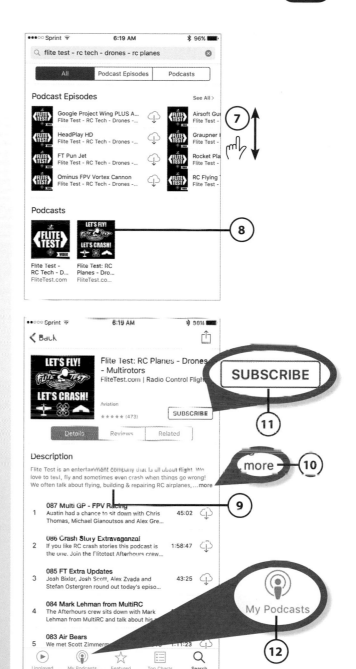

13 Tap the podcast to play it (details about finding and playing podcasts are in the following tasks).

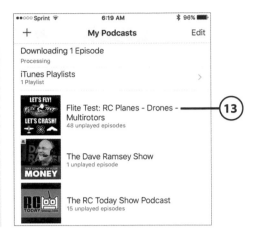

>>>Go Further
MORE ON PODCASTS

As you ponder podcasts, consider the following:

- You can browse for podcasts using the Featured and Top Charts buttons. These present groups of podcasts that you can filter by tapping the Categories button at the top of the screen and choosing the category of podcast in which you are interested. You can then browse the results and explore podcasts you might wish to subscribe to just like when you search for podcasts.

- The screen for some podcasts has three tabs: Details, Reviews, and Related. These tabs are just like the tabs for apps in the App Store (see Chapter 6).

- When you search for or browse for podcasts and you view one to which you are subscribed, you see the UNSUBSCRIBE button. To unsubscribe from a podcast without deleting all the episodes you've downloaded, tap UNSUBCRIBE.

- You can share a podcast by tapping the Share button, and then choosing how you want to share it (such as with AirDrop, Mail, or Messages).

- To unsubscribe from a podcast and delete all the episodes you've downloaded, tap My Podcasts. Tap the Edit button in the upper-left corner of the screen. Tap the podcast's unlock button (–) and tap Delete. The podcast and all its episodes are deleted from your library.

Choosing a Podcast to Listen To

When you're ready to listen, open the Podcasts app and tap My Podcasts. You can use the My Podcasts screen to quickly find the podcast you want to hear or see.

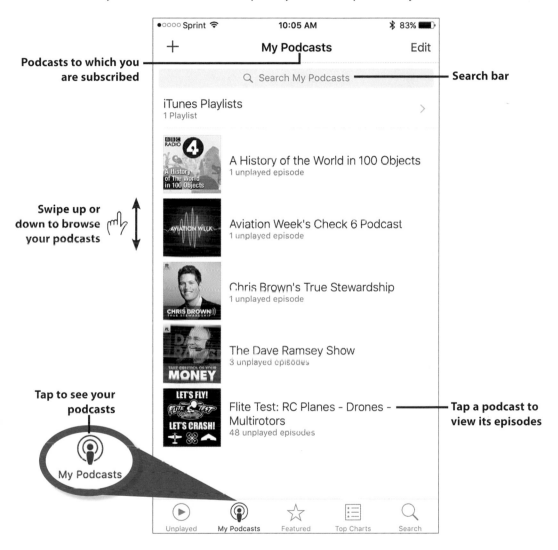

Podcasts to which you are subscribed

Search bar

Swipe up or down to browse your podcasts

Tap to see your podcasts

Tap a podcast to view its episodes

- Swipe up and down the My Podcasts screen to browse all the podcasts to which you are subscribed. You see a thumbnail for each podcast. Tap a thumbnail to see a podcast's page so you can select and play episodes (covered in the next task).

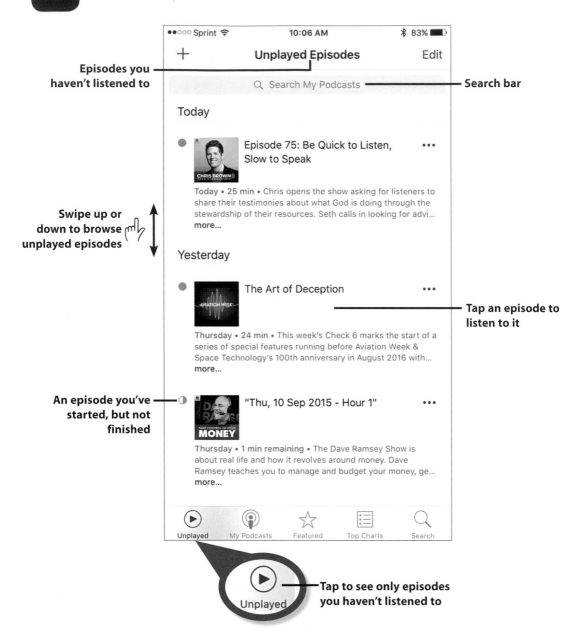

Episodes you haven't listened to

Search bar

Swipe up or down to browse unplayed episodes

Tap an episode to listen to it

An episode you've started, but not finished

Tap to see only episodes you haven't listened to

- To view a list of episodes you haven't listened to, tap Unplayed. You see the list by the date on which the episode was released. Swipe up and down the screen to find an episode in which you are interested. Tap an episode to play it (covered in the next task).

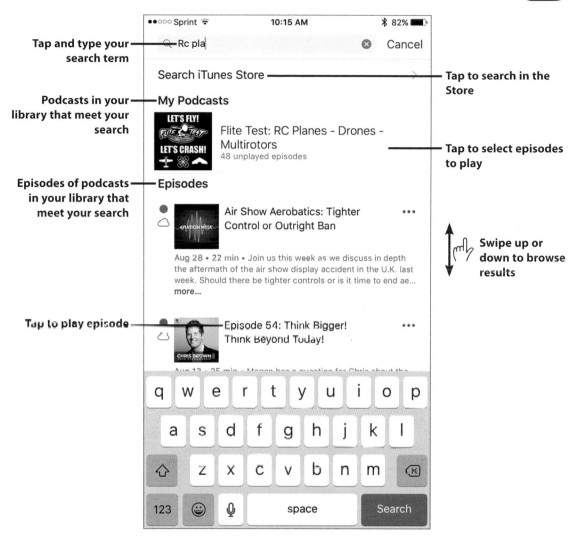

Tap and type your search term

Search iTunes Store — Tap to search in the Store

Podcasts in your library that meet your search — My Podcasts

Flite Test: RC Planes - Drones - Multirotors
48 unplayed episodes — Tap to select episodes to play

Episodes of podcasts in your library that meet your search — Episodes

Air Show Aerobatics: Tighter Control or Outright Ban

Aug 28 • 22 min • Join us this week as we discuss in depth the aftermath of the air show display accident in the U.K. last week. Should there be tighter controls or is it time to end ae... more...

Swipe up or down to browse results

Tap to play episode — Episode 54: Think Bigger! Think Beyond Today!

- You search for podcasts in your library or in the Store using the Search bar. Tap in the Search bar and type your search term. The podcasts and episodes of podcasts that meet your search criteria appear in the list of results. Tap a podcast to view and play its episodes, or tap an episode to play it. Tap Search iTunes Store to search there for podcasts related to your search.

Podcast Badge

When you see a badge on a podcast, the number indicates how many episodes you haven't viewed on a list, not how many you haven't listened to (which would make more sense).

Listening to Podcasts

The first step in listening to a podcast is to find the episode you want to listen to. You can see episodes individually, such as on a list of results from a search, or more commonly, when you view a podcast to which you are subscribed.

As you learned in the previous task, you can do this by tapping the podcast on the My Podcasts screen to open it.

When you open a podcast, you see that podcast's screen. At the top is the general information about the podcast. Below that is the list of episodes for the podcast. What you see on this screen depends on the settings for the podcast, such as how long you keep episodes. Episodes are grouped in various ways, again depending on your settings (see "Setting Your Podcast Preferences" earlier in this chapter for information on settings). You can browse the list of episodes.

Return to your podcasts

Podcast you are viewing

Episodes available for the podcast you are viewing

Episode that is playing

Tap to take action on an episode

Tap to listen to an episode

Swipe up or down to browse episodes

Unplayed episode

Miniplayer

Tap to move to the Now Playing screen

Tap the episode to which you want to listen. If it is not currently downloaded, it downloads and starts to play as soon as enough of it has been downloaded that it can play without stopping. If it is already stored on your phone, it starts playing immediately. At the bottom of the screen, you see the Miniplayer. As the episode plays, you can view its information or pause it by tapping the Pause button.

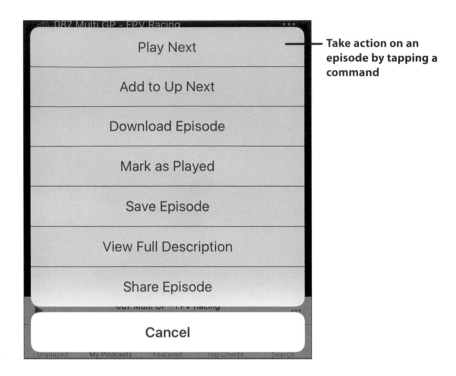

Take action on an episode by tapping a command

When you tap on the ellipsis next to an episode, you see a menu providing a number of commands you can apply to that episode, such as Play Next, Mark as Played, and so on.

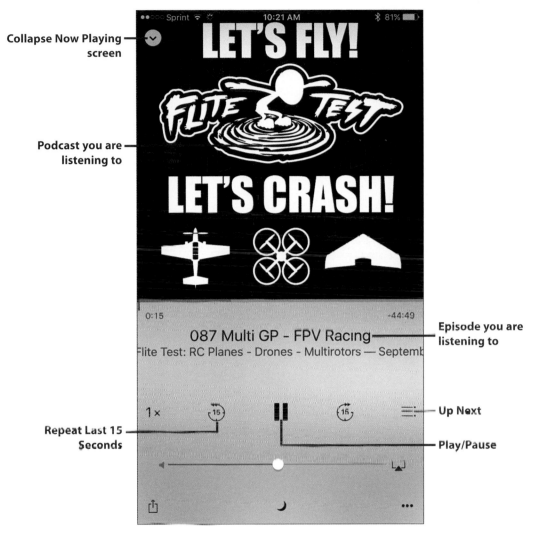

Collapse Now Playing screen

Podcast you are listening to

Episode you are listening to

Up Next

Repeat Last 15 Seconds

Play/Pause

When you tap the Miniplayer, you move to the Now Playing screen. On the Now Playing screen, you have the following controls:

- Tap the downward-facing arrow to move back to the podcast's screen and display the Miniplayer instead.

- Tap the Up Next button to see a list of episodes for the podcast you are playing or if you are viewing the Unplayed list, you see the list of unplayed episodes in the order they will play (you can tap an episode from the list to play it). You can add episodes to the end of this list by using the Add to Up

Next command or you can move an episode to the top of the list by using the Play Next command. Tap Done to close the Up Next list.

• Tap the Pause/Play button to pause a playing podcast or to play a paused one.

• Tap the Repeat Last 15 Seconds button to repeat the last 15 seconds of the episode.

Managing Podcasts and Episodes of Podcasts

Here are some pointers you can use to manage your podcasts:

- To manage a podcast and its episodes, move to its screen and tap Settings (the gear button) to move to the Settings screen for the podcast.

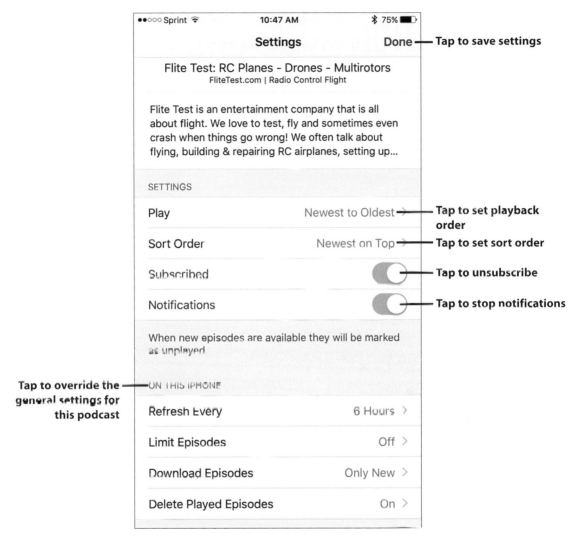

- The Settings tools enhance or override the general podcast preferences you set in the Settings app. Use the Play option to set the order in which the episodes play. Tap the Sort Order option to set the order in which they appear on the podcast's screen. Set the Subscribed switch to off (white) to stop downloading episodes; set it to on (green) to resume downloads. Use the Notifications switch to stop or resume notifications for the podcast (if you've disabled all notifications for the Podcasts app, this switch is disabled). Use the controls in the ON THIS IPHONE section to override the global settings; for example, you can use the Refresh Every option to change how the podcast is refreshed. When you are done configuring the settings, tap Done.

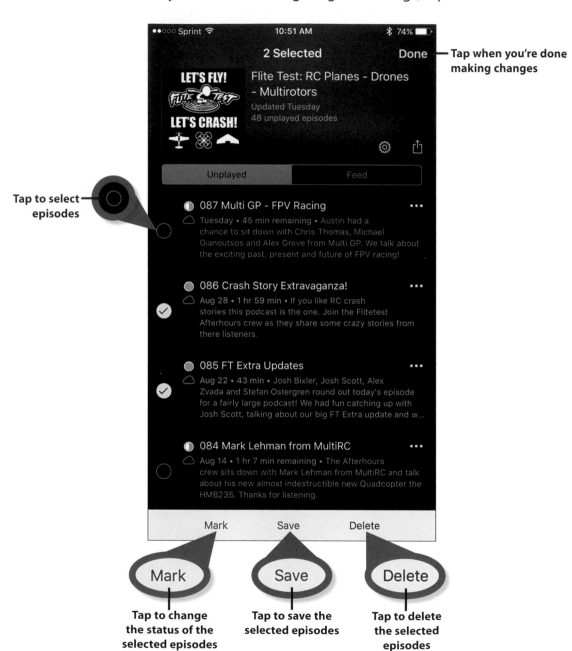

Tap when you're done making changes

Tap to select episodes

Mark
Tap to change the status of the selected episodes

Save
Tap to save the selected episodes

Delete
Tap to delete the selected episodes

- To manage a podcast's episodes, move to its screen and tap Edit (shown in an earlier figure). Selection circles appear next to each episode. Tap the episodes you want to manage. Tap Mark, and then tap Mark as Played or Mark as Unplayed to change the selected episodes' status; when you mark an episode as Played, it is immediately removed from the list if the app is configured to delete played episodes. To save episodes so they won't be deleted automatically, tap Save Episodes. To unsave episodes, tap Remove from Saved. Tap Delete to delete the selected episodes. Tap Done to exit the Edit mode.

- To delete individual episodes of a podcast, swipe to the left on the episode you want to delete and tap Delete.

- When a podcast is marked with an exclamation point badge, it has a problem. Tap the podcast to see an explanation of the problem at the top of the screen. Most commonly, it is that the app has stopped downloading the podcast because you haven't listened to any episodes in a while. Tap the message to refresh the podcast.

- You can also refresh all your podcasts by swiping down from the top of the My Podcasts screen, or refresh a specific podcast by swiping down from the top of its screen.

Finding Your Way with Maps

The Maps app enables you to find locations and view them on the map. However, the real power of the Maps app is that you can then get detailed, turn-by-turn, spoken directions to those places. You can use these directions to drive, walk, or even take public transportation to the places you find.

Generating directions with the Maps app is easy and quick to do as the following steps demonstrate:

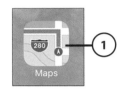

(1) On the Home screen, tap Maps.

(2) Tap in the Search bar, and type in the location you want to find. You can type in an address, a place name (such as Lucas Oil Stadium), or even a description of what you are looking for (e.g., Starbucks near me). As you type, the app presents a list of locations that meet your search.

(3) Tap the location you want to see on the map. The map appears and the location, or locations (if you do a more general search), for which you searched are marked with a pushpin.

(4) If there is more than one location shown in the map, tap the pushpin for the location in which you are interested; if only one location was found, it is selected automatically and you don't need to tap it. You see a summary of the location you selected, including an estimated time to go there from your current location (the car icon indicates the time is estimated based on regular vehicle travel).

(5) If you want directions from your current location to the selected location, tap the blue time estimate part of the summary pop-up and skip to step 13.

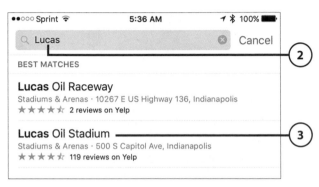

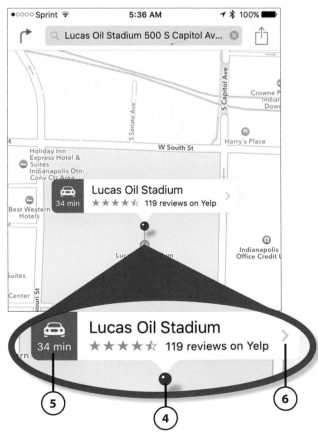

6 To generate directions starting from someplace other than your current location, tap the right-facing arrow. On the location's info screen, you see a variety of information about it, such as phone number, website, physical address, and so on (the information provided varies).

7 Browse up and down the screen to view information about the location. Links enable you to perform other actions related to it, such as tapping the phone icon to place a call to the number shown.

8 Tap Directions.

9 Tap in the top box and tap the clear button to erase the current start location, which is your current location by default.

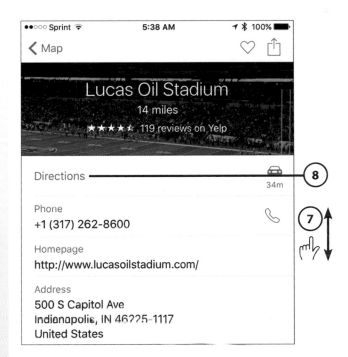

10 Type the location for the starting point of your route. The app searches for locations based on what you type; this works just like when you started this process.

11 Tap the location where you want the route to start.

12 Tap Route. When the app determines the route you selected, you see it in dark blue on the map; alternate routes are shown in other shades (you can tap an alternate route to use it instead).

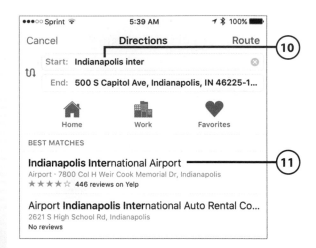

13 Tap Drive to get driving directions, Walk to get walking directions, or Transit to see routes available by public transportation.

14 Tap Start to have the app start navigating for you. The app shows you the part of the route you are on and announces when you need to do something else, such as when and where you need to turn. It gives you a "heads-up" warning when a change is coming up, such as a notice you will be exiting a highway 2 miles before the exit. The app guides you until you reach the destination. If you get off course, it recalculates the route for you automatically. This continues until you arrive at your destination.

15 As you navigate, you can tap the screen to show its controls.

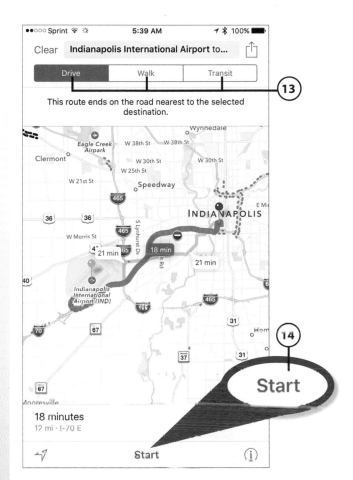

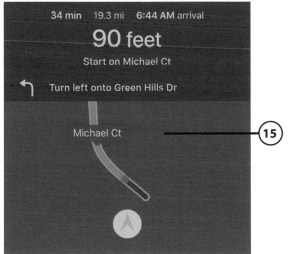

16 Tap End to end the navigation before you reach the destination; otherwise, navigation stops automatically when you reach the end of the journey.

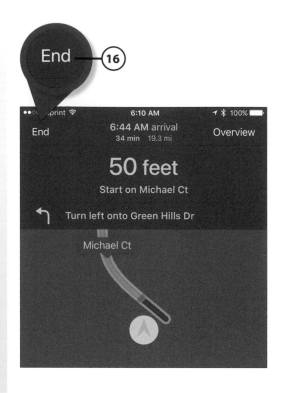

>>>Go Further

GET THERE WITH MAPS

Here are a few Maps pointers to help you along your way:

- To see an overview of your route, tap Overview. The map zooms out and you see the entire route. Tap Resume to go back to the navigation.

- To repeat the current step you are on, tap it. The app speaks the current step.

- Maps presents a 3D view of your route; tap 3D to turn this off or on. This view is difficult to describe so the best thing to do is to try it to see if you find it useful.

- To see the directions in text form, tap the List button, which appears in the center at the bottom of the screen. You see each step on the route. Tap Done to return to the map.

- To configure the voice used for navigation, tap the speaker button located in the bottom-right corner of the screen. You can change the volume level or set the Pause Spoken Audio switch to on (green) to temporarily stop the voice navigation. Tap Done to return to the map.

- You can use the standard zoom and swipe motions on the map to change your view. As you change the map's scale, you see the scale pop up at the top of the window. If you manipulate the map such that your current location is no longer shown, tap the arrow button to refocus the map so your location is in view. Tap it again to change into compass view so that true North "projects" from your icon on the map. You can then navigate with the map as you would with a compass.

- When you aren't navigating and are just viewing a location on the map, tap the Info button (i) to reveal options, such as Map that shows you the standard map view, Transit that shows you transit information for the location, Satellite that layers a satellite image on the map, Hide Labels and Hide Location that you can use to hide those elements, 3D Map that toggles the 3D view, and Drop a Pin that enables you to manually choose a location on a map. If Maps doesn't provide accurate information, you can tap Report an Issue to report the problem. Tap Done to close the Info screen without making changes.

- When you move into search mode, you see Nearby category buttons (for example, Food) at the top of the screen. Tap one of these to see locations in that category near you. Tap a result to see its information. If the category has sub-categories (for example, Coffee Shops when you tap Food), tap the sub-category to see locations of that type.

- Maps remembers your recent searches and presents them on the search list when you move into search mode. You can tap a recent search, such as a route, to repeat it.

- You can swap the starting and ending locations in a route by tapping the button just to the left of the Start and End fields on the search screen.

- You can tag locations as favorites and get back to them quickly by tapping Favorites on the search screen.

- As you navigate through a route, Maps identifies traffic or construction issues along the path and attempts to reroute you so that you avoid the trouble spots.

Working with the Wallet App and Apple Pay

New! The Wallet app manages all sorts of information that you need to access, from airline tickets to shopping and credit cards. Instead of using paper or plastic to conduct transactions, you can simply have your iPhone's screen scanned.

You also use the Wallet app to access your Apple Pay information to make payments when you are in a physical location, such as a store or hotel (Apple Pay is covered in detail in "Working with Apple Pay" later in this chapter). You can also use Apple Pay when you make purchases online using some apps on your iPhone.

Working with the Wallet App

You can store a wide variety of information in your Wallet so that it is easily accessible. Examples include boarding passes, membership cards (to a gym for example), store cards (such as Starbucks if you are an addict like me), and loyalty or discount cards (things like loyalty cards for grocery stores or gas stations). The Wallet app eliminates the need to carry physical cards or paper for each of these; instead, your information is available to you digitally and you can enter it as needed by scanning the iPhone's screen.

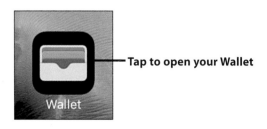

Tap to open your Wallet

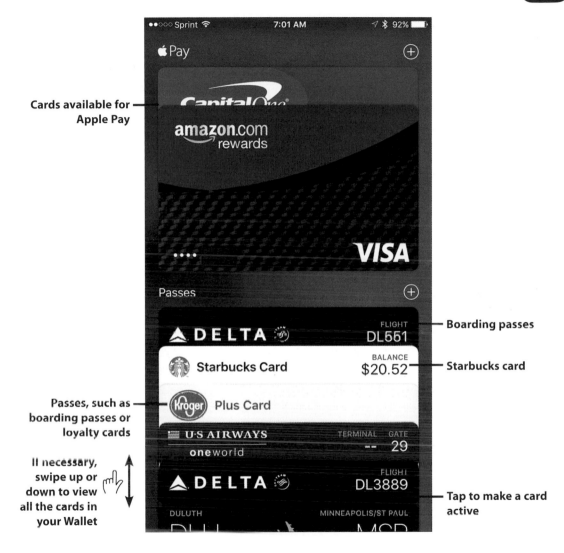

Cards available for Apple Pay

Passes, such as boarding passes or loyalty cards

If necessary, swipe up or down to view all the cards in your Wallet

Boarding passes

Starbucks card

Tap to make a card active

To open your Wallet, tap the Wallet icon. The Wallet app opens. At the top, you see the Apple Pay section that shows the cards you've enabled for Apple Pay. In the Passes section, you see other cards, such as boarding passes and loyalty cards.

As you add cards and boarding passes to your Wallet, they "stack up" at the bottom of the screen. Tap the stack to see the list of items available in your Wallet. The cards expand so that you can see at least the top of each card; if you have a lot of cards installed, swipe up or down on the screen to view all of them.

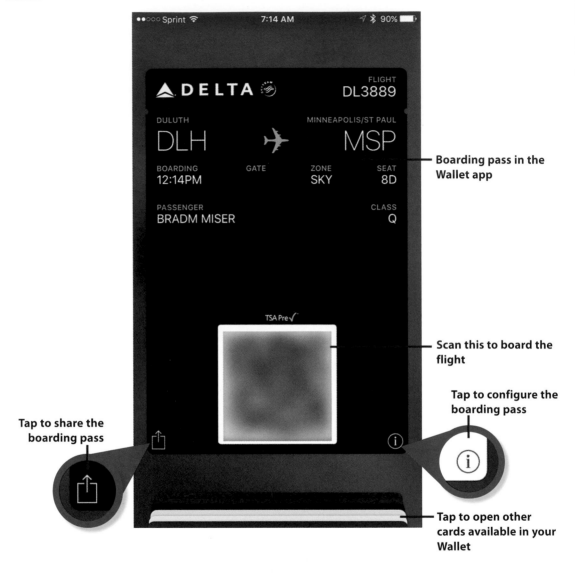

Boarding pass in the Wallet app

Scan this to board the flight

Tap to configure the boarding pass

Tap to share the boarding pass

Tap to open other cards available in your Wallet

To use a card in your Wallet, tap it. It becomes the active card and you can access its information. For example, you can quickly access a boarding pass by opening the Wallet app and tapping it. To board the plane, you scan the code on the boarding pass. Even better, boarding passes start appearing on the Lock screen a few hours before the take-off time. Swipe to the right on the boarding pass on the Lock screen and you jump directly to the boarding pass in the Wallet app (you don't even need to unlock your phone).

Most passes enable you to share them or information about them by tapping the Share button and using the standard sharing tools that appear.

Starbucks card

Current balance

Scan this to pay for Starbucks goodies

Tap to share the card

Tap to configure the card

Tap to delete the card from your Wallet

Tap to save your changes and close the Configure screen

Controls to configure the card

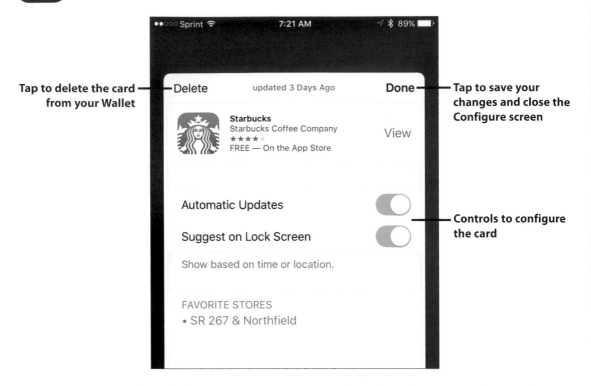

When you tap the Info button (i), you can use the controls on a card's Configure screen to adjust certain aspects of how the card works. For example, if you set the Suggest on Lock Screen switch to on (green), the card automatically appears on your Lock screen at the appropriate times. When you enable this for a card, such as Starbucks, it appears on the Lock screen when you are in close proximity to your favorite stores. And, some cards can be automatically refilled from your bank account or credit/debit card so that they always have a positive balance.

To delete a card from your Wallet (such as a boarding pass when the flight is finished), tap its Info button, tap Delete, and then confirm that you want to delete. The pass or card is removed from your Wallet.

When you're done configuring a card, tap Done. The Configure screen closes and you return to the card you were configuring.

There a couple of ways to add cards to your Wallet. The most frequent way to add a card is by using the Add to Wallet command in the app associated with the card (note that this might be called Add to Passbook in apps that haven't been updated for iOS 9 yet, but it does the same thing). In some cases, you may be able to scan the code on a card to add it.

Adding Passes or Cards to Your Wallet Using an App

If you are a frequent patron of a particular business (perhaps you are addicted to Starbucks coffee like I am) that has an iPhone app, check to see if it also supports the Wallet app. For example, when you use the Starbucks app configured with your account, you can add a Starbucks card to your Wallet as follows:

1. Open the app for which you want to add a pass or card to your Wallet.

2. Tap the app's command to manage its information; this command can be labeled with different names in different apps, it is the MANAGE command in the Starbucks app, or It may be accessed with an icon or differently named menu.

3. Tap Add to Wallet or Add to Passbook.

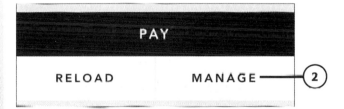

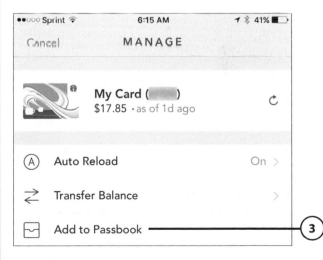

Wallet AKA Passbook

In prior versions of the iOS, the app now known as Wallet was called Passbook. In apps that haven't been updated for iOS 9 yet, you might see the Add to Passbook command instead of Add to Wallet. Add to Passbook does the same thing as Add to Wallet.

---

④ Tap Add. The card or pass is added to your Wallet and is ready to use.

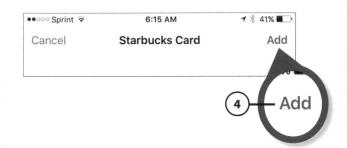

Finding Apps that Support the Wallet

You can search for apps that support the Wallet by opening the Wallet app, tapping the Add button (+) in the Passes section, and tapping Find Apps for Wallet. This takes you into the App Store app and you see apps that support the Wallet. You can then download and install apps you want to use as described in Chapter 6.

Adding Passes or Cards to Your Wallet by Scanning Their Codes

In some cases, you can add a card or pass to the Wallet by scanning its code. To do so, follow these steps:

① Open the Wallet app and tap the Add button (+) in the Passes section.

2 Tap Scan Code to Add a Pass.

3 Use the iPhone's camera to scan the code on the card by positioning the phone so that the white box encloses the code on the card. If the code is recognized and is available for the Wallet, the pass or card is added to the Wallet and is ready for use. If the code isn't recognized or doesn't support the Wallet, you see an error and you need to find an associated app for the card to use it with the Wallet.

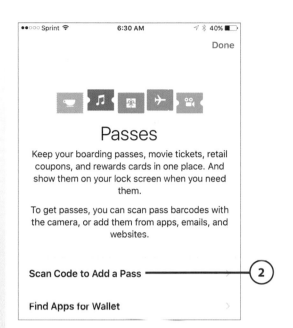

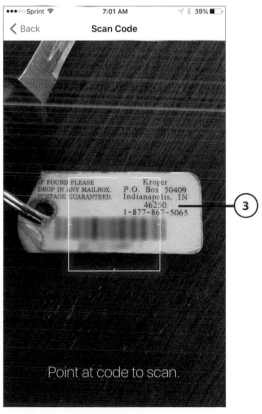

Working with Apple Pay

Cards available for Apple Pay

Tap the card you want to use for Apple Pay

When you see this, touch the Touch ID button to authorize payment

Apple Pay enables you to pay for things more easily and securely than with physical credit or debit cards. (Note that Apple Pay requires an iPhone 6, iPhone 6 Plus, or later.) When you are making a purchase in a physical store, you can simply hold your iPhone up to a contactless reader connected to the cash register and touch your finger to the Touch ID button. (The finger you use must be recognized for Touch ID; see Chapter 4, "Configuring an iPhone to Suit Your Preferences," for the details of configuring fingerprints for Touch ID.) The iPhone communicates the information required to complete the purchase.

When you are making a transaction in an app that supports Apple Pay, tap this to pay

Apple Pay also simplifies purchases made in online stores. When you use an app or a website that supports Apple Pay, you can tap the Buy with Apple Pay button to complete the purchase.

Apple Pay is actually more secure than using a credit or debit card because your card information is not passed to the device; instead a unique code is passed that ties back to your card, but that can't be used again. And, you never present your card so the number is not visible to anyone, either visually or digitally.

With Apple Pay, you can store your cards in the Wallet app, and they are instantly and automatically available to make purchases.

Apple Pay Support

In addition to requiring an iPhone 6/6s or iPhone 6/6s Plus, a credit or debit card must support Apple Pay for it to work with that card. The easiest way to figure out if your cards support it is to try to add a card to Apple Pay. If you can do so, the card is supported and you can use it. If not, you can check with the credit or debit card company to see when support for Apple Pay will be added so you can use it.

Adding Credit or Debit Cards to Apple Pay

To start using Apple Pay, add a credit or debit card to it:

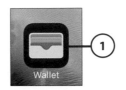

Wallet ①

(1) Open the Wallet app.

(2) Tap the Add button (+) in the Apple Pay section at the top of the screen.

(3) Tap Next.

(4) Position the iPhone so that the card is inside the white box. The app captures information from the card, which is highlighted in white on the screen. When it has captured all the information it can, you move to the Card Details screen.

Prefer to Type?

If you don't want to use the camera option, or if that option doesn't capture the information correctly, you can also type your card's information directly into the fields. To do this, perform step 3, and then tap Enter Card Details Manually, which is at the bottom of the Scan screen. You can use the resulting Card Details screens to manually enter the card's information.

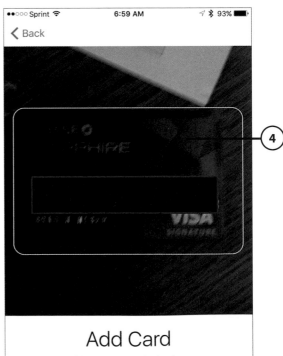

5 Use the keyboard or keypad to enter any information that wasn't captured or to correct any information that wasn't captured correctly.

6 Tap Next. The information for the card is verified. If it can't be verified, you see an error message. For example, if the card doesn't support Apple Pay, you see a message saying so. If this happens, tap OK to close the message and then wait for your card to support Apple Pay or enter a different card's information. When the card is verified, you see the Terms and Conditions screen.

7 Tap Agree.

8 Tap Agree at the prompt. The card's verification is complete and you see it in the Wallet app. You are ready to use Apple Pay.

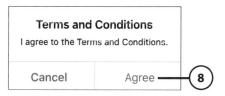

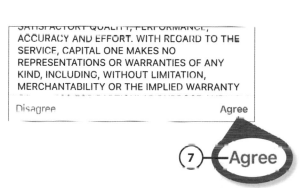

More Verification Required

In some cases, there may be an additional verification step after you tap Agree in step 8. When this is the case, the Complete Verification screen appears. Tap how you want to receive the verification code, such as via Email or Text Message, and then tap Next. The card configuration completes. You should receive a verification code. When you have the code, open the Settings app and tap Wallet & Apple Pay. Tap the card you need to verify, and then tap Enter Code. Enter the verification code you received; when you enter the correct code, the card is verified and becomes available for Apple Pay.

Managing Apple Pay

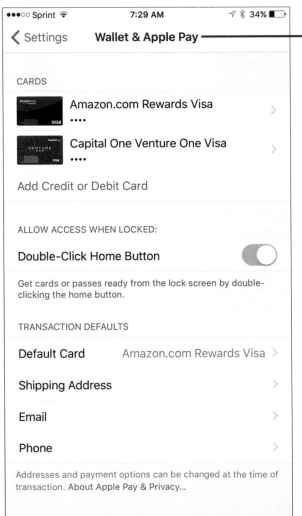

Use the Wallet & Apple Pay Settings screen to manage Apple Pay

To manage Apple Pay, open the Settings app and tap Wallet & Apple Pay. On the resulting screen, you can:

- Tap a card to configure it, such as to determine if notifications related to it will be sent. You also see a list of recent transactions for the card.

- Add a new credit or debit card.

- Use the Double-Click Home Button switch to determine if you can access the cards in your Wallet by pressing the Home button twice when the phone is locked. This makes using your Wallet even easier because you press the Home button twice and your cards appear; tap a card to use it or touch the Home/Touch ID button to pay for something with Apple Pay.

- Set your default Apple Pay card.

- Update your billing, shipping, and email addresses and phone numbers.

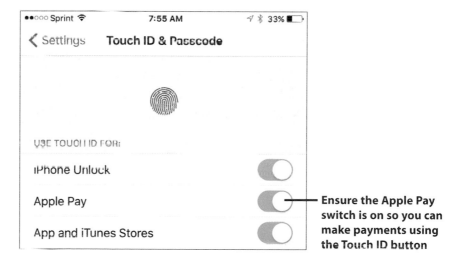

Ensure the Apple Pay switch is on so you can make payments using the Touch ID button

You should also make sure Apple Pay is set to use Touch ID. Open the Settings app, tap Touch ID & Passcode, and then enter your passcode. Ensure that the Apple Pay switch is on (green). This enables you to complete Apple Pay transactions by touching the Touch ID button.

Managing Your Health with the Health App

Apple's Health app does two things. One is that you can use it to store a Medical ID with your medical information in one place for easy access, for your reference or for the reference of others during an emergency. The other is that it can be a dashboard for other health-related apps you use. For example, if you use an app to help you lose weight, that app can provide information to the Health app. Likewise, apps you use to monitor your exercise can feed their results to the Health app so you can get all your health information in one place.

Using the Health App to Create a Medical ID

To configure a Medical ID in the Health app, perform the following steps:

(1) Tap Health to open the app.

(2) Tap the Medical ID button.

(3) Tap Create Medical ID.

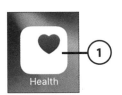

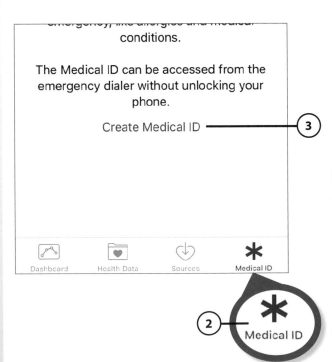

conditions.

The Medical ID can be accessed from the emergency dialer without unlocking your phone.

Create Medical ID — (3)

Dashboard   Health Data   Sources   Medical ID

(2) Medical ID

4 Set the Show When Locked switch to on (green) so that you or others can access your medical information when your iPhone is locked. For example, if someone needs to provide you with medical treatment, they can get to this information without having to unlock your phone.

5 Tap and complete each section of information to add it to your Medical ID. This information includes your birthdate, medical conditions, medical notes, allergies, medications, emergency contacts, blood type, and other important information.

6 Tap Done to save the updated information.

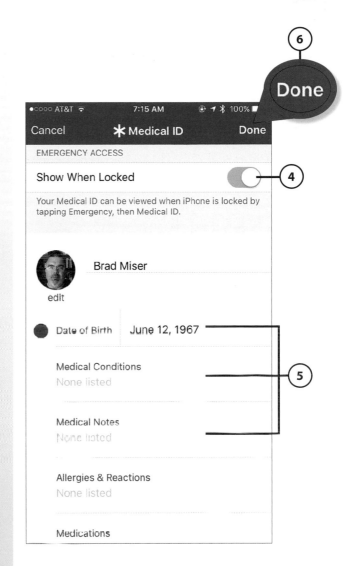

Accessing Your Medical ID

You can view your Medical ID information at any time by returning to the Medical ID screen (open the Health app and tap Medical ID). To update your information, tap Edit and change or add information.

If you enabled the Show When Locked feature in step 4, your Medical ID can be accessed while your iPhone is locked. This is especially useful for situations in which you are incapacitated and others need this information to treat you. To access this information while the phone is locked, wake the phone up, swipe to the right on the slider to move to the Touch ID or Enter Passcode screen. Tap Emergency; then, tap Medical ID.

Tap to access the Emergency screen without unlocking the phone

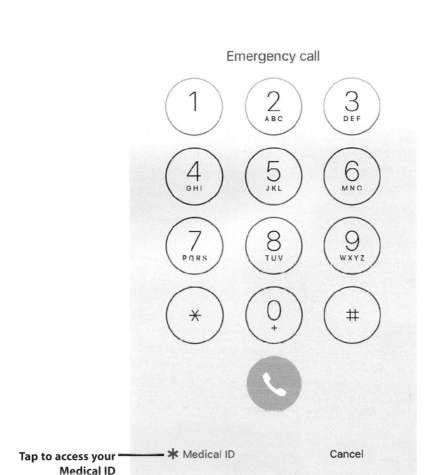

Tap to access your —————— ✳ Medical ID
Medical ID

Using the Health App for Health and Fitness Information

You can use the Health app to store all sorts of health and related information. This information can be entered directly into the Health app, or even more usefully, it can be automatically added from other apps you use, such as an app you use to monitor exercise or to lose weight.

Finding and Installing Health Apps

You can use the information in Chapter 6 to find and download health-related apps from the App Store. As you consider apps you may want to use, make sure they are compatible with the Health app; if an app is described as working with the Healthkit or Apple Health compatible, it can report its information to the Health app. You need to install these apps on your iPhone so they can work with the Health app. To get information about apps that can work with the iPhone's Health app, do a Web search for "apps that work with the health app." Or, search the App Store for "Healthkit." When you find apps you want to use, download and install them as detailed in Chapter 6.

Configuring Apps to Report to the Health App

You have to provide explicit permission for apps to report their data to the Health app so that you can view that information on the Health app's screens. This typically involves accessing the app's settings or configuration tools to set this permission. How you do this varies from app to app, but the following steps show how you do this in one app as an example.

(1) Open the app you want to connect to the Health app.

(2) Move into the app's Settings area; typically, you tap a button with the gear icon on it to do this.

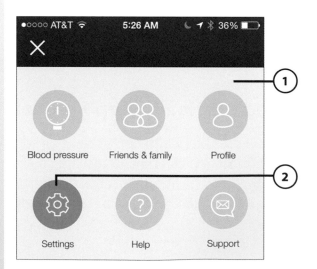

3. Set the Store in Health or similar option to on, such as by setting its switch to on (green). This enables the app to connect to the Health app to provide information to it.

4. If prompted to do so, choose the specific data you want the app to report into the Health app by setting the switches to on (green). When you enable data, it is reported to the Health app; if you disable data, it is not reported to the Health app.

5. Tap Done. The app begins reporting its information to the Health app.

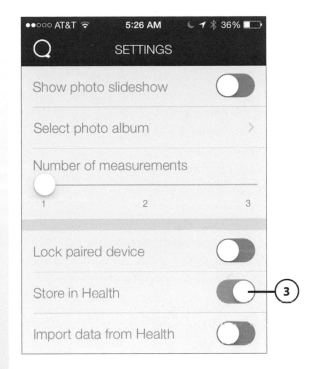

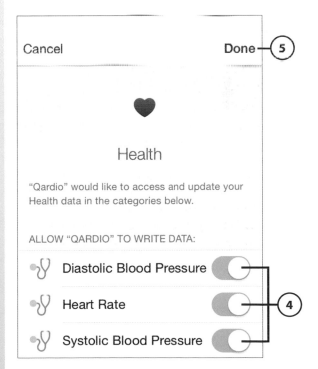

Using the Health App to View Health Information

You can use the Health app to view your health information. Because it consolidates the information from many other apps, there is a large amount of information available to you. You can view information in individual categories and view dashboards.

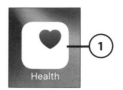

(1) Tap Health on the Home screen to open the app.

(2) Tap Health Data. You see the various kinds of information that the Health app can work with.

(3) Swipe up and down the screen to review all the categories of information available in the app.

(4) Tap the category you want to explore, such as Fitness. You move into that category and see its details.

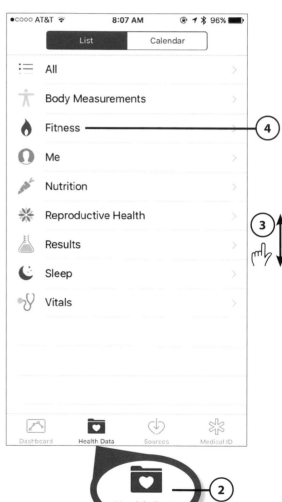

5 Swipe up and down the screen to review all the sub-categories of information available in the app.

6 Tap an area you are interested in, such as Workouts.

7 Tap the timeframe for which you want to view information, such as Week. The graph updates to show the timeframe you select and you can see the data for what has been collected in the Health app for that timeframe. For example, if you are viewing Workouts, you see the workout information for the current week.

8 If you want the information you are working with to be available on the Health app Dashboard, set its Show on Dashboard switch to on (green).

9 To see all the data in the category, tap Show All Data. On the All Recorded Data screen, you see all the information available in the category.

10 Tap Add Data Point to manually enter information. On the resulting screen, enter the information you want to add and tap Add.

11 To share the information you are viewing with other apps, tap Share Data, set the switches for the apps with which you want to share data to on (green), and tap the back button.

12 When you are done viewing the information, tap the back button.

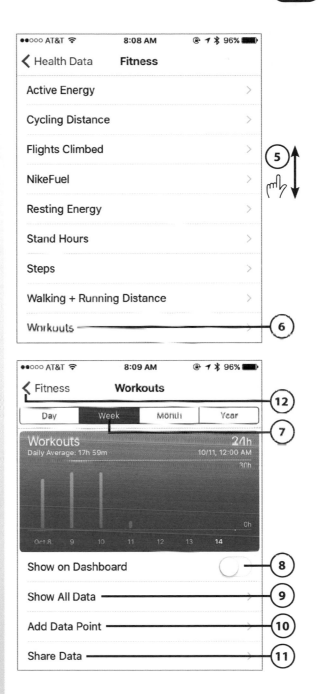

(13) Tap Dashboard. You see a compilation of dashboards showing all the data for which the Show on Dashboard switch is on (as described in step 8).

(14) Tap a tab to change the timeframe for the dashboards being displayed.

(15) Swipe up and down the screen to browse all of the dashboards.

(16) Tap a dashboard to view its detail and configure it.

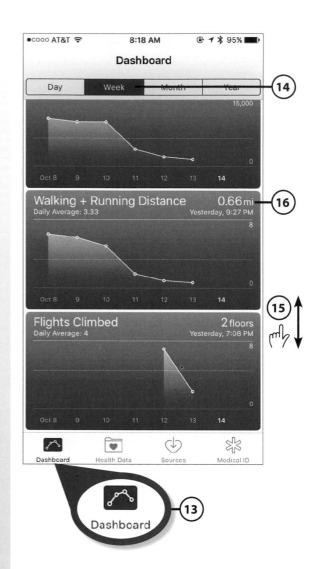

Managing Sources in the Health App

You can configure the sources of information being managed in the Health app on the Sources screen as follows:

1. Tap Sources. On the Sources screen, you see a list of apps that can share information with the Health app.

2. Tap an app to configure it.

3. Swipe up and down the screen to see all of the options.

4. Set the switches to on (green) for data that you want the app to provide to the Health app.

5. Set the switches to off (white) for the data that you don't want to be reported into the Health app.

6. Tap Sources and repeat steps 2 through 5 to configure the other Health app's use.

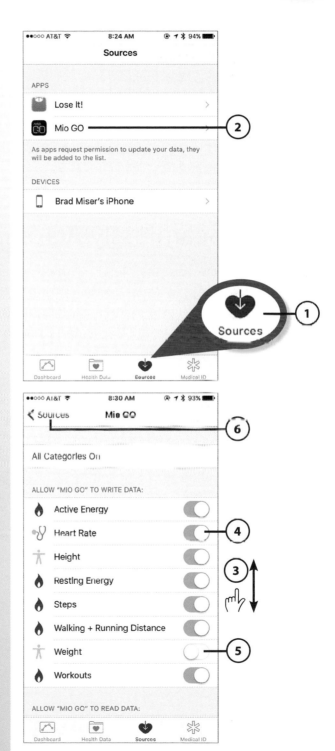

Configuring Health Devices

Some health devices can report their information directly into their apps, which can in turn report that data into the Health app. (Your iPhone can track your steps and report those to the Health app.) First, if necessary, pair the device with your iPhone (see Chapter 2, "Connecting Your iPhone to the Internet, Bluetooth Devices, and iPhones/iPods/iPads"). Second, open the Settings app, tap Privacy, and then tap Motion & Fitness. Use the settings on the Motion & Fitness screen to enable Fitness Tracking and to enable apps to access your Motion & Fitness activity.

Working Seamlessly Across Your Devices

Your iPhone can work seamlessly with other iOS devices running iOS 8 or later (such as iPads), Apple Watch, or Macs running OS X Yosemite or later. This enables you to change devices and keep working on the same tasks. For example, you can start an email on your iPhone and then continue it on your Mac without missing a beat.

You can also take phone calls to your iPhone on Apple Watch, iPads, or Macs.

Working with Handoff

Handoff enables you to work seamlessly between iOS devices, Apple Watch, as well as Macs running OS X Yosemite or later. Each device needs to be signed into the same iCloud account and have Handoff enabled. If you do not have an Apple Watch, multiple iOS devices running iOS 8 or later, or a Mac running OS X Yosemite or later, then there is no need to turn on this feature.

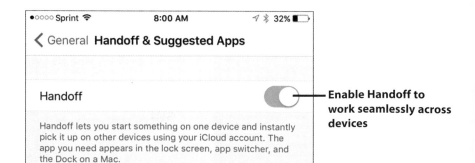

Enable Handoff to work seamlessly across devices

Ensure that Handoff is enabled on all the devices with which you want to use it. On iOS devices, enable Handoff by opening the Settings app, tapping General, and then tapping Handoff & Suggested Apps. Set the Handoff switch to on (green).

For Apple Watch, open the Apple Watch app on your iPhone and tap General. On the General screen, scroll down to Enable Handoff and make sure it is on (green).

To enable handoff on a Mac running OS X Yosemite or later, open the System Preferences app, and then open the General pane. Ensure that the Allow Handoff between this Mac and your iCloud devices check box is checked.

Using Handoff on iOS Devices

When Handoff is enabled on your devices, you can work on the same items on any device, as the following example of working with email shows:

1. Start an email on your iPhone (note this only works for iCloud email).

2. To work on the email on another iOS device, swipe up on the Mail icon on its Lock screen and unlock the device.

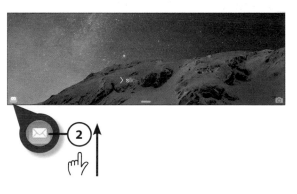

(3) Work on the email on the iOS device.

Handoff on a Mac

When your Mac detects activity associated with Handoff, an icon on the Dock appears. Click that icon to open the activity, such as an email, web page, Pages document, or other iCloud-based activity.

This works in the other direction, too. For example, if you open a web page on your Mac, you see the Safari icon on the iPhone's Lock screen. Swipe up on it and unlock your iPhone and the web page on your Mac opens on your iPhone.

Most Apple apps support Handoff and Apple has made it available to other software developers so they can add support to their apps, too.

Cancel	**Stinger Flights**	Send

To: Sir William Wallace

Cc/Bcc, From: bradmiser@icloud.com

Subject: Stinger Flights

Hey,

Awesome flights with the Stinger. The new brakes worked really well. I think it is dialed in now.

I was able to stop it very quickly.

Brad

Sent from my iPhone

(3)

Taking Phone Calls on Macs or iPads

A call coming in on your iPhone appears on the iPad

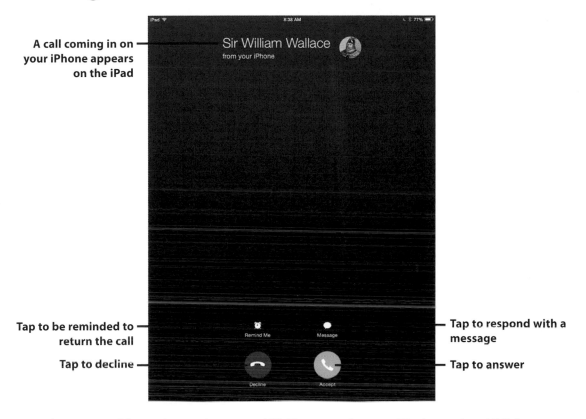

Tap to be reminded to return the call

Tap to decline

Tap to respond with a message

Tap to answer

When your iPhone is on the same Wi-Fi network as an iPad running iOS 8 or later, or a Mac running OS X Yosemite or later, you can take phone calls on those devices. When a call comes in to your iPhone, you see the call screen on the other devices and can take the call on one of those devices (see Chapter 8, "Communicating with the Phone and FaceTime Apps").

If you have an Apple Watch, it communicates with your iPhone using Bluetooth, so it is not necessary to be on Wi-Fi to take a call on the Watch instead of the iPhone.

Configuring Devices to Share iPhone Calls

To be able to take calls to your iPhone on other devices, open the Settings app and tap Phone. Tap Calls on Other Devices. Set the Allow Calls on Other Devices switch to on (green). To allow other devices to take calls, ensure those devices' switches are on (green). To prevent calls from going to a device, set its switch to off (white).

Index

Symbols

3D Touch, 10
  Quick Actions menu, opening, 14
  reading text messages, 400
  receiving/reading email, 334-335
  with Safari, 552-554
  selecting text, 36
  viewing
    events, 434-435
    photos, 594-595
3G networks, 58
4G networks, 58
30-pin port, 5

A

AARP app, 647
access restrictions, configuring, 155-161
accessibility options, configuring, 150-155
accessing. *See also* downloading
  cards in Wallet app, 674
  contact information, 257-262
  medical ID, 688
accounts
  deleting, 121
  email, configuring, 318

Facebook, 90, 114-116
Google, 90, 109-111
iCloud. *See* iCloud accounts
online. *See* online accounts
Accounts section (Mailboxes screen), 326
acronyms, text messaging, 417
activating Siri, 484
adding
  caller information to Favorites, 294-295
  cards
    to Apple Pay, 682-683
    in Wallet app, 676-679
  contact information to existing contacts, 249, 265
  contacts to Favorites, 259
  events to calendars, 436-448
  fields in contacts, 256
  icons to folders on Home screens, 170-171, 175
  locations in conversations, 410-411
  people to Family Sharing, 234-237
  photos
    to albums, 622-623
    to shared albums, 635-636
    to Wish List, 224
addresses
  email
    marking, 323
    removing, 339

FaceTime, managing, 307
formats for contacts, 256
verifying for iMessage, 376
AirDrop, 59, 81-82
  disabling, 83
  enabling, 82-83
  responding to share requests, 87
  security, 62
  sharing content, 84-86
AirDrop button, 25
airline apps, 647
Airplane mode, 50-51
AirPlay, streaming photos/videos to Apple TV, 629-632
AirPlay button, 25
AirPrint, 52-54
AirPrint for Windows, 53
alarms
  creating with Siri, 500
  managing, 470-471
  setting, 466-469
albums
  adding photos to, 622-623
  creating, 620-621
  managing, 623
  sharing, 633-641
  types of, 588-589
alerts, 26-27, 191-192
  banner alerts, replying from, 395
  dismissing, 453, 463

Messages app, 378
setting for events, 445-446
All Photos album, 588
answering calls, 289-292
App Store, 202
downloading and installing apps, 210-211
downloading previously purchased apps, 226-228
options, 205-206
related searches, 208
searching, 206-209
tips for using, 211
Trending Searches, 209
App Switcher, 16-17
Apple ID
for children, 237
iMessages, 369
managing, 205
signing in, 48-49
Apple Online Store, 92
Apple Pay, 672, 681. See also Wallet app
adding cards, 682-683
managing, 685
support for, 681
verifying cards, 684
Apple TV, streaming photos/videos to, 629-632
Apple Watch
peer-to-peer connectivity, 80-81
working seamlessly with iOS devices, 696-699
applying filters to photos, 609-610
apps, 13-18
AARP, 647
accessing contact information from, 261-262
airline apps, 647
App Store. See App Store
App Switcher, 16-17
AroundMe, 648
badges, 190
Calculator, 26, 646
Calendar. See Calendar app
Camera. See Camera app

Clock. See Clock app
Compass, 646
configuring, 211
Contacts. See Contacts app
contextual menus, 39
creating contacts from, 249
downloading
and installing, 210-211
previously purchased, 226-228
security, 62
Find Friends, 647
Find iPhone, 647
finding in App Store, 206-209
First Aid, 648
Flashlight, 25, 647
Foodler, 648
GateGuru, 648
Health. See Health app
health-related apps, finding and installing, 690
iBooks, 645
icons. See icons
iMovie, editing videos, 628
in-app purchases, preventing, 157
iTunes Store. See iTunes Store
launching, 13-15
Mail. See Mail app
Maps, 665-671
Messages. See Messages app
monitoring data usage, 72, 76
multitasking, 15
Music, 646
News, 646
Notes, 645
notifications. See notifications
opening
email attachments, 336
with Siri, 507
organizing into folders, 168-172
Photos. See Photos app
Podcasts. See Podcasts app
Quick Actions menu, opening, 14
quitting, 17
Reminders. See Reminders app
restrictions, configuring, 155-161
returning to, 18
Safari. See Safari

searching for Wallet support, 678
Settings. See Settings app
sharing with others, 211
Split-screen mode, 19
Stocks, 645
toolbars, opening Control Center, 24
TripAdvisor, 648
TripIt, 648
universal apps, 209
updating, 211
Urban Spoon, 649
user reviews, 209
using during calls, 288, 315
video previews, 209
Videos, 645
Voice Memos, 646
Wallet. See Wallet app
Watch, 646
Weather, 645
WebMD, 649
Yelp, 649
archiving email messages, 349
AroundMe app, 648
asleep/locked condition, 46-48
associating
events with calendars, 438, 443
photos with contacts, 250-251
attachments
to conversations, browsing, 412-413
email
downloading, 328
opening in apps, 336
embedded images versus, 408
saving, 359
sending images/video in text messages, 401-406
audio
FaceTime app, audio only, 268
in Messages app, 376
iTunes Store. See iTunes Store
kept audio messages, 391
listening in conversations, 390-391
music, auto-mute during calls, 292
podcasts. See podcasts
sending in conversations, 407-408

audio controls, 25

Auto-Brightness feature, 176

Auto-Capitalization, disabling, 140

Auto-Correction, 34-35, 140

Auto-Lock, configuring, 128-129

AutoFill, completing web forms, 557

automatic downloads from iTunes Store, 202-204, 226

automatic erase feature, 136

automatic prompting (Wi-Fi networks), 63

automatic signatures (email), configuring, 318-319

automatic sign in (websites), 558

B

Back button, browsing photos, 592

background, opening web pages in, 534

backing up to iCloud accounts, 92, 104

badges, 26-27, 190
   folders and, 172
   on podcasts, 658

banners, 26, 191
   replying from, 395

battery usage, screen brightness and, 164

birthdays in iCloud settings, 237

BIU button, 33, 38

blocking
   contacts from text messaging, 377-378
   FaceTime, 307

Bluetooth, 59, 77
   forgetting devices, 80
   pairing devices, 77-80

boarding passes. See cards

bookmarks
   browsing the Web, 521-523
   creating, 541-544, 550-551
   defined, 514
   deleting, 549

editing, 547
   as Favorites, 524-526
   organizing, 544-549
   syncing, 520, 544

brightness (of screen)
   adjusting, 176-179
   battery usage, 164

Brightness slider, 25

browsers. See web browsers

browsing. See also web browsing
   apps in App Store, 209
   attachments to conversations, 412-413
   iTunes Store content, 216-218
   photos, 585-592
   podcasts, 654

Burst mode
   managing photos in, 601-603
   taking photos in Camera app, 584
   with timer in Camera app, 584
   uploading to iCloud, 603

Bursts album, 589

C

Calculator app, 26, 646

Calendar app, 419. See also calendars
   configuring, 420-429
   Quick Actions feature, 449
   Siri and, 497-500
   viewing events with 3D Touch, 434-435

calendars
   adding events manually, 436-448
   associating events with, 438, 443
   configuring, 420-429
   iCloud storage, 91
   managing, 451-453
   multiple, 424
   navigating, 430
   Quick Actions feature, 449
   searching, 449-451
   viewing, 424, 430-434

Call Failed screen, 277

calls, 267
   adding information to Favorites, 294-295
   clearing Recents list, 293-294
   configuring phone settings, 268-273
   converting to FaceTime, 282, 309
   FaceTime. See FaceTime
   hanging up, 282
   headset, 296
   in-process calls, 281-288
   making calls, 273-281, 490
   missed calls, 303
   muting, 282
   on other devices, configuring, 269-270
   receiving, 289-292, 699
   roaming charges, 274
   sharing on Macs/iOS devices, 699
   on speaker, 282
   terminology, 268
   visual voicemail. See visual voicemail

camera, 4. See also photos
   Control Center, taking photos/video, 582
   HDR (High Dynamic Range) feature, 583
   Quick Access feature, taking photos/video, 581
   sensitivity, 584

Camera app, 26, 561. See also, photos; video
   associating photos with contacts, 251
   Burst mode, 584
   configuring settings, 562-567
   icons, explained, 570-572
   Live Photos, 572
   Location Services with, 584
   panoramic photos, 577-578
   Self-timer, 584
   types of photos/video, 568-569

Camera Roll album, 588

Caps Lock key, 35, 140

capturing screenshots, 585

cards
  accessing in Wallet app, 674
  adding
    to Apple Pay, 682-683
    in Wallet app, 676-679
  Apple Pay support, 681
  deleting in Wallet app, 676
  sharing in Wallet app, 675
  Suggest on Lock Screen option
    (Wallet app), 676
  verifying in Apple Pay, 684
  viewing in Wallet app, 673
Categories button (App Store), 205
cell phone functionality, 267.
  See also calls
  calls on other devices, configuring,
    269-270
  FaceTime. See FaceTime
  visual voicemail.
    See visual voicemail
cell phone providers, Wi-Fi
  networks, 70
cellular data networks, 58
  connecting iPhone to Internet,
    71-76
  connection speeds, 58
  data plans, 59
  overage charges, 59
  personal hotspots, 68
  roaming charges, 59
changing
  mailboxes, 359
  passcodes, 136
  text replacements, 143
  voice of Siri, 481-482
  voicemail password, 304
  Wi-Fi networks, 66
Character Preview, disabling, 140
children, Apple IDs, 237
Chrome, 514
clearing
  browsing history, 529
  History List (iTunes Store), 226
  Recents list, 293-294
  searches in iTunes Store, 215
Clock app, 26, 419-420, 465

configuring Date & Time settings,
  422-423
  managing alarms, 470-471
  setting alarms, 466-469
  Siri, creating alarms/timers, 500
  Stopwatch, 472-473
  Timer, 474-476
  World Clock, 469
Clock button, 33
closed Wi-Fi networks, connecting
  iPhone to Internet, 70
cloud-based accounts. See iCloud
  accounts
codes, scanning in Wallet app, 678-679
commands, contextual, 36
  in apps, 39
commenting on shared photos, 637
Compass app, 646
completed reminders
  marking, 464
  viewing, 464
composing email with Siri, 491-492
conditions, monitoring, 44-45
conference calls, 284-287
  limitation on callers, 285
configuring. See also customizing;
  Settings app
  accessibility options, 150-155
  access restrictions, 155-161
  Apple Pay, 685
  apps, 211
  Auto-Lock/TouchID/passcodes,
    128-136
  automatic downloads from iTunes
    Store, 202-204
  backups on iCloud, 104
  calendars, 425-429
  calendar settings, 420-423
  cellular data network usage, 73-76
  Contacts app settings, 244-246
  Date & Time settings, 422-423
  Dock, 172-173
  Do Not Disturb feature, 147-149
  email accounts, 318
  email settings, 318-320, 323
  Facebook accounts, 114-116

FaceTime settings, 305-307
Family Sharing, 232-234
Find My iPhone, 108
Google accounts, 109-111
Handoff feature, 696-697
Health app connections, 690-691
Health app information sources,
  695-696
health devices, 696
iCloud accounts, 91-92
iCloud Drive, 99-100
iMessage and text settings,
  369-378
keychain syncing on iCloud,
  105-107
Macs/iOS devices to share calls, 699
notifications, 190, 423
  global preferences, 194-195
  for specific apps, 196-199
online accounts, 111-120
phone settings, 268-273
Photos & Camera settings, 562-567
photo storage on iCloud, 101-103
Photo Stream, 102
podcast settings, 649-651
reminder settings, 422-423
Safari, 515-520
Siri, 481-484
connection speeds, cellular data
  networks, 58
connections, 57. See also
  Internet, connections
  AirDrop, 81-87
  Bluetooth, 77-80
  to Health app, configuring, 690-691
  peer-to-peer connectivity, 80-81
  security, tips for, 59-62
  terminology, 58-59
contacts
  accessing information, 257-262
  adding
    to existing, 249, 265
    to Favorites, 259
  answering calls from, 290
  blocking from text messaging,
    377-378

creating, 256
  from apps, 249
  from email, 247-248
  manually, 249-255
deleting, 265
dialing calls, 276
groups, 260
iCloud storage, 91
inviting to events, 444
photos on Call screen, 282
removing from text messages, 381
selecting for text messaging, 381
sharing, 259, 406
storing, 247
syncing, 256, 263
unblocking from text
  messaging, 378
updating, 263-265

Contacts app, 243-244. See
  also contacts
  accessing information, 257-259
  configuring settings, 244-246
  sending email, 337

content restrictions, configuring,
  155-161

contextual commands, 36, 39

Control Center, 24-26, 582

conversations (text). See also
  Messages app
  adding location information,
    410-411
  browsing images/video
    attachments, 412-413
  deleting, 414-416
  embedding images/video, 409
  listening to audio, 390-391
  managing, 397
    images/video in, 388-390
  sending
    audio in, 407-408
    images/video as attachments,
      401-406
  watching video, 392-394

converting voice calls to FaceTime,
  282, 309

cookies, 520

Copy key, 33

copying photos, 616

correcting mistakes with Siri, 504

costs, FaceTime calls, 307

created albums, 589

credit cards. See cards

Crop tool (Photos app), 603, 606-609

cropping photos, 606-609

current time, viewing on
  calendars, 433

customizing. See also
  configuring; Settings app
    Home screens. See Home screens,
      customizing
    keyboard, 137-143
    language and format preferences,
      143-147
    Lock screen, wallpaper, 180-185
    notifications, 147-149, 164
    screen, brightness/view/text size,
      176-179
    sounds, 164, 186-189

Cut key, 33

cutting text, 38

D

data plans, 59, 71

data retrieval, 90
  configuring, 116-120
  disabling, 121

data roaming
  charges, 72
  configuring, 74-75

data usage
  FaceTime calls, 307
  monitoring, 72-73, 76

Date & Time settings, configuring,
  422-423

debit cards. See cards

declining
  calls, 291
  FaceTime calls, 310

default Home screens, returning
  to, 175

deferring downloads, 223

deleted email messages, moving out
  of Trash, 348

deleted voicemails, listening to,
  302-304

deleting. See also removing
  alarms, 471
  bookmarks, 549
  cards in Wallet app, 676
  contacts, 265
    from text messages, 381
  email
    addresses, 339
    gestures for, 352
    messages, 348
  fields in contacts, 256
  folders, 175
  icons, 174-175
  keyboards, 141
  lists, 463
  messages and conversations,
    414-416
  online accounts, 121
  photo albums, 623
  photos, 576, 623-625
  podcast episodes, 665
  podcasts, 654
  reminders, 464
  text replacements, 143
  videos, 626
  voicemails, 302

designating VIPs in email, 363

dialing numbers
  contacts, 276
  Favorites, 277
  keypad, 275
  Recents list, 278-279
  SIRI SUGGESTIONS screen, 280-281

dictation. See also Siri
  disabling, 141
  with Microphone key, 39-41
  of text, 505-506

directions
  Maps app, 665-671
  with Siri, 503-504
disabling
  AirDrop, 83
  data retrieval, 121
  Find My iPhone, 108
  group messaging, 383
  notifications for conversations, 413
discoverable (for Bluetooth
  devices), 77
dismissing alarms, 471
Do Not Disturb feature, 29-30, 147-149
Dock, configuring, 172-173
docking port, 5
downloading
  apps, 62, 210-211
  email attachments, 328
  iTunes Store content, 221-223
    automatic downloads,
      202-204, 226
    previously purchased content,
      228 231
  previously purchased apps from
    App Store, 226-228
  shared content from Family
    Sharing, 240-241
draft email, saving, 341
dragging items, 8
driving directions
  Maps app, 665-671
  with Siri, 503-504
dynamic wallpaper, 181

E

EarPods headset, 296
editing
  bookmarks, 547
  email with Siri, 493
  events with Siri, 500
  photos, 603
    Crop tool, 606-609
    Enhance tool, 604

    Filters tool, 609-610
    red-eye removal, 611-612
    Rotate tool, 606-609
    Smart Adjustment tools (Photos
      app), 613-615
    Straighten tool, 606-609
  suggested recipients list, 384
  text, 35
  videos, 627-628
email, 317. See also iMessages;
  Mail app
  addresses
    marking, 323
    removing, 339
    verifying for iMessage, 376
  attachments
    downloading, 328
    opening in apps, 336
  configuring, 318-320, 323
  creating contacts from, 247-248
  gestures, 329, 349-352
  Google accounts, configuring,
    109-111
  iCloud address, 91
  large messages, handling, 346
  mailboxes
    changing, 359
    creating, 355
  notifications, 323, 331, 349
  phishing, 60-61
  printing, 344
  saving drafts, 341
  scam email, avoiding, 376
  sending via Handoff feature, 697
  signatures, configuring, 318-319
  Siri, 331
  threads
    disabling, 325
    reading, 327
    selecting, 357
embedded audio, sending in text
  messages, 407-408
embedded images
  attachments versus, 408
  in text messages, 409
emergency notifications, 192

Emoji key, 32
Emoji keyboard, 31-33, 137
emoticons, 33, 137
enabling
  AirDrop, 82-83
  Find My iPhone, 108
  iCloud syncing, 97-98
Enhance tool (Photos app), 603-604
enhancing photos, 604
episodes. See podcasts
Erase Data feature, automatic
  erase, 136
events
  adding manually, 436-448
  alerts
    dismissing, 453
    setting, 445-446
  associating with calendars,
    438, 443
  creating with Siri, 497 498
  editing with Siri, 500
  invitations
    to contacts, 444
    sending with Siri, 498
  managing, 451-453
  notifications, 453
  Quick Actions feature, 449
  searching calendars for, 449-451
  viewing
    with 3D Touch, 434-435
    with Siri, 500
existing contacts, adding information
  to, 265
Explore (App Store), 205
external features, 3-5

F

Facebook accounts, 90
  configuring, 114-116
FaceTime, 304-305
  audio only, 268
  configuring settings, 305-307
  converting voice calls to, 282, 309

making calls, 307-310
  with Siri, 491
managing
  addresses, 307
  calls, 312-313
receiving calls, 310
Siri, 310
tracking calls, 311
using apps during calls, 315
Family Sharing, 90-91, 98, 202, 211
  adding people to, 234-237
  configuring, 232-234
  downloading shared content,
    240-241
  managing, 237-239
  photo albums, 637
  reminder lists, 463
Favorites
  adding
    caller information to, 294-295
    contacts to, 259
  browsing the Web, 524-526
  dialing calls, 277
  folders, 522
  marking photos as, 621
Favorites album, 589
Featured tab (App Store), 205
fetch mode (data retrieval), 90, 116
fields (in contacts), 256
file sizes of video, changing, 563-564
files, iCloud Drive, 91
  configuring, 99-100
filters, applying to photos, 609-610
Filters tool (Photos app), 604, 609-610
Find Friends app, 647
Find iPhone app, 647
Find My iPhone, 60, 92
  disabling, 108
  enabling, 108
  iCloud accounts, 93
finding
  apps in App Store, 206-209
  health-related apps, 690

iTunes Store content
  by browsing, 216-218
  by searching, 213-215
photos
  by browsing, 585-592
  by searching, 593
videos, 625-627
voicemails, 300-302
fingerprints, 60
  access restrictions and, 157
  recording, 128-136
Firefox, 514
First Aid app, 648
fitness information
  storing, 689
  viewing, 692-694
fitness-related apps, finding and
  installing, 690
flagging email messages, 349
Flashlight app, 25, 647
folders
  adding icons on Home screens,
    170-171, 175
  badges and, 172
  creating on Home screens, 168-170
  deleting, 175
  email messages, viewing, 358
  moving on Home screens, 170
  navigating, 15
  removing icons on Home
    screens, 172
  renaming, 175
Foodler app, 648
force-quitting apps, 17
forgetting Bluetooth devices, 80
Format key, 33, 38
format preferences, setting, 143-147
formats of addresses for contacts, 256
formatting text, 38
forms. See web forms
forwarding
  email, 344-346, 494
  text messages, 415
frame rate of video, changing, 564

G

GateGuru, 648
gestures, email, 329, 349-352
giving apps to others, 211
global email settings, configuring, 319
global notification preferences,
  configuring, 194-195
Globe key, 32
Google, 515
Google accounts, 90
  configuring, 109-111
Google Chrome, 514
greetings (voicemail), recording,
  297-299
group messaging, disabling, 383
groups
  contacts, 260
  viewing, 381

H

Handoff feature, 643
  configuring, 696-697
  on Macs, 698
  sending email, 697
handyPrint for Mac, 53
hanging up
  calls, 282
  FaceTime calls, 313
HDR (High Dynamic Range)
  feature, 583
headphone jack, 5
headset, 296
Health app, 686
  configuring
    app connections, 690-691
    information sources, 695-696
  health and fitness information
    storing, 689
    viewing, 692-694

medical ID
  accessing, 688
  creating, 686-687
health devices, configuring, 696
health-related apps, finding and
  installing, 690
hearing impairment, accessibility
  options, 154
Hide All Calendars button, 430
High Dynamic Range (HDR)
  feature, 583
History
  clearing, 529
  tracking websites visited, 528-529
History List (iTunes Store), 224-225
  clearing, 226
Home button, 5, 46
  signing into Apple ID, 48-49
Home screens, 7, 18
  creating bookmarks, 550-551
  customizing, 163-165
    *adding icons to folders, 170-
    171, 175*
    configuring Dock, 172-173
    creating folders, 168-170
    deleting icons, 174
    moving icons, 165-168
    removing icons from folders, 172
    tips for, 175
    wallpaper, 180-185
  returning to default, 175
  rotating, 21
  SIRI SUGGESTIONS page, 23
  Spotlight Search tool, 21-22
hotspots. *See* personal hotspots

Find My iPhone, enabling, 108
keychain syncing, 105-107
obtaining, 92-95
photo storage, 101-103, 562, 633
  *adding photos to shared albums,
  635-636*
  *commenting on shared
  photos, 637*
  *inviting people to shared
  albums, 637*
  managing shared albums, 637-641
  sharing, 633-634
  uploading Burst mode photos, 603
signing in, 95-96
syncing with, 97-98
iCloud Drive, 91
icons
  adding to folders on Home screens,
    170-171, 175
  in Camera app, 570-572
  deleting, 174-175
  Emoji keyboard, 33
  Handoff feature, 698
  moving on Home screens, 165-168
  removing from folders on Home
    screens, 172
  in Status bar, 44-45
identifying songs with Siri, 224
identity theft insurance, 62
images. *See also* photos
  attached to email messages,
    saving, 359
  browsing conversation
    attachments, 412-413
  of contacts as wallpaper, 290
  embedding in conversations, 409
  managing in conversations,
    388-390
  sending in conversations as
    attachments, 401-406
  stills, 181
  wallpaper, changing, 180-185
iMessages, 368
  adding location information,
    410-411
  blocking contacts, 377-378
  browsing images/video

attachments, 412-413
configuring settings, 369-378
conversations, managing, 397
deleting, 414-416
embedding images/video, 409
forwarding messages, 415
listening to audio in, 390-391
managing images/video in,
  388-390
reading messages, 386-387
  with 3D Touch, 400
  on iPhone 6/6s Plus, 398-399
receiving messages, 385
  with 3D Touch, 400
  on iPhone 6/6s Plus, 398-399
replying to messages, 394-396
sending
  audio in, 407-408
  *images/video as attachments,
  401-406*
  messages, 379-384, 396-397
  text messages versus, 378-379
text shorthand, 417
unblocking contacts, 378
undelivered messages, 395
watching video in, 392-394
iMovie app, editing videos, 620
In-app purchases, preventing, 157
in-process calls, 281-282
  conference calls, 284-287
  entering numbers during, 283
  using apps during, 288
Inbox screen
  gestures, 349-352
  organizing email messages,
    356-357
Inboxes section (Mailboxes
  screen), 326
information retrieval. *See* data retrieval
inserting photos/videos in email, 344
installing
  apps, 210-211
  health-related apps, 690
  third-party keyboards, 139
interface. *See* multi-touch interface;
  software

iBooks app, 645
iCloud accounts, 90
  backing up to, 104
  birthdays in settings, 237
  configuring, 91-92
  file storage, 99-100

Internet, 520
  3D Touch features, 552-554
  automatic sign in, 558
  bookmarks, 521-523
    creating, 541-544
    creating on Home screen, 550-551
    deleting, 549
    organizing, 544-549
  completing web forms, 554
    AutoFill, 557
    manually, 555-556
  configuring Safari, 515-520
  connections, 57
    cell phone provider Wi-Fi
      networks, 70
    cellular data networks, 71-76
    changing networks, 66
    closed Wi-Fi networks, 70
    open Wi-Fi networks, 63-65
    personal hotspots, 68
    public Wi-Fi networks, 68-70
    security, 59-62
    Siri and, 480
    terminology, 58-59
  Favorites, 522-526
  managing pages in tab view,
    536-538
  opening pages, 534-535
  Private mode browsing, 538
  screen orientation, 549
  searches, 539-540
  tracking visited sites, 528-529
  URLs, 526-528
  viewing websites, 530-533
Internet Explorer, 514
introduction to iPhone. *See* touring
  iPhone
inviting
  contacts to events, 444, 498
  people to shared albums, 637
iOS devices, working seamlessly
  between, 696
  Handoff feature, 696-697
  receiving calls, 699
  sending email, 697
iOS operating system, 6

iPads
  AirDrop, 81-82
    disabling, 83
    enabling, 82-83
    responding to share requests, 87
    sharing content, 84-86
  peer-to-peer connectivity, 80-81
iPhone
  introduction to. *See* touring iPhone
  security, tips for, 59-62
iPhone 6/6s Plus
  3D Touch
    with Safari, 552-554
    viewing photos, 594-595
  Live Photos, 572
  Quick Actions feature
    calendar events, 449
    sending text messages, 396-397
    taking photos/video from, 583
  receiving/reading
    email, 331-335
    text messages, 398-400
  split-pane web browsing, 549
iPods
  AirDrop, 81-82
    disabling, 83
    enabling, 82-83
    responding to share requests, 87
    sharing content, 84-86
  peer-to-peer connectivity, 80-81
iTunes Radio, 224
iTunes Store, 202, 212
  automatic downloads, configuring,
    202-204
  browsing , 216-218
  downloading
    content , 221-223
    previously purchased content ,
      228-231
  Family Sharing
    adding people to, 234-237
    configuring, 232-234
    downloading shared content,
      240-241
    managing, 237-239
  History List , 224-225
  iCloud accounts, 92

  previewing content, 219-221
  searching , 213-215
  tips for using , 225-226

J-K

Junk folder, moving email messages
  to, 349, 365
junk mail, 365

kept audio messages, 391
keyboard
  customizing, 137-141
    text replacements, 142-143
  deleting, 141
  iPhone 6 Plus keys, 33
  multiple keyboards, 31-32
  orientation, 32-33
  text, 30-39
Keychain, 92
keychain syncing iCloud accounts,
  105-107
keypad, dialing calls, 275
kids, Apple IDs, 237
known networks, 67

L

language, setting, 143-147
large email messages, handling, 346
launching apps, 13-15
Lightning port, 5
links
  defined, 514
  opening web pages,
    515-516, 531, 534-536
  options, 532
listening
  to audio in conversations, 390-391
  to deleted voicemails, 302-304
  to podcasts, 658-662
  to voicemail, 299-302

List view (calendars), 451

lists, organizing reminders, 461-463

Live Photos, 181-182, 572

Location Services
  with Camera app, 584
  creating calendar events, 437
  with Reminders app, 459

locations
  Maps app, 665-671
  sending in conversations, 410-411
  tagging in photos, 584

Lock passcode, 157

Lock screen
  customizing wallpaper, 180-185
  notifications, 27
  taking photos/video from, 581

locked/asleep condition, 46-48

logging in. *See* signing in

loyalty cards. *See* cards

LTE networks, 58

M

Macs
  Handoff feature icons, 698
  working seamlessly with iOS
    devices, 696
    Handoff feature, 696-697
    receiving calls, 699
    sending email, 697

Mail app, 324. *See also* email
  archived messages, 349
  checking for new messages, 347
  creating contacts from, 247-248
  deleting messages, 348
  determining status of
    messages, 347
  emailing photos, 617-619
  flagging messages, 349
  forwarding email, 344-346
  gestures, 349-352
  inserting photos/videos, 344
  junk mail, 365

managing multiple messages,
  352-354

marking as read/unread, 349

moving messages
  out of Trash, 348
  to Junk folder, 349, 365

multiple email accounts, 325, 338

notifications, configuring, 196-199

organizing messages
  Inbox screen, 356-357
  Message screen, 354

receiving/reading email,
  326-331, 336
  with 3D Touch, 334-335
  on iPhone 6/6s Plus, 331-334

replying to email, 342-343

saving attached images, 359

searching email, 360-362

sending email, 337-340, 344

setting preferences, 318-320, 323

Siri
  composing email, 491-492
  editing email, 493
  forwarding email, 494
  reading email, 493
  replying to email, 492
  retrieving email, 494

suggested recipients, 341-342

viewing messages in
  mailboxes, 358

VIP features, 199, 362-364

mailboxes
  changing, 359
  creating, 355
  email messages, viewing, 358

Mailboxes screen (Mail app), 325

managing
  alarms, 470-471
  Apple ID, 205
  Apple Pay, 685
  Burst mode photos, 601-603
  calendars, 451-453
  Contacts app, 243-244
    accessing information, 257-259
    configuring settings, 244-246
    creating contacts, 247-256
    deleting contacts, 265

    storing contacts, 247
    syncing contacts, 256, 263
    updating contacts, 263-265
  FaceTime calls, 312-313
  Family Sharing, 237-239
  images and video in conversations,
    388-390
  in-process calls, 281-282
    conference calls, 284-287
    entering numbers during, 283
    using apps during, 288
  junk mail, 365
  multiple email messages, 352-354
  online accounts, tips for, 121
  photo albums, 623
  podcasts, 662-665
  reminders, 463-464
  shared albums, 637-641
  text conversations, 397
  text messages with Siri, 497
  voicemail, 299
  web pages in tab view, 536-538

manual configuration, online accounts,
  112-114

manual entry
  Apple Pay cards, 682
  calendar events, 436-448
  completing web forms, 555-556
  contacts, 249-255
  deleting contact information, 265
  reminders, 456-461
  updating contact information,
    263-265

manual mode (data retrieval), 90, 116

Maps app, 665-671

marking
  completed reminders, 464
  email as read/unread, 349
  email addresses, 323
  photos as Favorites, 621
  VIPs in email, 363

medical ID
  accessing, 688
  creating, 686-687

medical information (Health app), 686
  accessing medical ID, 688

configuring
  app connections, 690-691
  information sources, 695-696
creating medical ID, 686-687
storing health and fitness
  information, 689
viewing health and fitness
  information, 692-694

merging conference calls, 285

Message screen
  managing email, 348-349
  organizing email messages, 354

Messages app, 367-368
  adding location information,
    410-411
  audio/video messages, 376
  blocking contacts, 377-378
  browsing images/video
    attachments, 412-413
  configuring, 369-378
  deleting messages, 414-416
  embedding images/video, 409
  forwarding messages, 415
  listening to audio in, 390-391
  managing
    conversations, 397
    images/video in, 388-390
  notifications, 378
  reading texts, 386-387
    with 3D Touch, 400
    on iPhone 6/6s Plus, 398-399
  receiving texts, 385
    with 3D Touch, 400
    on iPhone 6/6s Plus, 398-399
  replying to texts, 394-396
  sending
    audio in, 407-408
    images/video as attachments,
      401-406
    texts, 379-384, 396-397
  sharing contacts, 406
  Siri
    managing messages, 497
    reading messages, 494-495
    replying to messages, 495
    sending messages, 496

text messages versus iMessages,
  378-379
text shorthand, 417
unblocking contacts, 378
undelivered messages, 395
watching video in, 392-394

Microphone key, 39-41

missed calls, 303

mistakes, correcting with Siri, 504

MMS messages, limitations, 402

mobile versions of web pages, 523

monitoring
  data usage, 72-73, 76
  iPhone conditions, 44-45

movement of camera, sensitivity
  to, 584

moving
  between web pages, 532
  email messages out of Trash, 348
  folders on Home screens, 170
  icons on Home screens, 165-168

multi-touch interface, 6
  apps, 13-18
  Home screen, 7
  types of touch, 8-13

multimedia, accessibility options, 155

multiple calendars, 424

multiple email accounts, 325, 338

multiple email messages, managing,
  352-354

multiple iCloud accounts, 95

multiple keyboards, 31-32

multiple online accounts, 114

multiple web pages
  managing in tab view, 536-538
  opening
    in background, 534
    in tabs, 534-535

multitasking apps, 15

music
  auto-mute during calls, 292
  identifying with Siri, 224
  playing with Siri, 502-503

Music app, 646

mute switch, 4
muting
  calls, 282
  FaceTime calls, 312
  music during calls, 292
  phone, 291-292

N

naming folders, 175
navigating
  calendars, 430
  folders, 15
  with Maps app, 665-671
networks
  3G, 4G/LTE, 58
  cellular data, 58
    connecting iPhone to Internet,
      71-76
    connection speeds, 58
    data plans, 59
    overage charges, 59
    personal hotspots, 68
    roaming charges, 59
  roaming charges, 274
  Wi-Fi, 58

new email messages, checking for, 347
News app, 92, 646
Notes app, 92, 645
Notification Center, 27-28, 193
notifications, 26-27
  alerts, 191-192
  badges, 190
  banners, 191
  configuring, 190, 423
    global preferences, 194-195
    for specific apps, 196-199
  for conversations, disabling, 413
  customizing, 164
  Do Not Disturb mode, 29-30,
    147-149
  email, 323, 331, 349
  emergency notifications, 192
  of events, 453

Lock screen, 27
Messages app, 378
Notification Center, 27-28, 193
sounds, 192
vibrations, 192
viewing more information, 28
numbers, entering during calls, 283

O

obtaining iCloud accounts, 92-95
online accounts
   configuring, 111
     manually, 112-114
     updates, 116-120
   deleting, 121
   disabling data retrieval, 121
   Facebook, 90, 114-116
   Google, 90, 109-111
   iCloud. See iCloud accounts
   management tips, 121
   storing contacts, 247
   terminology, 90
open Wi-Fi networks
   changing networks, 66
   connecting iPhone to Internet,
    63-65
opening
   apps with Siri, 507
   Control Center, 24
   email attachments, 336
   Quick Actions menu, 14
   Settings app, 124-125
   web page links, 515-516, 531,
    534-536
   web pages
    in background, 534
    in tabs, 534-535
optional characters on keyboard, 35
organizing
   apps in folders
    badges, 172
    on Home screens, 168-170
   bookmarks, 544-549

email messages
   Inbox screen, 356-357
   Message screen, 354
photos
   adding to existing albums, 622-623
   managing albums, 623
   in new albums, 620-621
   reminders with lists, 461-463
orientation
   keyboard, 32-33
   screen, 33
   web browsing, 549
Orientation Lock button, 25
original photo, reverting to, 610
overage charges, 59, 71

P

pages of Home screens, 18
pairing Bluetooth devices, 77-80
pairing codes for Bluetooth devices, 77
Panoramas album, 589
panoramic photos, 569
   taking in Camera app, 577-578
Passbook. See Wallet app
passcodes, 60
   configuring, 128-136
   restarting iPhone, 46
   types of, 157
passkeys for Bluetooth devices, 77
passwords
   creating with Safari, 559
   entering for voicemail, 300
   typing, 66
   voicemail password, resetting,
    299, 304
Paste key, 33
pasting text, 38
pausing downloads, 223
payment methods. See Apple Pay;
  Wallet app
Peeks, 10, 13
peer-to-peer connectivity, 80-81

personal hotspots, connecting iPhone
  to Internet, 68
personalizing. See configuring;
  customizing
Perspective view for wallpaper, 182
phishing, 60-61
Phone app, configuring,
  268-273
phone calls. See calls
phone settings, configuring, 268
photo albums
   adding photos to, 622-623
   creating, 620-621
   managing, 623
   sharing
    adding photos to, 635-636
    commenting on shared
     photos, 637
    via iCloud, 633-634
    inviting people to, 637
    managing shared albums, 637-641
Photo Stream, configuring, 102
photos. See also Camera app;
  images; Photos app
   associating with contacts, 250-251
   contact photos on Call screen, 282
   iCloud, 91, 101-103, 562, 633
    adding photos to shared albums,
     635-636
    commenting on shared
     photos, 637
    inviting people to shared
     albums, 637
    managing shared albums, 637-641
    sharing photos, 633-634
    uploading Burst mode photos, 603
   inserting in email, 344
   iPhone capabilities, 561-562
   Live Photos, 181-182
   reverting to original, 610
   tagging locations, 584
   as wallpaper, 180-185
Photos app, 561, 585
   applying filters to photos, 609-610
   available actions, 616
   configuring settings, 562-567

copying photos, 616

deleting
photos, 624-625
videos, 626

editing
photos, 603
videos, 627-628

emailing photos, 617-619

enhancing photos, 604

finding photos
by browsing, 585-592
by searching, 593

marking photos as Favorites, 621

photo albums
adding photos to, 622-623
managing albums, 623
organizing photos, 620-621

red-eye removal, 611-612

sharing videos, 629

Smart Adjustment tools, 613-615

straightening/rotating/cropping photos, 606-609

streaming photos/videos via AirPlay, 629-632

viewing photos
with 3D Touch, 594-595
in slideshows, 595, 598-600

watching videos, 625-627

Photos source, 585

physical controls, 3-5

physical impairment, accessibility options, 153

PIN for Bluetooth devices, 77

pinching screen, 8

playing music with Siri, 502-503

Podcasts app, 649
browsing podcasts, 654
configuring settings, 649-651
deleting podcasts, 654
listening to podcasts, 658-662
managing podcasts, 662-665
searching for podcasts, 652-653, 657
selecting podcasts, 655-657
sharing podcasts, 654
subscribing to podcasts, 652-654
unsubscribing from podcasts, 654

Pops, 12-13

ports, 5

Predictive Text, 31-34
disabling, 141

preordering iTunes Store content, 225

previewing iTunes Store content, 219-221

previous screen, returning to, 439

previously purchased apps, downloading from App Store, 226-228

previously purchased iTunes content, downloading, 228-231

printing
AirPrint, 52-54
email, 344

priority ratings for reminders, 460

privacy
access restrictions, configuring, 155-161
AirDrop, 82
keychain syncing, 107

Private mode (Safari), 538

private Wi-Fi networks, security, 61

prompts, public Wi-Fi networks, 69

public Wi-Fi networks. *See also* open Wi-Fi networks
connecting iPhone to Internet, 68-70
security, 61

punctuation, 35

push mode (data retrieval), 90, 116

Q

quality of video, changing settings, 563-564

Quick Access feature (camera), taking photos/video, 581

Quick Actions menu
calendar events, 449
opening, 14
sending text messages, 396-397
taking photos/video from, 583

Quick Website Search feature, 540

quitting apps, 17

R

rating systems, 158

reading
email, 326-331, 336
with 3D Touch, 334-335
on iPhone 6/6s Plus, 331-334
with Siri, 493
text messages, 386-387
with 3D Touch, 400
on iPhone 6/6s Plus, 398-399
with Siri, 494-495

receiving
calls, 289
answering, 289-291
answering during call, 292
on Macs/iPads, 699
email, 326-331, 336
with 3D Touch, 334-335
on iPhone 6/6s Plus, 331-334
FaceTime calls, 310
text messages, 385
with 3D Touch, 400
on iPhone 6/6s Plus, 398-399

Recently Added album (screenshots), 585

Recents list
clearing, 293-294
dialing calls, 278-279

recommended content, browsing in iTunes Store, 218

recording
fingerprints, 128-136
video
Camera app, 567, 579-580
from Control Center, 582
from Lock screen, 581
from Quick Actions menu, 583
slow-motion video, 584
time-lapse video, 585
voicemail greeting, 297-299

red-eye removal, 611-612

red line on calendars, 433

refreshing
    podcasts, 665
    web pages, 532

related searches (App Store), 208

reminders, 453-455
    creating, 456-461
        with Siri, 499
    of declined calls, 291
    via iCloud, 91
    managing, 463-464
    organizing with lists, 461-463

Reminders app, 419-420, 453-455
    configuring
        notifications, 423
        settings, 422-423
    creating reminders, 456-461
    managing reminders, 463-464
    organizing reminders with lists,
        461-463
    Siri, creating reminders, 499

Remove red-eye tool (Photos app),
    604, 611-612

removing. *See also* deleting
    contacts from text messages, 381
    email addresses, 339
    fingerprints, 136
    icons from folders on Home
        screens, 172
    online accounts, 121
    red-eye from photos, 611-612
    restrictions, 161

renaming
    fingerprints, 136
    folders, 175

renting movies, 225

repeated reminders, creating, 458

repeating events, creating, 439-441

replying
    to email, 342-343, 492
    to text messages,
        394-396, 495

resetting voicemail password, 299, 304

resolution (video), changing, 563-564

restarting iPhone, 46

restrictions, configuring, 155-161

Restrictions passcode, 157

retrieving
    data, 90
    email with Siri, 494

returning
    to apps, 18
    to default Home screens, 175
    to previous screen, 439

reverting to original photo, 610

ringer, adjusting volume, 292

ringtones
    browsing in iTunes Store, 218
    customizing, 186-189

roaming
    charges, 59, 72, 274
    configuring, 74-75

Rotate tool (Photos app), 603, 606-609

rotating
    Home screens, 21
    phone, 10
    photos, 606-609

S

Safari, 513-514, 520
    3D Touch features, 552-554
    automatic sign in, 558
    bookmarks, 521-523
        creating, 541-544
        creating on Home screen, 550-551
        deleting, 549
        organizing, 544-549
    completing web forms, 554
        AutoFill, 557
        manually, 555-556
    configuring, 515-520
    Favorites, 522-526
    iCloud usage, 91
    managing pages in tab view,
        536-538
    opening pages
        in background, 534
        in tabs, 534-535

passwords, creating, 559
    Private mode, 538
    screen orientation, 549
    searches, 539-540
    tracking visited sites, 528-529
    URLs, 526-528
    viewing websites, 530-533

saving
    bookmarks, 541-544
    email drafts, 341
    images attached to email
        messages, 359

scams
    avoiding, 376
    email phishing, 60-61

scanning codes in Wallet app, 678 679

screen
    battery usage, 164
    customizing brightness/view/text
        size, 176-179
    Home screens. *See* Home screens
    orientation, 33, 549
    returning to previous, 439
    Standard view, 164, 177
    Zoomed view, 164, 178

screenshots, capturing, **585**

Screenshots album, 589

Search button (App Store), 205

search engines, 515

searches
    Internet, 539-540
    Spotlight Search tool, 21-22

searching
    for apps
        in App Store, 206-209
        with Wallet support, 678
    calendars, 449-451
    email messages, 360-362
    iTunes Store content, 213-215
    photos, 593
    for podcasts, 652-653, 657
    reminders, 464
    Settings app, 125-126
    with Siri, 501-502
    with SIRI SUGGESTIONS screen, 509
    for text replacements, 143

security
  access restrictions, configuring, 155-161
  AirDrop, 82
  Auto-Lock/TouchID/passcodes, configuring, 128-136
  keychain syncing, 107
  passcodes
    restarting iPhone, 46
    types of, 157
  passwords, creating with Safari, 559
  tips for, 59-62
selecting
  contacts for text messaging, 381
  email threads, 357
  photos in slideshows, 596
  podcasts, 655-657
  text, 36-37
  web form data, 555
Self-timer, taking photos in Camera app, 584
Selfies album, 589
sending
  audio in conversations, 407-408
  email, 337-340, 344
    via Handoff feature, 697
    suggested recipients, 341-342
  images and video
    in conversations as attachments, 401-406
    embedding in conversations, 409
  locations in conversations, 410-411
  photos via email, 617-619
  text messages, 379-384, 396-397
    with Siri, 496
sensitive information, keychain syncing, 107
sensitivity of camera, 584
Settings app, 51. *See also* configuring
  accessibility options, 150-155
  access restrictions, 155-161
  Auto-Lock/Touch ID/passcodes, 128-136
  Do Not Disturb feature, 147-149
  keyboard, 137-141
    text replacements, 142-143

  language and format preferences, 143-147
  opening, 124-125
  searching, 125-126
  Split-screen usage, 126-128
Shared source (photos), 587
sharing
  via AirDrop, 81-87
  apps with others, 211
  calls on Macs/iOS devices, 699
  cards in Wallet app, 675
  contacts, 259, 406
  iTunes content. *See* Family Sharing
  photos
    commenting on shared photos, 637
    via email, 617-619
    via iCloud, 633-636
    inviting people to shared albums, 637
    managing shared albums, 637-641
  podcasts, 654
  reminder lists, 463
  security for, 62
  videos, 629
Shift key, 35
shooting video. *See* recording, video
shortcuts
  text, 36
  typing URLs, 527
shorthand, text messaging, 417
Show All Calendars button, 430
shutting down iPhone, 46
signatures (email), configuring, 318-319
signing in
  Apple ID, 48-49
  to iCloud accounts, 95-96
  to websites, automatic sign in, 558
silencing ringer, 291-292
silent alarms, 468
Siri, 41-43, 479-480
  activating, 484
  alarms, creating, 500
  changing voice, 481-482

  composing email, 491-492
  configuring, 481-484
  contacts, 260
  correcting mistakes, 504
  driving directions, 503-504
  editing email, 493
  email, 331
  events
    creating, 448, 497-498
    editing, 500
    viewing, 500
  FaceTime calls, 310
  forwarding email, 494
  how to use, 484-489
  identifying songs, 224
  Internet connections and, 480
  making calls, 490
  opening apps, 507
  playing music, 502-503
  reading email, 493
  reminders, creating, 461, 499
  replying to email, 492
  retrieving email, 494
  searching for information, 501-502
  text messages
    managing messages, 497
    reading, 494-495
    replying to, 495
    sending messages, 496
  time management with, 500
  timers, creating, 500
SIRI SUGGESTIONS screen, 23, 507-510
  dialing calls, 280-281
  FaceTime calls, 310
size of text, adjusting, 164, 176-179
sleep mode, 46-48
slideshows, viewing photos, 595, 598-600, 632
Slo-mo album, 589
slow-motion video, 569
  recording in Camera app, 584
  watching, 627
Smart Adjustment tools (Photos app), 604, 613-615
smileys, 33, 137
Snooze button, 469

social media (Facebook), 90, 114-116

software, 6
   Control Center, 24-26
   Home screens, 18
      SIRI SUGGESTIONS page, 23
      Spotlight Search tool, 21-22
   multi-touch interface, 6
      apps, 13-18
      Home screen, 7
      types of touch, 8-13
   Split-screen mode, 19

songs, identifying with Siri, 224

sounds. *See also* notifications
   music, auto-mute during calls, 292
   customizing, 164, 186-189
   as notifications, 192

sources for Health app, configuring, 695-696

spam mail, 365

speaker, calls on, 282

speaking text, 505-506
   with Microphone key, 39-41
   Siri, 41-43

speed of connections, cellular data networks, 58

spell checking feature, 39
   disabling, 140

Split-screen feature, 19
   reading text messages, 398-399
   receiving/reading email, 331-334
   in Settings app, 126-128
   for web browsing, 549

Spotlight Search tool, 21-22

square photos, 569

Standard view, 164, 177

Status bar icons, 44-45

status of email messages, determining, 347

stills, 181

Stocks app, 645

stopping Family Sharing, 239

Stopwatch, 472-473

Store. *See* App Store; iTunes Store

storing
   contacts, 247
   health and fitness information in Health app, 689

Straighten tool (Photos app), 603, 606-609

straightening photos, 606-609

streaming photos/videos via AirPlay, 629-632

subscribing to podcasts, 652-654

Suggest on Lock Screen option (Wallet app), 676

suggested recipients (Mail app), 341-342
   editing, 384

Suggestion option, 37

surfing the Internet. *See* web browsing

swiping screen, 8. *See also* gestures

symbols, 35

syncing
   bookmarks, 520, 544
   contacts, 256, 263
   with iCloud accounts, 97-98, 105-107

T

tab view (Safari), managing web pages, 536-538

tabs
   managing web pages in, 536-538
   opening web pages in, 534 535

tagging photo locations, 584

taking photos
   Camera app, 567, 573-576
      Burst mode, 584
      panoramic photos, 577-578
      Self-timer, 584
   from Control Center, 582
   from Lock screen, 581
   from Quick Actions menu, 583

tapping screen, 8

telephone calls. *See* calls

text
   cutting, 38
   dictating, 39-41, 505-506. *See also* Siri
   editing, 35
   formatting, 38
   keyboard, 30-39
   pasting, 38
   Predictive Text, 31-34
   selecting, 36-37
   shortcuts, 36
   sizing, 164
   typing, 30. *See also* keyboard

text messaging, 367-368. *See also* Messages app
   adding location information, 410-411
   blocking contacts, 377-378
   browsing images/video attachments, 412-413
   configuring iMessage and text settings, 369-378
   conversations, managing, 397
   deleting, 414-416
   embedding images/video, 409
   forwarding messages, 415
   iMessages versus, 378-379
   listening to audio in, 390-391
   managing images/video in, 388-390
   reading texts, 386-387
      with 3D Touch, 400
      on iPhone 6/6s Plus, 398-399
   receiving texts, 385
      with 3D Touch, 400
      on iPhone 6/6s Plus, 398-399
   replying to texts, 394-396
   responding to calls with, 291
   sending
      audio in, 407-408
      images/video as attachments, 401-406
      texts, 379-384, 396-397
   shorthand, 417
   Siri
      managing messages, 497
      reading messages, 494-495

replying to messages, 495
sending messages, 496
unblocking contacts, 378
undelivered messages, 395
watching video in, 392-394
text replacements, 142-143
text size, adjusting, 176-179
text tones, customizing, 186-189
third-party keyboards, installing, 139
threads, email
    disabling, 325
    reading, 327
    selecting, 357
time
    checking, 47
    viewing, 433, 465
Time-lapse album, 589
time-lapse video, 569
    recording in Camera app, 585
    watching, 627
time management with Siri, 500.
    See also Calendar app; Clock app;
    Reminders app
time zones, World Clock, 469
Timer, 474-476, 584
timers, creating with Siri, 500
Today view (calendars), 451
toolbars, opening Control Center, 24
tools
    Camera app, 570-572
    Photos app, 603
Top Charts (App Store), 205
top-level domains in URLs, 527
Touch ID, 60
    access restrictions and, 157
    in Apple Pay, 685
    configuring, 128-136
Touch ID button, 5, 46
    signing into Apple ID, 48-49
touch screen, types of touch, 8-13
touring iPhone, 3
    Airplane mode, 50-51
    AirPrint, 52-54
    Control Center, 24-26

external features, 3-5
Home screens, 7, 18
    SIRI SUGGESTIONS page, 23
    Spotlight Search tool, 21-22
iOS operating system, 6
keyboard, 30-39
monitoring conditions, 44-45
multi-touch interface, 6
    apps, 13-18
    types of touch, 8-13
notifications, 26-30
Settings app, 51
Siri, 41-43
Split-screen mode, 19
text dictation, 39-41
Touch ID button, signing into
    Apple ID, 48-49
volume control, 49-50
Wake/Sleep button, 47-48
tracking
    FaceTime calls, 311
    websites visited, 528-529
Trash, moving email messages
    from, 348
travel time, adding to events, 441
Trending Searches
    App Store, 209
    iTunes Store, 213
trimming videos, 627-628
TripAdvisor app, 648
TripIt app, 648
troubleshooting
    configuring app notifications, 199
    Family Sharing, 237
    moving icons on Home
        screens, 166
    podcasts, 665
    Siri, 480, 504
    undeliverable text messages,
        395, 406
turn-by-turn directions, Maps app,
    665-671
turning off iPhone, 46
TV. *See* Apple TV
types of touch, 8-13

typing
    text, 30. *See also* keyboard
    passwords, 66

U

UI (user interface). *See* multi-touch
    interface; software
unblocking contacts from text
    messaging, 378
undeliverable text messages, 395, 406
Undo key, 33
undoing photo edits, 609-610
Uniform Resource Locators. *See* URLs
universal apps, 209
unlocked/wake condition, 46-48
unsubscribing
    from podcasts, 654
    from shared albums, 641
Updates (App Store), 205
updating
    apps, 211
    contact information, 263-265
    disabling updates, 121
    online accounts, 116-120
uploading Burst mode photos to
    iCloud, 603
Urban Spoon app, 649
URLs (Uniform Resource Locators)
    browsing the Web, 526-528
    defined, 514
    viewing, 530
user reviews of apps, 209

V

verification requests via email, 60-61
verifying
    addresses for iMessage, 376
    cards in Apple Pay, 684
versions of web pages, 523

vibrations, 26-27
  creating, 189
  customizing, 186-189
  as notifications, 192
video previews for apps, 209
videos
  accessibility options, 155
  browsing conversation
    attachments, 412-413
  Camera app, 567, 579-580
    icons, explained, 570-572
    Live Photos, 572
    slow-motion video, 584
    time-lapse video, 585
    types of video, 568-569
  embedding in conversations, 409
  inserting in email, 344
  iPhone capabilities, 561-562
  iTunes Store. See iTunes Store
  managing in conversations,
    388-390
  in Messages app, 376
  Photos app
    deleting videos, 626
    editing videos, 627-628
    marking as Favorites, 621
    sharing videos, 629
    streaming via AirPlay, 629-632
    watching videos, 625-627
  quality settings, 563-564
  recording, 581-583
  sending in conversations as
    attachments, 401-406
  watching in conversations, 392-394
Videos album, 589
Videos app, 645
viewing. See also watching
  attachments to conversations,
    412-413
  Burst mode photos, 601
  calendars, 424, 430-434
  cards in Wallet app, 673
  completed reminders, 464
  email messages in mailboxes, 358
  events
    with 3D Touch, 434-435
    with Siri, 500

groups, 381
health and fitness information in
  Health app, 692-694
notification information, 28
photos
  with 3D Touch, 594-595
  on Apple TV, 629-632
  in slideshows, 595, 598-600
time, 465
URLs, 530
VIP email messages, 363
websites, 530-533
views (screen), setting, 176-179
VIP features (email), 199,
  362-364
virtual keyboard, 30-39
vision impairment, accessibility
  options, 151-152
visual alarms, 468
visual notifications, 26
visual voicemail, 268, 296
  deleting voicemails, 302
  finding voicemails, 300-302
  initial setup, 298
  listening/managing voicemails, 299
  listening to deleted voicemails,
    302-304
  recording greeting, 297-299
  resetting password, 299, 304
voice calls. See calls
Voice Memos app, 646
voice of Siri, changing, 481-482
voice recognition with Siri, 41-43
volume, adjusting, 281, 292
volume button, 5, 49-50

W-Z

Wake/Sleep button, 4, 47-48
wake/unlocked condition, 46-48
Wallet app, 672. See also Apple Pay
  accessing cards, 674
  adding cards, 676-679
  deleting cards, 676

iCloud storage, 92
  opening, 673
  sharing cards, 675
  Suggest on Lock Screen
    option, 676
  viewing cards, 673
wallpaper
  changing, 180-185
  contact images as, 290
  dynamic wallpaper, 181
Watch app, 646
watching videos, 625-627. See also
  viewing
  on Apple TV, 629-632
  in conversations, 392-394
Weather app, 645
web browsers, 514
web browsing, 520. See also Safari
  3D Touch features, 552-554
  automatic sign in, 558
  bookmarks, 521-523
    creating, 541-544
    creating on Home screen, 550-551
    deleting, 549
    organizing, 544-549
  completing web forms, 554-557
  configuring Safari, 515-520
  Favorites, 522-526
  managing pages in tab view,
    536-538
  opening pages, 534-535
  Private mode, 538
  screen orientation, 549
  searches, 539-540
  tracking visited sites, 528-529
  URLs, 526-528
  viewing websites, 530-533
web forms, completing, 554
  AutoFill, 557
  manually, 555-556
web pages
  automatic sign in, 558
  defined, 514
  mobile versions, 523
  opening links, 515-516, 531,
    534-536
  searches on, 541

WebMD app, 649

websites
    defined, 514
    iCloud usage, 91
    viewing, 530-533

Wi-Fi networks
    Airplane mode, 51
    cell phone provider Wi-Fi
      networks, 70
    changing networks, 66
    closed Wi-Fi networks, 70
    defined, 58
    open Wi-Fi networks, 63-65
    private Wi-Fi networks, 61
    public Wi-Fi networks, 61,
      68-70

Wish List, adding to, 224

World Clock, 469

writing email. *See* sending, email

Yelp app, 649

Zoomed view, 164, 178

zooming
    taking photos, 575
    web page views, 531